Django in Action

CHRISTOPHER TRUDEAU

FOREWORD BY MICHAEL KENNEDY

MANNING

SHELTER ISLAND

For online information and ordering of this and other Manning books, please visit
www.manning.com. The publisher offers discounts on this book when ordered in quantity.
For more information, please contact

    Special Sales Department
    Manning Publications Co.
    20 Baldwin Road
    PO Box 761
    Shelter Island, NY 11964
    Email: orders@manning.com

Manning Publications Co.	Development editor: Connor O'Brien
20 Baldwin Road	Technical editor: Asif Saif Uddin
PO Box 761	Review editor: Kishor Rit
Shelter Island, NY 11964	Production editor: Deirdre Hiam
	Copy editor: Christian Berk
	Proofreader: Jason Everett
	Technical proofreader: Ninoslav Cerkez
	Typesetter and cover designer: Marija Tudor

ISBN 9781633438163
Printed in the United States of America

For Michelina

brief contents

contents

Appendix E containing sample exercise solutions is available in the ePDF and ePUB versions of this book, and you can read it online in liveBook

foreword

Welcome to *Django in Action*! I'm sure you're excited to begin your Django journey. First, though, let me give you a little background on my friend, Christopher Trudeau, who has put a huge amount of effort into writing this book for you.

Christopher has a passion for communicating technical details, especially around Python and Django. Christopher has been on my podcast, *Talk Python to Me*, where his appearances have ranked in the top 10% of episodes, spanning almost 10 years of interviews. He frequently co-hosts the *Real Python* podcast. Christopher has also written and recorded many courses (much of them focusing on Django), and he has worked in such industries as cloud computing, gaming, travel, and finance, to name a few. In short, he doesn't just talk the talk—he has experience to back it up.

With this book, you hold the key to the fascinating world of Python web development. There are many types of applications you could choose to build: desktop GUI apps, mobile apps, embedded apps, and more. But web applications, the kind you build with Django, are special. They are immediately accessible to everyone, everywhere. There is no approval process, nor are there any gatekeepers or developer fees. You have an idea. You figure out how to build it with Python. You publish it to the web, and you're on your way.

So why Django? Django is one of the "big three" web frameworks in the Python space, which together represent the vast majority of adoptions. The people behind Django have spent years building their community.

Only Django, amongst the web frameworks, has the Django Software Foundation, a 501(c)(3) nonprofit foundation, to ensure the community remains strong and provides direction for the project. Only Django has outreach programs, such as Django Girls, a nonprofit foundation that organizes free Python and Django workshops for women interested in coding, and Djangonauts, a community mentorship program that helps people become contributors to Django.

So what you will learn in this book is how to build web apps with Django. But, perhaps unknowingly, you'll also be dipping your foot into this rich and supportive community behind Django. It's quite special, and there are few places like it.

I know you'll enjoy your journey into Django, both the technology and the community. And Christopher will be an excellent guide to lead you. Build something amazing and have a great time along the way!

—MICHAEL KENNEDY
FOUNDER, TALK PYTHON

preface

I was in university when the World Wide Web first came to be, and I remember using the Mosaic browser in its early form. When I entered grad school, we were already using the web to write content for students, including both static HTML and early CGI. I graduated from single Perl scripts to working with Java, eventually working with large teams of developers, writing scaled systems for the banking and telecom sectors.

In 2008, I was managing development teams at a company that got acquired, and during the transition, I had a lot of time on my hands. I decided to pick up a new language: Python. I used it to solve a couple of smaller problems we had at work and pretty much have never looked back. My next company was a start-up, building web tools. I looked around in the Python ecosystem for a web framework and landed on Django. Even back in its 1.1 days, Django was a complete system. It included everything we needed to build websites, which allowed my team and me to concentrate on the code specific to our clients.

Django's core is based on mapping a URL to some code, running the code that generates a page and returning that page as a response. The page can be built using Django's template engine, meaning HTML can be composed like code, removing the need for repetition. Most websites require some storage mechanism, and Django's object relational mapping (ORM) abstracts away the database, making it easier to query and manipulate data in Python.

This alone would be enough to recommend Django to build websites, but it contains much more. Out of the box, Django is built for multiuser websites, meaning it includes mechanisms for authentication, authorization, and user management. It comes with tools to help write automated tests, both at the unit level and with hooks for tools like Selenium for doing cross-site integration testing.

It doesn't stop there. Django is built using a pluggable architecture, which makes it easier for you to build content, but it also means there are plenty of people who've written tools you can take advantage of. The Django Packages site currently lists over 5,000 add-ons you can take advantage of. Need to write an API for your site? Django Ninja and the Django REST Framework have your back. Need a CMS? Wagtail and Django CMS are ready for you. Leveraging all these tools allows you to concentrate on what is unique to your project, rather than having to re-invent the wheel.

Django has been around for a long time, but it is still growing and adapting. Whether you need to put together a quick website prototype or write something to scale, Django is a great choice.

Django's documentation is already excellent, so why write a book? Django is so comprehensive that it can be difficult to wrap your mind around all its pieces. This book is based around a single project, adding to its features as you progress. This gives you a better understanding of how all the pieces fit together as well as practical advice on how to build your own site. My intent isn't to replace the documentation but to act as a companion, hopefully helping you along your learning journey.

acknowledgments

You and I have something in common: I also read everything in a book, including the acknowledgments. As a reader, I'd always wondered just how much the author was expected to say—and how much was genuine. Now that I find myself writing my own acknowledgments section, I find myself at a loss: How do I properly express gratitude to all those deserving?

Cliche as it may be, I'll start with my wife. She had unwavering enthusiasm throughout this project and confidence when mine was waning. Her support means everything to me. I'm a very lucky man.

Although my parents think Python has something to do with slithering animals, I'm still grateful for everything they have provided me. Whether nature or nurture, they can take more credit than most.

Before starting on this journey, I was ignorant of the fact that the term "editor" actually refers to a collective. Michael Stephens is my procurement editor, which means he was responsible for challenging me with doing this in the first place. Without him, none of this would have got started. Connor O'Brien is my development editor; he's what you think of when you hear the word "editor." He was my first reader, my guide, and a very patient man. He agreed to sign on when things were rough, at the beginning, and I'm grateful he took the chance on me. Thank you, Connor; it wouldn't have gotten done without you. And to complete the triumvirate, is Christian Berk, my copy editor, making me sound far more literate than I am. He diligently replaced every "which" with "that" and vice versa—I never seem to get those right.

To fellow Manning author (that's fun to write) and Real Python alumni, Dane Hillard, thanks for lending me your setup, saving me days of technical work, and listening to my moaning. Your perspective was invaluable.

There are loads more people at Manning who helped out along the way: Deirdre Hiam, my project editor; Jason Everett, my page proofer; technical editor, Asif Saif Uddin; reviewing editor, Kishor Rit; and technical proofreader Ninoslav Cerkez. Thanks to all of you for helping to turn some random scribbling into a professional affair.

Finally, to my internal reviewers and those who participated in the Manning Early Release Program, I send a giant thank you: Alfredo Alessandrini, Ankit Anchlia, Carmelo San Giovanni, Gregor Zurowski, Henry Stamerjohann, Ian De La Cruz, James Matlock, Jason Li, Jeff Smith, Jelte Derksen, Jereme Allen, Jonathan Reeves, Laud Bentil, Mafinar Khan, Mike Baran, Nitendra Bhosle, Omar Ebrahim, Oren Zeev Ben Mordehai, Patrick Regan, Radhakrishna MV, Richard Meinsen, Richard Tobias, Rodney Weis, Rupa Lahiri, Shahnawaz Ali, Simone Sguazza, Sudeep Batra, Sudheer Kumar Reddy Gowrigari, and Walter Alexander Mata López. Your feedback along the way helped me make better content and find those parts that needed more work. I'm sure some problems remain, but I'll take the blame for that.

about this book

Django in Action was written to help you learn how to use Django to build multiuser websites. Throughout the book, you'll be building *RiffMates*, a musicians' classifieds site. You'll start by creating a basic site with a few simple pages and eventually progress to multiuser capabilities.

How this book is organized: A roadmap

The book is divided into three parts. Part 1 gives the basic structure of all Django projects, teaching you how to get started.

- Chapter 1 provides a background on how Django sites work and introduces you to the differences between writing with a framework and writing using a library.
- Chapter 2 gets you started writing code, showing you how to create your first project and build your first web page.
- Chapter 3 does a deep dive into the Django Template Engine, which allows you to compose and re-use HTML, like you would with object-oriented code.
- Chapter 4 is all about the object relational mapping (ORM), an abstraction to a database, giving you the ability to write Python classes to interact with database tables and queries.
- Chapter 5 shows you the Django Admin, an out-of-the-box web tool for administering ORM classes. This includes both those you write and those which are built-in, such as the user management classes.

Once through part 1, you'll have enough to build your own single-user site. Part 2 introduces you to more advanced features in Django, including multiuser sites, accepting user content, testing, and the database migration system.

- Chapter 6 is about user management. You learn how to add and control users as well as all the work involved in password resets.
- Chapter 7 shows you how to deal with content for your site: data submitted by users; files uploaded by users; and static content, such as images, CSS, and JavaScript files.
- Chapter 8 covers the testing tools that come with Django. Unit testing a website requires extra work, but Django provides mechanisms to ensure you can write good automated tests with a high degree of coverage.
- Chapter 9 describes the Django management command interface: command-line tools you use to manage your site. It also shows you how to write your own custom commands.
- Chapter 10 does a deep dive on how Django manages changes to your ORM classes through its migration system. When you add fields to your database abstraction, the migration system keeps the corresponding database tables in sync.

The chapters in part 3 are independent of each other and show you how to use third-party tools to add capabilities to your website. If you've covered parts 1 and 2, you have enough knowledge to cherry-pick the chapters of interest in part 3.

- Chapter 11 shows you how to add API capabilities to your website, allowing your users to access data through programmatic interfaces. This chapter concentrates on the third-party Django Ninja tool but also points you toward the Django REST Framework as well as tools for GraphQL.
- Chapter 12 introduces you to writing more dynamic web pages using HTMX. In this chapter, you learn how to do search-as-you-type, lazy loading, infinite scroll, and more.
- Chapter 13 covers a wide variety of third-party Django tools that help you write less code and be more productive when you're building and debugging your sites.
- Chapter 14 gives a brief listing of other useful features in Django as well as third-party libraries that allow you to build more functionality into your websites.

Django In Action also includes a deep set of appendices, covering how to get Python and Django environments going, considerations when putting your code in production, and two quick-reference guides for template tags and ORM fields.

About the code

Throughout the book, you'll be building RiffMates, a musicians' classified site. Since Django is a framework, most code snippets will not work on their own—you've got to put it into the context of a project. You'll be guided on how to do this along the way, but a version of the project is available at https://github.com/cltrudeau/django-in -action.

The sample code is divided into sections, which correspond to chapters, or parts of chapters. For example, `code/ch04a_bands` contains the first few examples from chapter 4, while `code/ch04d_relationships` contains all the changes done in chapter 4.

Every chapter includes exercises for you to test what you've learned, and the sample code contains answers. For example, `code/ch04e_exercises` contains all the code from chapter 4, including the answers to the exercises.

As RiffMates gets built while you go along, each subsequent directory includes code for everything before it. The `ch05a_admin` directory includes all the code, including all the exercise answers from chapters 2 through 4. Spoiler alert, if you go digging around in the directories for later chapters, you may come across some exercise answers. Sample code was processed using the Black formatter (https://pypi.org/project/black/), and as such, you may find cosmetic differences between it and code generated by the Django framework itself.

Source code and commands you need to run are represented in the book using a `fixed width font`. Code listings may include line-continuation markers (➡) for code that is too long to fit on a single line. Code annotations accompany most of the listings, highlighting important concepts.

Writing about a framework is a moving target. The code in this book was written and tested against Django 5.0. Django's version numbering system uses what is referred to as "loose semantic versioning," offering a new release every 8 months. Each major version number (the 5 in 5.0) corresponds to three releases. For the 5 family, that's 5.0, 5.1, and 5.2. The .2 release is a long-term support version, meaning that's where the bug fixes will go for a 28-month support period. A full list of release timings and support windows is available on the downloads page: https://www.django project.com/download/.

Don't let major release numbers scare you; they may or may not correspond to breaking changes. When I started writing the book, I was coding against 4.2, and upgrading to 5.0 required no changes in the project. Between versions, features may get deprecated—see the release documentation for specifics if you're upgrading a project.

Django releases are tied to Python versions. I tested using Python 3.12, but as long as you're using a version that matches the Django release, you'll be just fine. I intentionally avoided any Python syntax changes only available in more-recent releases. A table showing which Python versions are supported with which versions of Django is available on the FAQ page: https://docs.djangoproject.com/en/dev/faq/install/#what-python-version-can-i-use-with-django. You can get executable snippets of code from the liveBook (online) version of this book at https://livebook.manning.com/book/django-in-action. The complete code for the examples in the book is available for download from the Manning website at https://www.manning.com/books/django -in-action, and from GitHub at https://github.com/cltrudeau/django-in-action.

liveBook discussion forum

Purchase of Django in Action includes free access to liveBook, Manning's online reading platform. Using liveBook's exclusive discussion features, you can attach comments to the book globally or to specific sections or paragraphs. It's a snap to make notes for yourself, ask and answer technical questions, and receive help from the author and other users. To access the forum, go to https://livebook.manning.com/book/django-in-action/discussion. You can also learn more about Manning's forums and the rules of conduct at https://livebook.manning.com/discussion.

Manning's commitment to our readers is to provide a venue where a meaningful dialogue between individual readers and between readers and the author can take place. It is not a commitment to any specific amount of participation on the part of the author, whose contribution to the forum remains voluntary (and unpaid). We suggest you try asking the author some challenging questions lest his interest stray! The forum and the archives of previous discussions will be accessible from the publisher's website as long as the book is in print.

Other online resources

Django's documentation is great, and it's the best place to start to get more information: https://docs.djangoproject.com/. Note that the documentation is divided by release number. Visiting the main URL automatically points you at the most-recent release version. Additionally, the "dev" version of the docs is one step ahead of the release, being the target for the next version. This book uses the dev version of the URL when pointing at any documentation.

For example, the following three URLs all point to information about the django-admin command, but for the dev, 5.0, and 4.2 versions, respectively:

- https://docs.djangoproject.com/en/dev/ref/django-admin/
- https://docs.djangoproject.com/en/5.0/ref/django-admin/
- https://docs.djangoproject.com/en/4.2/ref/django-admin/

The bottom-right corner of any Django documentation page has a Documentation Version widget that allows you to view the same page but for another release. Above the documentation widget, there is also a Language widget, showing the available translations for any given release.

The Django project's home page is also a great place to learn about what is going on in the Django world:

- *Django's News page*—https://www.djangoproject.com/weblog/
- *Django's Community page*—https://www.djangoproject.com/community/

There are also plenty of other sites that report on the Django ecosystem:

- Django News (https://django-news.com/) is a weekly email newsletter.
- Django Chat (https://djangochat.com/) is a biweekly podcast from two of the core developers.

For inspiration on what to build or to learn about the many packages out there, see

- *Django Projects*—https://builtwithdjango.com/projects/
- *Django Packages*—https://djangopackages.org/

about the author

CHRISTOPHER TRUDEAU is a fractional-CTO, who helps companies with both their tech stack and the processes their development teams use to build things. He is a co-host of the *Real Python* podcast, he is author of over 50 online Python and Django courses, and he has taught over 4,000 students about tech and technical processes.

Christopher has been writing code for over 40 years in a variety of languages and has been building websites using Django since its 1.1 days. In his spare time, he dabbles in photography, reads everything he can get his hands on, cycles the streets of his Toronto home, wrestles Komodo dragons, and enjoys adding lies in his bio.

about the cover illustration

The figure on the cover of *Django in Action*, titled "Le Créole," is taken from a book by Louis Curmer published in 1841.

In those days, it was easy to identify where people lived and what their trade or station in life was just by their dress. Manning celebrates the inventiveness and initiative of the computer business with book covers based on the rich diversity of regional culture centuries ago, brought back to life by pictures from collections such as this one.

Part 1

Django essentials

The first part of the book is all about getting you going with Django, giving you the tools you need to write a website. You'll learn how coding with a framework is different from writing against a library, how to create a Django project, how to use the Django Template Engine to compose and re-use HTML, how to interact with databases using Django's object relational mapping (ORM), and how to take advantage of the built-in Django Admin tool. When you're finished with this part of the book, you'll have written the first part of the RiffMates project and have enough knowledge to write Django-based websites.

Django unfolds

This chapter covers

- What the Django Framework is and why to use it
- The actions Django performs when you enter a URL in your browser
- Server-side rendering vs single-page applications
- The kinds of projects you can complete with Django

You've written a brilliant Python script that runs on your local machine, and now you want other people to be able to use it. You can use magical packaging tools and send your program to your users, but then, you're still stuck with the challenge of whether they have Python installed. Python does not come by default on many computing platforms, and you have the added problem of making sure the Python version your script requires is installed on your user's machine.

Alternatively, you can turn your Python program into a web application. In this case, your user's interface becomes a web browser, and those are installed everywhere. Your users no longer even need to know what Python is; they simply point their browser at the right URL and can use your software. To do this, your program needs to be adapted to run on a web server. This requires a bit of work, but using a single environment also has a distinct advantage: you are in full control over what version of Python gets run.

If you already have some experience with Python, a great answer to building web applications is Django. Django is a third-party Python framework that lets you write code that runs on a web server. Using Django, you write Python code, called a *view*, that is tied to a URL. When your users visit the URL, the Django view runs and returns results to the user's browser. Django does a lot more than that though—it includes tools for doing the following:

- Routing and managing URLs
- Encapsulating what code gets run per page visit
- Reading and writing to databases
- Composing HTML output based on reusable chunks
- Writing multiuser-enabled sites
- Managing user authentication and authorization to your site
- Web-based administrative tools that manage all these features

Django started out as a tool for writing newspaper articles at the *Lawrence Journal-World* in Lawrence, Kansas. Rather than having each article be a single file on a web server, the newspaper wanted a way to reuse pieces of HTML. You don't want to write the newspaper's banner in every file—you want to compose it like you would with code. You also probably don't want your reporters writing HTML; it isn't their expertise.

Django evolved as both a coding framework and a series of tools to manage web content. Among other things, the framework provides the ability to compose HTML out of reusable pieces solving the banner problem, and one of the tools it includes is a web-based interface for the creation of content. Reporters can write articles without worrying about HTML. Django's tools are built on top of the framework, giving you the power to customize them to suit your needs.

The robustness of the Django framework has led to widespread industry adoption. Reddit, YouTube, *The Onion*, Pinterest, Netflix, Dropbox, and Spotify are just a few of the organizations that use Django. Sites like these need scale, and Django has proven itself. Whether you want to build something small or hope to become a massive site, Django can help you. It is a mature platform with a vibrant community, focused on maintaining and evolving a well-tested, secure framework. To top it all off, the original developers at the *Journal-World* made it open source, meaning it is freely available for you to both use and modify for your needs.

1.1 Django's parts

Let's start with a high-level view of what makes up Django, knowing that each of these topics is covered in detail later in the book. One way to understand Django is to think about it in three parts:

1 A mapper between URLs and view code
2 An abstraction for interacting with a database
3 A templating system to manage your HTML-like code

Of course, Django is way more than just three parts, but all the other parts are built using these three concepts. Django includes tools like a web interface for modifying content in the database and the code needed to write multiuser sites. Each of these is built on those same three ideas. This means once you've learned the key concepts, you can incorporate the tools into your site and customize them using the same knowledge you use to write your web application.

The first of the three ideas is about how code gets invoked when a user visits a web page. When a browser hits a URL, a web server is responsible for replying. Django isn't a web server; it is a framework called by a web server. The web server is configured to map certain URLs to certain content, and in the case of Django, some of the URLs get passed to the framework. This handoff is completed through a generic Python web interface called the *Web Server Gateway Interface* (WSGI).

When you visit a Django URL, the web server calls the framework through WSGI, at which point Django is responsible for generating the page response. The first core part of Django determines what code to call based on the URL. This is done through a mapping in your Django project. The mapping is between URLs and response handlers, known as *views*. A view is a function or class that generates content, which Django then parcels as a response to the web browser. You'll write your first view in chapter 2, shortly after you've created your first Django project.

The complete request flow from browser to response is shown in figure 1.1. It starts with the browser interacting with the web server, the web server calling Django through WSGI, Django mapping the visited URL to a view, and the view formulating a response.

The mapping between URLs and views is accomplished through a list data structure inside a Python file. Each mapping gets defined through the construction of a path object, which contains the URL to map and a reference to a view function. Mappings can be given names, so you can reference them elsewhere in your code; you use the name in your code, or in your HTML, and Django replaces it for you. This way, changing a URL only needs to be done in one place.

Visiting a URL causes Django to loop through all its mappings and look for a match. If a match is found, the corresponding view gets invoked. If no match is found, Django shows a 404 error page.

The vast majority of code you write for a Django project is the actual view code. Views return a response object that encapsulates the information to send back to the browser. The most common of these objects is HttpResponse, which returns text over HTTP, the body of which is typically HTML.

Inside your view, you determine what your visitor sees on the web page. This may involve interacting with a database. Your database might contain the inventory in your warehouse, a list of the books in your library, or the names of users who can access

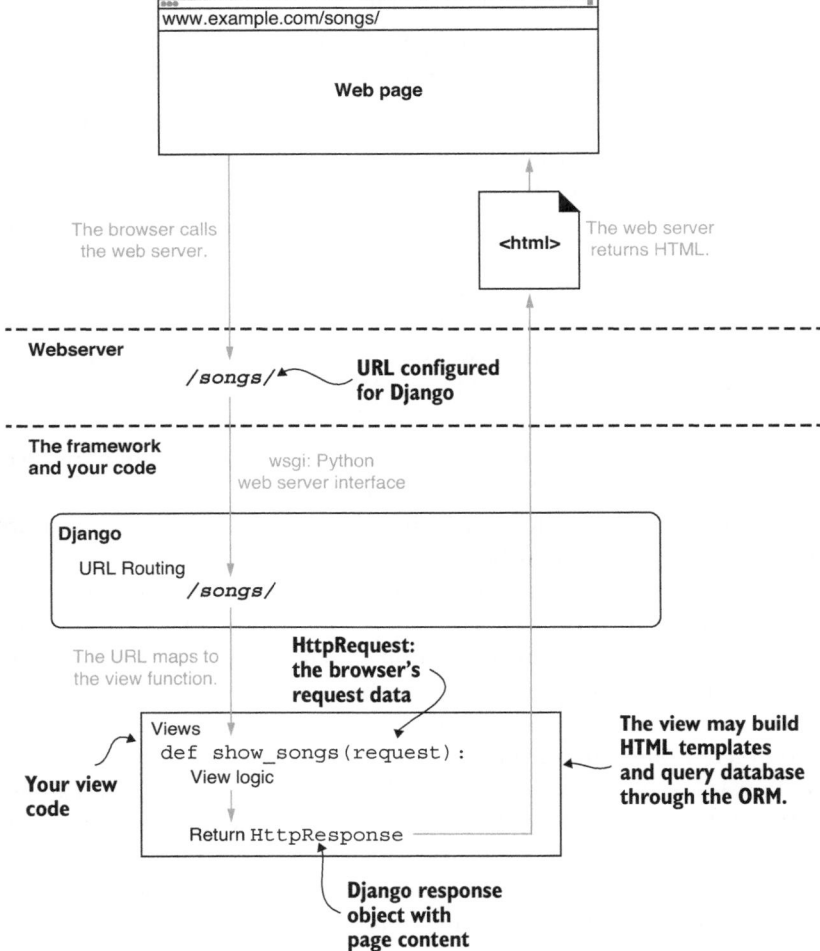

Figure 1.1   Django handling a page visit

particular pages. To facilitate communication with a database, Django includes an *object relational mapping* (ORM), the second of the three core parts. This is an abstraction that allows you to manage content in a database through Python classes and objects. If your web page requires information from the database, the ORM is used to look up a QuerySet object that contains database results. How to use the ORM as well as how it maps to a database are covered in chapter 4.

The third core part of Django is the templating engine, which helps you create and manage the HTML within your page response. HTML is a fairly verbose text format often containing a lot of repeated content. Using the templating engine, you define HTML templates that describe parts of a web page. The parts get assembled, composed, and reused to form the response to the user.

For example, navigation bars or footers that appear on every page only need to be defined once, and then the template engine helps you include them everywhere. Templates are not HTML-specific; they also get used for populating email content and anywhere else you wish to manage text, like reusable code. Figure 1.2 shows a view in more detail and its interactions with the ORM, database, and templating engine.

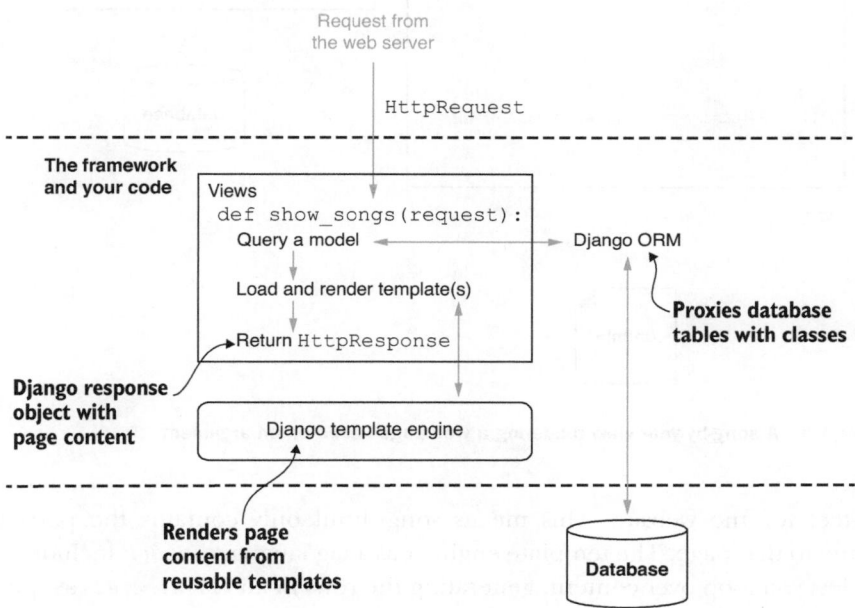

Figure 1.2   A view interacting with the database and template engine.

Consider a web page that shows the songs released in a given year. The URL for all the songs in 1942 might be http://example.com/song_by_year/1942/. The code for displaying this page starts with a mapping between the /song_by_year/ portion of the URL and a function to handle the response. The mapping is capable of parsing the /1942/ portion of the URL as a parameter and passing it into the view function that generates the page. Figure 1.3 shows the parts of the URL handled by the view and how the view interacts with the ORM.

The song_by_year view does a look-up in the database for all the songs in 1942. The database query gets abstracted through a Song class in the ORM, and a query gets performed by invoking a function on that class. The result from the database gets encapsulated in a QuerySet response object containing all the corresponding songs.

With the data in hand, the view creates the HTML response. It loads the songs.html template, which inherits from a common template that defines the look-

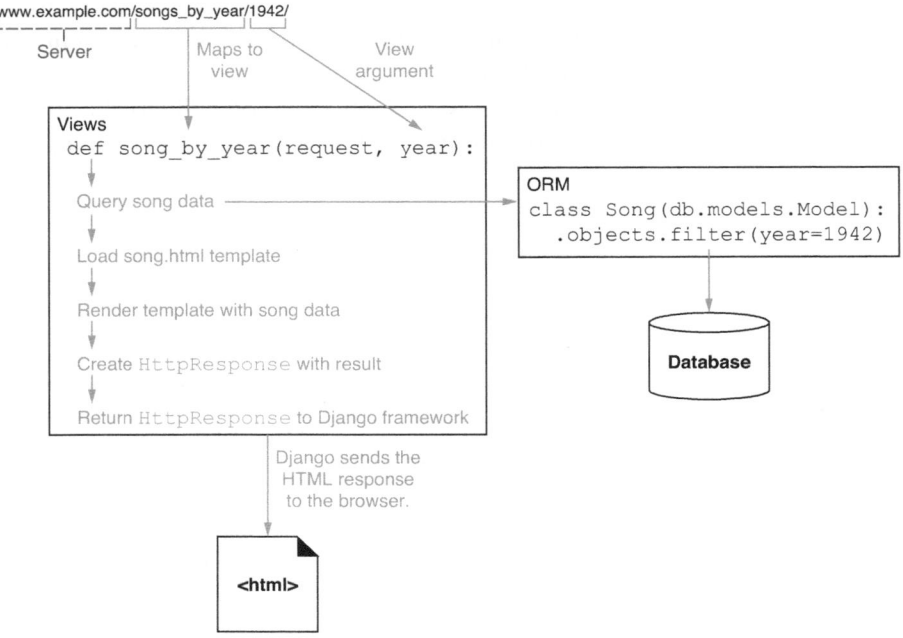

Figure 1.3   A song-by-year view rendering a web page based on an argument

and-feel for the website. This means songs.html only contains the parts that are unique to that page. The template engine has a tag language, which includes a feature that lets you loop over content, generating the rows in an HTML <table>, populating each row with the information from a song from 1942. You'll learn all about Django templates, their tags, and how to compose them together in chapter 3.

Once the HTML has been rendered, it gets packaged in an HttpResponse object and sent back to the Django framework. The loading and rendering of a template is so common that Django provides shortcuts to do this.

Django uses the response object to construct the data the web server needs for the browser. This includes all the HTTP headers and the body containing the HTML. The content gets returned to the web server through WSGI, and the server sends it down to the browser. That's how you see your page full of songs.

1.1.1   *Mapping URLs, Django views, and the MVC model*

The simplest form of any website is a mapping between a file and a URL. A web page that shows a picture of a kitten is at least two files: one for the HTML document and one for the image of the kitten. Simple file-to-URL mapped sites like this are called *static sites*. If you want your users to be able to upload their own images or add comments to your page, your site can no longer be just static files. A *dynamic site* is one that determines a page's content when it gets visited.

Dynamic sites are more complicated than static ones; they need an interface for the users to interact with, somewhere to store data like uploaded pictures and comments, and logic for knowing how to combine these into content. Django's primary purpose is building dynamic websites. In doing so, it uses a common architectural pattern for user interfaces known as the *model—view—controller* (MVC) method. This method breaks software into three pieces, as shown in the following list and figure 1.4:

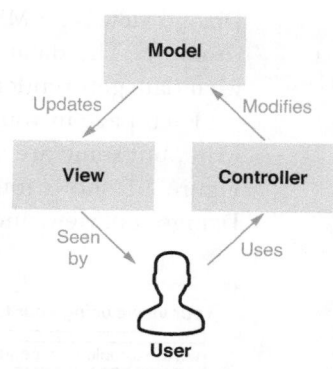

1 *Model*—Represents the logic and data of an application independent of its user interface
2 *View*—Presents data to the user, possibly with multiple views for the same data

Figure 1.4 Model—view—controller architectural pattern

3 *Controller*—An input and control mechanism the user uses to interact with models and views

The MVC is a good way of thinking about how software interacts with users, but Django is more inspired by it than strictly governed by it. The line between what is a view and a controller is a little fuzzy. This fuzziness provides the added benefit of creating entertaining debate on the internet.

When a web server passes a URL request to Django through WSGI, Django looks that URL up in its master mapping file, named urls.py, and as the name implies, it is just Python. The file can be renamed, but there really isn't any reason to do so. The urls.py file contains a variable called urlpatterns, which is a list containing Django path objects. Each path object either maps a URL to a Django view or loads another file containing more mappings.

A Django view is just Python code. It can be a function that returns a response document or a class with methods that do the same. Each view takes at least one argument, called the request. This variable contains information about the HTTP Request that was made. The request object includes the URL that was hit; any query parameters in the URL; HTTP method information; HTTP headers; and in the case of pages with forms, the data the user filled in. Not every view needs all this information, but it is there when you require it.

Key steps in Django's request handling process straddle the boundaries defined by the MVC. Django mapping a URL to the code that handles it is considered an MVC controller. Django's view, which returns the HTML document, is a hybrid of the MVC view and controller. Inside a Django view, models get queried, which makes it an MVC controller, but it also returns HTML, which makes it an MVC view. Just because Django names it *view* doesn't mean it is an MVC view—don't let the overlapping names confuse you.

Consider the prior song-by-year page example. The same Django view outputs different results, depending on the year passed in. The HTML template used in the

Django view is an MVC view; it is responsible for formatting the look and feel of the response. The database lookup in the Django view is an MVC controller, changing what data gets rendered by the MVC view based on the year argument.

Each page in your web application is generated by a view. Most are views that you write, but some are views you configure, taking advantage of tools built into Django. Figure 1.5 shows four web pages—two of which are views you would write, one is a Django tool view, and the other is a hybrid of the two.

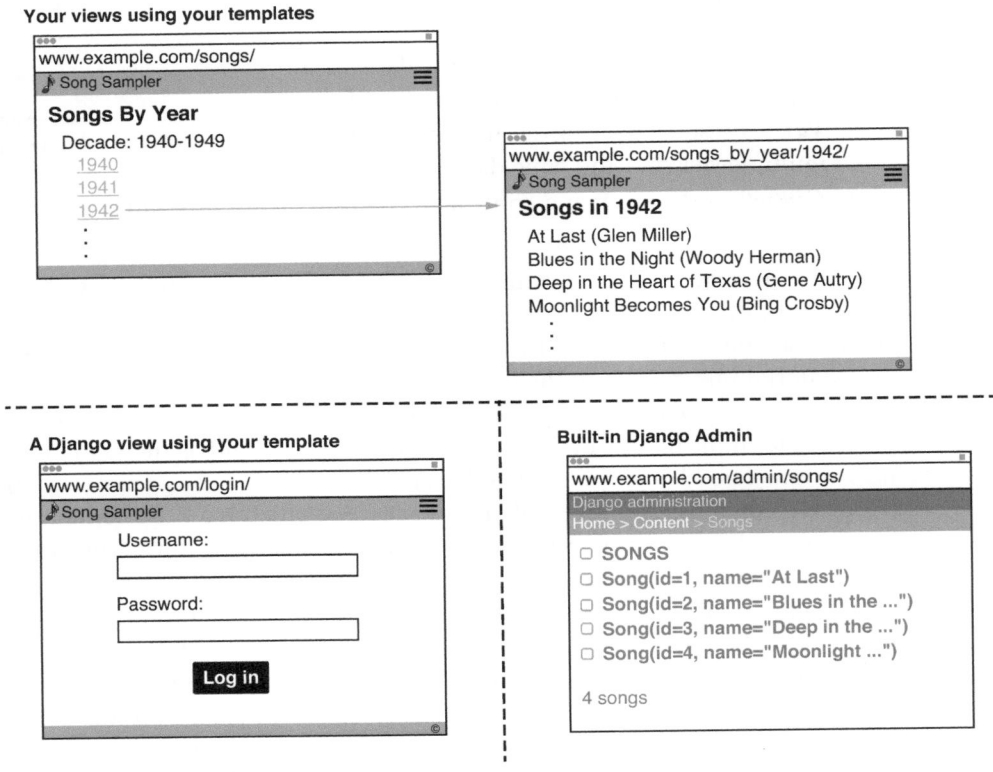

Figure 1.5   Most pages will be your views with your templates, but Django provides tools to reduce your work

A typical view is responsible for querying data out of a database; making logic decisions about output; and then loading, rendering, and returning the result of a template. In the "Songs By Year" page, the view reads all the years from the song database and groups them by decade. The grouped data is sent to the template engine that renders the page, including links to each corresponding detail page with "Songs in 1942" being just one example. The same view generates all "Songs in" pages, with the year being passed as an argument. The argument changes how the MVC controller works but uses the same MVC view for the output.

1.1.2   Databases: Dynamic sites need data

Views are key to the *dynamic* part of a dynamic website. They can create what is on a page based on data or input from the user. That data might be products in a catalog, the score of last night's game, or your latest recipe for gnocchi. In all these cases, your data has to live somewhere. Enter the database.

Databases are a field in computing in their own right. There are different kinds, each with its advantages and disadvantages. There are many implementations of each kind and specialty languages written just for communicating with them. All of this can be a little overwhelming. Django implements an ORM to abstract this away.

Consider a database containing information about books, like the one shown in figure 1.6. You are going to have different kinds of data: an author (that's me), a publisher (that's Manning), and a book (that's what you're holding). There are many authors, many books, and many publishers. Some books have multiple authors, and some authors have written multiple books. A relational database stores this information in tables similar to a sheet in an Excel spreadsheet. It then expresses relationships between these items with keys. The Author table might reference the Book table using a key that is a unique identifier for a Book.

Item tables

Book table

ID	Title	Year
10	Martian Chronicles, The	1950
11	Farenheit 451	1953
12	Carrie	1974
13	Firestarter	1980
14	Talisman, The	1984
15	Mystery	1993

Unique key for each item

Author table

ID	Last_name	First_name
1	Bradbury	Ray
2	King	Stephen
3	Straub	Peter

Publisher table

ID	Name
23	Viking Press
24	Doubleday
25	Ballantine
26	Dutton

Relationship tables

Book-publisher table

ID	Book_ID	Publisher_ID
40	10	24
41	11	25
42	12	24
43	13	23
44	14	23
45	15	26

Doubleday published both the Martian Chronicles and Carrie.

Keys relate Books to Publishers.

Book-author table

ID	Book_ID	Author_ID
80	10	1
81	11	1
82	12	2
83	13	2
84	14	2
85	14	3
86	15	3

Two Authors, one Book

Keys relate Books to Authors.

Figure 1.6   Tables store either item information or relationship information

An ORM is an object-oriented way of representing different data elements and the relationships between them. Each row in a database table gets expressed as an object. Instead of thinking about the Book table, you think about the Book class. An ORM lets you query a specific book as well as link to the book's associated author and publisher, which themselves are objects. Django automatically creates reverse relationships, so if you have an Author object, you can query all the author's books without having to write any additional code. The relationships between the Book, Author, and Publisher objects are shown in figure 1.7, along with their corresponding database table representations.

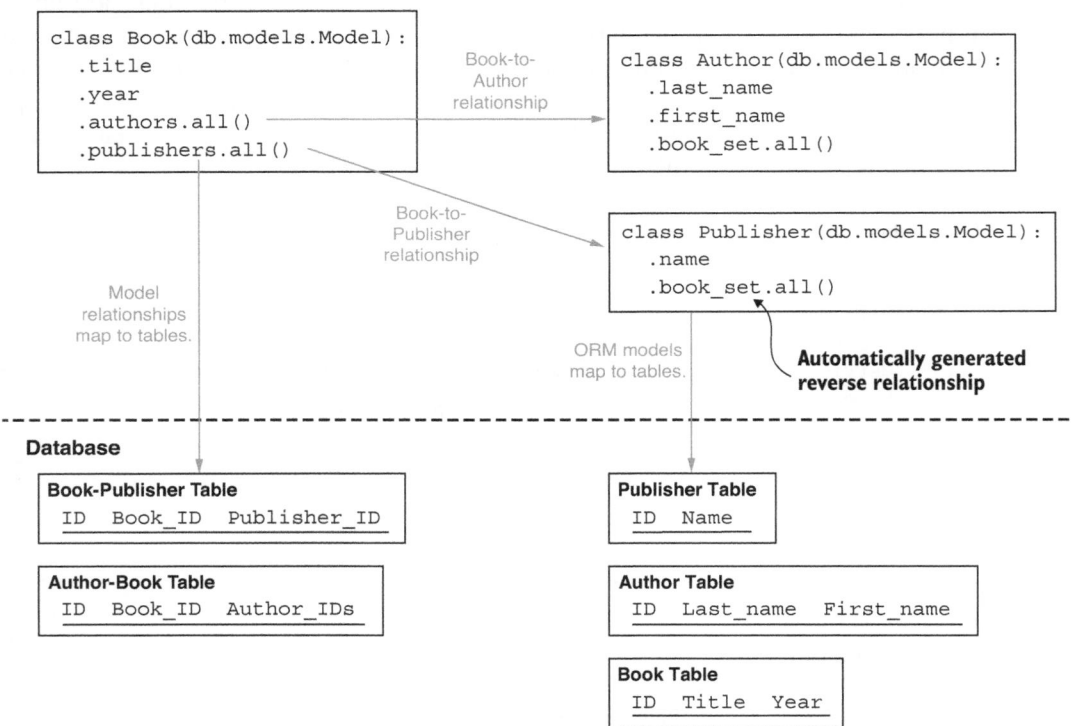

Figure 1.7 ORM Models are data objects that map to underlying item and relationship tables

Django's ORM allows you to define data models that map to tables in a database. You create rows in those tables by creating and saving objects. You can create, read, update, and delete data using the ORM, never having to touch the database itself.

Django's ORM comes with support for multiple databases, including PostgreSQL, MariaDB, MySQL, Oracle, and SQLite. There are also many third-party plugins for other databases. There are even plugins for non-relational databases, like the

MongoDB NoSQL server. One of the beauties of an ORM is that it abstracts this away; your code is the same regardless of what database is connected underneath.

When a Django view requires information out of the database it uses one or more ORM classes that have been defined by the programmer. Each class inherits from an ORM base class called `Model`. The base class provides methods for querying the database. For example, calling `.objects.filter(last_name__startswith="A")` on `Author` returns all the authors with a last name beginning with `"A"`. Query results get represented by a common Django object called a `QuerySet`. The `QuerySet` can be passed as part of a data context to the template engine. The template engine generates HTML using the results. A list of authors might generate a bullet-point list in the output. Django also provides a way to deal with the database directly if the abstraction is insufficient in specific cases.

1.1.3   Structuring HTML for reuse

Your Django view is responsible for returning content to the browser, which most of the time is HTML. HTML was originally designed for physicists to write easily accessible articles for other physicists. Modern web pages have more in common with marketing brochures than physics articles. Each page in a website tends to include a lot of repetition—for example, the navigation header that appears on every page.

Django includes a templating engine. The engine's job is to compose pieces of content together into a page. Using it, you only have to write the navigation header once, and then it can be included in every page of your site. To change the navigation header, you only have to do it in one place.

Your view likely wants to show some of that previously mentioned data on your page. Lists of things can get quite repetitive. In Python, if you want to print a long list, you don't hardcode it. Instead, you put a `print` statement inside a `for` loop that iterates on the list. The templating engine lets you do the same using *tags* and *filters*. Tags are instructions to the engine for conditional rendering, while filters change how data is displayed. Using these, you can create loops, conditionally render blocks, print a date in your user's format, and much more. Figure 1.8 shows how templates are composed and how to use tags, denoted by `{% %}`. All of this is covered in detail in the chapter on the template engine.

Django is able to interact with different template engines. The original templating language that ships with Django, understandably, is called the *Django Templating Language* (DTL). Django also ships with the popular third-party templating language Jinja2. This isn't maintained by the Django core team, and won't be covered in this book, but is included in the framework for the convenience of those familiar with it.

The DTL interface has three concepts: variable rendering, tags, and filters. Variable rendering replaces values in the template with data sent into the engine. Tags are like functions and provide looping, conditional blocks, and a number of operations on your templated text. Filters are variable modifiers changing values before they are displayed. For example, one filter takes a date object and formats it to a desired output. The DTL is also pluggable, allowing you to write your own tags and filters.

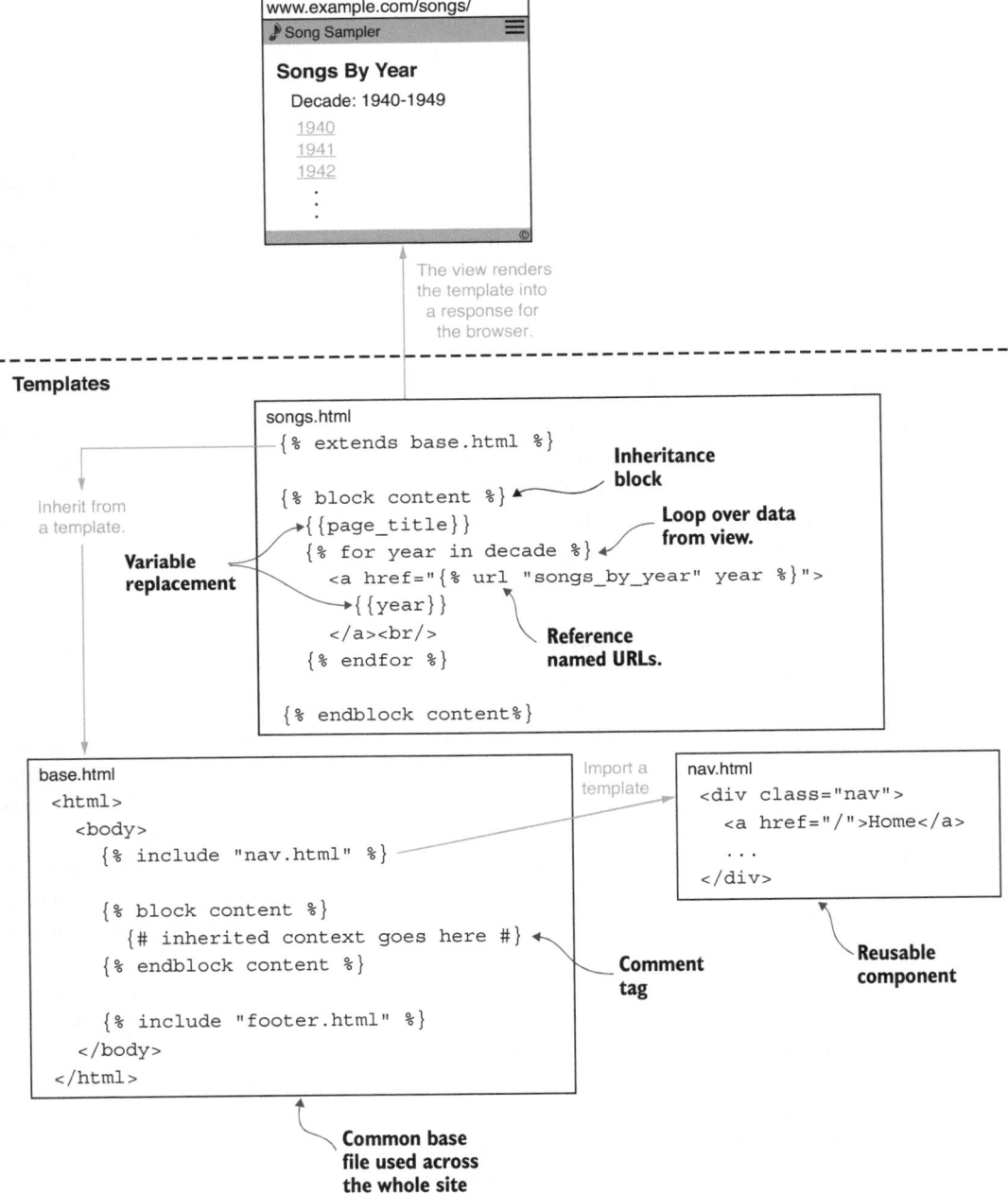

Figure 1.8   Composing HTML templates into a rendered page

The output from a Django view is a response object—a web page uses one called `HttpResponse`. Django provides shortcut functions that wrap the process of loading and rendering a template and embedding the result in an `HttpResponse` object. The view returns an object to Django, and Django then uses the object to formulate the content that is sent back to the browser. This includes any HTTP headers along with the body containing the HTML.

1.1.4 Multiuser sites

From the very beginning, Django was meant for multiple users. The *Lawrence Journal-World's* web application consists of views for the readers, showing the newspaper pages as well as views for the journalists. The journalists' views are the tools they use to write articles.

Both the readers and the journalists are users, each using a different part of the web application. A regular reader should not be able to edit articles; they should only be able to read them. Controlling who can do what in a website can be broken into two parts: authentication and authorization. *Authentication* is the process of the user proving who they are, and *authorization* refers to the permissions associated with that user. Django provides tools for managing all of this.

User identities really are just another kind of data, so a multiuser Django site uses the ORM to track user accounts. Authentication compares a username and password from a login page with a known set of values in the database. Because users tend to be forgetful, you need more than just a login page—you also need a password reset screen. To manage users, you want tools for listing and editing them. You need pages for creating new users, either by an administrator or through self-sign-up. As users are people, you likely need to occasionally block one of them from logging in. Temporarily, of course—I'm sure they'll see the error of their ways. Django comes with tools to help you do all of these things. You'll learn all about users and the complications they cause in chapter 6.

In addition to providing user-management tools, Django includes a general tool called the Django Admin, which is a web-based administration interface for the database. Anything that you construct with the ORM can be managed through the Django Admin, including all of your user accounts. Having the Django Admin is a huge advantage and can save a large amount of time when building sites. The Django Admin is built on the same coding concepts as your own site: Django views, the ORM, and a series of templates. The tools that come with Django are built using the core parts of Django. You'll see how quickly you can create a site with a full administration interface in chapter 5.

1.2 What can you do with Django?

Django's original purpose at the *Lawrence Journal-World* was as a tool allowing journalists to upload articles to the web. The generic term for this kind of software is a *content management system.* Django is a general web framework, but it has a heavy leaning toward content management. For the journalists, the content in question is newspaper articles. For a blog site, the content is a blog post. In both of these cases, the content is text that makes up the page, but that isn't the only choice.

An e-commerce website has pages of items for sale, a shopping cart, and payment processing. This isn't really considered a content management system, but it does have some things in common. The catalog pages query the database for available items and display them—the "content" here is the merchandise. A shopping cart is a special case of this, where the contents of the cart are specific to the user and this visit.

Consider what blog and e-commerce sites have in common: there are "things" stored in the database (blog posts or merchandise), and users visit pages that display one or more of those things. The Django ORM provides an object-oriented abstraction for database storage, making it easier to code and manage these things, and the Django Admin provides a web interface for interacting with instances of them. Django views use the ORM to show the user either the blog posts or merchandise appropriate to the page and construct the page through the template engine. Its general approach of objects plus views rendering templates makes Django a good fit for any multipage website.

1.2.1   *Server-side, single-page, and mixed-page applications*

As web applications have evolved, the architectural choices in building them has grown. Inside a Django view, the template engine gets called to render HTML to be sent to the browser. This is called *server-side rendering*. By contrast, a *single-page application* (SPA) moves this rendering and some application logic into the browser itself. An SPA's approach to the MVC model is for the view and controller parts to be entirely in the web browser.

> **Server-Side Rendering vs. SPAs**
>
> The phrase *server-side rendering* can be a little confusing. Of course, in all situations, your browser displays the HTML. However, the distinction between server-side rendering and SPAs is where the HTML is composed. In server-side rendering, the server is responsible for assembling all of the pieces of the HTML and sending it down to the browser. The template engine runs on the server side, composing the parts of the template into a result, like in figure 1.8.
>
> By contrast, SPAs create the HTML in the browser. All the logic for page creation happens in the browser, so you can think of this as a browser-based template engine. The server sends the code for building the templates to the browser as well as the data necessary, but all page composition happens on the client side.

This doesn't mean Django can't be used to build SPAs. When a user visits an SPA-based site, a JavaScript bundle gets downloaded. The bundle contains the complete user interface and a lot of the business logic for the application. The JavaScript presents a dynamic interface hosted in a single web page, hence the name. The application still needs the web server as a data store and to execute certain kinds of business logic, and this part of the architecture can be done with Django.

In a Django-based SPA, a view doesn't render HTML; instead, it serves data to the SPA. This is typically done using JSON. Plugin libraries like the *Django REST Framework* and *Django Ninja* provide features for building APIs based on views as well as tools for serializing your ORM data objects into a form the JavaScript application can consume.

The world isn't binary. There are degrees between a traditional server-side application and a full single-page application. Using libraries like Vue.js, to trigger API calls, or HTMX, which uses pieces of HTML, you can augment server-side rendering with client-side flexibility. Django fits this naturally, with views rendering full pages, supporting APIs, and HTML snippets, as required.

1.2.2 *When and where you should use it*

There are lots of choices in the Python world for writing web applications. A popular alternative to Django is *Flask*. Flask is smaller than Django and only directly offers the routing and view portion. Flask tends to require other libraries to build out a full system. It is often paired with SQLAlchemy for an ORM and Jinja2, for templating. By contrast, Django comes with an ORM and templating engine already. You may be able to get going with Flask a little faster than Django, but if your application grows, you're going to need the other pieces as well. With the routing, views, template rendering, and ORM all coming in one package, you don't have to worry about how and whether things will work together.

The flip side of this argument is that Django isn't really meant to be used in pieces. Although the ORM is fantastic, if you're not building a web application and only want the ORM, Django isn't the best fit. Django is intended to build web projects. You can use it as a tool for other things, but you'll find you're fighting it.

SPAs are designed with a backend server that only provides data, while the GUI component gets handled by the browser. The FastAPI library specializes in providing REST APIs and is a popular choice if you are using Python for the backend of an SPA.

If you are writing SPAs, there is a strong argument for using Node.js on the server side. Having JavaScript as both the client and server language has advantages. If you write your server in Python, you're going to have to duplicate some code, usually code for object to data conversion. Personally, my preference for Python far outweighs this extra work.

Django is sometimes viewed as a server-side only technology because that was what it was originally written for. The URL-maps-to-views approach has come full circle. Originally, it was how you built web pages. Then, single-page applications came along, and this approach was considered older tech. The same site structure works well for APIs though. This means Django can be used as a backend for single-page applications, as the server component for mobile apps, and when machine-to-machine communication is important. The availability of libraries like the Django Rest Framework and Django Ninja (heavily inspired by FastAPI) make writing APIs with Django relatively quick and painless. Being able to have both web pages and APIs in the same project means less code for you to write and maintain. How to use APIs with Django is covered in chapter 11.

Django has been around for a long time; its first release at the *Lawrence Journal-World* was in 2003. It can no longer be described as "the new kid on the block." The programming world has a tendency toward rejecting the old, but a distinction should be made between dinosaurs and sharks. Dinosaurs are extinct. Sharks were around with the dinosaurs, but they are still mean, eating machines today. Django is actively being developed and still releases major versions annually. Recent releases have focused on redesigning the underlying technology to better support asynchronous coding, making Django competitive with newer web development stacks.

Django isn't just a shark but a shark with accessories; it's modular in design and supports plugins. There are thousands of plugins available—one of which may already do what you were going to code for yourself. The Django Packages site (https:// djangopackages.org/) has over 4,000 installable libraries that cover topics such as analytics, data tools, e-commerce, feed aggregation, forums, payment processing, polls, reporting, and social media. Whatever web application you want to build, there is likely a package that can help you.

Django's vast ecosystem is a real advantage, but even outside the Python world, there are things making Django better. HTMX is a JavaScript library that allows you to replace part of an active page with a snippet of HTML. You do this without having to write any JavaScript at all. Suddenly, Django's ability to serve and handle pieces of HTML, when combined with HTMX, means a resurgence of dynamic webpages without resorting to heavier, single-page application frameworks. Making your pages more dynamic using HTMX is covered in chapter 12.

1.2.3   *Potential projects*

There are many types of websites out there, and depending on what you're building, you may end up using different parts of the Django framework. The following is an incomplete list of the types of projects you might be interested in:

- *Blogs*—These are a natural fit for Django, with the ORM storing article content and views responsible for showing articles and table-of-contents pages. Wiki sites and newspapers are a variation on this, where instead of blog posts, you have encyclopedic information or newspaper articles as content.
- *e-commerce sites*—These sites are all about the catalog. The ORM stores information about your merchandise, while the views present them to the users. In complex sites, you may be interacting with an inventory backend instead or exporting shopping patterns for data analysis. The Django Admin provides an out-of-the-box inventory management system by working in conjunction with the ORM.
- *Content sites*—Many websites are repositories of specialty information. Consider the Internet Movie Database (IMDB); it is really a frontend to a database entry describing information about a movie. Django's ORM and the Django Admin make it a good tool for these kinds of sites.

- *Document management*—This is a broad class of sites where some content gets served from the filesystem instead of in the ORM. Typically, the ORM contains a lightweight object that points to the file on the server or CDN. Users then interact with pages to see or download the documents. Video sites are a version of this, where the document is a movie file. Data scientists use this kind of site for presenting reports or results from their analysis.
- *Utility sites*—It is quite common for developers and system administrators to create utility scripts solving specific problems in an organization. Often, these scripts are difficult to share, as they're environment specific. Creating a web frontend for these kinds of utilities makes them useful to a wider audience within an organization. Similarly, most companies have share folders full of Excel files that are ad-hoc solutions to a problem. Excel can be a fragile beast; there is seldom any input validation, and a small change in the wrong cell can produce the wrong result. Processes like this that are used by many people call out for a web version, converting the logic in Excel into a web application providing input validation and robustness.

Orthogonal to the type of site, is your architectural approach. Your project may use one or more of the following design concepts:

- *Single-page applications*—Not so much a type of project but a design approach, SPAs can be built with Django as their API backend. Third-party libraries, like Django Ninja, simplify the creation of these kinds of projects.
- *Multiuser sites*—Django includes user account management out of the box. The Django Admin can be used to administer user accounts, and Django provides views for login and password management.
- *Multilingual sites*—Django includes mechanisms for handling multiple written languages and localization, such as date and currency format. This can be especially powerful when mixed in with multiuser capabilities, as users see the site in their native language.
- *Static-page sites*—For speed of interaction, nothing beats a static website, where the server feeds the user straight HTML. Of course, maintaining these kinds of sites can be painful, unless you use tools that allow you to compose the page. The third-party library django-distill is a site generator; you build a Django site like you normally would then use distill to output it as a static site. This gives you all the advantages of the Django template engine while keeping the performance gain of a static site.

1.2.4 *The RiffMates project*

Books are great (you should buy multiple copies for your friends), but practice is where you really learn things. This book presents a project called *RiffMates*, where you help your cousin build a musicians-seeking-musicians personals site. This project is primarily the content site type, but it mixes in some document management aspects, all in a multiuser context. Coding along will help you better understand how to build your own projects. Each chapter includes exercises to test your progress, and sample code and answers are available online at https://github.com/cltrudeau/django-in -action.

This book is divided into three parts. The first part covers Django's core components, the second part delves into Django's built-in tools, and the third part covers how to use third-party libraries to build different kinds of sites.

In part 1, you start to build RiffMates. You will write views and register them against URLs. You'll learn about the template engine and how to load and render templates in your views to output HTML to the browser. You will also learn how to interact with the database doing queries on musician and venue data, while using the Django Admin to manage it all.

Part 2 shows you the power of Django and all the nifty stuff built into it. You'll turn RiffMates into a multiuser site and learn how to customize the provided views dealing with logins and password management. Once you've got user accounts happening, you will add the ability to get input from your users, including uploaded files.

Part 3 focuses on how key third-party libraries can help you extend the functionality of your website. Django was originally designed as a content management system framework, but its community has created all sorts of pluggable tools to do other things. You can build websites with REST APIs; deal with data import and export; and interact with popular JavaScript frameworks, like HTMX.

Happy web coding!

Summary

- Django maps a URL to a view, which is either a function or a class that returns a document to the browser.
- A Django view can render a document by composing pieces of HTML through a template engine.
- The model—view—controller architectural pattern divides the parts of a program into three pieces. The model contains data and business logic, the view is for visualizing the data, and the controller is for interacting with it.
- An object relational mapping is a way of abstracting database tables with programming classes.
- Django includes tools for managing multiuser websites.
- Single-page applications move the view and controller parts of the MVC into the browser.
- Django can be used as the backend for a single-page application.

Your first Django site

This chapter covers

- Creating a Django project
- Django projects and apps
- Creating a Django app
- Running the development server
- Writing a Django view

In this chapter, you'll start your Django coding journey by taking the first steps toward building a website for musicians and bands. You'll create your first web page using the Django framework: a credits page showing who built the site.

2.1 The RiffMates project

Your cousin Nicky is a guitarist, and she has a great idea for a website: classifieds for musicians. The site will cater to musicians looking for bands, bands looking for musicians, venues looking for bands, and bands looking for gigs. Nicky even has a name picked out, *RiffMates*. Over coffee, you and Nicky have talked at great length about what the site needs, including the following:

- Profile pages for musicians, bands, and venues
- Classified ad listings
- Announcement listings for tryouts
- Search capabilities based on instruments played and style of music
- Messaging between potential matches

Nicky has confidence in your coding skills because you've talked excitedly about the Python you've learned in the past. As you think about the problem, you realize that those features are just the business requirements. To build a working website that can do all those things, you'll also need features that are common to most websites, such as

- Public-facing and private-only web pages
- Logins
- Ability for users to submit both text and image content
- User sign-up
- Password management
- A database for storage
- Admin pages for managing the site

A lot goes into what seems like a simple website. Asking around, you've heard that Django provides all those capabilities for you, so you've decided to learn Django to help you build RiffMates.

Django is a *framework*. Programming with a framework is different than programming with a library. In the case of a library, your code determines the order of execution. By contrast, when you're building inside a framework, execution control belongs to the framework. If you were building a house, a library would contain the pieces you needed for the house, whereas a framework is already the rough outline of the house. Working within a framework means your application designs are more constrained, but what you lose in flexibility, you gain in efficiency—there is less code for you to write.

The partially completed building that you get with Django is the structure of a website. Django calls this a *project*. A Django project is what interacts with a web server to respond when a user visits a URL. Your code lives inside the project and gets invoked by Django. Each time you want to create a new site, you create a new project, and you need to have the project in place before you can start adding pages to it. The rest of this chapter covers creating a project and writing your first web page inside it.

2.2   *Creating a Django project*

The Django framework includes a command-line tool that is used for creating new projects, called `django-admin` (not to be confused with the Django Admin, the web tool for managing your data). Django is published on PyPI (https://pypi.org/) and can be installed in a Python virtual environment using the command `python -m pip install  django`. Once you've got the package installed, you use the command `django-admin` to create a skeleton framework for your project.

Using virtual environments

Each time you install a package in Python, you're making it available to the entire system. As different projects have different needs, this can cause conflicts. To deal with this, Python uses *virtual environments*, which are self-contained Python setups that are isolated from each other. It is important to use a virtual environment when writing Python to avoid packaging conflicts.

Appendix A contains a brief overview of installing packages in Python virtual environments. For a full explanation on the technology, see http://mng.bz/JZVZ.

Each Django project is a Python program, but because it is built using a framework, the project provides the execution paths. When you create a new project, Django installs the bare minimum you need inside a new directory with the name that you give it.

At the heart of a Django project is a file named wsgi.py. WSGI, a Python specification that describes how code interacts with a web server, stands for *Web Server Gateway Interface.* You really don't need to know much about this, especially when you're working in your development environment; the file gets generated for you. Inside wsgi.py is a short program responsible for interfacing between your code and the web server. When you're ready to put your project in production, you'll configure your web server to point at this application in your project. This is why Django is considered a framework rather than a library: wsgi.py is the entry point, and most of the code you write will be called through it. Figure 2.1 shows you how the WSGI protocol acts as a bridge to your code through the wsgi.py file.

When you build RiffMates, or any other website, what you're really trying to do is make web pages. Each page lives at a URL, and each time a user visits a URL, you're going to want some code called to generate the page. In Django, this code is called a *view*.

When you load a page, or in some cases interact with one, your web browser is communicating with a web server. In the case of a Django project, the web server communicates with the WSGI application defined in wsgi.py. The WSGI application triggers the Django framework code. Django runs a view that is responsible for returning content that Django turns into an HTTP response for the browser.

Django needs to know what view to call for each URL on the website. This is done by mapping URLs to views. Within the framework, a URL sometimes is known as a *route*. Each Django project has a main urls.py file that contains a list of URL mappings, called `urlpatterns`. The list contains `django.urls.path` objects that specify a pattern that matches one or more URLs and what view to call when that URL gets visited.

The wsgi.py and urls.py files are key to your Django project. Every new website you build with Django requires its own copy of these files. To make your life easier, the `django-admin` command that comes with the package creates these files for you, customizing them based on your project name.

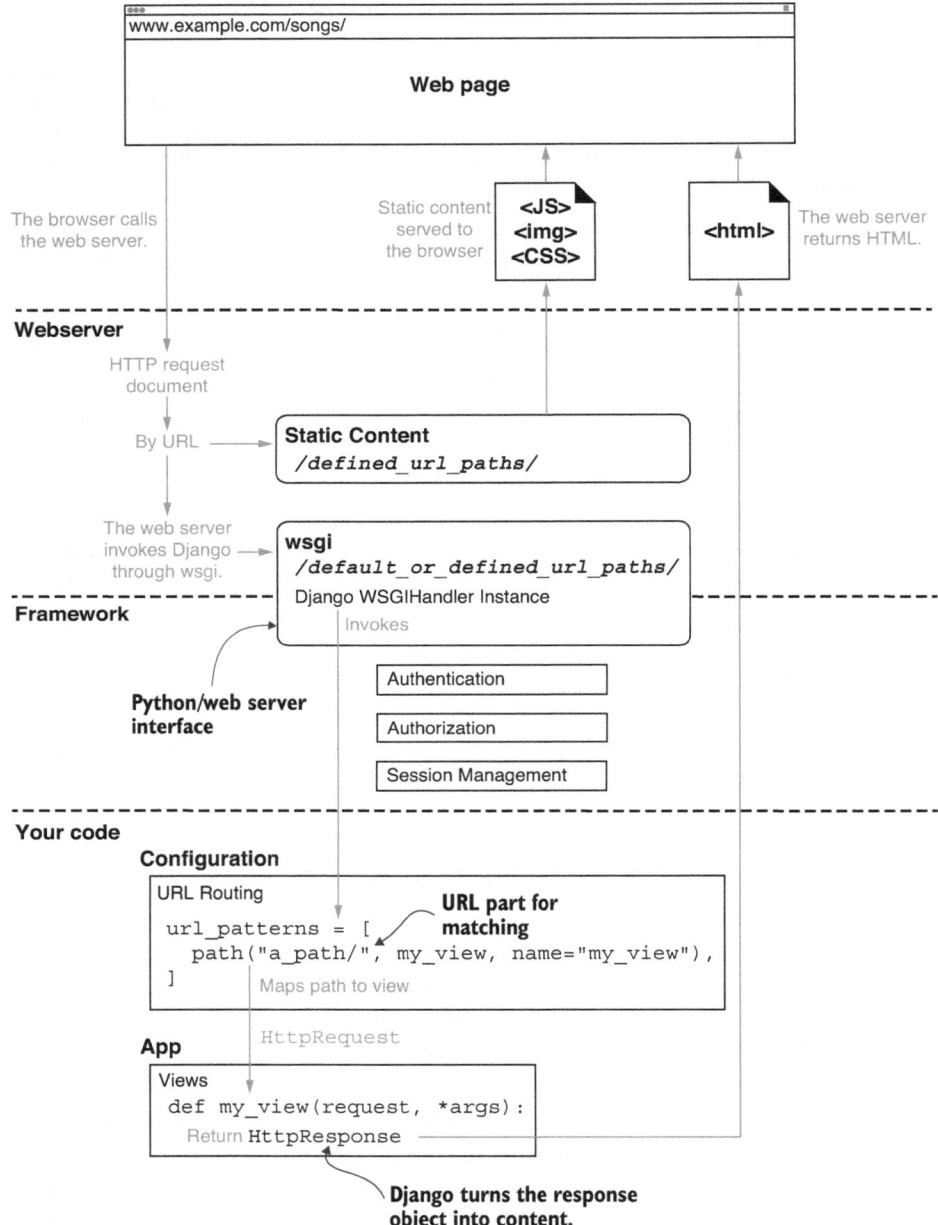

Figure 2.1   A web server invokes Django through WSGI, Django calls your code, and then it formats the response for a browser

The django-admin program is actually the entry point for a number of configuration activities. Each activity gets invoked using a command provided as an argument to djago-admin. To create a new Django project, you use the `startproject` command, giving it the name of your project. By default, `startproject` creates a new directory for your project, copies a script called manage.py inside, and creates a configuration directory. The manage.py script is similar to `django-admin` and is used to run various control and configuration actions in the project. The configuration directory contains wsgi.py, urls.py, and other files.

The configuration directory is confusingly named: it has the same name as your project. When you create RiffMates, you're going to get both a RiffMates directory and a RiffMates/RiffMates directory. It is unclear to me why the Django folks didn't name this something like *config*, as this causes confusion when you're talking to someone else about the code: Are you in the RiffMates directory? "Yes." Which one?

Naming your project

Python modules are typically named using *snake case*, or lowercase words separated by underscores. I'm not sure where I picked up the habit of naming my Django projects in violation of this convention—it may be because I'm an ex-Java programmer. If seeing *RiffMates* makes you cringe, feel free to name your project in a more "Pythonic" fashion.

Because your Django project is a directory itself, you have some flexibility about where you put your Python virtual environment. Some virtual environment tools prefer keeping all the environments together in a common directory, whereas others keep the environment with the project. In this latter case, you can put your virtual environment inside your project folder, which is what I'll be doing in the example here.

To create your first Django project, you're going to do the following:

1 Create a virtual environment.
2 Install Django into that virtual environment.
3 Use the Django `django-admin` tool to create your RiffMates project.

Once you've done all of this, you will be able to start the development server and point your browser at your new site. Open a command-line terminal, and change to the directory where you normally keep your code. Inside the terminal, create a directory for your project and a virtual environment inside of it:

```
$ mkdir RiffMates          ◁──┘ Create a directory
                                for your project.
$ cd RiffMates
RiffMates$ python3.12 -m venv ./venv    ◁──┘ Create a virtual
                                             environment.
```

NOTE Most of this book will be spent in Python, but to get going, you need to run some command-line scripts. All command-line examples use Unix syntax with dollar-sign ($) denoting the prompt. The value before the dollar-sign indicates the current directory and whether a virtual environment has been activated. For details on how to install Unix-compatible tools on Windows, see appendix A.

With the project directory and virtual environment in place, the next step is to install Django. Activate the virtual environment, and then run `pip install`:

```
                                    ┌── Activate your virtual
                                    │   environment.
RiffMates$ source venv/bin/activate    ◄─┘
(venv) RiffMates$ python -m pip install django    ◄─┤ Install Django.
```

Django is dependent on a couple of other packages. The `pip install` command will install the dependencies. Your results will look something like this:

```
Collecting django
  Using cached Django-5.0.2-py3-none-any.whl.metadata (4.1 kB)
Collecting asgiref<4,>=3.7.0 (from django)
  Using cached asgiref-3.7.2-py3-none-any.whl.metadata (9.2 kB)
Collecting sqlparse>=0.3.1 (from django)
  Using cached sqlparse-0.4.4-py3-none-any.whl (41 kB)
Using cached Django-5.0.2-py3-none-any.whl (8.2 MB)
Using cached asgiref-3.7.2-py3-none-any.whl (24 kB)
Installing collected packages: sqlparse, asgiref, django
Successfully installed asgiref-3.7.2 django-5.0.2 sqlparse-0.4.4
```

Now that you have Django installed, the last step is actually creating your project. Run the `startproject` command:

```
                                                    ┌── Create your
                                                    │   Django project.
(venv) RiffMates$ django-admin startproject RiffMates .  ◄─┘
```

Virtual environment placement and Django projects

The previous steps created the RiffMates project directory manually. It was done this way so that the virtual environment directory could be in the project directory.

By default, the `django-admin startproject` command creates your project directory for you. Some coders prefer to keep their virtual environments in a central location, rather than putting them inside the project. If you prefer this organization, you can skip the project directory creation step and use `django-admin startproject RiffMates` without the period at the end, instead:

```
code$ source ~/wherever-your-RiffMates-venv-is/bin/activate
(RIFF) code$ python -m pip install django
Collecting django
  Using cached Django-5.0.2-py3-none-any.whl.metadata (4.1 kB)
Collecting asgiref<4,>=3.7.0 (from django)
  Using cached asgiref-3.7.2-py3-none-any.whl.metadata (9.2 kB)
Collecting sqlparse>=0.3.1 (from django)
  Using cached sqlparse-0.4.4-py3-none-any.whl (41 kB)
Using cached Django-5.0.2-py3-none-any.whl (8.2 MB)
Using cached asgiref-3.7.2-py3-none-any.whl (24 kB)
Installing collected packages: sqlparse, asgiref, django
Successfully installed asgiref-3.7.2 django-5.0.2 sqlparse-0.4.4
(RIFF) code$ django-admin startproject RiffMates   ◄─┐ startproject without
(RIFF) code$ ls                                      │ the trailing period (.)
RiffMates/
```

Running the `django-admin startproject` command creates a skeleton of your project. The new RiffMates project directory looks like this:

```
RiffMates/
├── RiffMates
│    ├── __init__.py
│    ├── asgi.py
│    ├── settings.py
│    ├── urls.py
│    └── wsgi.py
└── manage.py
```

The project directory (RiffMates) contains the confusingly named configuration directory (RiffMates/RiffMates), the virtual environment, and the manage.py command. The manage.py command does pretty much the same things as `django-admin`, except it is connected to, and aware of, your project.

The RiffMates/RiffMates configuration directory contains the previously mentioned wsgi.py and urls.py files, along with a few others. Your project is a Python program, so the configuration directory is a module, meaning it contains an __init__.py file.

The asgi.py file is an asynchronous version of WSGI. Depending on the kind of web server you're using, you might point to asgi.py instead of wsgi.py. More details on when these two files get used is covered in appendix B.

The final file in the configuration directory is settings.py; it contains configuration values for changing the behavior of Django. (We'll have more on that in a bit.)

You've created your first Django project, and now, you actually have a website! Albeit, it's a very small, rather boring website, but it exists. You haven't built any pages yet, but Django provides a default one for you, and it has a fancy rocket ship on it! To see the website and bask in the glory of the rocket ship, you need a web server. Django ships with one, and when you're developing your site, this is the server to use.

You start the Django development server using the manage.py script and the `runserver` command. Note that you do this inside the RiffMates project directory, not the RiffMates/RiffMates configuration directory! Start the Django development server by running the following command:

```
(venv) RiffMates$ python manage.py runserver
```

Type less on Unix

Throughout this book, when it is time to run a Django management command, the instructions are to type python manage.py, as this is compatible across all operating systems. On Unix systems, including Linux and macOS, manage.py is executable, so you can use ./ execution. For example, the development server command gets shortened to the following:

```
(venv) RiffMates$ ./manage.py runserver
```

There are a number of management commands you'll be using frequently, so you may want to add tab completion to your shell. On bash, run the following (or add it to your .bash_profile or .bash_rc file):

(continued)

```
$ complete -f -d -W "runserver createsuperuser test shell dbshell \
migrate makemigrations loaddata dumpdata" ./manage.py
```

This allows you to type manage.py, the first letter of a management command, and then press TAB to auto-complete the name of the command, saving even more typing. Other shells have equivalent completion mechanisms; in fact, some versions of zsh ship with auto-completion for the Django command built-in.

Once going, the development server shows you some debug info and then tells you its base URL. By default, the server listens on port 8000 of your local machine. If you prefer a different port number, you can provide it as part of the `runserver` command (e.g., `python manage.py runserver 8800`). The output from the server command looks like this:

```
Watching for file changes with StatReloader
Performing system checks...                                    A warning that can
                                                               be ignored for now
System check identified no issues (0 silenced).

You have 18 unapplied migration(s). Your project may not work properly  ←
until you apply the migrations for app(s): admin, auth, contenttypes,
sessions. Run 'python manage.py migrate' to apply them.

Django version 5.0.2, using settings 'RiffMates.settings'
Starting development server at http://127.0.0.1:8000/        ←   Listening on
Quit the server with CONTROL-C.                                  port 8000
```

Don't worry about the `18 unapplied migration(s)` message—you'll deal with it shortly. Remember that `localhost` is an alias to the IP address 127.0.0.1, so you can also use the English alias http://localhost:8000/ to visit your site. Enter the base URL into your browser and see the rocket ship on the default Django project page (figure 2.2).

Dev servers are for development

For convenience, Django includes a web server. This means you don't need to install and manage one when you're creating and maintaining your website. This is not a hardened web server though, and it should never be put into an untrusted environment.

Do not expose the Django development server directly to the internet, and if you're using it internally at a company, speak with your IT department about whether it should be hosted behind your firewall. Furthermore, the default configuration for a Django project is in debug mode, which also should not be used in production. Appendix B discusses what you need to know to put your Django project into a hardened production environment. It is right there in the name: the *development server* should only be used for *development*!

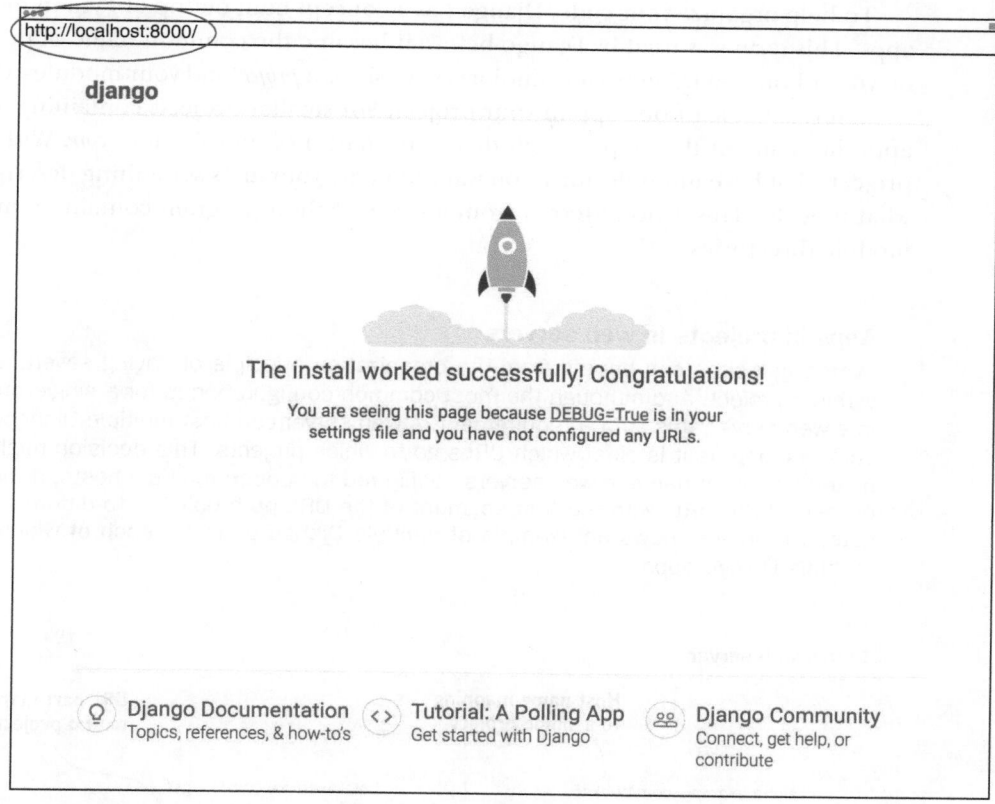

Figure 2.2   Django Rocket Page

At the moment, your website only responds to the base URL (/) because you haven't defined any views. Without views, Django shows you its version of "Hello, World!": the Django rocket ship. It is a pretty small site, but maybe boring was under-selling it—rocket ships are fun!

As fun as rocket ships are, they have nothing to do with musicians. Nicky might be happy to see you've built something, but you're going to want to replace that ship with your own content. To do that, you'll have to write your own view. In Django, views go inside modules called *apps*. Exit the Django development server with CTRL-C, and let's go create an app.

2.3   *Projects vs. apps*

Each page in your website is likely to have its own view. I've mentioned the main urls.py file where routes get registered, mapping a URL pattern to code. In theory, you can write a view, or use a built-in one, right inside the urls.py file. Your entire website could be inside the files the startproject command created for you. In practice, this is a horrible way of organizing things, and urls.py would quickly become unwieldy.

To help organize your code, Django has a concept built on top of Python modules: apps. This term was used by Django before it became the common name of programs on your phone. In Django's terminology, your site is a *project* and your modules are *apps*.

You need at least one app in your project. For smaller projects containing a single app, the name of that app isn't all that important. I often call mine *core*. With larger projects that have multiple apps, you want to name your apps something descriptive of what they do. This is no different from a larger Python program containing multiple module directories.

Apps in projects in web servers

Even small sites can benefit from the organization principle of having several apps within a project. And although the most common configuration is for a single project in a web server, this isn't a requirement. A web server can host multiple Django projects, as long as it is clear which URLs go to which projects. This decision might be based on a host name in web servers configured to support multiple hosts, or based on part of the URL, with the first segment of the URL path pointing to different projects. The figure shows an example of multiple Django projects, each of which has multiple Django apps.

Single web server

Host name mapping to a single project

URL part mapping to two projects

alpha.example.com/books/

beta.example.com/songs/
/paintings/

Books project		Songs project		Paintings project	
authors	book_stores	recordings	sheet_music	museums	artists_mgmt
				donations	

Multiple apps in a project

Multiple projects in a web server

Multiple apps per project, multiple projects per server

You should design your Django apps to be self-contained. The idea of an app even extends to third-party libraries. You can install apps written by other people, and there are thousands of them available to you out there. How you organize your apps and how much they reference each other is up to you, but the structure is in place to help you stay organized.

Similar to creating a project, there is a command for creating an app. When you create a new app, Django automatically creates skeleton files inside the app directory. The files have the following names expected by Django:

- *apps.py*—App-specific configuration
- *views.py*—Code that outputs web page content
- *models.py*—Code that defines database objects
- *tests.py*—Unit tests for your app
- *admin.py*—Code for managing your database objects
- *migrations/*—A folder containing scripts to manage the database

Figure 2.3 provides an overview of the files that are generated.

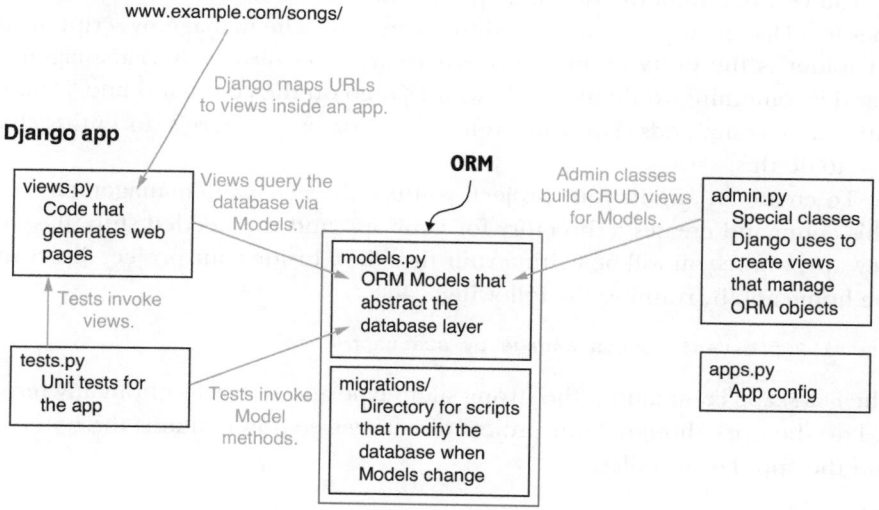

Figure 2.3 Anatomy of a Django app

The apps.py file contains default configuration for the app which helps Django identify your directory as an app, and you'll likely never need to touch it. The other four Python files are stubs that contain an `import` statement for the Django module most commonly used in that type of file.

Every time you create a new app, you get these files, but not every app needs all of them. If your app doesn't interact with the database, you don't need models.py, admin.py, or the migrations directory. If you're not a fan of tests, you can remove tests.py, but if you do, somewhere, a kitten might die. You should always have tests. For the sake of the kittens, writing good tests for your Django project gets covered in a later chapter.

Your first app, containing your first view, will be named *home*. It will contain your project's Home page, About page, and other similar content.

2.4 *Your first Django app*

Normally, when building software, it is a good idea to build a minimally viable product (MVP). You want feedback on your code as quickly as possible, and the sooner you get in front of users, the sooner you can adapt to their needs. Instead of taking an MVP approach, here you'll be taking an MUT approach. What's MUT (besides something I just made up)? It is *minimal understanding of technology*. Instead of approaching your site with the best bit of customer functionality, here, you'll be taking an approach based on the minimal amount of understanding you need to get things going. As such, the first web page you're going to build for RiffMates is the Credits page. It's not terribly exciting, but it requires the least amount of work to build.

You've already got the RiffMates project in place, but almost all your project's code goes in a Django app, so you'll need to create one. The manage.py script in your project folder is the entry point to Django *management commands*. A management command is something you'd like to do with Django on the command line. Django comes with many commands. You can even write your own—there's an entire chapter on how to do this!

To create an app in your project, you use the `startapp` management command. This command creates a directory for your app and the needed stub files, including views.py, where you will be writing your first view. Inside your project directory, create the home app by running the following:

```
(venv) RiffMates$ python manage.py startapp home
```

The `startapp` command is the strong silent type and returns without any response—it did do the work though. Your project directory tree now contains the home directory and the app skeleton files:

```
RiffMates/
├── RiffMates
│   ├── __init__.py
│   ├── asgi.py
│   ├── settings.py
│   ├── urls.py
│   └── wsgi.py
├── home
│   ├── __init__.py
│   ├── admin.py
│   ├── apps.py
│   ├── migrations
│   │   └── __init__.py
│   ├── models.py
│   ├── tests.py
│   └── views.py
└── manage.py
```

Your home app is a Python module, hence the __init__.py file. The other skeleton files for the app got created as well. Unfortunately, creating the app is not sufficient. You also need to tell Django about it. The settings.py file in your RiffMates/RiffMates configuration directory is a Python script containing variable declarations that define Django's behavior.

The settings.py file comes with dozens of configuration values, and you can add your own and access them through the `django.config.settings` module. To register your app, modify the `INSTALLED_APPS` configuration value, which is a `list` of strings that are the names of all the apps in your project.

The developers of Django have consciously made a choice here: instead of auto-discovering all the modules and treating them like apps, you have to explicitly register an app. Although this is an extra step, it means Django doesn't have to differentiate between regular Python modules and Django apps, which are also modules. By doing it this way, your project can contain modules that aren't apps, if you wish.

Django has its own apps, which come with the framework. A new project has several of them already included in `INSTALLED_APPS`. To register your newly created home app, open RiffMates/RiffMates/settings.py and add your app's name to the `list`, as in the following listing.

Listing 2.1   Tell Django about your home app

```
# RiffMates/RiffMates/settings.py
...                          ◁──────────
INSTALLED_APPS = [
    'django.contrib.admin',
    'django.contrib.auth',
    'django.contrib.contenttypes',
    'django.contrib.sessions',
    'django.contrib.messages',
    'django.contrib.staticfiles',
    'home',              ◁──┐
]
...
```

Throughout the book, you'll see ... to indicate this listing has code before or after it. Conveniently, this is also valid Python, and your compiler will ignore it if you copy it into your source.

Add the home app to the INSTALLED_APPS list.

Django is now aware of your app. You're ready to add a view to show your Credits page.

2.5   *Your first Django view*

Each view is responsible for creating content that Django returns when the view's corresponding URL gets visited. Django provides some built-in views, but most of the time, you're going to want your own. You can write views as either functions or classes. I prefer function-based views, as I find it clearer to understand a URL calling a function than it corresponding to one or more methods in a class. I'll be sticking with function-based views throughout the book.

Recall that when you visit a URL, your web browser is opening up a network connection to a web server. It knows which web server based on the host portion of the URL (known as the *domain*). The language that the browser uses to speak to the web server is called the *HTTP protocol*; it's a set of rules specifying how the browser and web server communicate. The HTTP protocol is split into two parts: the request from the browser to the server and the response from the server to the browser. Django encapsulates both of these in objects, helpfully named `django.http.HttpRequest` and `django.http.HttpResponse`.

A function-based view has two requirements: it takes at least one argument, an `HttpRequest` object, and returns an `HttpResponse` data structure (or something like it). Django uses the `HttpResponse` to produce the response document, including headers and HTML body for your browser.

By convention, the `HttpRequest` argument gets called `request` and contains many of the headers your browser sent the web server, including the URL. Your view function can take more arguments than just the request. Django supports a way of specifying multiple parameters inside a URL and mapping these to your function arguments. It also supports query parameter—that's everything after the question mark (?) in a URL. Query parameters get embedded in the request object. You'll learn more about both these techniques in future chapters.

To keep it simple, your Credits page will contain your name and Nicky's, and not much else. To keep it really simple, it will be plain text, rather than HTML. Your view is only a few of lines of code: a function that takes a `request` object, declares a string, and returns an `HttpResponse` object. Figure 2.4 shows the files that need to be changed to declare your view.

The `HttpResponse` you return needs two arguments: the content to return, and the type of that content. The content, in this case, is a string containing your credits. The second argument is `content_type`, and it changes the MIME type of the response.

Web browsers are capable of displaying all kinds of different content: HTML, images, CSS, and more. An HTTP response can contain a MIME-type header that indicates just what the content is. MIME stands for *multipurpose internet mail extensions* and, as the name implies, originally came about to define how to attach different kinds of content to an email message. By default, the `HttpResponse` object uses a MIME type that indicates HTML, as the credits page returns plain text, the `HttpResponse` object needs to be told this by setting `content_type="text/plain"`. To write your first view, open RiffMates/home/views.py, and replace the stub code with the content of the following listing.

Listing 2.2   Credits view

```
# RiffMates/home/views.py
from django.http import HttpResponse
```
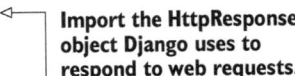
Import the HttpResponse object Django uses to respond to web requests.

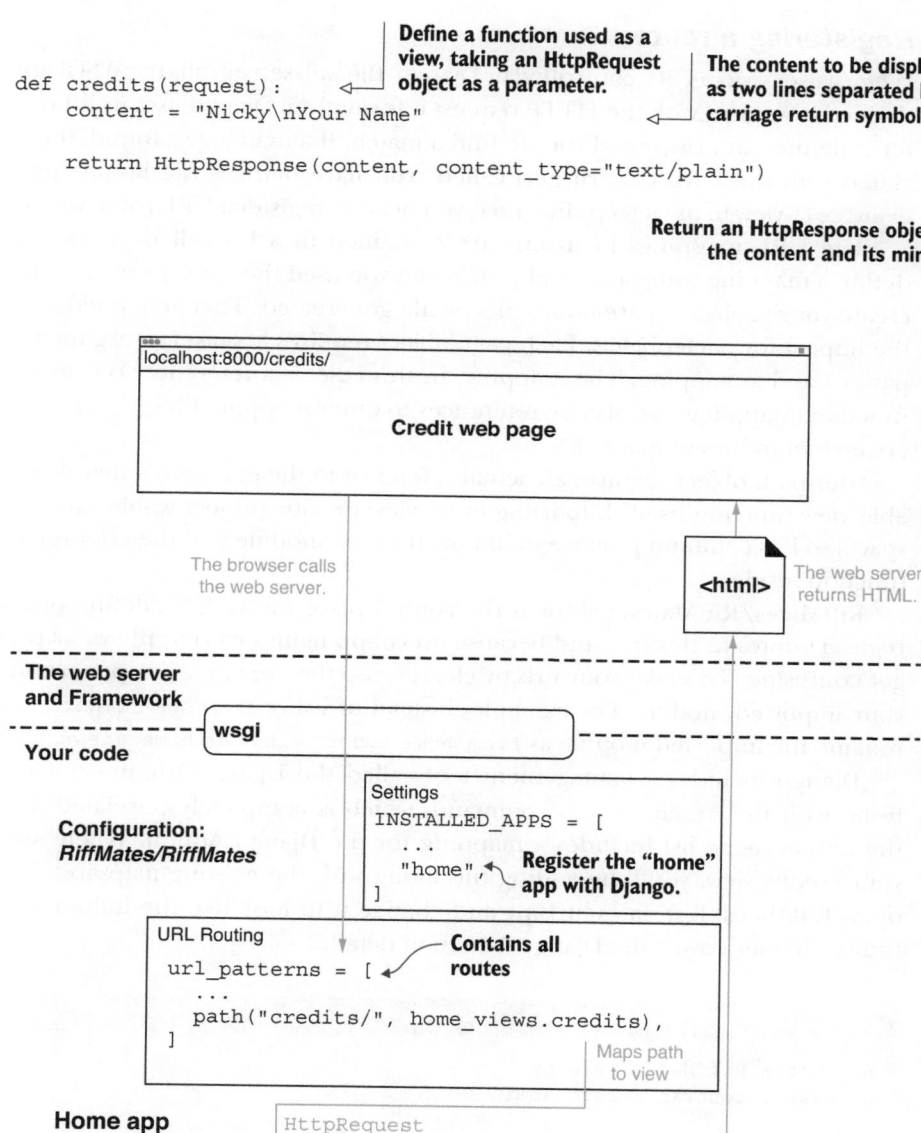

Figure 2.4 The credits() view within your *RiffMates* Django project

You're not quite done yet. Although you have a view, you haven't mapped it to a URL.
You do that by modifying urls.py.

2.6   *Registering a route*

When a user visits a URL controlled by Django, the web server calls the WSGI application defined in wsgi.py with the HTTP request information. Django uses its list of URL patterns defined in urls.py and tries to find a match. If a match gets found, the view associated with the URL pattern gets called. You have defined the home app with the credits() view in its views.py file; now, you need to register a URL route with that view.

The URL mappings in urls.py are contained in a list called urlpatterns. You define a mapping using a path object. When you used the startproject command to create your project, a bare-bones urls.py file got created. That generated file includes the import for path objects. Each path object requires at least two arguments: a URL pattern and a mapping. The mapping, in this case, is a reference to your credits() function. Mappings can also be references to other mapping files, giving the ability to create hierarchies of maps.

Your path object requires an actual reference to the credits() view—yes, the callable view function itself. Importing every view in your project would take up a lot of space, so it is common practice to import the view module and then dot-reference the function inside.

RiffMates/RiffMates/urls.py is the central place for all URL definitions. All apps register routes in this file, and because every app names its view file views.py, this can get confusing. To make your urls.py clearer, use the import ... as pattern to rename your imported module. For example, instead of using from home import views, you rename the imported module as from home import views as home_views.

Django includes a management tool called the Django Admin—not to be confused with the django-admin command, which is completely unrelated. By default, the urlpatterns list includes a mapping for the Django Admin. When you register your credits view, you'll be adding this along with the existing mapping. To do this, open RiffMates/RiffMates/urls.py and change it to look like the following listing. A future chapter covers the Django Admin in detail.

Listing 2.3   Register your view

```
# RiffMates/RiffMates/urls.py
from django.contrib import admin

from django.urls import path

from home import views as home_views          ←┘ Import the home
                                                  app, aliasing it.

urlpatterns = [                                    Register the credits view
    path("admin/", admin.site.urls),               function in the home app
    path('credits/', home_views.credits),      ←┘ against the 'credits/' path.
]
```

Note the lack of a leading slash (/) in the path pattern. Django prefixes the leading slash for you. The URL /credits/ is registered using path("credits/"). To register that URL subpath against your view, you pass a reference to the credits function to the path object. Remember, as it is a reference to a function, you aren't calling it, and don't use parentheses—it is credits, not credits().

In this code, I import the module and use a dotted reference to the view: home_views.credits. Instead, you could import the view from the module, but as you add more views to home/views.py, that would require a lot of importing.

Other ways of specifying paths

Older versions of Django provided a different mechanism for specifying the structure of a URL to register against that looked like a regular expression. Some programmers still prefer the power of regular expressions when registering routes, so re_path exists if you prefer that style or have a particularly fancy route not covered by path. I recommend switching to the newer style, as it is generally easier to read and use. For more information on re_path, see http://mng.bz/wxy5.

2.7 Visiting your view

You're almost ready to go. The last time you ran the development server, you got a warning message: 18 unapplied migrations. Django tracks when you make changes to database models and creates special scripts, called *migrations*, for making database changes. The unapplied migrations are scripts for built-in apps, like the Django Admin. In later chapters, you'll write your own database objects, but for now, you can run a migration to get rid of the warning.

The management command to run database migrations is migrate. Before running the development server, run python manage.py migrate to remove the unapplied migrations warning:

```
(venv) RiffMates$ python manage.py migrate
```

Running migrate produces a lot of output; you will see a list of the apps that required migration (Apply all migrations: admin, auth, contenttypes, sessions), along with the output from each migration app. The output will include the full name of the app and migration script. For example, Applying admin.0001_initial... OK indicates the script 0001_initial for the admin app was run successfully.

The migrate command applies migration scripts across several modules. You'll learn all about this in detail in a future chapter.

Restart the development server. This time, you won't get the warning:

```
(venv) RiffMates$ python manage.py runserver
Watching for file changes with StatReloader
Performing system checks...

System check identified no issues (0 silenced).

Django version 5.0.2, using settings 'RiffMates.settings'
Starting development server at http://127.0.0.1:8000/
Quit the server with CONTROL-C.
```

With the development server running, you can see the results of your hard work by visiting: http://localhost:8000/credits/. If you've wired everything together correctly, it should look like figure 2.5. When you're done admiring your accomplishment, press CTRL-C to exit the development server.

```
http://localhost:8000/credits/
Nicky
Your Name
```

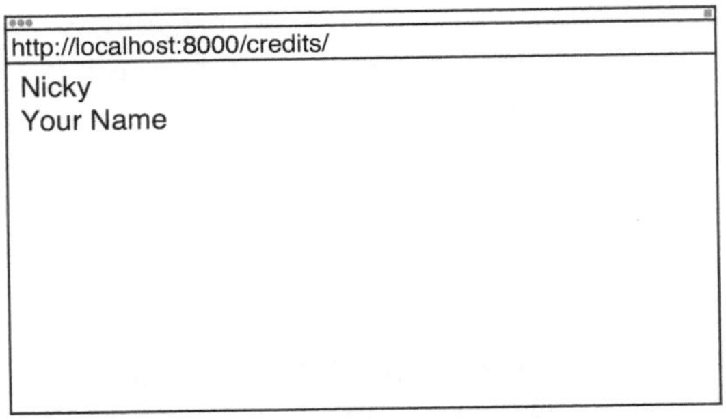

Figure 2.5   Your first Django view

You've got your first project built and your first view written, and you have enough information to build an entire website. Everything else is about how to make fancier and fancier views, but the cornerstone has been laid. Each page you add to your site will be another view. Instead of your view returning plain text, you can return HTML. HTML is verbose. Because of this, Django includes tools to manage it more like code, through the use of templates. You can write reusable parts and compose them together. That is the next step.

2.8   Exercises

For a bit of practice, try to adapt your code to do the following:

1   Add an About page to the site, using the same techniques as you did for the Credits page. Instead of using plain text, have the content block contain valid HTML content.

2   Add a Version Info page that contains the version number of your site. Instead of using plain text, return valid JSON. You can do this by adapting the MIME type or using a `django.http.JsonResponse` object instead. Details on the `JsonResponse` object can be found in the documentation: http://mng.bz/qOox.

Summary

- Django is a framework, rather than a library, meaning your code gets called by Django, not the other way around.
- Django calls a website a *project*.
- You create a Django project using the `django-admin startproject` command. This creates skeleton files for your website.
- Django projects contain a configuration directory that has the same name as the project directory. This directory includes the URL mapping file (urls.py) and a script that specifies configuration settings (settings.py).
- The code for your website goes in modules that Django calls *apps*.
- You create a new app using the `python manage.py startapp` command. This creates skeleton files for your app.

- Your app must be registered by adding it to the INSTALLED_APPS value in settings.py.
- URLs get mapped to functions, known as *views*, responsible for returning web content.
- To write a view, add a function to the views.py file in an app. The function takes at least one argument, an HttpRequest object, named request by convention. The function returns an HttpResponse object specifying the content returned to the browser. Your view gets registered in urls.py, using a path object to map a URL to a reference to the view function.

Templates **3**

This chapter covers
- Managing HTML-like code through templates
- Rendering templates based on context data
- Template tags and filters
- Using the `render()` shortcut inside views
- Composing and inheriting templates for HTML reuse

This chapter introduces you to adding HTML content to your website. Django includes a templating engine that can compose and control text content, allowing you to create reusable pieces of HTML, managing it like you would manage your code.

3.1 Where to use templates

In the previous chapter, you learned how to start a simple website by creating a Django project. Inside the project, you created your first app and your first view. To keep things simple, an important thing got left out: HTML. A website isn't much of a website without it. The purpose of a Django view is to return content, typically for a single web page. Your first view was the Credits page, showing the website's authors. This view used plain text; however, instead of returning plain text, most of your views will return HTML.

The Django Template Engine is a collection of tools that allow you to compose and control text in a way similar to how inheritance works in object-oriented programming. A header or footer can be declared in a separate file and then included in each page that is rendered. This isolates the text, and any changes automatically get propagated throughout your site.

On a web page with a navigation menu, you might want to highlight the current page. Instead of different header blocks for each page, Django includes conditional rendering. It supports the equivalent of Python `if` and `else` statements, allowing you to change the rendering of the navigation bar based on Python objects passed as arguments to the template engine.

> **NOTE** The template engine is not HTML specific—it operates on any text. The vast majority of the time, you will be using it to manage HTML, but you can also templatize email messages, personalize prefilled text in forms, or perform any other text manipulation you come up with.

The interface to the template engine is composed of two key objects, both found in the `django.template` module: `Template` and `Context`. The `Template` object represents a piece of text written in the template language, while the `Context` object provides data to the template engine for rendering the result.

3.2 Context objects and the parts of a Template

Using the Django Template Engine breaks down into three steps:

1 Create or load a template.
2 Define the context.
3 Render a template using the context.

When you create or load a template, you get a `django.template.Template` object as a result. The contents of this object are actually a compiled version of the text you want in the template. To get the output from the template, you need to render it. Rendering requires a `django.template.Context` object that contains any data used in the template. For example, if you are using a template for a navigation menu and want to highlight the current page, the context might contain a variable indicating the name of the current page. Inside the template, a conditional block checks the value of the current page variable and changes the rendering of the menu as needed. Pieces of templates can be composed together, so a template is often part of a page—it doesn't have to be the whole thing.

`Context` objects get built using dictionaries. Anything you can put inside a Python dictionary can be used as context. If the template references something not found within the context, it is rendered as an empty string. The effect is that errors are handled silently. This is both a feature and a frustration. Blank spots on the page are less problematic for your users, but it may be a bit trickier to find bugs, as the evidence is sneakily silent.

The simplest possible template is text containing no special characters. When rendered, you will get exactly the text you gave the template—what you put in is what you get out. This is of limited value. To have your template change based on the context, Django provides four constructs:

- *Variable rendering via matched double braces*—`{{ name }}`
- *Script actions, like conditionals and loops using tags*—`{% now "Y" %}`
- *Comments*—`{# a comment #}`
- *Output modification via filtering data*—`{{ name | upper }}`

A set of matched braces, sometimes known as *mustache braces*, gets used to display a variable. The name given inside the braces is used as a key in the context dictionary and replaced with the corresponding value.

A variable can be referenced using dot-notation to get at the contents of an object. Consider a `Person` class with a `last_name` attribute. If the context contained an object named `person`, then `{{ person.last_name }}` uses the person object and dereferences the `last_name` attribute on that object.

Tags in the template language get used to perform logic actions inside the template. Some tags get used on their own, and some are paired. The `{% now %}` tag renders as the current date. This tag takes a parameter that indicates the format of the date. Rendering `{% now "Y" %}` results in the current year.

Paired tags typically control the rendering of the block between the tags. One such pair is `{% if %}` and `{% endif %}`, which surround a block that is conditionally rendered. The `{% if %}` tag takes a condition to be evaluated as an argument and behaves similarly to the if statement in Python. For example, `{% if num > 3 %}` Lots `{% endif %}` renders Lots if the key num exists in the context dictionary, is a number, and has a value greater than 3. A variety of common tags are covered later in this chapter.

Filters are a way of modifying data in a variable. Remember, variables get displayed via paired double braces. You apply a filter to a variable by using the pipe (`|`) operator. For example, `{{ name | upper }}` applies the `| upper` filter to the value contained within name. The `| upper` filter is similar to `str.upper()`, returning the contents of name in capital letters. Several filters and their use are covered later in this chapter.

There are over 80 tags and filters built into the Django template language. Appendix C is a glossary of the tags and filters built into Django and points you to the online documentation. The template language is also extensible, meaning you can even write your own tags and filters (https://docs.djangoproject.com/en/5.0/howto/custom-template-tags/). Many third-party libraries, written and shared by fellow community members, are available to install as Django apps. For example, the Django Packages website has a listing dedicated to template tag packages: https://djangopackages.org/grids/g/templatetags/.

3.3 Django shell

As templates are typically rendered through a view, learning and experimenting with them might mean having to write a lot of throwaway code. Instead of creating a dummy view, you can use the Python read, evaluate, print loop (REPL). If you haven't come across the REPL yet, it's built into Python and allows you to immediately see the results of a line of code. In the REPL, you type some code (the tool *reads* it), and then the tool *evaluates* it, *prints* the results, and *loops* to do it all over again.

For regular Python, you enter the REPL by running `python` without any arguments. With Django being a framework, you can't just fire up the Python REPL within a Django context. There are several steps to be performed to get you into "Django land," including importing and activating the framework. Luckily, Django provides a command, so you don't have to do this by hand. Instead of calling `python`, you call the `manage.py` command named `shell`:

```
(venv) RiffMates$ python manage.py shell
```

When you run the command, you get a regular Python REPL, except it is Django aware. Because Django is a framework, if you used the default Python REPL on its own, you'd have to run some commands to get it to load and understand the Django environment; instead, the `shell` command takes care of this for you. When started, the command reports version information and then sends you to the `>>>` prompt, awaiting your instructions:

```
(venv) RiffMates$ python manage.py shell
Python 3.12.1 [Clang 13.0.0 (clang-1300.0.29.30)] on darwin
Type "help", "copyright", "credits" or "license" for more information.
(InteractiveConsole)
>>>
```

If you need to experiment with some Django code, using the `shell` command to enter the REPL is less work than trying to implement your idea in a view. It is also less error prone; you don't have to remember to remove your experiment afterward. Now, let's use the `shell` to play with some templates.

> **NOTE** The REPL supports the use of the up arrow to retrieve previous commands. This can save a lot of typing if you're doing repetitive work. If you are using the REPL a lot, you may want to search for third party replacements, such as `bpython`, `IPython`, and `ptpython`, that include advanced code editing tools and macro capabilities.

3.4 Rendering a Template

`Template` objects are, well, objects. You can instantiate them like any other object. In practice, you're more likely to use a shortcut that loads a file containing the template content, but let's deal with the objects directly first to better understand how they work. You'll learn about using shortcuts to load and render template content from file a little later in the chapter.

`Context` objects contain the data that is used by the template when it is rendered. They take a dictionary containing the data you want in the context as an argument. To render a template, you call `Template.render()`, which returns the resulting string.

In keeping with a grand programming tradition, your first template is "Hello, World!". Figure 3.1 illustrates the concept. A `Template` object is instantiated with a template string, `Hello {{ name }}`; then a `Context` object is created with a dictionary with the key `name`; and then the `Template` object's `.render()` method is called with the `Context` as an argument. The result is the rendered template. Figure 3.1 shows this interaction.

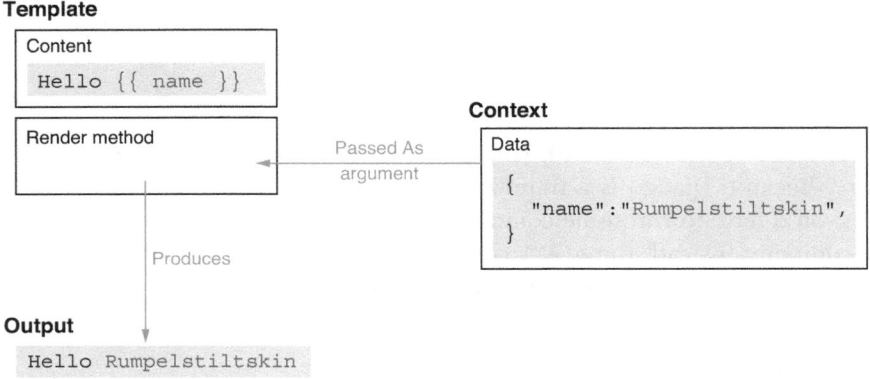

Figure 3.1   **The `render()` shortcut saves you code**

Double braces indicate variable replacement in a template. In this example, the `{{ name }}` causes the template engine to look for a key called `name` in the `Context`. The contents of the corresponding value are used to replace the double-brace content in the template.

Let's play with this in the Django REPL. Use the `shell` management command like you did earlier to start a new session. Once in the REPL, import the `Template` and `Context` from `django.template`. Instantiate a `Template` object, passing in `"Hello {{ name }}"` as the template to be rendered. This is the same as in figure 3.1. Now, instantiate a `Context` object, passing in a `dict` with key `name` and a corresponding value for your name. Call the `.render()` method on the `Template` object, passing in your `Context` object. This will render the template, returning the output string. The following listing shows just that.

Listing 3.1   Rendering a template in the Django REPL

```
>>> from django.template import Template, Context
>>> t = Template("Hello {{name}}")
```

A **Template** object with the
template text Hello {{ name }}

```
>>> c = Context({"name":"Rumpelstiltskin"})
>>> t.render(c)
'Hello Rumpelstiltskin'
```

◁——— **A dictionary containing data for the context**

Render the template using the given context. The result replaces {{ name }} with Rumpelstiltskin.

The template language allows you to access the attributes on objects, the items in lists and tuples, and the values in dictionaries. All of these are done using a dot notation, even those parts that would require square brackets to access in Python. For example, {{ person.name }} works for both a person object and a person dictionary, accessing the name attribute or key, respectively. The third item in a list of fruit is accessed using {{ fruit.2 }}.

Dot notation also gets used for callables without arguments. For example, {{ person.show_name }} invokes the person.show_name() method and renders its results.

In addition to doing variable replacement with double braces, you can use template tags to control the content of your rendered result. The most common tags are conditional blocks and loops, but some are for straight replacement as well. The {% lorem %} tag gets rendered as *lorem ipsum* text, a chunk of Latin often used in the printing industry to indicate placeholder text. On your website, you might use the {% lorem %} tag when you're waiting on someone else to write some copy, dropping the tag in so that the page renders with some content taking up space on the page, instead of just leaving the area blank. This may not be the most popular tag, but it is a good example to help learn how tags work.

In the REPL, create a new Template object that uses the {% lorem %} tag. As your template doesn't have any data, use an empty dictionary to instantiate the Context. The following listing contains the code and the resulting Latin.

Listing 3.2   Using the {% lorem %} tag in the Django REPL

```
>>> t = Template("Cicero said: '{% lorem %}', amongst other things")
>>> t.render(Context({}))
"Cicero said: 'Lorem ipsum dolor sit amet, consectetur
adipisicing elit, sed do eiusmod tempor incididunt ut labore et
dolore magna aliqua. Ut enim ad minim veniam, quis nostrud
exercitation ullamco laboris nisi ut aliquip ex ea commodo
consequat. Duis aute irure dolor in reprehenderit in voluptate
velit esse cillum dolore eu fugiat nulla pariatur. Excepteur
sint occaecat cupidatat non proident, sunt in culpa qui officia
deserunt mollit anim id est laborum.', amongst other things"
```

Like many tags, {% lorem %} takes optional arguments, allowing you to control how much text results. The first two arguments are a count and a method. The method can be w, p, or b, for *words, paragraphs,* or *blocks.* The value of the count tells you how many of the words, paragraphs, or blocks to include. Render another template in the REPL, this time telling {% lorem %} to display five words. The following listing shows the code the and resulting, much shorter, text.

Listing 3.3   The `{% lorem %}` tag with arguments in the Django REPL

```
>>> t = Template("{% lorem 5 w %}")
>>> t.render(Context({}))
'lorem ipsum dolor sit amet'
```

Tags are kind of like functions, and like functions, the choice of arguments is specific to the tag. Some tags interpret their arguments as the names of variables, while others, like `{% lorem %}`, take them verbatim. You'll see the difference as you learn a few of the more common tags in the next section.

3.5   *Common tags and filters*

Although Django comes with many tags and filters, there are a few that you will find you use over and over again. Let's cover a few you're likely to use while building Riff-Mates.

3.5.1   *Conditional blocks*

It was probably early on in your programming journey when you first came across the need for `if` statements. You'll find the same need in templates. The basic conditional statement is a block, which means it uses paired tags: `{% if %}` and `{% endif %}`.

The `{% if %}` tag takes a condition, which if true means the block gets rendered. The simplest condition is the name of a variable. In this case, the variable gets evaluated for "truthiness," following the same rules as `if` statements in Python. The following renders the `<h1>` content if `first_page` evaluates to `True`:

```
{% if first_page %}
    <h1> Welcome to <i>RiffMates</i> </h1>
{% endif %}
```

If `first_page` contains zero, `False`, an empty container (`list`, `set`, `dict`, etc.), or doesn't exist in the context, the block gets excluded from the render. All other values of `first_page` result in the enclosing block getting shown.

Block tags generally don't care about newlines or spacing. The `{% if %}` and `{% endif %}` tags can appear on the same line. I frequently have a conditional block in my `<title>` tag, optionally appending a page name to a default shorter title:

```
<title>RiffMates{% if title_suffix %} &mdash; {{title_suffix}}
➡ {% endif %}</title>
```

The `{% if %}` tag supports the same comparison operators as Python. You can use `==`, `!=`, `<`, `>`, `<=`, `>=`, `in`, `not in`, `is`, and `is not` to compare variables or values. Comparing the value of `num_drummers` to a constant is similar to Python:

```
{% if num_drummers > 1 %}
    <b>You only need one drummer!</b>
{% endif %}
```

When the variable in a comparison is not in the context, the condition gets treated as False. If num_drummers is not in the context in the preceding example, the comparison fails and the block does not get shown.

Conditional clauses can be combined using Boolean operators, like those in Python. You can use and, or, and not in an {% if %} tag. The same order of precedence as Python gets applied. If and and or are in the same clause, and gets higher precedence. The following code checks for the "truthiness" of musicians and compares num_venues to three:

```
{% if musicians and num_venues > 3 %}
    You have lots of choice!
{% endif %}
```

More complex conditional blocks can be constructed by adding {% elif %} and {% else %} tags to your conditional. These tags behave like their Python counterparts. As you might expect, the comparison clauses that work in {% if %} work in {% elif %} as well. The following checks for num_musicians being greater than 0 and less than 6, and then if that condition fails, it checks if num_musicians is greater than or equal to 6, and if that condition fails, you are told that you have zero musicians:

```
{% if num_musicians > 0 and num_musicians < 6 %}
    Band sized
{% elif num_musicians >= 6 %}
    Big-band sized
{% else %}
    Your band needs people
{% endif %}
```

3.5.2 Looping blocks

Consider a case in which you have a list of instruments that you want to output in an HTML bullet list. To do this cleanly, you need to loop over your data. The {% for %} tag is similar to a for statement in Python, allowing you to iterate over a container. Just like Python, the tag takes the name of a variable used inside the looping context and an object to iterate over. The value in the looping context gets used like any other variable, often displayed using double braces.

One use of the {% for %} tag is to construct <ul>, <ol>, or <table> structures in HTML. In all these cases the {% for %} tag goes inside the containing structure, with the contents of the {% for %} block being what you want to be repeated. The following code outputs a <ul> tag with its insides constructed by looping over the instruments value, rendering <li> tags:

```
<ul>
    {% for instrument in instruments %}
        <li> {{instrument.name}}: {{instrument.cost}}</li>
    {% endfor %}
</ul>
```

Remember that variable rendering supports dot notation. For the preceding to work, `instruments` must be iterable and contain objects that have `name` and `cost` attributes.

If the iterable given to `{% for %}` is empty, nothing in the block will be displayed. Depending on your situation, this might result in an empty list or table. You can either wrap the enclosing HTML in an `{% if %}` block or use the optional `{% empty %}` feature of the loop. Anything within the `{% empty %}` section of a `{% for %}` tag only gets rendered if there was nothing in the iterable being looped over:

```
<ul>
    {% for instrument in instruments %}
        <li> {{instrument.name}}: {{instrument.cost}}</li>
    {% empty %}
        <li> <i>No instruments found</i> </li>
    {% endfor %}
</ul>
```

In addition to the loop variable you define in `{% for %}`, there is an implicit variable as well: `forloop`. This is an object that contains attributes with information about the state of the loop as it is being iterated. The `forloop.counter` attribute is a 1-based count of the loop iteration. The Boolean values `forloop.first` and `forloop.last` indicate whether it is the first or last iteration of the loop, respectively. You can turn the previous example's `<ul>` into a sentence instead:

```
My favorite instruments are:
{% for instrument in instruments %}

    {% if forloop.last %} and {% endif %}

    {{ forloop.counter }}. {{instrument.name}}

    {% if forloop.last %}. {% else %}, {% endif %}
{% endfor %}
```

I've included extra newlines and indentation in this example to make the template readable—for HTML this wouldn't matter. If `instruments` contained two objects named `Bassoon` and `Oboe`, the result (stripped of newlines and extra spaces), would be

```
My favorite instruments are: 1. Bassoon, and 2. Oboe.
```

All the forloop attributes

The following is a complete list of the attributes available in the internal `forloop` object:

- `forloop.counter`—The iteration count of the loop, starting at 1
- `forloop.counter0`—The iteration count of the loop, starting at 0
- `forloop.revcounter`—The number of iterations remaining in the loop, with the last being 1
- `forloop.revcounter0`—The number of iterations remaining in the loop, with the last being 0

- `forloop.first`—A Boolean that is `True` for the first iteration
- `forloop.last`—A Boolean that is `True` for the last iteration
- `forloop.parentloop`—The `forloop` object for the surrounding loop, in the case of nested loops

3.5.3   Comment blocks

There are two ways to write a comment in the Django template language: inline and using a multiline tag. *Inline comments* use matching {# and #} braces, while *multiline comments* use a {% comment %} block tag. The multiline form is useful for temporarily commenting out parts of a template while you are debugging. This code has an inline comment beside `Guitar` and has commented out the `Oboe` and `Bassoon` tags:

```
<ul>
    <li> Guitar {# cool instrument #} </li>
    <li> Drums </li>
    {% comment "For orchestras only" %}
    <li> Oboe </li>
    <li> Bassoon </li>
    {% endcomment %}
</ul>
```

When the preceding HTML gets rendered, the opinion next to `Guitar` is not shown. Likewise, neither of the symphony instruments appear in the list. The {% comment %} tag takes an optional argument of a string used as a note about the comment. Yes, you can comment your comment. It might seem silly, but if you are commenting out a large block of a template, it is sometimes helpful to leave yourself a note reminding yourself why.

3.5.4   Verbatim blocks

One thing almost every coder enjoys writing about is coding. Many characters that are meaningful in HTML you will also find in your code. This can make for some messy HTML. Writing a Python `if` statement with comparison operators in a web page requires entities like > and < to display properly.

This problem is even worse if you're writing a website about Django or JavaScript templating. Both of these cases use characters that are special to HTML or the Django Template Engine itself. There is a tag that solves this: {% verbatim %}. This block tells the template engine to render everything contained within exactly how it is. You can even name a {% verbatim %} block so that you can wrap {% verbatim %} blocks. The following code contains {{ }} operators and a {% verbatim %} tag that are ignored by the Django Template Engine, as they're all inside a {% verbatim %} block:

```
{% verbatim myblock %}
    Many JavaScript templates use {{ }} operators which overlap
    with the Django Template Engine. A similar problem exists if
    you wish to show a tag like {% verbatim %}.
{% endverbatim myblock %}
```

3.5.5 Referencing URLs

There are many situations in which URLs appear inside HTML. You may be linking to another page, referencing a CSS file, or showing an image. In most of these cases, your URL will be pointing to another Django view or an asset under Django's control. You can hardcode the URL in your HTML, but if you decide to refactor your URL mapping, you'll end up with a lot of work—or worse: some broken links.

To help solve this problem, Django provides a way of naming URL mappings. Recall the `django.urls.path` objects inside urls.py that map a URL to a view. These objects have an optional argument allowing you to name the `path`. You can reference a URL in your code using this name or in a template via the `{% url %}` tag.

To see this in action, first, you will need to name one of your URLs. Open Riff-Mates/RiffMates/urls.py and modify the `path` object for the Credits page, adding the `name` attribute, like in the following listing.

Listing 3.4 Naming a URL mapping

```
# RiffMates/RiffMates/urls.py
...
from home import views as home_views
...
urlpatterns = [                                    Naming the
    ...                                            mapping for the
    path('credits/', home_views.credits, name="credits"),  ◁─┘ credits view
]
```

By adding the `name="credits"` argument to the `path` object, this URL mapping can now be referenced with the string `"credits"` elsewhere in your code and templates. To access the resulting URL in a template, use the `{% url %}` tag, giving it `'credits'` as an argument. Note the surrounding quotes; the `{% url %}` can take either a variable or a hardcoded string. The most common use for the `{% url %}` tag is inside a link in your HTML:

```
<a href="{% url 'credits' %}">Credits Page</a>
```

The preceding anchor tag's `href` parameter gets rendered using the URL for your Credits page. If you decide to change the URL for the `credits()` view, you only do this in the urls.py file, and the `{% url %}` tag takes care of the rest.

Always name your routes

You should always use named URLs in your code. Doing otherwise is like not using constants in your code.

Take careful note of the use of the single and double quotes in this example. As HTML uses double quotes to demark a tag's attributes, you need to use single quotes inside the `{% url %}` tag.

3.5.6 *Common filters*

Tags are sometimes used to render a specific value, like with {% now %} or {% url %}, but are mostly used for control flow, like {% if %} and {% for %}. Often, you want to perform an action on some data, modifying how it will be displayed. Consider a datetime object in Python: it stores date and time information, but when you want to print it out, you have a large number of choices for formatting the display. By changing the arguments to the .strftime() method, you change how the date is shown. Filters in Django templates are a generic way of doing this kind of action on all kinds of data.

Filters apply inside double-brace surrounded variables with the filter's change applied to the variable before it is rendered. You use a filter through the pipe (|) operator within the double braces. The input to a filter is the contents of the variable, while its output is an action applied to the data.

Two commonly used filters are | upper and | lower. These behave like the str.upper() and str.lower() calls, changing the case of the corresponding string. The template {{ word | upper }} results in rendering the contents of word after changing all its letters to upper case.

The following are some other common filters:

- {{ num | pluralize }}—Returns s if the value of num is greater than 1
- {{ words | first }}—Returns the first item in a list
- {{ words | last }}—Returns the last item in a list

The {{ | pluralize }} filter is useful for composing counting sentences. For example, the template text You have {{ num }} message{{ num | pluralize }} gets rendered as "You have 3 messages." when num contains three. The {{ | first }} and {{ | last }} filters are handy when you need items out of a list. You can always use {{ words.0 }} to also get the first, but as the template language doesn't support negative indexing, the only way to get the last item is with this filter.

Like tags, filters can take arguments. You pass arguments to a filter using the colon (:) character. The | join filter works like Python's str.join() method, taking a list and constructing a string from the result. This filter takes an argument specifying the separator between the joined items, most commonly a comma (,). The template {{ words | join:"," }} is equivalent to the Python ",".join(words).

You've now seen how to create Template objects, how to render them using a Context, and an overview of some key tags and filters. Doing all of this in a view would make your Python code rather unwieldy. Almost every view you write is going to want to render a template to return some HTML to your user. Because this is such a frequent activity, Django provides a shortcut method, called render(). This shortcut loads a template from a file, creates a Context object based on a dictionary, and returns an HttpResponse object, all in a single line of code.

3.6 *Using render() in a view*

Each time someone visits a page on *RiffMates* your view will return some HTML to their browser. The vast majority of your views will do a bit of logic processing and then load and render a template containing the HTML for their page. The `django.shortcuts.render()` function encapsulates most of what you need to render some HTML in a single call. Figure 3.2 shows the code savings you get by using the shortcut.

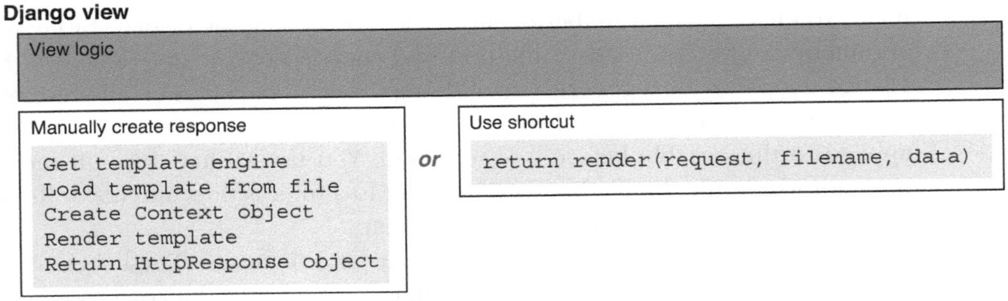

Django view

```
View logic
```

```
Manually create response                 or    Use shortcut
Get template engine                             return render(request, filename, data)
Load template from file
Create Context object
Render template
Return HttpResponse object
```

Figure 3.2   The `render()` shortcut saves you code

The `render()` function has two required arguments: the `HttpRequest` object passed into the view and the name of a template to load from disk. You tell Django where to look for templates by changing configuration in settings.py—more on that in a moment. The `render()` function also has optional arguments for providing a context dictionary, specifying the MIME type of the response and changing the HTTP status code.

The view for your Credits page consisted of a hardcoded string using plain text. You want RiffMates to contain more complicated pages than that. Let's add a view that shows your users the latest happenings on the site with a News page, this time using HTML.

You'll need a view for your News page. Call it `news()`, and put it in RiffMates/home/views.py along with your views for the Credits and About pages (if you did the exercises at the end of chapter 2). The `news()` view uses the `render()` shortcut, which needs to be imported at the top of the file.

The signature for `news()` is the same as `credits()`, taking a `request` object as an argument. Inside the view, a dictionary holds a list containing the news shown on the page. This dictionary gets passed to `render()` as context for the template. The result from `render()` is an `HttpResponse` object, which the view then returns. The `render()` shortcut takes three arguments:

- The `request` object
- The name of an HTML page, news.html in this case
- A reference to the data dictionary to be used as the template context

Modify RiffMates/home/views.py, adding the import for `render()` and the new code for `news()`, as in the following listing.

Listing 3.5   Adding a view for the news page

```
# RiffMates/home/views.py
from django.shortcuts import render
...
def news(request):
    data = {
        'news':[
            "RiffMates now has a news page!",
            "RiffMates has its first web page",
        ],
    }

    return render(request, "news.html", data)
```

Like all views, `news()` must be registered as a route. You need a `path` object inside Riff-Mates/RiffMates/urls.py for the `news()` view, similar to how you did for `credits()`. Add the new `path` object to `urlpatterns`, like in the following listing.

Listing 3.6   Registering the `news()` view as a route

```
# RiffMates/RiffMates/urls.py
...
urlpatterns = [
    ...
    path('news/', home_views.news, name="news"),      ⟵┐ New path object mapping "/
]                                                         news/" to the news() view
```

The `render()` shortcut in the `news()` view looks for an HTML template named news.html. Before creating that template, you must tell Django where to look for templates. You do this by modifying the `TEMPLATES` configuration in RffMates/RiffMates/ settings.py. The `TEMPLATES` value is a dictionary containing four keys that control how templates work in Django:

- `BACKEND` *specifies which template engine to use in your project.* Django ships with the original Django Template Engine as well as a popular third-party template engine, named Jinja2. You can also install other third-party engines if you prefer. I'll be sticking with the default throughout this book.
- `DIRS` *is a list of directories in which Django looks for templates.*
- `APP_DIRS` *is a Boolean value.* When `True` (the default), Django will look for template directories within the app directories. Note that the apps are searched in order of their appearance in the `INSTALLED_APPS` configuration value.
- `OPTIONS` *is a nested dictionary to pass configuration options to the template engine.* The default values for this are sufficient.

By default, the `DIRS` property is an empty `list` and needs to be changed to wherever you decide to put your templates. The most common place to put your templates is in your project folder in a directory named *templates*. Use your file explorer or the command line to add such a directory. Note that this goes in your project folder, since it is a sibling of your home app directory; it does *not* go in the RiffMates/ RiffMates configuration folder. The following listing shows the complete folder structure so far.

Listing 3.7   The new templates directory and the soon-to-be-created news.html

```
RiffMates/
├── RiffMates
│   ├── __init__.py
│   ├── asgi.py
│   ├── settings.py
│   ├── urls.py
│   └── wsgi.py
├── home
│   ├── __init__.py
│   ├── admin.py
│   ├── apps.py
│   ├── models.py
│   ├── tests.py
│   └── views.py
├── manage.py
└── templates
    └── news.html
```

Template locations: A common location vs. app directories

The APP_DIRS option in the TEMPLATES configuration allows you to tell Django to look inside your apps for templates. When APP_DIRS is True, Django will look for a directory named templates in each of your app directories. Whether you keep all of your templates with their corresponding apps or put them in a common location is a matter of style.

When I first started writing Django, I tended to keep my templates with their corresponding apps. I only used the common folder for reusable template blocks. Over time, I have drifted in the other direction. For most projects I have found it simpler to keep all the HTML in one place.

The one exception is if the app itself is reusable. Reusable apps are beyond the scope of this book, but you can write Django apps that can be installed like other Python projects. In this case, any templates the app needs must be shipped with the app and, thus, go in the app's templates directory.

The DIRS property list expects a fully qualified path to your template directory. Paths like this are common in the settings.py file. As most paths in your project will be relative to the project directory, Django declares a configuration option near the top of settings.py, called BASE_DIR. By default, the value of BASE_DIR is the fully qualified path of your project directory inside a pathlib.Path object. Older versions of Django used `os.join()` and strings to specify a path, so be careful if you are dealing with older code. Modify the `DIRS` option of the `TEMPLATES` configuration in settings.py to point your newly created RiffMates/templates directory. The resulting configuration for `TEMPLATES` is shown in the following listing.

Listing 3.8　Change your settings to point at the new templates directory

```
# RiffMates/RiffMates/settings.py
...
TEMPLATES = [
    {
        'BACKEND': 'django.template.backends.django.DjangoTemplates',
        'DIRS': [ BASE_DIR / 'templates', ],
        'APP_DIRS': True,
        'OPTIONS': {
            'context_processors': [
                'django.template.context_processors.debug',
                'django.template.context_processors.request',
                'django.contrib.auth.context_processors.auth',
                'django.contrib.messages.context_processors.messages',
            ],
        },
    },
]
```

Add your templates directory to the list of directories where Django looks for templates.

If APP_DIRS is used at the same time as DIRS, the app directories will be searched after the DIRS directories.

Your view is in place, and you have told Django where to look for news.html. The only thing left is to create `news.html`. This template is relatively small, containing a header and a `{% for %}` loop inside a `<ul>` tag. The `{% for %}` loop iterates over the `newslist` in the context dictionary and creates an `<li>` item for each list entry. Create RiffMates/templates/news.html according to the following listing.

Listing 3.9　HTML template to be rendered by the `news` view

```
<!-- RiffMates/templates/news.html -->
<!doctype html>
<html lang="en">
<head>
  <title>RiffMates News</title>
</head>
<body>
  <h1>RiffMates News</h1>

  <ul>
    {% for item in news %}
      <li>{{ item }}</li>
    {% endfor %}
  </ul>
</body>
</html>
```

With all these changes in place, it is time to see the results. Run the development server using `python manage.py runserver`, and then visit http://localhost:8000/news/. It should look something like figure 3.3.

You're much closer to having a real website now. Each web page you wish to host gets its own view. Each view gets a corresponding URL as a registered route and an HTML page. The HTML gets rendered from a template in your project's RiffMates/RiffMates/templates folder. However, there are two more things that will make your HTML writing easier: escaping special characters and composing templates. Let's start by dealing with those pesky special characters.

Figure 3.3   Your `news()` view

3.7   *Escaping special characters*

HTML uses angle brackets to make tags. Unfortunately, angle brackets can also function as greater-than and less-than signs. Your text may need to include these symbols, so HTML provides entities to work around this. If you want to write a greater than symbol in HTML, you use `&gt;`.

Template variables are data. Data comes from all sorts of places and may contain characters special to HTML. To display your data on the page as it is meant to appear, a transformation has to happen. Django has your back and automatically does the transformation. This is known as *escaping characters*.

To play with escaping, you're going to need another template. Earlier, you used the Django REPL to directly instantiate a `Template` object; for historical reasons, this version of the object does not do auto-escaping. When you load a template file into the engine through the `render()` shortcut, you are actually using a different version of a `Template` object that does auto-escape. To build a realistic experiment, you need a little snippet of a template file in your RiffMates/RiffMates/templates directory—I named mine experiment.html. Create your own experimental file, like in the following listing. My version renders a single variable.

Listing 3.10   Mini-template experiment.html for playing with auto-escape
---

```
I love the sound a {{ instrument }} makes.
```

With this template in place, you can load and render it in the REPL. You're going to do that a bunch using different values of `instrument` to see the results of auto-escaping.

Remember, you can get to Django's version of the REPL using the `manage.py` `shell` command. This time, instead of creating a `Template` object, load one using the template engine based on your experiment.html file.

Django supports multiple template engines. You retrieve the one currently configured in your settings using `Engine.get_default()`. `Engine` objects have a `get_template()` method that loads a template similar to the `render()` shortcut.

Once you have a `Template` object, call `.render()`, passing in a `Context` object, like you did earlier in the chapter. Do this with different values for `instrument` to see the results of auto-escaping. The following listing renders the template twice, once with `trombone` and once with `tuba > baritone`.

Listing 3.11 Experimenting with special HTML characters in the Django REPL

```
>>> from django.template import Engine, Context
>>> engine = Engine.get_default()
>>> t = engine.get_template("experiment.html")
>>> data = {"instrument":"trombone"}
>>> t.render(Context(data))
'I love the sound a trombone makes.\n'
>>> data = {"instrument":"tuba > baritone"}
>>> t.render(Context(data))
'I love the sound a tuba &gt; baritone makes.\n'
```

Note how changing the value of `instrument` from `trombone` to `tuba > baritone` causes auto-escaping to execute. The greater-than symbol (`>`) is rendered as `&gt;`, making it safe to display in HTML.

Django gives you several ways to control auto-escaping. The `| safe` filter indicates that a value should not be escaped. You do this if what you're rendering has HTML in it and you want it to display as HTML rather than be escaped. The `| escape` filter does the opposite, causing the filtered value to be auto-escaped. The `{% autoescape %}` tag allows you to turn auto-escaping on or off for a block. To see these in action, add a few more lines to experiment.html:

```
I love the sound a {{ instrument }} makes.
A shiny {{ instrument | safe }} is good.

{% autoescape off %}
Don't put a {{ instrument }} too close to your ear.
{% endautoescape %}
```

The template engine compiles and caches templates; if you modify experiment.html, you may or may not get the latest copy in the REPL. The Django development server watches your files and will reload edited templates, but that isn't guaranteed in the REPL. Exit the REPL after making the previous changes, and then run it again to see the effect of your new tags. Your results should look like those in the following listing. When you're done, don't close your REPL session; you're going to play around some more, using the same template in a moment.

Listing 3.12   Rendering experiment.html after your changes in the Django REPL

```
>>> from django.template import Engine, Context
>>> engine = Engine.get_default()
>>> t = engine.get_template("experiment.html")
>>> data = {"instrument":"flute"}
>>> t.render(Context(data))
"I love the sound a flute makes.\n
↪ A shiny flute is good.\n\n\n
↪ Don't put a flute too close to your ear.\n\n"
>>> data = {"instrument":"<b>sax</b>"}
>>> t.render(Context(data))
"I love the sound a &lt;b&gt;sax&lt;/b&gt; makes.\n
↪ A shiny <b>sax</b> is good.\n\n\n
↪ Don't put a <b>sax</b> too close to your ear.\n\n"
```

Without modification, the <b> tags get escaped. Using either the | safe filter or the
{% autoescape %} tag allows you to include HTML inside your data.

There is one more way to affect auto-escaping behavior: change the data. Django
has a subclass of a Python str called SafeString. You get a SafeString by calling the
mark_safe() utility method on a string. Alternatively, If you are dynamically building
snippets of HTML, you can use format_html(), which also returns a SafeString. Any
string marked as safe will not be escaped. Operations on SafeString objects return
regular str objects; if you need to modify a SafeString, you will have to mark it as
safe again.

Let's play with these utilities in the same REPL session. Use the same template as
before, but this time, modify the context data to contain a string marked as safe. The
mark_safe() function takes the string you want to mark safe as an argument. Add a
safe string with a <br/> tag to the instruments context, and then render it, as in the
following listing.

Listing 3.13   Using mark_safe() to mark data as safe in the Django REPL

```
>>> from django.utils.safestring import mark_safe
>>> instrument = mark_safe("drum<br/>")
>>> data = {"instrument":instrument}
>>> t.render(Context(data))
"I love the sound a drum<br/> makes.\n
↪ A shiny drum<br/> is good.\n\n\n
↪ Don't put a drum<br/> too close to your ear.\n\n"
```

The format_html() function works like str.format(), using braces as placeholders
and passing in arguments used to populate the string. The format_html() method
can save a lot of typing if you're building a chunk of HTML, where you'd otherwise
need to compose and use mark_safe() on individual pieces. In the same REPL session, build a phrase that contains paired <i> tags with a placeholder between them,
like in the following listing.

```
>>> from django.utils.html import format_html
>>> instrument = "bass"
>>> instrument = format_html("big <i>{}</i>", instrument)
>>> data = {"instrument":instrument}
>>> t.render(Context(data))
"I love the sound a big <i>bass</i> makes.\n
➥ A shiny big <i>bass</i> is good.\n\n\n
➥ Don't put a big <i>bass</i> too close to your ear.\n\n"
```

User input and the safety of strings

Escaping strings becomes that much more important when you start dealing with user input. Malicious users could input data that intentionally damages your web pages. Be careful using any of the tools that turn off escaping, and make sure you know what you will be allowing on your page.

There are even more string management utilities in `django.utils.html`, which deal with rendering JSON, doing tag processing, and addressing those pesky strings input by users. See the documentation for more details: http://mng.bz/7dZQ.

Escaping is all about the micro level of HTML: making sure your data gets rendered as you intended. At the macro level, you have a different problem: HTML is repetitive. The Django template language includes a way to compose and inherit blocks to help you write less HTML.

3.8 Composing templates out of blocks

Modern HTML pages tend to have a lot of moving parts, navigation bars, footers, sidebars, breadcrumbs, and more. In addition to having lots of pieces, the structure of web pages can be complex so that it's responsive across different platforms and browsers. Much of the source used to manage this complexity gets repeated on most pages across a website. To help with this, the Django Template Engine allows you to define a system of reusable components, called *blocks*.

A template block labels a section of a page with a name using paired {% block %} and {% endblock %} tags. Template pages can be composed together in an inheritance hierarchy with children gaining the structure of their parent. Any blocks in a child page with the same name as the parent page replace the block in the parent page.

Consider the `<title>` tag in head section of an HTML page. General pages in your site might set the title "RiffMates," while some pages may want to replace this with more specific information. In a parent template, you could declare a block with the name `title`, and then any inheriting child page could override this block with the specific name.

You perform inheritance with the {% extends %} tag. A child page declares that it extends a parent and inherits its parent's structure. The most common use of this is to have a base page that defines the look of your site with some placeholder blocks for content. Regular pages then extend the base page and only declare the blocks that need overriding. I typically call my main parent page base.html. This main parent page contains all the boilerplate HTML that defines the look and feel of a site. Included in the boilerplate is a block named content, which is empty. Any other page on the site then extends the base page, declaring a content block that contains the details for that page.

For more complicated sites, you may want to have a couple of variations on the main page. A common pattern is to have a main page without navigation, a page that inherits from that with navigation, and then your actual site pages. Figure 3.4 shows an About page using this hierarchy.

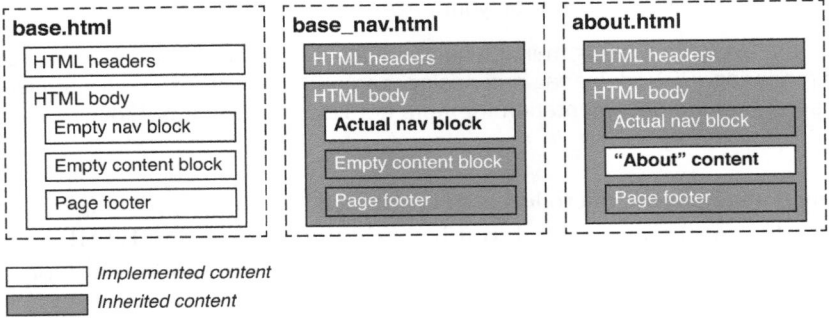

Figure 3.4   **Page inheritance for component reuse**

3.8.1   *Writing a base template file*

To put all this into practice let's write a parent page for your website. This page contains the HTML common to all pages on the site. It defines two blocks: one for the title area, and a second for content. Call the file base.html and put it with your other templates in the RiffMates/templates directory. Listing 3.15 shows example content for this parent. If you want prettier web pages, this is the place to insert code for your favorite web style framework, like Bootstrap or Tailwind.

Listing 3.15   Base HTML template for inheritance

```
<!-- RiffMates/templates/base.html -->
<!doctype html>
<html lang="en">
<head>
  <title>
    {% block title %}RiffMates{% endblock %}
  </title>
</head>
```

```
<body>
  {% block content %}
  {% endblock content %}
</body>
</html>
```

The closing {% endblock %} can optionally include the same name as its correspond-ing {% block %} tag. If you don't specify the name, the most recent block gets closed. By including the name of the block in the closing tag, you make your code clearer in the case of nested blocks.

To use your new base.html, you create a child page containing the {% extends %} tag. This tag takes a single argument: the name of the template it is extending. Inside the child file, you override the blocks declared in the parent and insert the corre-sponding content. Create news2.html, a new version of the News page. This file declares two blocks: one to override the title and the other to override the content.

Inside a block, there is a handy context variable named {{ block.super }}. This variable contains the content of the parent block. This is useful if you want to add to the parent block rather than completely replace it. Inside news2.html write content similar to that in the following listing.

> **Listing 3.16   A new 'News' file**

```
<!-- RiffMates/templates/news2.html -->
{% extends "base.html" %}

{% block title %}
  {{block.super}}: News
{% endblock %}

{% block content %}
  <h1>RiffMates News (2)</h1>

  <ul>
    {% for item in news %}
      <li>{{ item }}</li>
    {% endfor %}
  </ul>

{% endblock content %}
```

Because you added a new template file instead of modifying the existing one, you need to update your news() view. Edit RiffMates/home/views.py and change the render() call to point to the newly created news2.html file.

Once you have done that, run the development server and visit http://localhost :8000/news/ again to see the change. The page will be similar to before but this time with the 2 tacked onto the <h1> tag to prove it worked. Although the result in the browser is the same, news2.html is shorter than news.html, and if you start styling to your base page, it will be applied across every template that inherits from base.html.

Inheritance is useful for creating common base files and reusing structure throughout your web pages, but you may want to have a chunk of HTML repeated within your page instead. A nice companion to inheritance is the ability to include other templates inside your HTML.

3.8.2 *Including an HTML snippet*

I heard you want to have templates in your templates. Well, there is a tag for that. The `{% include %}` tag loads a subtemplate into your template. There are two common uses for this: organizing your template files and reusable components. HTML files have a tendency to get overly long. If you want to organize them in pieces, you can compose a page from a series of included subtemplates. The simplest use of `{% include %}` takes a single argument: the name of the template to be included. The following listing shows a sample file that includes two subtemplates.

Listing 3.17 An HTML file that includes two subtemplates

```
<!-- Sample template using include -->
{% extends "base.html" %}

{% block content %}

    <h1>Nicky's Blog</h1>

    {% include "blog1.html %}

    {% include "musicians_list.html" %}

{% endblock content %}
```

Once you have subtemplates, you can include them in multiple files, giving you reusable components. This is similar to a function call in your code: you encapsulate some HTML together and then compose it into other templates as needed. Like a function, you can even declare arguments to your subtemplate. The `{% include %}` tag has an alternate form that uses the keyword `with`. This form gives you the ability to declare key–value pairs as context in the subtemplate.

Consider a case in which you are using a third-party comment section, such as Disqus, on your website or including page view tracking JavaScript. In both cases, you need to include some HTML that is parameterized for the given page. You can build this in a reusable fashion by creating a subtemplate with a variable and then use the `with` clause when instantiating the `{% include %}` tag.

The following is a subtemplate that is part of a pagination footer. The view rendering the template takes a query string specifying a page number. You'll learn how to write this kind of view in a later chapter. For now, imagine a view that renders different content based on a query parameter named `page`. Each instance of the subtemplate contains links to the previous and next page. The subtemplate in listing 3.18 has two links, based on variables named `prev` and `next`. All of this is wrapped in `{% if %}` tags;

each link only shows for nonempty values. Remember that empty values are treated as `False` for the purposes of the {% if %} tag.

Listing 3.18   A pagination footer

```
                            Check if there is
{% if prev %}       ◄─┘     a previous page.
    <a href="?page={{prev}}">Prev</a>         ◄─┐
{% endif %}                                       If so, link to the current page
{% if next %}                                     with a new query parameter
    <a href="?page={{next}}">Next</a>             containing the page number.
{% endif %}
```

The preceding subtemplate can be reused in any web page via {% include %}. To populate the values, the tag uses the `with` format providing numbers for `prev` and `next`. The following listing shows the use of the subtemplate for page 5.

Listing 3.19   Including a subtemplate with values

```
<h3> More Content </h3>

{% include "pagination.html" with prev=4 next=6 %}
```

Normally, the first argument to {% include %} is a string containing the name of the subtemplate to include. The tag also supports the use of variables to specify the subtemplate name. If you're doing something particularly dynamic, you can get the subtemplate name from the data context. That means you can include different subtemplates, based on the context set in your view.

Templates are a powerful tool to manage HTML in a manner similar to Python. Instead of writing large files with lots of repetition, you build composable parts. Instead of hardcoding content, you build segments that include conditional rendering and loops that change the page based on the context data passed in from a view. All of this results in more maintainable code. The next step is to extend this power to your views: instead of using hardcoded data dictionaries, you retrieve content from a database.

3.9 *Exercises*

Practice makes perfect. Here are some activities you can try on your own:

1 Create a new base HTML file using your favorite web style framework, such as Bootstrap or Tailwind. Once you have something pretty, test it out by changing news2.html to extend from it.

2 Write a more advanced version of the News page by adding a `news_advanced()` view to home/views.py. Each data item in this view is a tuple containing the date and subject of the news. Create a news_adv.html template that shows the data in a table. Look-up the {% cycle %} tag and the |date filter in appendix C, and

apply them to your table, using {% cycle %} to apply striping to the table and | date to format the news item's date.

Summary

- The Django Template Engine is a system that allows you to compose and render text (typically HTML) like code.

- Django has its own templating language that supports rendering variables, conditional segments, looping, inheritance, and composition.

- Templates get rendered using a context that provides data for the result.

- Template objects can be created directly, but the more common case is to use the render() shortcut in your views

- Tags provide a way to control how your content gets rendered (like conditionals or loops), or they can act as function calls returning data (like inserting a named URL).

- Filters work in conjunction with rendered variables, modifying them in place. This allows you to change the appearance of data inside the template itself, rather than in the view.

- URLs can be named and then referenced in your code or in a template without hardcoding a value.

- The TEMPLATES section in settings.py controls which template engine gets used and where that engine looks for template files.

- The Django Template Engine automatically escapes characters that are meaningful to HTML. You can control what is an isn't escaped through a variety of tags, filters, and the SafeString object.

- Templates can inherit from other templates. This gives you a way to create a common base file with your boilerplate HTML and keeps your actual pages smaller.

Django ORM

This chapter introduces you to Django's *object relational mapping* (ORM), an object-oriented abstraction for interacting with databases. Django provides a way to create, read, update, and delete both data and tables in a database to add storage capabilities to your website.

4.1 Interacting with a database

Until now, RiffMates has been composed of mostly static content. You learned how to write views that are called when a user visits a URL, and inside those views, you created small dictionaries to provide context for rendering templates. Hardcoding data dictionaries in a view is rather limited. Most websites have a storage layer that is queried inside the view. Storage gets used for

- User accounts
- Inventory
- E-commerce transactions
- Experience customization
- User-created content
- Site data

If the phrase *site data* seems vague to you, that's because it is. Many websites store and display data that is specific to that site. For example, a movie site has data for movies, and a book site has data for books. For Nicky's RiffMates site you need

- Musicians
- Bands
- Classifieds
- Venues
- Venue lineups

As RiffMates grows, so will this list. There are a variety of approaches for storing this data, but by far, the most common is to use a relational database. You'll recall that a relational database stores content in a series of tables similar to how a spreadsheet works. The columns in a table have a data type, typically storing strings or numbers. To represent a band, your columns might include the band name and the date they were formed. Each row in the table corresponds to a single band. To be able to reference a band, the table includes an identity column, typically an auto-incrementing number provided by the database. This identity is called the table's *primary key*.

Columns can also indicate a relationship between data items, hence the term *relational* in *relational database*. To represent a song, your columns include the name of the song and, like the bands, a unique identifier. To link a band and a song, either the band or song table includes a column that references the other's unique identifier. The unique identifiers are often *primary keys*: special numbers the database creates for you. You can see an example of object relationships in figure 4.1.

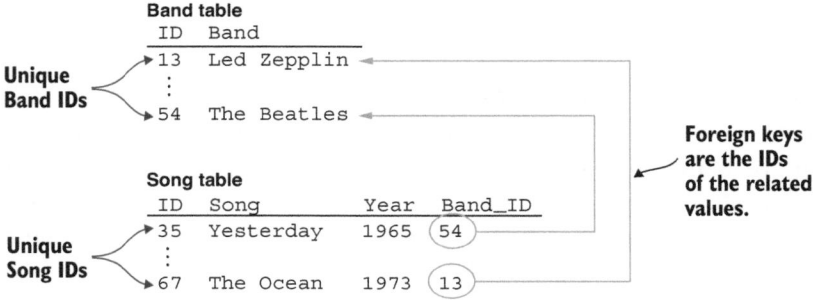

Figure 4.1   Inter-table relationships between bands and songs

Relational databases have their own programming language, called *Structured Query Language* (SQL). SQL includes structural directives for managing tables and query directives for handling the data inside the tables. One way of dealing with storage for your website is to write SQL embedded inside your Python, executing it through a connection to your database. In this case, when you query the table with song data, you get back a series of rows from the song table. Any reference to a band identifier would mean another SQL query, this time to the band table.

Creating tables means writing scripts in SQL. If you decide to add a *composer* column to the song table, that means another SQL script. It doesn't take long before you are writing a lot of SQL, but fortunately, there is an alternative.

ORM is a programming technique that maps content in a relational database to object-oriented code. Instead of thinking in terms of tables, you write classes representing the data in your project. A `Musician` class contains attributes for first name, last name, and date of birth, and then the ORM maps this class to tables in the database. This abstraction means you don't need to write a single line of SQL.

The downside of this mapping is you are now defining the structure of your data in two places: your classes and the database. Adding a stage name to your musician means changing the class but also keeping the database in sync. Django's ORM includes a table management feature called *migration*. The migration process tracks changes you make to your classes and writes the corresponding SQL scripts for you.

Figure 4.2 shows how the ORM fits into your Django code. You build models in your app; those models are managed through migration scripts; and then inside of your views, you interact with the database to populate content for your pages.

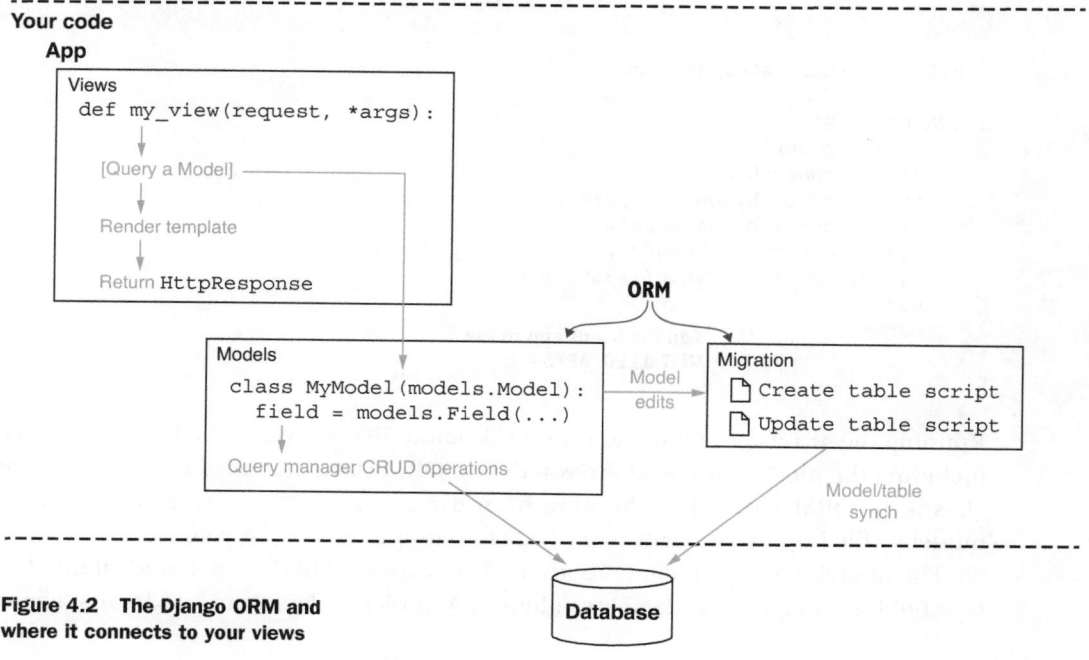

Figure 4.2   The Django ORM and where it connects to your views

Understanding databases is a deep topic in its own right and beyond the scope of this book. This chapter will give you enough background in relational databases to understand how to use the ORM, but you may want to dig deeper into databases.

4.2   *ORM Models*

At the heart of an ORM is a mapping between Python classes and tables in a relational database. Unlike Python's dynamic typing, where you can define what kind of data goes in a variable at run time, relational databases are picky about the data types of a column. To define a mapping between a class and a table, you need to be explicit about the data type of the columns. Django's ORM provides a base class you inherit from and a series of fields that specify the types of data for the mapping.

Let's start by defining a musician class that contains the first name, last name, and date of birth of the musician. The first question is: Where do you put this? In chapter 2, when you created a Django app, one of the skeleton files built for you was models.py. This file is where Django expects you to build you ORM models. Currently, you only have the home app that contains general content for your site. Create a new app to contain the data definitions and views for musicians and their bands, and call it *bands*. Remember, you do this with the `manage.py startapp` command:

```
(venv) RiffMates$ python manage.py startapp bands
```

In addition to creating the app, recall that you need to tell Django about it by adding it to the `INSTALLED_APPS` configuration value inside RiffMates/RiffMates/settings.py, like in the following listing.

> **Listing 4.1   Tell Django about your bands app**

```
# RiffMates/RiffMates/settings.py
...
INSTALLED_APPS = [
    'django.contrib.admin',
    'django.contrib.auth',
    'django.contrib.contenttypes',
    'django.contrib.sessions',
    'django.contrib.messages',
    'django.contrib.staticfiles',
    'home',
    'bands',          ⟵┐  Add the bands app to the
]                        │  INSTALLED_APPS list.
...
```

Running the `startapp` command created skeleton files for you in the bands directory, including the models.py file where you define ORM classes. You tell Django that your class is an ORM model by inheriting from `django.db.models.Model`. The skeleton model.py file imports the `models` package into its namespace for you.

The models package includes both the base class for ORM models and all the data type fields for mapping to database columns. A musician class that includes first name, last name, and date of birth needs three attributes, each of which is a field that corresponds to the stored data type. These attributes serve a dual purpose: they both define the data type of the column in the corresponding database table, and they are used to access the content of the field during a query. A `first_name` attribute with the field type `CharField` both states that the first name gets stored as a character field in the database and is the access point for getting a musician's first name when you query the database.

To represent a musician, you create a `Musician` class and map three fields for the first name, last name, and date of birth. Unlike Python, in which strings can have an arbitrary length, many relational databases want you to be specific about string sizes. The `CharField` requires a `max_length` argument to indicate the size of the column. There are text fields that don't have this limit, but their storage tends to be inefficient;the best practice is to use the `CharField` for fields like names. Your first and last name fields are both `CharField`, while the date of birth gets stored using a `DateField`.

How much space?

Deciding how much is a reasonable size for any field is somewhat based on experience (read: guesswork). In the old days, using 10 characters for a first name was quite common. Christopher, for example, has 11 characters. I used to frequently receive mail addressed to *Christophe*. Names are culture specific, and making assumptions about them can get messy quickly. With disk space being cheap now, being more generous with your field lengths is achievable.

To define your first `Model` class, edit RiffMates/bands/models.py, and change it to look like the following listing.

Listing 4.2 Musician ORM Model class

```
# RiffMates/bands/models.py
from django.db import models

class Musician(models.Model):
    first_name = models.CharField(max_length=50)
    last_name = models.CharField(max_length=50)
    birth = models.DateField()
```

Defining the model is only the first step. Now, you need to create the corresponding table in the database. To map your `Musicians` class to a table, the ORM needs to execute some SQL on the database. Django abstracts this SQL using some Python called a *migration script*. As you make changes to your ORM models, Django tracks the changes and creates new versions of the migration scripts. You then apply the migration scripts to the database. Both the creation and running are done through management commands. The mapping for the `Musicians` model to the table created in the database after the migration gets performed is shown in figure 4.3.

Django ORM Model for Musician

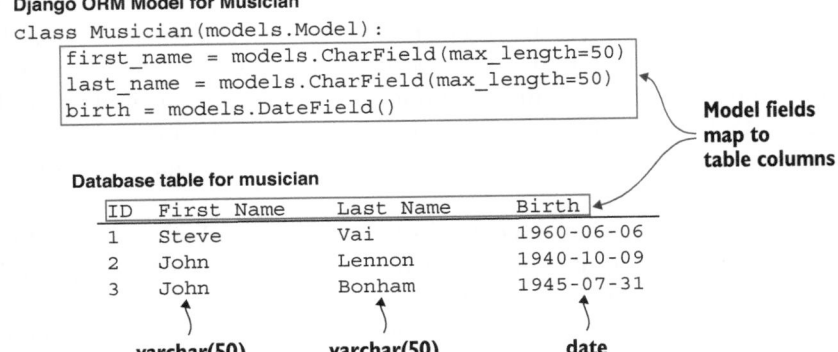

```
class Musician(models.Model):
    first_name = models.CharField(max_length=50)
    last_name = models.CharField(max_length=50)
    birth = models.DateField()
```

Model fields map to table columns

Database table for musician

ID	First Name	Last Name	Birth
1	Steve	Vai	1960-06-06
2	John	Lennon	1940-10-09
3	John	Bonham	1945-07-31

varchar(50)   varchar(50)   date

Figure 4.3 Musicians ORM Model object to database table mapping

The command that creates migration scripts is `makemigrations`. The first time you run this, it creates a migrations directory in the app and an initial migration script. Subsequent calls to the command detect any changes to the model and if found, adds more migration scripts.

Run the `makemigrations` command on the `bands` app using the following command:

```
(venv) RiffMates$ python manage.py makemigrations bands
```

Django responds by telling you what it did—in this case, it created the initial migration script containing a model named `Musician`:

```
Migrations for 'bands':
  bands/migrations/0001_initial.py
    - Create model Musician
```

The migration scripts are Python programs and part of your project like any other code file. The details of these scripts and how and when you might modify them by hand gets covered in a later chapter.

With the initial script in place, you use another management command to perform the migration. The `migrate` command runs any outstanding migration scripts that have not previously run on the database. Under the covers, Django is storing the state of migrations in the database itself, and it knows what scripts have been run and which are new.

Recall from chapter 2 the `18 unapplied migration(s)` warning when first running the development server. Django ships with several apps that help you manage users and the database. These apps themselves have models and corresponding migration scripts. When you first ran the development server, Django was telling you it had detected the presence of migrations that haven't been run. To fix the warning, you ran the `migrate` command. Now that you have your own migration script, you do the same thing to sync your model changes with the database. Run the following:

```
(venv) RiffMates$ python manage.py migrate
```

Django tells you what migrations ran and on what apps:

```
Operations to perform:
  Apply all migrations: bands
Running migrations:
  Applying bands.0001_initial... OK
```

If you skipped the migration step in chapter 2 because you didn't care about the warning, the command also runs the migrations for the `admin`, `auth`, `contenttypes`, and `sessions` apps. Your project now contains a db.sqlite3 file: the SQLite single-file database. This file can be examined with appropriate tools to see the results of the ORM executing.

4.3   SQLite and dbshell

By default, Django is configured to use SQLite as its database. *SQLite* is a local, single-file database. *Local*, in this case, means on your machine (as opposed to over the network), and *single file* means the whole database resides in a file on your file system. SQLite is one of the most popular embedded databases out there, and even if you've never used it before, you've probably used it before. It is very likely that one of the apps on your phone uses SQLite as its storage.

> **NOTE** Django supports several databases besides SQLite and third-party libraries add even more connectivity support. For details on how to configure Django for a database besides SQLite, see appendix B on running Django in a production environment.

When using the default SQLite database, the first time you use the ORM, Django creates the database file, calling it db.sqlite3. If you have SQLite installed on your computer (available from https://www.sqlite.org), you can use the `sqlite3` command to open the database. If you don't want to install another tool on your machine, that's OK; Django has a management command that does the same thing.

The `dbshell` command invokes the database's equivalent of a REPL. Django supports multiple databases with `dbshell` mapping to the database currently configured for your project. This means you don't have to remember your database's specific command, since you can always just run `dbshell`. This is a convenience, but once inside the command, you are using the database's interactive tool. The operations you perform on the database and how you perform them are specific to the database's tool.

Run the `dbshell` command to enter SQLite's interactive program:

```
(venv) RiffMates$ python manage.py dbshell
```

When SQLite starts, it gives you its version information and prompts you with `sqlite>`:

```
SQLite version 3.43.2 2023-10-10 13:08:14
Enter ".help" for usage hints.
sqlite>
```

Inside the SQLite shell, you can run SQL queries directly. To differentiate shell commands from SQL, SQLite uses a dot (.) prefix for its own commands. The welcome message tells you to use the `.help` command to find out more. The output of `.help` is rather lengthy—it is a full listing of everything you can do in the shell.

One of the commands available to you allows you to see all the tables in the database. Try the `.tables` command:

```
sqlite> .tables
```

Are there a few more tables than you expected? Remember, Django provides several built-in apps that you migrated, each of which resulted in a table. There are also system tables; `django_migrations` is where the ORM tracks which migrations have run. Your `Musician` class gets mapped in the `bands_musician` table:

```
auth_group                   bands_musician
auth_group_permissions       django_admin_log
auth_permission              django_content_type
auth_user                    django_migrations
auth_user_groups             django_session
auth_user_user_permissions
```

Django ORM Models name their tables *app*, underscore *(_), classname.* For your `Musicians` class, that results in the *band* app name and the *musician* model name. This is only the default; you can control your table names if you wish (https://docs.django project.com/en/5.0/ref/models/options/#db-table).

The `.schema` command shows you the SQL that was executed to create a table. Run this for the `bands_musician` table:

```
sqlite> .schema bands_musician
```

If you're new to SQL, the output can be a little daunting:

```
CREATE TABLE IF NOT EXISTS "bands_musician" ("id" integer NOT NULL
➥ PRIMARY KEY AUTOINCREMENT, "first_name" varchar(50) NOT NULL,
➥ "last_name" varchar(50) NOT NULL, "birth" date NOT NULL);
```

The advantage of an ORM is that you don't have to be an expert in SQL. Figure 4.4 breaks the statement down into its component parts.

The SQL that creates the table includes the CREATE TABLE command; the name of the table to be created (bands_musician); and four columns, id, first_name, last_name, and birth. Your `Musicians` model did not define an `id` attribute, as Django does that for you automatically. It uses an integer and declares that it can't be

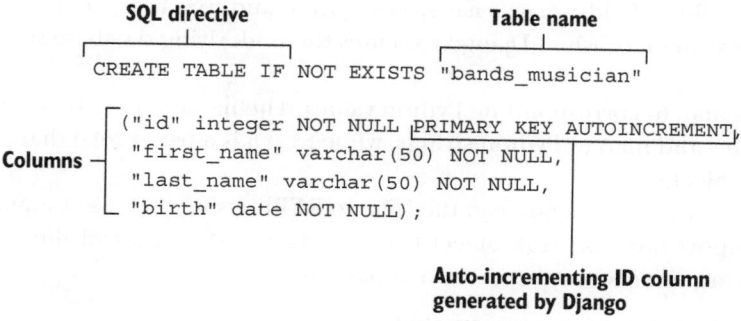

Figure 4.4   SQL used to create the table storing musicians info

empty (NOT NULL), it is the identifier other tables use to reference it (PRIMARY KEY), and it automatically increments when new rows get added (AUTOINCREMENT). The first_name and last_name columns are varchar(50). A varchar is what SQL calls the CharField, and the 50 is the max length defined in your model. The birth field is of type date.

Not only is the id field not allowed to be empty (NOT NULL), but your three attribute fields are the same. This is the default behavior. You can control this through additional options to the field declaration (more on this later).

You can use the SQLite command-line tool to directly enter SQL queries. Your Musician class doesn't have any data yet, so there is nothing to see. You could write an SQL INSERT statement, but that isn't the ORM way of doing things. Leave the SQLite tool by running .quit, and learn the ORM way.

4.4 Model queries

Each Model class is both declarative and functional. Inheriting from models.Model and using the fields from the models package defines the structure of the tables that the ORM creates and manages for you. The base class also comes with a *query manager*, an interface for interacting with data in the database. You can create your own query manager, but for the vast majority of what you'll do with the ORM, the default query manager will be sufficient. The default, named *objects*, is attached to the base class.

The query manager is a class itself, and its methods get used for operations relating to your Model. You've created Musician and seen the resulting table in the database; now it is time to make some data. The .create() method on the query manager does exactly this. The arguments to .create() are the fields in your class that you wish to populate. As the .create() method is generic, you can't use positional arguments for the fields; you have to use keyword arguments for everything.

The other complication with arguments is which fields are required and which are optional. Because .create() is generic, the compiler can't tell if you're missing an argument. Musician doesn't have optional fields, so you need to provide keyword arguments for all the fields: `first_name`, `last_name`, and `birth`. If you miss one, you will only receive an error when Django executes the underlying database statement at run time.

Field types map to corresponding Python values. The names in `Musician` are `Char-Field` attributes and map to Python strings, while `birth` is a `DateField` that maps to a Python `date` object.

To create your first Musician, run the Django REPL, using the `shell` management command; import the `Musician` object from `bands.models`; and call the `.create()` method, with arguments for your favorite musician:

```
(venv) RiffMates$ python manage.py shell
Python 3.12.1
Type "help", "copyright", "credits" or "license" for more information.
(InteractiveConsole)
>>> from bands.models import Musician
>>> from datetime import date
>>> steve = Musician.objects.create(first_name="Steve",
       last_name="Vai", birth=date(1960, 6, 6))
```

Using the .objects query manager to create a musician passing in string and date keyword argument values

The `.create()` call inserts the content into the database and returns a corresponding `Musician` object. You can display the value of `steve` in the REPL:

```
>>> steve
<Musician: Musician object (1)>
```

The result isn't too friendly. When you display an object like this, the Django REPL casts the object into a string to show the result. The `Model` base class implements `.__str__()`, the special method called when an object gets cast to a string. The provided implementation shows the class name and the object's `id` in parentheses. Your first `Musician` object got an `id` of 1.

To make it easier to view and debug your objects, it is best practice to override the base class's `.__str__()` method. Exit the Django shell, open RiffMates/bands/models.py, and add the contents of listing 4.3 to your `Musician` class, as shown in the following listing.

Listing 4.3   Overriding `.__str__()` in your `Musician` class

```
# RiffMates/bands/models.py
...
class Musican(models.Model):
    ...
    def __str__(self):
        return f"Musician(id={self.id}, last_name={self.last_name})"
```

Override the special method called when casting Musician to string.

Save the file and re-enter the Django shell. The database is meant as permanent storage; you've already created Mr. Vai, and now you want to fetch him back. The `.objects` query manager provides several methods for querying data out of the database and returning them as objects or groups of objects. One of the simpler queries is `.objects.first()`, which returns the first item in the database of that object type. I don't find I use this method much in my views, but it can be handy if you're mucking around in the REPL and need a quick piece of data to play with.

To fetch Mr. Vai's `Musician` object, you'll first need to re-import `Musician`, as closing the shell before will have lost the import state. Once you have the `Musician` class, you run the `.first()` method on the `.objects` query manager, and it returns the first (and only) `Musician` object:

```
(venv) RiffMates$ python manage.py shell
Python 3.12.1
Type "help", "copyright", "credits" or "license" for more information.
(InteractiveConsole)
>>> from bands.models import Musician
>>> steve = Musician.objects.first()
>>> steve
<Musician: Musician(id=1, last_name=Vai)>
```

With your new `.__str__()` in place, the display value of `steve` in the REPL is more readable. Steve is kind of lonely; use `.create()` to add a few more musicians to your database:

```
>>> from datetime import date
>>> Musician.objects.create(first_name="John", last_name="Lennon",
➥ birth=date(1940, 10, 9))
<Musician: Musician(id=2, last_name=Lennon)>
>>> Musician.objects.create(first_name="John", last_name="Bonham",
➥ birth=date(1948, 7, 31))
<Musician: Musician(id=3, last_name=Bonham)>
```

You have some data to play with and a fantasy rock trio that would make any record company salivate. As you might guess, to go along `.first()`, you'll need a `.last()` query, which returns the most recent item added to the database. Try it out on your own. Fetching a single object is kind of boring though, so you can get sets of data and filter the content as well.

4.4.1 Using .all() and .filter() to fetch QuerySet results

To find all the objects in a table, you call the query manager's `.all()` method. This returns a `QuerySet` object, a wrapper to the query you ran. Try it out yourself:

```
>>> Musician.objects.all()
<QuerySet [<Musician: Musician(id=1, last_name=Vai)>, <Musician:
➥ Musician(id=2, last_name=Lennon)>, <Musician: Musician(id=3,
➥ last_name=Bonham)>]>
```

Individual items, or a subset of the result of a `QuerySet`, can be accessed using square brackets, similar to a `list` or `tuple`. Re-run the `.all()` query, store the result, and then access the second item using `[1]`:

```
>>> result = Musician.objects.all()
>>> result[1]
<Musician: Musician(id=2, last_name=Lennon)>
```

The `QuerySet` object is a lazy object. That descriptor isn't meant to be rude—*lazy* means it waits as long as possible to be evaluated. You might have hundreds or thousands of musicians in your database. Running `.all()` could result in a large amount of data coming back. The `QuerySet` object wraps the query but doesn't execute it immediately. You can further refine your query by performing operations on a `QuerySet`. Accessing an item in the `QuerySet` is what causes it to be evaluated. In the Django shell, running `.all()` directly casts the result as a string, invoking the evaluation.

Achieving laziness

When you call a method on a query manager, it returns a `QuerySet` object that represents an SQL statement that has not yet been run on the database. This can take a little getting used to. Read that again: calling a query method doesn't actually query the database. This is named *lazy execution*, which means the database call doesn't happen until you actually need the data.

Although this can be a little strange to wrap your head around, it's a good thing. It means you can refine a query and build it up over multiple lines of code, and it won't fire until you actually need it to. This is much more efficient than running multiple queries.

In the previous example, when you ran `Musician.objects.all()`, Django created a `QuerySet` object in response. When you access the result by printing it out, converting it to a list, or accessing one of its members, Django then calls the database.

By contrast, you could run the same code, `Musicians.objects.all()`, and then call `.first()`. This is another query method, which returns the first item in a query set. Django is smart enough to optimize the underlying call: rather than fetching all the data and then giving you the first item, it only asks the database for the first item. This is far more efficient.

Likewise, you could call `.count()`, which returns the number of items in a `QuerySet`. Note that this isn't like calling `len()`. Turning the result into a list and determining the length of the list could take a lot of processing, especially if there is a lot of data. The `.count()` query method happens on the database side, and databases are good at counting results. By calling `.count()` on a `QuerySet`, the only data coming back to Django is the number of items in the `QuerySet`, not the values being counted.

Both `.first()` and `.count()` cause the query to be executed as they return data, but not all query methods do so. You can chain calls to `.filter()`, narrowing down the resulting data as you go. Each call adds more to the underlying SQL statement, and it isn't until you perform an action that requires data to be returned that the statement gets executed.

Databases are optimized for searching and filtering on items. As much as possible, you want the database to do the work. You can ask for all musicians and search the result for those with first name *John*, but this is inefficient. Not only do you have to write the search code yourself, but if the database you are using is on the network, all the data has to be sent over the wire. Instead, you want to ask the database to run queries like this for you.

The query manager provides the `.filter()` method for accessing a subset of the objects from a table. The arguments to `.filter()` are key–value pairs, where the keys are the fields you are searching and the values are the content you are looking for. To find all the musicians with the first name *John*, you call `.filter()` using `first_name="John"` as the argument:

```
>>> Musician.objects.filter(first_name="John")
<QuerySet [<Musician: Musician(id=2, last_name=Lennon)>, <Musician:
➥ Musician(id=3, last_name=Bonham)>]>
```

Because `QuerySet` objects are lazy, you can chain them together. Rerun the previous query, store the result, and then call `.first()` on the result:

```
>>> result = Musician.objects.filter(first_name="John")
>>> result.first()
<Musician: Musician(id=2, last_name=Lennon)>
```

The `.filter()` method is extremely powerful. You can perform matches on substrings or do comparative matching on numeric or date values. All of this is performed by altering the arguments to the method.

4.4.2 Field look-ups

You called `.filter()` to find an exact match using `first_name="John"`, but what if you want everyone who has a first name that begins with *J*? Querying `.filter(first_name="J")` doesn't work, as that looks for an exact match: a first name containing only the letter *J*.

In Python code, if you had a list of names, you could compare each string using an operator. `"John" >= "J"` is `True`, so *John* starts with something grater than or equal to *J*. The problem is you aren't doing this in Python; you're trying to get a database to do it for you.

If you're familiar with SQL, you're probably mumbling "WHERE clause" under your breath right now. If you're not familiar with SQL, a WHERE clause is a restriction on the bounds of a query—for example, a first name beginning with the letter *J*.

Django supports these kinds of restrictions through *field look-ups*. A field look-up is a modification to a query argument expressed through a double underscore (__). For example, the __startswith field look-up changes a query from looking for an exact match to looking for fields that begin with the given value. You use a field look-up by appending it to the argument name. To find everyone whose first name begins with *J*, you specify `first_name__startswith`:

```
>>> Musician.objects.filter(first_name__startswith="J")
<QuerySet [<Musician: Musician(id=2, last_name=Lennon)>, <Musician:
➥ Musician(id=3, last_name=Bonham)>]>
```

This can take a little getting used to. I have caused many bugs by forgetting that the base behavior looks for an exact match or sticking an asterisk into the string intending a "starts-with" semantic. Field look-ups can feel a little "anti-Pythonic": it is just weird to change the name of function's argument to change the behavior of the function. With practice, though, you'll get used to it.

There are many field look-up modifiers. All value comparison is done using field look-ups: greater than, less than, greater than equal, and so on. Although it might feel more natural to specify *J**, that syntax won't work for nonstring values. Consider the queries *after this date* and *smaller than this number*, you just can't stick a star on the end of those. The field look-up mechanism works regardless of the type of data being queried. For example, to find all musicians born in 1945 or later, you use __gte to find dates greater than or equal to a Python date object containing January 1, 1945:

```
>>> Musician.objects.filter(birth__gte=date(1945, 1, 1))
<QuerySet [<Musician: Musician(id=1, last_name=Vai)>, <Musician:
➡ Musician(id=3, last_name=Bonham)>]>
```

Some of the more commonly used field look-ups are in table 4.1.

Table 4.1   Commonly used field look-ups

Field Look-up	Name	Description
__contains	Contains	Text field contains the given value
__icontains	Case-insensitive contains	Text field contains the given value, ignoring case
__gt	Greater than	Objects with a field greater than the given value
__gte	Greater than equal	Objects with a field greater than or equal to the given value
__in	In iterable	Objects with a field value matching one of the values given in an iterable. Example: id__in=[1, 4, 6] matches objects with an ID field of 1, 4, or 6.
__lt	Lesser than	Objects with a field lesser than the given value
__lte	Lesser than equal	Objects with a field lesser than or equal to the given value
__startswith	Starts with	Text field starts with the given value
__istartswith	Case-insensitive starts with	Text field starts with the given value, ignoring case
__endswith	Ends with	Text field ends with the given value
__iendswith	Case-insensitive ends with	Text field ends with the given value, ignoring case

Database dependencies

Not all field options work as advertised, due to underlying database implementations. For strings containing ASCII, SQLite only does case-insensitive matching for substrings. For strings containing values outside the ASCII range, SQLite only does exact matching. Aren't computers fun? For a full list of the peculiarities of Django interacting with your database of choice, see http://mng.bz/ma28.

There are many more field look-ups built into Django, including one for querying ranges of values and some specific to dealing with dates and times. The whole list is available in the Django documentation: http://mng.bz/5lm7.

4.5 *Modifying your data*

You've created and queried data, but that's just not enough. Data changes over time, so you need to be able to edit and delete data. To demonstrate, create another `Musician` object:

```
>>> Musician.objects.create(first_name="Joseph", last_name="Trudeau",
➥ birth=date(1938, 2, 22))
<Musician: Musician(id=4, last_name=Trudeau)>
```

This new object has two problems: first, my dad was born on the 23rd, not the 22nd. Second, he doesn't qualify as a musician. I love him dearly, but his relationship to pitch is a challenging one. Deal with the first problem first: as I didn't store the result of the `.create()` in a variable, I need to run a query to get the object back. The `.get()` method of the query manager retrieves a single object but only if there is a single match. Run a query using `.get()`, giving `id=4` and store that in a variable this time:

```
>>> dad = Musician.objects.get(id=4)
>>> dad
<Musician: Musician(id=4, last_name=Trudeau)>
```

With the object in hand, you can alter the attributes on the object. This, on its own, is not sufficient, you are only changing the object in memory. The `.save()` method on your object executes the underlying SQL to sync your object up with the database. Change the `birth` value to the 23rd, and then call `.save()` to update the database:

```
>>> dad.birth
datetime.date(1938, 2, 22)
>>> dad.birth = date(1938, 2, 23)
>>> dad.save()
```

Querying the same object into a new variable proves the value in the database has changed:

```
>>> joseph = Musician.objects.get(first_name="Joseph")
>>> joseph.birth
datetime.date(1938, 2, 23)
```

Recall that .get() only returns a single match. If there is no match or there are multiple matches, .get() raises an exception. Try querying an id that doesn't exist yet:

```
>>> Musician.objects.get(id=42)
Traceback (most recent call last):
  File "<console>", line 1, in <module>
  File "RiffMates/venv/lib/python3.12/site-packages/django/db/models/
➥ manager.py", line 85, in manager_method
    return getattr(self.get_queryset(), name)(*args, **kwargs)
           ^^^^^^^^^^^^^^^^^^^^^^^^^^^^^^^^^^^^^^^^^^^^^^^^^^^^^

  File "RiffMates/venv/lib/python3.12/site-packages/django/db/models/
➥ query.py", line 650, in get
    raise self.model.DoesNotExist(bands.models.Musician.DoesNotExist:
➥ Musician matching query does not exist.
```

Or querying with first_name="John", you get the following:

```
>>> Musician.objects.get(first_name="John")
Traceback (most recent call last):
  File "<console>", line 1, in <module>
  File "RiffMates/venv/lib/python3.12/site-packages/django/db/models/
➥ manager.py", line 85, in manager_method
    return getattr(self.get_queryset(), name)(*args, **kwargs)
           ^^^^^^^^^^^^^^^^^^^^^^^^^^^^^^^^^^^^^^^^^^^^^^^^^^^^^

  File "RiffMates/venv/lib/python3.12/site-packages/django/db/models/
➥ query.py", line 653, in get
    raise self.model.MultipleObjectsReturned(
bands.models.Musician.MultipleObjectsReturned: get() returned more
➥ than one Musician -- it returned 2!
```

As my dad himself will admit, he doesn't belong in our musicians table; it is time to fix the second problem. The .delete() method on your object instance deletes the corresponding object from the database. Note that unlike the other database operations you've performed, this one is directly on the instance itself. Use the joseph value you queried before and delete it:

```
>>> joseph.delete()
(1, {'bands.Musician': 1})
```

The .delete() method returns a tuple containing the number of objects deleted and a dictionary with key–value pairs for the type and number of objects deleted. Most of the time, you just ignore the response from .delete().

Calling .delete() does not change your object—it only affects the database. While the joseph object is within scope, you can still access all of its attributes. In fact, you can create a new entry in the database with the same values as the old one by calling .save() on the object. The value of the unique ID field will change, but all the other fields would be back. To see the effect of delete on the database, run a query looking for my non-musician father; you'll notice the entry is no longer there.

Your users aren't going to have access to your database, or they better not— that is just asking for trouble. To display your data, you need a view. The query methods you've learned so far can be implemented in views for display to your users.

4.6   Querying models in views

Many of the views you want to write need to be parameterized. You wouldn't write a view for every musician in the database; instead, you want to write a single view that takes a musician as an argument. There are two ways to parameterize a view:

- URLs based arguments
- Query parameters

Figure 4.5 shows both types of parameterized URLs.

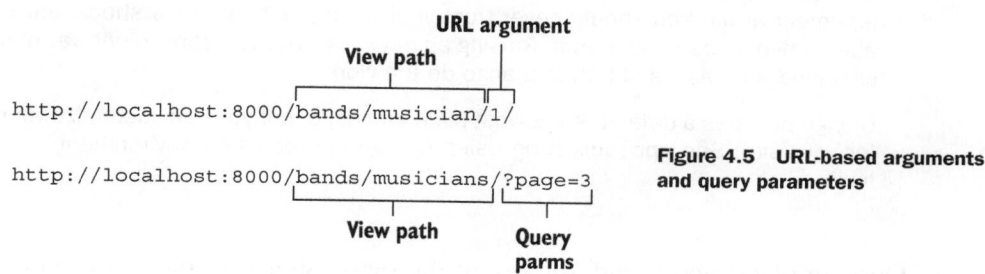

Figure 4.5   URL-based arguments and query parameters

You may be more familiar with query parameters if you've ever seen key–value pairs in a URL after a question mark. Django supports these but also allows you to capture parts of a URL as arguments to your view. Captured parts is the recommended way of using arguments with your URL, but query parameters still get used for optional behaviors in a view.

4.6.1   Using URL arguments

Let's start with Django's preferred case: URL based arguments. To build a page that displays information for a single musician, you need a way of specifying which musician. As your database already has a unique identifier for each musician, the typical solution to this problem is to use the database ID as the argument to the view.

A view to show musician details uses the ID of a `Musician` object as an argument. Remember that the URL `path` object is what defines the mapping between the URL in the browser and the called view. To support arguments to the view, you specify this in the `path` object declaration, indicating the arguments and their type using angle brackets. Inside the view, you perform a look-up of the `Musician` object for the given ID from the database. The resulting object gets rendered through a template.

Django provides a shortcut named `get_object_or_404()` to help you fetch an object or error out if the argument is invalid. This shortcut takes two or more arguments. The first argument is the `Model` object to query—in this case, the `Musician`. The second and subsequent arguments get used to form the look-up query. They use the same format as the query manager's `.get()` method, as that's what the shortcut is calling for you. The most common case is `id=object_id`, searching for a single object that has the corresponding ID, usually passed in as an argument to the view.

Why 404?

If the arguments to `get_object_or_404()` don't result in a single object, either the arguments match multiple arguments or one isn't found, the shortcut raises an `Http404` exception. Django automatically handles this, showing a `404` page instead of the result of the view.

This mechanism is rather important. Although your site probably won't show links with bad arguments, URLs are part of the public space: your users could type any argument at all. You should never trust your users, and your view should always be able to handle bad arguments. Raising an `Http404` error is a convenient way of short-circuiting your view and letting Django do the work.

Django provides a default, somewhat plain `404` page, but you can customize your own for your site. See appendix B on using Django in production environments to learn how.

Once an object gets found, the rest of the view is similar to the views you've written before. You use the `render()` shortcut to render a template, passing in your object as context. The following listing is a view that looks up a `Musician` object by ID and renders RiffMates/templates/musician.html.

> **Listing 4.4   A view for displaying a `Musician` object based on an argument**

```
# RiffMates/bands/views.py
from django.shortcuts import render, get_object_or_404      ◁─┐ Import
                                                              │ get_object_or_404().

from bands.models import Musician      ◁─┐ Import the Musician
                                         │ object to be queried.
def musician(request, musician_id):
    musician = get_object_or_404(Musician, id=musician_id)      ◁─┐

    data = {                                                    Find a Musician object
        "musician": musician,      ◁─┐ Add the Musician object   with the argument's ID
    }                                │ to the context dictionary.  or raise a 404 error.

    return render(request, "musician.html", data)
```

Like your other views, this one needs to be registered. The `path` object is a little different from those you've seen before. This one includes a capture specifier to indicate that part of the URL is to be used as an argument. Capture specifiers are inside of angle brackets and consist of the type of the argument and the name used in the view. For example, `<int:musician_id>` indicates the argument is an integer and is named `musician_id` in the view. All URLs are text; by including the data type in the capture specifier, Django can automatically cast the given argument to your desired data type.

Django supports several capture types, with the three most common being the following:

- `str`—Any non-empty string excluding the forward-slash (/) path separator
- `int`—Any integer zero or more
- `slug`—A special string value consisting of letters, numbers, and hyphens

The capture specifier is part of the path-matching process. If your URL specifies an integer component, but your user sends in a non-integer, the path does not match. This means your view doesn't get called. Django treats it as a `404` without you needing to worry about it.

Up until now, you have registered your URL `path` objects directly in the main urls.py file. It is actually good practice to associate the URLs for an app with the app. You can do this by creating a new URL-routing file in the app and then including its contents in the main file.

A URL pattern file in an app uses the exact same structure as the main file. Create `RiffMates/bands/urls.py` like you see in the following listing.

Listing 4.5   App specific URL pattern declaration file for bands

```
# RiffMates/bands/urls.py
from django.urls import path

from bands import views                          A path object with an
                                                  integer capture specifier
urlpatterns = [
  path('musician/<int:musician_id>/', views.musician, name="musician"),
]
```

Using separate URL-routing files for each app tends to simplify the code you need in the file. Without them, the main file needs to alias the view module, as all apps have the same name for their views: views.py. Having a bands-app-specific URL file only uses the bands app's views.py file, so the alias is unnecessary.

Django does not automatically find and register app specific URL routing files—you need to register them. The `django.urls` module provides a function called `include()` that enables you to include all the URLs in a module. The `include()` function gets used as part of a `path` object, registering all the URLs in the included module under a path. This way, all the URLs in a module start with the same path prefix. To avoid the need to import many modules, the `include()` function takes a string that names the module whose content is to be included. Open RiffMates/RiffMates/urls.py, and make the changes you see in the following listing.

Listing 4.6   Registering all the URL routes in the bands app

```
# RiffMates/RiffMates/urls.py
...
from django.urls import path, include          Add the include() function
...                                             to the import line.
```

```
urlpatterns = [
    ...
    path('bands/', include("bands.urls")),
]
```

Register all the routes in bands.urls.py
under the bands/ prefix.

When adding more views to the `bands` app, you now only need to register the URL in RiffMates/bands/urls.py. Any new URL routes there are included under `bands/` through the above change to the main route file.

To complete your view, you'll need a template. Recall from listing 4.2 that the `render()` shortcut passed in `musician.html` as the template to be rendered. Feel free to be more creative, listing 4.7 contains a bare-minimum template. Create a new file named RiffMates/templates/musician.html for this content.

Listing 4.7   Template for musician detail information

```
<!-- RiffMates/templates/musician.html -->
{% extends "base.html" %}

{% block title %}
  {{block.super}}: Musician Details
{% endblock %}

{% block content %}
  <h1>{{musician.first_name}} {{musician.last_name}}</h1>

  <p> Was born {{musician.birth}}. </p>
{% endblock content %}
```

Your new view is ready to go. Fire up the old development server and visit the web page at http://localhost :8000/bands/musician/1/ to see Steve Vai's musician Details page. It will look something like 4.6, depending on how seriously you took the challenge to be creative.

By editing the URL and changing the numeric value, you can query different musicians in the database. Shortly, you'll be creating

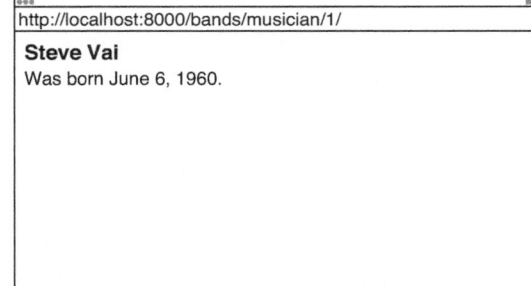

Figure 4.6   Musician view showing Steve Vai

a listing page that has links to many musicians, but you want to make sure the Details pages work before you get there. Test a few different `Musician` ID values.

You should also check an ID value that doesn't exist, first to ensure the error handling code is working and second so you can experience the wonder that is a Django Error page. When your code raises an `Http404` exception, Django does one of two things, depending on the value of DEBUG in your configuration RiffMates/RiffMates/ settings.py file. In a production environment, where DEBUG=False, Django shows a generic `404` page with very little information on it. You don't want to expose the details of your code to the untrustworthy public.

In a development environment, where `DEBUG=True`, Django shows you a debugging error page, complete with information on what went wrong. In the case of a bad `Musician` ID, the error is *No Musician matches the given query.* The error page also includes a list of all the URLs Django attempted to match. This can be handy if you're trying to figure out why the URL you typed is causing a `404` error. In the case of a `404` raised by `get_object_or_404()`, you'll see the URL that got matched, but that the argument wasn't valid. Figure 4.7 contains the debug error page for a musician ID that doesn't exist in my database.

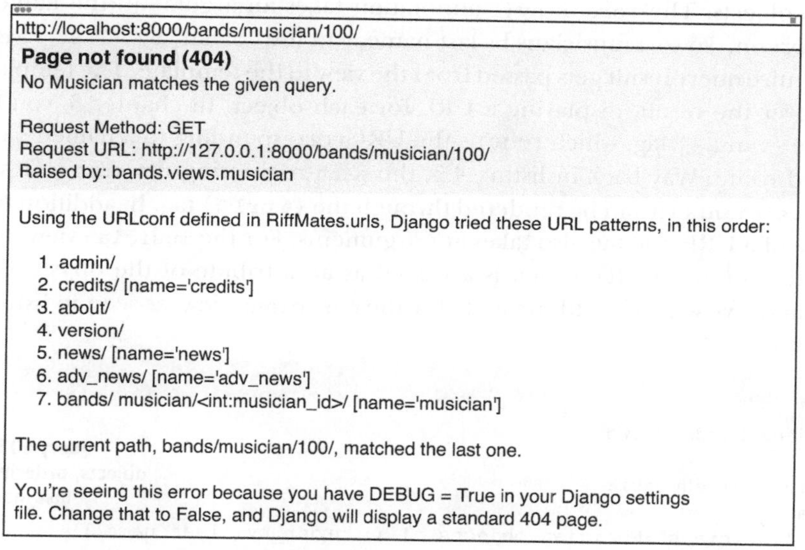

```
http://localhost:8000/bands/musician/100/

Page not found (404)
No Musician matches the given query.

Request Method: GET
Request URL: http://127.0.0.1:8000/bands/musician/100/
Raised by: bands.views.musician

Using the URLconf defined in RiffMates.urls, Django tried these URL patterns, in this order:

   1. admin/
   2. credits/ [name='credits']
   3. about/
   4. version/
   5. news/ [name='news']
   6. adv_news/ [name='adv_news']
   7. bands/ musician/<int:musician_id>/ [name='musician']

The current path, bands/musician/100/, matched the last one.

You're seeing this error because you have DEBUG = True in your Django settings
file. Change that to False, and Django will display a standard 404 page.
```

Figure 4.7   Page not found, as no musician exists with ID 100

Getting a 500 error

Pointing to a bad URL, or passing invalid arguments to one, results in a `404` page. Coding errors result in a 500 error. If `DEBUG=True`, the 500 error page is similar to the `404` and includes a stack trace of your code, showing the offending line and a variety of information about the calling state. Like with the `404`, in production mode, the 500 error is generic, showing very little information, and it also can be customized for your application.

The visitors to your site probably aren't interested in guessing the ID of the musician they're looking for. In addition to your musician's details page, you're going to want some sort of index listing as well.

4.6.2   Listing pages

A view doesn't have to take arguments to take advantage of the database. An index listing page could query all, or some, of the objects in the database and display them to the user. Each object in the result can then link to the corresponding detail page.

It is common practice to have the object page named in the singular and the listing page in the plural. The `musician()` view you wrote previously displays a single musician. The corresponding listing view would be called `musicians()` (plural). The database query inside the `musicians()` view looks for all the `Musician` objects in the database.

It is good practice to sort the contents of your listing pages. You do this by appending `.order_by()` to your query. This is called an *annotation*. Annotations interact with query results, changing their behavior or augmenting the information on the returned objects. The `.order_by()` annotation takes an argument: the name of the field to sort on. To sort musicians by last name, you use `.order_by("last_name")`.

The entire query result gets passed from the view to the template. The template then iterates over the result, displaying a URL for each object. In chapter 3, you learned about the `{% url %}` tag, which returns the URL corresponding to a named `path` for a registered route. Way back in listing 4.5, the `path` registering the `musician` view got named `musician`, so it can be rendered through the `{% url %}` tag. In addition to taking the name of a URL, the tag also takes any arguments. For the `musician` view, the argument is the musician's ID, which is accessed as an attribute of the object. Edit RiffMates/bands/views., and add the code for the `musicians` view, as seen in listing 4.8.

Listing 4.8   Index page for `Musician` objects

```
# RiffMates/bands/views.py
...
def musicians(request):
    data = {
        'musicians':Musician.objects.all().order_by('last_name'),
    }

    return render(request, "musicians.html", data)
```

> Query all Musician objects, ordering by the last_name field.

You'll need to register the route for your new view. As you now have a URL file specific to the bands app, that is the best place to register the URL. This time the URL has no argument, so you're back to the simpler form. Edit RiffMates/bands/urls.py, and add the new `path` object like in the following listing.

Listing 4.9   Adding the `musicians` index view to the bands app URL file

```
# RiffMates/bands/urls.py

urlpatterns = [
...
    path('musicians/', views.musicians, name="musicians"),
]
```

Listing 4.10 contains a simple template for your view. Create RiffMates/templates/ musicians.html, and add content similar to the listing's.

Listing 4.10   Template for the `musicians` view

```
<!-- RiffMates/templates/musicians.html -->
{% extends "base.html" %}

{% block title %}
  {{block.super}}: Musician Listing
{% endblock %}

{% block content %}
  <h1>Musicians</h1>

  <ul>
    {% for musician in musicians %}
      <li> <a href="{% url 'musician' musician.id %}">
        {{musician.last_name}}, {{musician.first_name}}
      </a> </li>
    {% empty %}
      <li> <i>No musicians in the database</i> </li>
    {% endfor %}
  </ul>

{% endblock content %}
```

> The {% url %} tag points to the musician view and passes in the ID as an argument.

With the view written, the route registered, and a template defined, you're all set to visit your musician's listing page. Start your development server, and go to http://localhost :8000/bands/musicians/. The output should be similar to figure 4.8.

When you have more content in your database, the listing page will become cumbersome. There are a few ways of dealing with this; one is to limit the number of results in a page and support multiple pages.

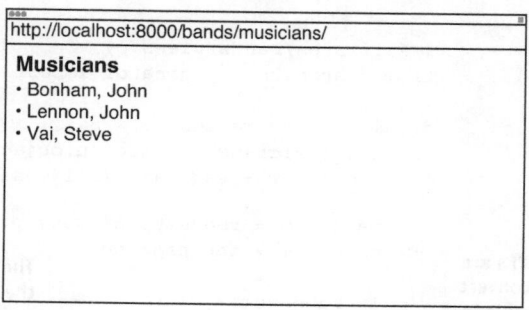

Figure 4.8   Musician listing page

4.6.3   Using query parameters for pagination

It is bad practice to support an unlimited number of objects in a query. Not only does this become information overload for your users, but it can be detrimental to your database. Django provides a utility to carve your queries up into pieces, allowing you to show a subset on the page. The `Paginator` class takes an iterator of objects and a limiter. The iterator can be a `QuerySet`, so you can pass the result of an object query directly to a `Paginator`. The limiter specifies the maximum number of objects per page.

Once you have a `Paginator` instance, you access page objects inside it. Each page object indicates the items on the page and whether there are pages before or after the page. This allows you to build a template with *previous* and *next* links to continue in the pagination.

The number of the current page in a pagination sequence is a perfect use of URL query string parameters. By using a URL parameter, rather than an embedded argument, you can specify default behavior more easily.

Query parameters are accessible as part of the `HttpRequest` object that is the first argument of every view. Your request contains a special dictionary, named `GET`. This dictionary is actually an instance of a Django class called `QueryDict`, but for our purposes, you can treat it like any other dict. For any query parameters in the URL, there is a corresponding key–value pair in the `GET` dict.

To add pagination to the `musicians` view, the view needs to

- Add a `Paginator` object populated by the musicians listing
- Check for a page number query parameter
- Handle out of range page numbers
- Pass the current page to the template for rendering

The code in the following listing is the new version of the `musicians` view, applying all of these features.

Listing 4.11   Musicians listing view supporting pagination

```
# RiffMates/bands/views.py                              Import the          Create a
from django.core.paginator import Paginator   <──┘   Paginator class.    Paginator using
...                                                                       the query,
def musicians(request):                                                   limiting two
    all_musicians = Musician.objects.all().order_by('last_name')          objects per page.
    paginator = Paginator(all_musicians, 2)    <──

    page_num = request.GET.get('page', 1)      <──     Fetch the page key from the
    page_num = int(page_num)                           GET dictionary, defaulting
                                   The minimum value for  to 1 if the key does not exist.
    if page_num < 1:           <──  the page number is 1.
        page_num = 1                                   The maximum value for the page
    elif page_num > paginator.num_pages:       <──     number is the number of pages.
        page_num = paginator.num_pages
                                           Fetch the page object
    page = paginator.page(page_num)   <──  containing the subset of items.

    data = {                                   To keep the template code easy to read,
        'musicians':page.object_list,  <──     pass the list of objects in as musicians.
        'page':page,               <──
    }                           Pass the page object in to access
                                page number information.
    return render(request, "musicians.html", data)
```

URLs are text, convert any value to an integer. → (annotation for `page_num = int(page_num)`)

The template for this view must change as well. You need to add links at the bottom for any "previous" and "next" pages. The `page` object passed into the template has methods to help you: `.has_other_pages()`, `.has_next()`, `.has_previous()`, and `.next_page_number()`. Using these inside conditional blocks allows you to appropriately render links that point to other pages in the pagination result. Remember that object methods get accessed the same way as attributes in the template language, so you won't need any parenthesis.

Listing 4.12 shows the conditional block that goes on the bottom of RiffMates/templates/musicians.html. As the `musicians` view passes in `pages.object_list` as `musicians` in the context, the rest of the page can remain unchanged.

Listing 4.12   Musicians listing view supporting pagination

```html
<!-- RiffMates/templates/musicians.html -->
<!-- ... -->
    {% if page.has_other_pages %}
      {% if page.has_previous %}
        <a href="{% url 'musicians' %}?page={{page.previous_page_number}}"
          >Prev</a>    
      {% endif %}
      {% if page.has_next %}
        <a href="{% url 'musicians' %}?page={{page.next_page_number}}"
          >Next</a>
      {% endif %}
    {% endif %}
```

> **Link to the musicians view (this page) with a query parameter for the previous page.**

> **And a query parameter for the next page**

With the changes in place, you have a paginated version of your musicians listing page. Run your development server and revisit the page. Try the URL with and without the `page` query parameter. You may also want to modify the `Paginator` object, changing how many items per page to see how the page changes.

Musicians are great, but to make a great tune, you need to group them together. To capture a band in your database, you need to create relations between musicians.

4.7   Model relations

A single object in the database will only get you so far. The *relational* in *relational database* is all about the connections between objects. There are two ways to relate objects to each other in a database. The first is to add a relationship column to your object table. The relationship column contains the ID of the related object, which is known as a *foreign key*. Foreign key relationships are one to many. This means multiple things can be related, but they are related through a single object. A music venue can have multiple rooms, each with its own schedule, but each room can only be associated with a single venue. That association between one venue and many rooms creates our one-to-many relationship.

The second way to interrelate objects in a database is to add a new table. The new table has the sole purpose of specifying object-to-object relationships. This kind of table has three columns: a unique ID, a foreign key to the first kind of object, and a foreign key to the second kind of object. Each row in the database expresses the relation between two objects. This allows for many-to-many relationships. As musicians are a fickle bunch, they might belong to more than one band at a time. To express this relationship in the database you need a dedicated table that associates a musician with a band. To associate a musician with multiple bands you need multiple rows that contain the musician's ID and each related band. You can see the difference between one-to-many and many-to-many relationships in figure 4.9.

One-to-many relationships

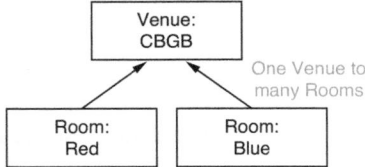

Many-to-many relationships

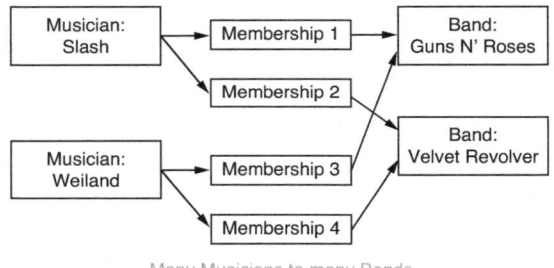

Figure 4.9   One-to-many vs. many-to-many relationships

Django supports both foreign-key and many-to-many relationships. It does this using `Model` fields named `ForeignKey` and `ManyToManyField`.

4.7.1   *One-to-many relationships*

A foreign-key relationship can feel a little backward. In writing, you might describe a venue containing multiple rooms. You're less likely to say there are multiple rooms all belonging to the same venue—it just doesn't flow as well. But that's how you do it in a database. This all comes down to which table contains the relationship column. If you put a *rooms* column on the venue table, you can only associate each venue with a single room. Remember, each row in the venue table is for a single venue. If instead, you put a *venue* column on the room table, each row describing a room can point at a single venue. This allows a venue to be associated with many rooms but a room only to be associated with a single venue.

   Expressing a foreign key relationship in Django requires the addition of a field to your `Model`. The `ForeignKey` field requires at least two arguments. The first is a reference to the related `Model` object. This reference can either be the `Model` class itself or, optionally, a string naming the class. The string format is useful to avoid having to import models from other modules and solve potential circular import problems. If the relationship is between models in the same file, you can use the class itself. If the relationship is between models in different files (and likely different apps), you should use the string specifier.

The second argument to the `ForeignKey` field is the `on_delete` parameter. In older versions of Django, this was optional, but it is now a required argument. This parameter specifies how Django is to behave if the associated object gets deleted. The choices for `on_delete` are a series of constants defined in the `django.db.models` module. The two most common choices are

- `CASCADE`—The associated object also gets deleted.
- `SET_NULL`—Set the field to `NULL`.

Other choices are available as well, including being able to define a function called when the model gets loaded. See http://mng.bz/679R for a complete listing. Up until now, all the fields you defined were required fields. To use `on_delete=SET_NULL`, the field must be allowed to contain a `NULL` value. To do this, pass `null=True` to the field constructor. Without it, the default of `null=False` is assumed.

Django comes with a web-based tool for managing the objects in your database, called the Django Admin. You can create objects in the tool, including specifying inter-object relationships. The Django Admin allows you to define whether the UI permits a relationship to be empty. To give you fine-grained control, Django distinguishes between `NULL` in the database and an empty value in the Django Admin. To allow empty values, you pass `blank=True` to the field constructor. You'll learn more about the Django Admin and these controls in chapter 5.

Let's add two new models to RiffMates: one for our venues and one for the rooms in those venues. Both the venues and the rooms need to have names, and additionally, the room needs to specify its associated venue. The `Room` model uses a `ForeignKey` field to create this relationship. If a venue gets removed from the database, it doesn't make sense to keep the associated rooms, so the `on_delete` value for the `Room` is `CASCADE`. Open RiffMates/bands/models.py, and add the `Venue` and `Room` models shown in the following listing.

Listing 4.13 Venue and Room models and their one-to-many relationship

```
# RiffMates/bands/models.py
...
class Venue(models.Model):
    name = models.CharField(max_length=20)

    def __str__(self):
        return f"Venue(id={self.id}, name={self.name})"

class Room(models.Model):
    name = models.CharField(max_length=20)
    venue = models.ForeignKey(Venue, on_delete=models.CASCADE)

    def __str__(self):
        return f"Room(id={self.id}, name={self.name})"
```

Foreign key relationship between Venue and Room

Remember that a Django `Model` is only a proxy to the table in the database, just because you updated your code doesn't mean the database has magically changed. To sync your code with the database, you need to create a new migration file. This is done using the `makemigrations` management command:

```
(venv) RiffMates$ python manage.py makemigrations bands
```

The output from the command tells you what was done:

```
Migrations for 'bands':
  bands/migrations/0002_venue_room.py
    - Create model Venue
    - Create model Room
```

With the new migration file in place, you apply the changes using the `migrate` management command:

```
(venv) RiffMates$ python manage.py migrate
```

Running `migrate` causes the changes to be synchronized to the database. The output from the command details which migrations got performed:

```
Operations to perform:
  Apply all migrations: admin, auth, bands, contenttypes, sessions
Running migrations:
  Applying bands.0002_venue_room... OK
```

With the database ready, you can go into the Django REPL and create some objects. You want to create a `Venue` instance first, so it is available to be passed into any `Room` objects. As `Room` does not specify the `null` argument, the default value of `False` is used. A `Room` can't be `NULL` and must be associated with a `Venue`. The following REPL session creates a `Venue` and two associated `Room` objects. Don't exit it yet; you'll be doing a bit more in a second.

```
(venv) RiffMates$ python manage.py shell
Python 3.12.1
Type "help", "copyright", "credits" or "license" for more information.
(InteractiveConsole)
>>> from bands.models import Venue, Room
>>> cbgb = Venue.objects.create(name="CBGB")
>>> red = Room.objects.create(name="Red", venue=cbgb)
>>> blue = Room.objects.create(name="Blue", venue=cbgb)
```

Each instance of your `Room` object can directly access its associated `Venue` object. Using dot notation, you can get at the properties of the `Venue`:

```
>>> red.venue
<Venue: Venue(id=1, name=CBGB)>
>>> red.venue.id
1
>>> red.venue.name
'CBGB'
```

What should be unique?

The relationship between the `Venue` and `Room` objects is based on their ID values, which are automatically generated by the database. Two different venues could both have rooms named `Red` without a problem, as the ID is what determines the relationship, not the value of the `name` field.

In fact, there is nothing currently stopping you from creating two `Room` objects with the same name and pointing them both at the same `Venue`. Django provides mechanisms for controlling this, which are discussed later in this chapter.

In your best Ron Popeil voice, read the next sentence out loud. *But wait, there's more!* In addition to the forward relationship being accessible, you can go backward as well. The object that a `ForeignKey` field points to automatically gets a query manager to access the associated objects. The query manager is named after the associated model with _set stuck on the end. Your `Venue` model has a `.room_set` query manager. All the queries you learned to use on the `.objects` query manager apply to this one, with the difference being the objects queried are only those associated through a foreign key. Run the `.all()` query on the `Venue` instance's `.room_set`:

```
>>> cbgb.room_set.all()
<QuerySet [<Room: Room(id=1, name=Red)>, <Room: Room(id=2, name=Blue)>]>
```

Because `.room_set` is an attribute and queries are callables, you can pass a `Venue` object into a template and iterate over the associated rooms using `{% for room in venue .room_set.all %}`. In fact, one of the exercises in this chapter asks you to do just that.

The related name

You can control what Django calls an associated model by adding the `related_name` parameter to the field. For example, to use `my_rooms` instead of `room_set` in the previous example, you would add `related_name="my_rooms"` to the `venue` ForeignKey field on the `Room` class. You can also change how the name appears in a query using the `related_query_name` field in a similar manner.

Generally, you shouldn't rename this relationship without a good reason; you'll only cause confusion for the people maintaining your code. There are two cases where this comes in handy. One, if your model includes two `ForeignKey` relationships to the same model, one needs to be renamed. The other is a special case: by setting `related_name="+"`, the reverse relationship is turned off, which you may wish to do for efficiency. For details, see the documentation: http://mng.bz/oe5D.

In section 4.4.2 you learned about field look-ups. A similar mechanism using double underscores (__) can also be used to query based on fields and relationships. For example, you can query for a `Venue` by filtering on `room__name="Red"`. This finds any `Venue` objects that have an associated `Room` object with `Red` as their `name` attribute.

These can also be combined with field look-ups: room__name__startswith="R" filters for a Venue with a Room with a name starting with R.

Sometimes one-to-many relationships just aren't not enough. To allow musicians to belong to several bands, you need many-to-many relationships.

4.7.2   *Many-to-many relationships*

Foreign keys in a database are a column that contains the ID of a row either in the same or a different table. A ForeignKey field in Django constructs one of these columns on the table corresponding to your Model. As the column is on the Model, you can at most create a one-way relationship. To create a many-to-many relationship, you need an entirely separate table. Technically, these tables contain foreign keys, but in Django, you don't use a ForeignKey field to construct them. In fact, you don't have to construct the table at all. The ManyToManyField is used to create many-to-many relationships. This field is a little different from the other fields you've used so far. Every other field results in a single column on the object's table. The ManyToManyField doesn't result in a new column but a new table.

To be able to relate musicians to bands (both plural), you need a many-to-many relationship. The ManyToManyField can go on either the Musician or Band class. When Django sees this kind of field, it creates a relationship table with three columns: a unique ID for the relationship and a column for each of the two keys of the related objects. The table is named based on the app and the two models participating in the relationship.

Besides establishing my age and musical preferences, figure 4.10 shows three tables, for musicians, bands, and their many-to-many relationship. Famous guitarist

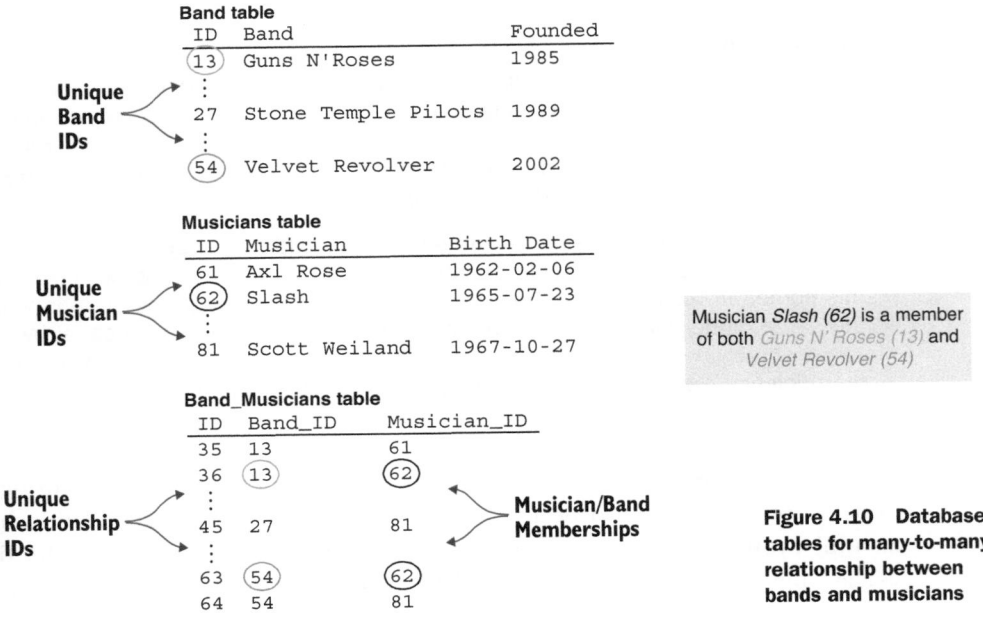

Figure 4.10   Database tables for many-to-many relationship between bands and musicians

Slash (id = 62) is a member of both Guns N' Roses (id = 13) and Velvet Revolver (id = 54). Singer Scott Weiland (id = 81) is a member of both Stone Temple Pilots (id = 27) and Velvet Revolver (still id = 54). The `Band_Musicians` table is how the band memberships get expressed. There is a row for Slash and Guns N' Roses (id = 36), a row for Slash and Velvet Revolver (id = 63), a row for Scott and STP (id = 45), and a row for Scott and Velvet Revolver (id = 64).

As a many-to-many relationship is two-way, you can put the `ManyToManyField` on either of the two participating objects and get a similar result. Semantically though, it tends to be clearer if the object representing a conglomerate is where the relationship gets placed. A band is a group of people, so it feels clearer if the `ManyToManyField` is on the `Band` object. Besides the relationship, the `Band` model also needs a name field. Open RiffMates/bands/models.py, and add the code for the `Band` object shown in the following listing.

Listing 4.14   Venue and Room models and their one-to-many relationship

```
# RiffMates/bands/models.py
...
class Band(models.Model):
    name = models.CharField(max_length=20)
    musicians = models.ManyToManyField(Musician)

    def __str__(self):
        return f"Band(id={self.id}, name={self.name})"
```

As with earlier changes to Django `Model` classes, you need to run the `makemigrations` and `migrate` management commands to sync the database with your `Model` code:

```
(venv) RiffMates$ python manage.py makemigrations bands
Migrations for 'bands':
  bands/migrations/0003_band.py
    - Create model Band
(venv) RiffMates$ python manage.py migrate
Operations to perform:
  Apply all migrations: admin, auth, bands, contenttypes, sessions
Running migrations:
  Applying bands.0003_band... OK
```

`ForeignKey` fields get populated as an attribute when you create an object, like you did passing a `Venue` into your `Room` object. In a many-to-many relationship, the relation is in a separate table, meaning the relation needs to be created as a separate step. Before doing anything else, you need a `Band` object; enter the Django REPL, and create it as follows:

```
>>> from bands.models import Band
>>> beatles = Band.objects.create(name="The Beatles")
```

To add Mr. Lennon to The Beatles, you need a reference. You can query him based on his ID if you remember it, or as his last name is currently unique, you can run a `.get()` query based on that:

```
>>> from bands.models import Musician
>>> lennon = Musician.objects.get(last_name="Lennon")
>>> lennon
<Musician: Musician(id=2, last_name=Lennon)>
```

Now that you have a reference to a musician and a band, you can associate the two together. The `Band` class has a query manager named after the `ManyToManyField`: `musicians`. The `.add()` method on the `.musicians` query manager adds a `Musician` to the `Band`:

```
>>> beatles.musicians.add(lennon)
```

As `.musicians` is a query manager, you can run queries on it. Running `.all()` returns all the `Musician` objects currently associated with the `Band`. In this case, that's only Mr. Lennon:

```
>>> beatles.musicians.all()
<QuerySet [<Musician: Musician(id=2, last_name=Lennon)>]>
```

But wait, there's more! Yep, still more—sort of the same kind of more. You can also go backward. The `Musician` class now has a query manager named `band_set`. Using this query manager, you can determine which bands a given musician belongs to:

```
>>> lennon.band_set.all()
<QuerySet [<Band: Band(id=1, name=The Beatles)>]>
```

Because this is a many-to-many relationship, musicians can be associated with multiple bands. Let's create a supergroup trio band, named *Wishful Thinking*, and add all three of our musicians:

```
>>> vai = Musician.objects.get(last_name="Vai")
>>> bonham = Musician.objects.get(last_name="Bonham")
>>> wishful = Band.objects.create(name="Wishful Thinking")
>>> wishful.musicians.add(lennon, vai, bonham)
>>> wishful.musicians.all()
<QuerySet [<Musician: Musician(id=1, last_name=Vai)>,
 <Musician: Musician(id=2, last_name=Lennon)>,
 <Musician: Musician(id=3, last_name=Bonham)>]>
```

Recall that with the `ForeignKey` field, you need to be explicit about the behavior when a related object gets deleted. Deleting a `Venue` without deleting the corresponding `Room` objects doesn't make a lot of sense, so you `CASCADE`. With a many-to-many relationship, this problem doesn't exist. If you wanted to delete Mr. Lennon, Django takes care of removing any associated `Band` relationships. Note that this does not remove the `Band`. If you delete all the members of Wishful Thinking, you will still have a Wishful ThinkingBand object—it just won't have any related `Musicians`. If you are trying to remove all the musicians and their associate band, you need to make separate explicit delete calls on both object types.

4.8   Model fields

Django 5 ships with 29 data fields and 3 relationship fields. Some fields map directly to an SQL data type, while others are a convenient abstraction adding features on top of the SQL data type. For example, the `EmailField` is usually implemented as text in the underlying database, but it also provides validation to ensure the text input meets the standard format of an email address.

When you define a field, you can pass in arguments that control the construction of the underlying column. You saw this with `max_length` on a `CharField`. Some arguments can be used with all fields, and some are field specific. This section highlights frequently used fields and their arguments. For a complete listing, see the Django Model field reference document: http://mng.bz/nged.

4.8.1   Popular cross-field field options

In the section on one-to-many relationships, you learned abou the `null` and `blank` field options. Both of the options are available across all fields.

The `null` option specifies whether the column in the database can contain the `NULL` value. This is a Boolean option and defaults to `False`. `NULL` in SQL indicates a lack of a value. Depending on the column, this can get a little confusing. A `DateField` configured with `null=True` has two types of state: empty and containing a date value. By contrast, a `CharField` with `null=True` has three types of state: empty (`NULL`), empty string (`''`), and containing a string. Generally it is advised to use an empty string with text and leave `null=False`.

Closely related to `null` is the `blank` option. The `null` option specifies the behavior in the database, whereas the `blank` option specifies the behavior in the Django Admin and web forms. A value of `blank=False` (the default) means the Django Admin and web-based forms treat this field as required. It is possible to have `blank=True` and `null=False` if you are programmatically populating a field between form submission and writing the value to the database. This combination is unusual though—typically the values of these two options are the same.

The separation between `null` and `blank` exposes a design feature of Django: the differentiation between database and model validation. The fields in your `Model` may validate their data. `Model`-level validation happens before values get saved to the database. This is done both to help ensure the content can be saved to the database and to add additional validation for some fields. The `EmailField` example mentioned earlier does this. `Model`-level validation ensures the content meets the format for an email address, whereas the database validation may only care if the content is text. How this is implemented may vary between databases. If your database provides an email data type, Django generally will take advantage of it. If it does not, it will use model validation and then store it as text.

If you are frequently setting a field to the same value, the `default` option can be useful. When set, you no longer need to provide a value for this field when constructing a model. If you do not provide a value, the given default is used instead.

The `choices` field configuration option is a `Model`-level validation that provides a set of values the field can contain. This option takes an iterable of pairs, usually written as a list of tuples. Each pair specifies the value stored in the database and a display string to go with it. For example, a field containing a country code could specify `choices=[("US", "United States"), ("CA", "Canada"), ("MX", "Mexico")]`, if you only supported countries in North America. When this field gets shown in the Django Admin or in a web form, a `<select>` drop-down box gets used, with the full string of the country's name visible to the user and the resulting value for the `<select>` being the corresponding two-letter country code.

It is common practice to build an attribute into your `Model` class that specifies the choices value. An `Address` class could contain a `COUNTRY_CHOICES` attribute specifying the previous example's listing. The `choices` option would then point to the attribute. Doing it this way makes the list of choices available anywhere the model gets imported. There are third-party libraries that define frequently used tuple sets. For example, the "django-localflavor" (https://pypi.org/project/django-localflavor/) package includes submodules for many countries and choices-compatible listings for states and provinces within them.

Databases improve look-up performance through the implementation of a special data structure known as an *index*. Indexes are similar to dictionaries, in that they provide a quick way of looking up a given value based on a key, rather than scanning an entire list. The ID field of your Django `Model` is indexed by default. This ensures that `.get(id=obj_id)` performs quickly. If a field is going to be frequently used to look up a row, that field may need an index. For example, if you add search capabilities to your site allowing a musician to be found by last name, adding an index to the `last_name CharField` will make a significant performance improvement. The `db_index` field option is a Boolean; setting it to `True` causes Django to add an index on the corresponding column.

There are times when you want the value of a field to be unique within a table. Django provides several field options to enforce this: `unique`, `unique_for_date`, `unique_for_month`, and `unique_for_year`. The `unique` field operates at both the `Model` validation level and applies a constraint to the database. When `unique=True`, only one object in the table will be allowed to have the value found in that field. Any attempt to save another object with the same value will result in an exception. Django automatically applies an index to this column, as it needs to look values up on every save of an object to ensure uniqueness. The `unique_for_date`, `unique_for_month`, and `unique_for_year` options are special cases for `DateTimeFields`. The uniqueness constraint gets applied to the date, month, or year portion of the field, while the other parts (e.g., the timestamp) are not considered.

4.8.2   *Popular fields*

The field you've used so far is probably the most popular one out there: `CharField`. There are several variations on this field that are essentially text storage mechanisms but with different validation and default values. The `EmailField`, `URLField`, and

SlugField all inherit from CharField, adding validation for email addresses, URLs, and slug identifiers (mixes of letters, numbers, and dashes, often used as part of a URL). The EmailField defaults to a max length of 254, the URLField to 200, and the SlugField to 50. Validation for these three variants almost always get done at the Model level unless the underlying database has a special storage type for them.

A close relative of the CharField is the TextField. A CharField requires a fixed amount of allocated space, whereas the TextField is an open block. This variation is due to an implementation detail at the database level. Some databases implement both of these fields as the same data type, while others treat them separately. In the Django Admin or in web forms, the CharField is presented as an entry widget, while the TextField is presented as a multiline text widget. This is default behavior and is under your control if you wish. You'll learn more about this in chapter 7, which covers forms and user input.

Django provides a wide variety of numeric fields, but they all boil down to either integer or float storage. The IntegerField and FloatField are the base mechanisms for storing ints and floats, while variations, such as BigIntegerField and Positives-mallIntegerField, change the validation and possibly the amount of storage required by the data. The latter is database dependent.

Chapter 6 covers user data, and in it you will learn about file uploads. These use a field that holds a file path with file management on your server. The general version of this is the FileField, while the ImageField adds validation that the uploaded content was a recognized image format.

A recent addition to the list of fields is the JSONField. Although you could store JSON as text generally, some databases have implemented a datatype that is JSON aware. The advantage of this field is you access the corresponding attribute as if it is a Python object. Under the covers, the field automatically serializes the object into JSON and stores the result as encoded text. There are limitations to which database and database version support this field, and any Python object in the field must be serializable to the JSON format. SQLite is compatible with the JSONField if a particular extension is enabled. The extension is called JSON1, and whether it is on by default depends on the SQLite distribution and the operating system you're working on. See http://mng.bz/v8Xa for information on how to determine if you can use this extension in your environment.

4.9 Fixtures

Manually entering data into your system is tedious. Django provides two management commands that let you import and export data. Django calls the serialized data a *fixture*. Fixtures come in a variety of formats, including JSON, JSONL, and XML. You can also use YAML if you have the PyYAML library installed.

A fixture is a text version of the data you have in your database. This includes all the information needed to create the exact state of the tables involved. Object IDs are in the fixture, both as primary keys of an object and to express inter-object relationships. The dumpdata management command outputs the fixture data to the screen in

JSON format by default. The command optionally takes a list of apps whose data you are interested in. As the data is in JSON, the `json.tool` module built into Python can be handy; running it directly through `python -m` pretty prints the output. The following line dumps the band app to the screen in JSON, in a human readable format:

```
(venv) RiffMates$ python manage.py dumpdata bands | python -m json.tool
```

The output is a JSON representation of all the musicians, bands, venues, and rooms you created in the database. The content is serialized as a JSON list. The following shows two portions of the output, the serialized Steve Vai `Musician` object and the serialized Wishful Thinking `Band`:

```
[                                    The fixture content
    {                                is a JSON list.
        "model": "bands.musician",            A string indicates the app and
        "pk": 1,                              name of the model for this object.
        "fields": {
            "first_name": "Steve",        The fields dictionary serializes
            "last_name": "Vai",           the fields for the object.
            "birth": "1960-06-06"
        }
    },
    ...
    {
        "model": "bands.band",
        "pk": 2,
        "fields": {
            "name": "Wishful Thinking",
            "musicians": [1, 2, 3 ]          A many-to-many relationship
        }                                    is represented as a list of keys.
    },
    ...
]
```

The pk is the primary key, in this case the unique ID.

The companion to `dumpdata` is intuitively named `loaddata`. You specify what data to load via a filename or an app name. Dump the data again, this time without the pretty printing, and redirect the content into a file named bands.json:

```
(venv) RiffMates$ python manage.py dumpdata bands > bands.json
```

When your IDE is not your friend

You have to be careful not to accidentally corrupt a fixture output by `dumpdata`, as you might make it impossible to load back in again later. Although a fixture is just a text file, there are text files, and then there are *text files*. Different operating systems use different characters to indicate a newline. Some editors will insert a *byte-order mark* (BOM) (https://www.unicode.org/faq/utf_bom.html#bom1) when encountering Unicode content.

This challenge isn't unique to Django. Moving text files between operating systems or having an editor add a BOM when not expected can make text unreadable by any program. I've run into cases where the addition of the BOM meant Django couldn't load the fixture anymore.

Be especially careful when editing a fixture file, as the settings for your IDE may mess it up. This is complicated by the fact that some IDEs automatically open the file for you when they detect it has been created. This is more likely if you ran the `dumpdata` command inside your IDE's command window. When the IDE opens the file, it "fixes" it by adding the BOM. Using a terminal external to the IDE should provide a work-around for this problem.

This next bit can be a little nerve racking. It is time to delete your database. As the fixture stores exactly what is in the database, loading it will overwrite the content that is there. You won't see any difference. If you delete your database (or rename it, if that makes you more comfortable), you can then use the fixture to re-create it.

Deleting your database sets you to zero, though. Those migrations you ran won't exist. After deleting your database, but before loading the fixture, you need to run the `migrate` command. The following sequence removes and then restores your database from the fixture:

```
(venv) RiffMates$ rm db.sqlite3
(venv) RiffMates$ python manage.py migrate
Operations to perform:
  Apply all migrations: admin, auth, bands, contenttypes, sessions
Running migrations:
  Applying contenttypes.0001_initial... OK
  Applying auth.0001_initial... OK
  Applying admin.0001_initial... OK
  Applying admin.0002_logentry_remove_auto_add... OK
  Applying admin.0003_logentry_add_action_flag_choices... OK
  Applying contenttypes.0002_remove_content_type_name... OK
  Applying auth.0002_alter_permission_name_max_length... OK
  Applying auth.0003_alter_user_email_max_length... OK
  Applying auth.0004_alter_user_username_opts... OK
  Applying auth.0005_alter_user_last_login_null... OK
  Applying auth.0006_require_contenttypes_0002... OK
  Applying auth.0007_alter_validators_add_error_messages... OK
  Applying auth.0008_alter_user_username_max_length... OK
  Applying auth.0009_alter_user_last_name_max_length... OK
  Applying auth.0010_alter_group_name_max_length... OK
  Applying auth.0011_update_proxy_permissions... OK
  Applying auth.0012_alter_user_first_name_max_length... OK
  Applying bands.0001_initial... OK
  Applying bands.0002_venue_room... OK
  Applying bands.0003_band... OK
  Applying sessions.0001_initial... OK
(venv) RiffMates$ python manage.py loaddata bands.json
Installed 8 object(s) from 1 fixture(s)
```

Your data has been restored. Poke around in the Django REPL to prove this to yourself.

Fixtures are commonly used during testing. It is good practice to know the state of a database before performing a test—that way you can determine whether the result was what you expected. To standardize this process, you can associate fixture files with an app. You do this by creating a *fixtures* directory in the app. In this case, instead of passing a filename to the `loaddata` command, you specify the name of the app. Create a fixtures directory in the bands app and move bands.json inside of it. With that done, you can delete your database again and repeat the restoration process. This time, use the app's name instead of the filename directly:

```
(venv) RiffMates$ mkdir bands/fixtures          ←┐ Create a fixtures directory
(venv) RiffMates$ mv bands.json bands/fixtures/  ←  in the bands app.
(venv) RiffMates$ rm db.sqlite3                       ← Move the bands.json fixture
(venv) RiffMates$ python manage.py migrate            into the new directory.
Operations to perform:
  Apply all migrations: admin, auth, bands, contenttypes, sessions
Running migrations:
  Applying contenttypes.0001_initial... OK
  Applying auth.0001_initial... OK
  Applying admin.0001_initial... OK
  Applying admin.0002_logentry_remove_auto_add... OK
  Applying admin.0003_logentry_add_action_flag_choices... OK
  Applying contenttypes.0002_remove_content_type_name... OK
  Applying auth.0002_alter_permission_name_max_length... OK
  Applying auth.0003_alter_user_email_max_length... OK
  Applying auth.0004_alter_user_username_opts... OK
  Applying auth.0005_alter_user_last_login_null... OK
  Applying auth.0006_require_contenttypes_0002... OK
  Applying auth.0007_alter_validators_add_error_messages... OK
  Applying auth.0008_alter_user_username_max_length... OK
  Applying auth.0009_alter_user_last_name_max_length... OK
  Applying auth.0010_alter_group_name_max_length... OK
  Applying auth.0011_update_proxy_permissions... OK
  Applying auth.0012_alter_user_first_name_max_length... OK
  Applying bands.0001_initial... OK
  Applying bands.0002_venue_room... OK
  Applying bands.0003_band... OK
  Applying sessions.0001_initial... OK           ←┐ Load the fixture using the app
(venv) RiffMates$ python manage.py loaddata bands   name instead of the filename.
Installed 8 object(s) from 1 fixture(s)
```

Fixtures are a great way to insert or overwrite some data in your database, but they are a little fragile. Because inter-object relations are all specified using ID numbers, editing a fixture can be a delicate process. If you need to edit a field, like `Band.name`, that isn't too bad. If you want to add a new object, you need to make sure you use the right value for the ID. A fixture that contains the same ID for two different objects of the same type will result in an error. Fixtures are helpful for dealing with small amounts of data, and loading previously dumped content is useful. I recommend against using them to create new objects or managing large amounts of data.

4.10 *Danger zone, or know thy SQL*

When working with Django `Model` classes, it can be easy to forget that everything is a proxy to the database. The abstraction is helpful and allows you to quickly write Python to solve your data storage needs. The query manager attached to your `Model` allows you to do wonderfully complex queries. All of this is good, right up to the point where it is not.

If you start thinking of a `Model` as a Python object, rather than as a proxy to a table, you could end up with some very inefficient SQL. An extreme example of this happens when you map conceptual objects to a `Model`. Consider a website for a school, where you have students, teachers, and staff. From an object-oriented perspective you might design a student object, a teacher object, and a staff object. Translated into a Django `Model`, that results in three tables. If each of those has a name field, it is easy to make a mistake and have each field be a different length. If you want to add address information, you have to add it in three different places.

A flatter design is better. Instead of students, teachers, and staff, you have a person. The person has a role attribute to indicate whether someone is a student, teacher, or staff. This design results in all the people being in the same table.

This is an overly simplified example, but the object-oriented tools and design techniques you use in Python may not translate well to a database. You need to consider the resulting database structure when thinking about your Django `Model` design.

The impact of the database structure affects the performance of your database. Consider the many-to-many relationship you built in this chapter, between musicians and bands. To query the members of a band, a look-up gets done on the many-to-many table. As Django returns objects, rather than just their IDs, the corresponding band members must also be looked up in the musician table. To fetch a single band and its four members, a query is done to the band table to find the band, a query with four results gets done on the band/musician many-to-many table, and a query gets performed on the musicians table for each of the four musicians. Clever SQL can reduce the performance cost of all this work, and Django does a pretty decent job of completing this for you. The more inter-relationships your objects have, the messier all of this becomes.

For production systems with high volumes, or any system with a lot of data, the underlying SQL can make a huge difference on the performance. The better you understand SQL and what the ORM is doing on your behalf, the better your results. This does not mean you need to be an SQL expert tomorrow, but be aware that although it feels like you're writing Python, you're actually writing SQL.

4.11 *Exercises*

1 Modify the `musicians` index view to take an additional query parameter that specifies the number of objects per page. Make sure to support reasonable default and maximum values.

2 Using the musician index and detail pages as a reference, create similar pages for your `Band` objects. Inside the template, use the `musicians` relationship to show the members of the band.

3 Add a page that lists all `Venue` objects along with their corresponding rooms. You will need to iterate over the `room_set` query manager in the template.

Summary

- The Django ORM provides an object-oriented abstraction to a relational database.

- You inherit from `django.db.models.Model` to define a class to be mapped to the database.

- Your `Model` class uses fields to both define the type of data stored in the database and access to that data once queried.

- The `makemigrations` management command creates a Python file that describes the changes to the database needed by your models.

- The `migrate` management command runs any migration files that describe changes to models that have happened since the last invocation.

- Django's default database is SQLite, an embedded, single-file database.

- A database's query tool can be accessed using the `dbshell` management command.

- `Model` objects have a query manager named `.objects` that is used to query contents from the database for that model. The `.create()` method is used to create objects, while the `.first()`, `.last()`, and `.all()` methods return the first item, last item, and all the items for the object, respectively.

- A subset of values can be queried using the `.filter()` method, specifying key–value pairs for the filter. A value of `first_name="John"` returns all objects for which the `first_name` attribute is exactly `"John"`.

- The arguments to `.filter()` can be augmented to specify comparisons instead of exact matches. Suffixing a keyword with `__startswith` causes `.filter()` to return partial matches. A value of `first_name__startswith="J"` returns all objects for which the `first_name` field begins with the letter `"J"`.

- After modifying a `Model` instance, you call `.save()` on the object to update the database.

- The data for an object can be removed from the database using the `.delete()` method on the object itself. The Python proxy continues to exist after `.delete()` is called.

- Views can be parameterized to take arguments. Arguments can be given through URL query parameters or captured out of the URL itself.

- The `get_object_or_404()` shortcut retrieves an object from the database or raises an `Http404` exception in a single call.

- `Paginator` objects slice a query result into pages, allowing you to paginate the output in your templates.

- Django supports both one-to-many and many-to-many relations in the database. One-to-many relationships are defined using `ForeignKey` fields, while many-to-many relationships use the `ManyToManyField`.

Django Admin

5

This chapter covers

- Using the Django Admin to manage your `Model` content
- Creating a superuser
- Customizing the Django Admin
- Linking between `Model` objects in the Django Admin
- `Model Meta` properties

This chapter covers the Django Admin, a built-in, web-based tool for managing your object relational mapping (ORM) `Model` objects. The Django Admin gives you screens to list, add, edit, and delete the objects in the database.

5.1 Touring the Django Admin

In the previous chapter, you learned how to use the ORM to add storage capabilities to your Django site. Along the way, you used two techniques to construct data: the `.create()` method on a `Model` object and fixtures. Wouldn't it be nice if you had a graphical interface to manage your objects? Django comes with a tool that

105

does this for you. The *Django Admin* is a customizable, web-based interface that allows you to create and modify your `Model` objects with very little code.

Figure 5.1 shows a Django Admin screen that lists all of the `Musician` objects in the database. The code I wrote to generate that screen is less than 80 lines long. With it, you have multifield sorting, field search, filtering, custom columns, and all the actions you need to be able to add, update, and delete musicians from the database.

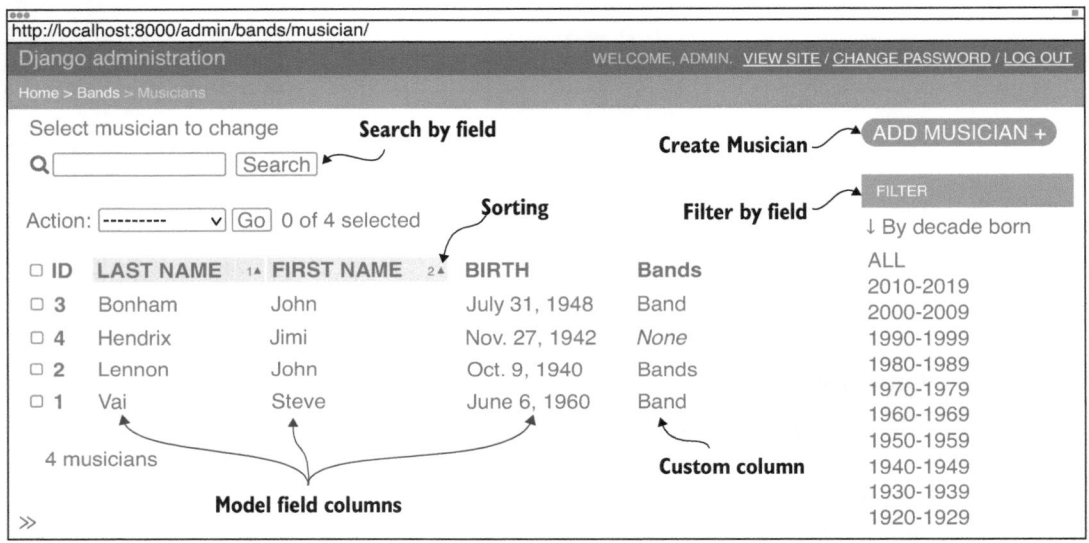

Figure 5.1   Parts of the Musician Listing page in the Django Admin

As the name implies, the Django Admin's purpose is administering your website. Its interface isn't the prettiest, and its design is optimized for users who control your site. Before using the Django Admin, you need to understand the basics of user permissions. Django is a multiuser framework, meaning you can create websites that have user accounts, and each account can be restricted to a subset of activities. Django has fine-grained permission control, and you can get quite specific about who can do what, but it also has a high-level mechanism that is good enough for most situations. Django divides users into three classes:

- General users
- Staff
- Admins

So far, when visiting RiffMates, you've been acting as an anonymous general user: one who isn't logged in. All the pages you've built have been public, so all users, including anonymous ones, are allowed to visit them. You'll learn all about building pages with restrictions in a later chapter.

The Django Admin is behind a login wall, since you don't want just anybody modifying your data. A user marked as *staff* is allowed to log in to the Django Admin. What they can do inside the Django Admin is dependent on their permissions. A user marked as *admin* automatically has permission to do everything in the Django Admin.

django-admin, Django Admin, admins, and superusers

Django uses the word *admin* a lot—and to mean different things. As you might imagine, this can be a bit confusing.

Term	Meaning
`django-admin`	The management script used to create new Django projects
Django Admin	The web interface allowing administrators to manage `Model` objects
Admin	The permission level applied to users with unrestricted access to the Django Admin
Superuser	Another term for an admin user, mostly used in the `createsuperuser` management command

Personally, I've never built a Django site for which I bothered with the staff designation. For sites that are complicated enough to have varying permission levels, I typically find that I want more control over the interface than the Django Admin provides. In this case, I end up building my own pages for staff-type activities. The admin user, though, is quite valuable. You can go a long way in being able to manage your site without having to write very much code, using the Django Admin and admin users.

NOTE I will continue referring to *admin* in the singular, but it is a property of a user account. You can have as many users with admin permission as you'd like.

5.1.1 Creating an admin user

The Django Admin allows you to create and manage users, but you have a bootstrapping problem: you have to be able to log in to the Django Admin to use the Django Admin. To get around this, there is a management command for creating a user with admin privileges. The `createsuperuser` command asks you a few questions and gets you going:

```
(venv) RiffMates$ python manage.py createsuperuser
Username (leave blank to use 'ctrudeau'): admin
Email address: admin@example.com
Password:
Password (again):
The password is too similar to the username.
This password is too short. It must contain at least 8 characters.
This password is too common.
Bypass password validation and create user anyway? [y/N]: y
Superuser created successfully.
```

I'll tell you a secret: I was a little naughty when selecting my password. Django has a set of rules for password strength, but the `createsuperuser` command allows you to ignore them. It prompts to confirm you're OK with being naughty, and then it lets you proceed.

> **WARNING**   When running a production site, you must guard access to the account that hosts your Django project. Anyone who can run commands can create a user with admin permissions and then will have full access to your site. With your newly created admin user in hand, you can now visit the Django Admin web interface.

5.1.2   *The default Django Admin*

If you were paying close attention, you might have noticed that the default `INSTALLED_APPS` configuration setting includes an app called `django.contrib.admin`. Likewise, the default main urls.py file also registers a `path` object for `admin/`. The Django Admin web interface is ready to go out of the box. If you don't want the Django Admin, you can remove it by modifying those two files.

As the Django Admin is already configured, and you created an admin user, you can visit it by running the development server and going to http://localhost:8000/admin/. The page prompts you with a login screen.

I'm quite certain you've seen a login page before, and hopefully, know just what to do. Use the username and password you gave to the `createsuperuser` command, and authenticate to the Django Admin.

Once inside, you will see the home page, which shows you all the objects registered with the Django Admin, grouped by their app. As you haven't registered any `Model` files yet, you see the two defaults: *Users* and *Groups*, as in figure 5.2.

You can explore these links if you like, but a later chapter deals with managing users and will cover this information in more detail. If you click the Users link, you will see a list of all your users, which, at the moment, is just the newly created admin account. If you are exploring, you can always get back to the home page by clicking the "Django administration" logo in the top-left corner. The right side of the page mentions actions, which include changes made to objects recently. As you haven't

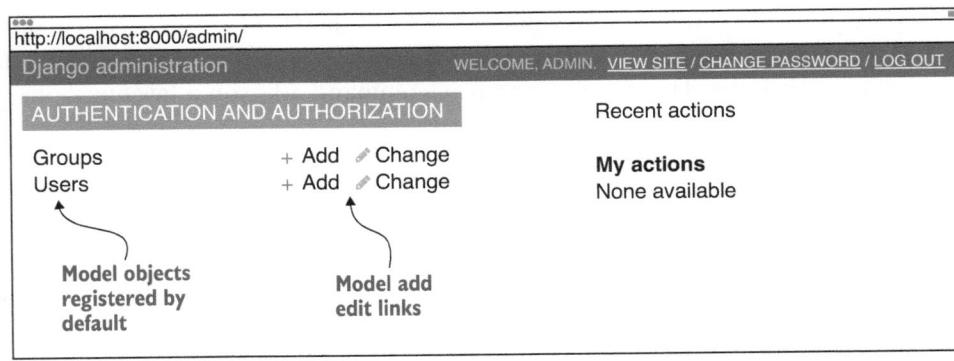

Figure 5.2   Django Admin home page with links for User and Group `Model` objects

done anything yet, the Actions list is empty. When you add, edit, or delete an object, you will see information on that in this list.

5.1.3   *Adding your own models*

Any ORM `Model` you define can be added to the Django Admin with just a few lines of code. When you created your app using the `startapp` command, Django created models.py and admin.py files for you. You've used the models.py file to define `Model` classes, and the admin.py file is where you declare that you want a `Model` to participate in the Django Admin. To make this declaration, create an `admin.ModelAdmin` class, and then register it against the `Model` class you want in the Django Admin. Figure 5.3 shows the relationship between the Django Admin app, the `admin.ModelAdmin` and `Model` classes in your app, and the resulting web interface.

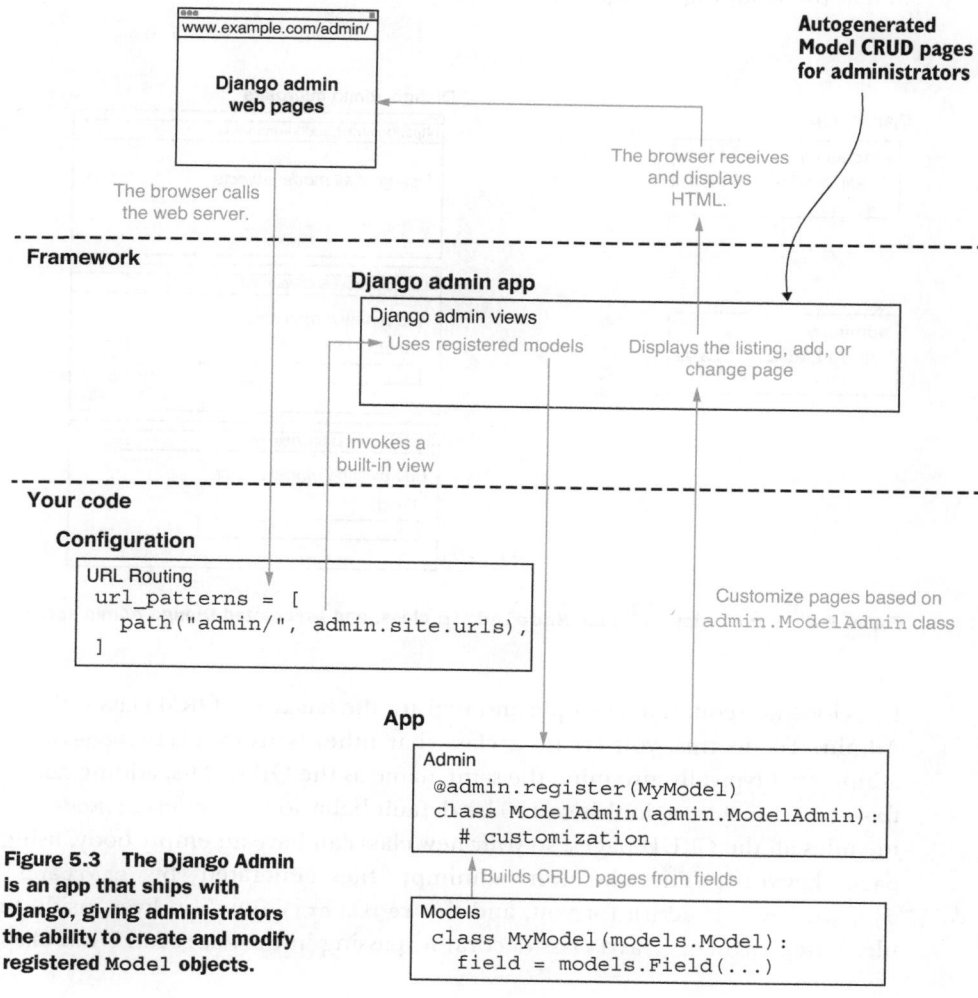

Figure 5.3   The Django Admin is an app that ships with Django, giving administrators the ability to create and modify registered `Model` objects.

When Django loads your app, it looks for admin.py files the same way it looks for models.py files. To add a `Model` to the Django Admin, you create a class that inherits from `admin.ModelAdmin` and call the `register()` function to associate the class with the model. The `register()` function can also be used as a class decorator. This is my preference, as it keeps the registration close to the `admin.ModelAdmin` class declaration.

Each registered `admin.ModelAdmin` class gets a set of *CRUD pages*. CRUD, besides being a very fun acronym, stands for *create, read, update, and delete,* which refers to the actions you take on most pieces of data. The *Listing page* acts as one of the Read pages, showing all the objects for the given `Model` class. Each listed object is a link, taking you to a *Change page*, where you can update the fields of the given object. The Django Admin also has links to an *Add page*, which allows you to create new objects, as well as a *Delete page*, which—as you might have guessed—allows you to delete existing objects. Figure 5.4 shows the relationship between the `Model` and `admin.ModelAdmin` classes as well as the resulting Django Admin screens.

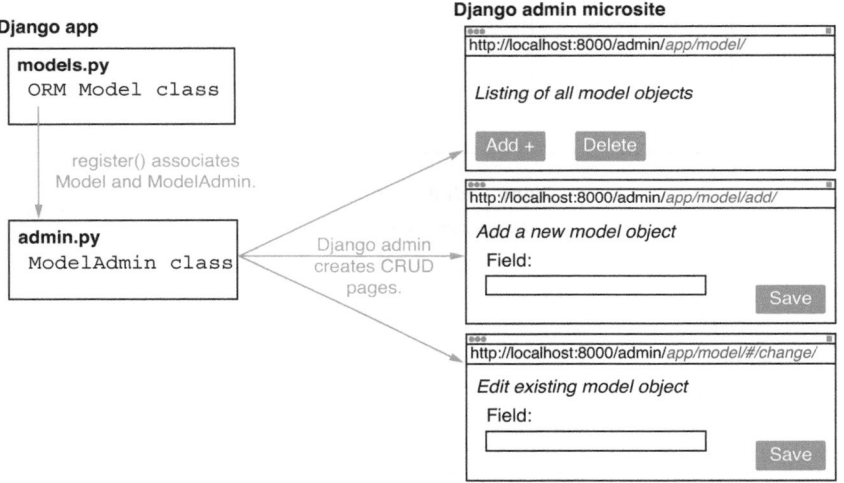

Figure 5.4 `Model` **class,** `admin.ModelAdmin` **class, and associated Django Admin screens**

Let's look at a concrete example and register the `Musician` ORM class with the Django Admin. To do this, you create a class that inherits from `admin.ModelAdmin` inside admin.py. I typically give mine the same name as the ORM class, adding `Admin` as a suffix—`MusicianAdmin`, in this case. The default behavior of the `admin.ModelAdmin` class includes all the CRUD pages, so your new class can have an empty body, using just the `pass` keyword. The skeleton admin.py file generated by `startapp` imports `django.contrib.admin` for you, and the `register()` function lives inside that module. I use `register()` as a class decorator, passing in the `Musician` ORM class itself to make the association between the new admin class and the ORM. That's it. One class import and three lines of code gives you a complete set of CRUD pages behind a secure login wall. The following listing shows the code you need inside admin.py to get this all to work.

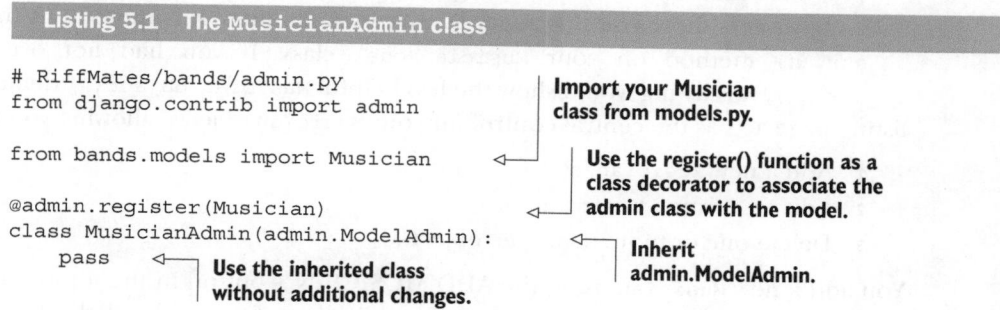

Listing 5.1   The `MusicianAdmin` class

```
# RiffMates/bands/admin.py
from django.contrib import admin          Import your Musician
                                          class from models.py.
from bands.models import Musician    ◄─
                                          Use the register() function as a
                                          class decorator to associate the
@admin.register(Musician)                 admin class with the model.
class MusicianAdmin(admin.ModelAdmin):  ◄   Inherit
    pass   ◄─ Use the inherited class         admin.ModelAdmin.
              without additional changes.
```

Fire up your development server, and return to the Django Admin Home page: http://localhost:8000/admin/. The page now has a new section for the Bands app and contains links to add a `Musician` object, and view the Musician Listing page. Go ahead and click Musicians to view the page, which contains a listing with the data you created in chapter 4. The result is similar to figure 5.5. The listing page has a navigation menu on the left-hand side similar to the home page; it is collapsible; and for the sake of space, I have collapsed it. The small chevron (») icon can be clicked to expand the nav.

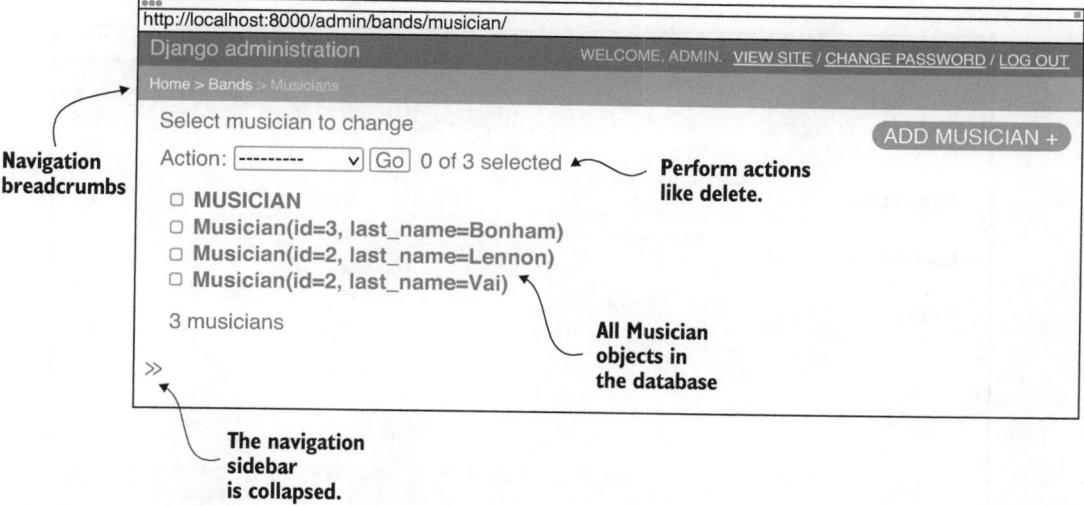

Figure 5.5   Listing page showing all `Musician` objects in the database and corresponding CRUD operations

On the Musician Listing page, underneath the header, a breadcrumb navigation widget is now displayed. This navigation aid has links to the home page, a page similar to the home page containing only the Bands app objects, and the name of the screen you are currently on.

The main feature of the listing page is the listing of `Musician` objects. Note how each object gets shown on this page. Does it look familiar? It is the output from the `.__str__()` method on your `MusicianModel` class. If you had not overridden `.__str__()`, this listing would show the less helpful `Musician object(#)` default. The listing page acts as the central control for your `Musician` objects, allowing you to

1 Add a new `Musician`.
2 Edit an existing `Musician`.
3 Delete one or more `Musician` objects.

You add a new `Musician` using the ADD MUSICIAN + button in the top-right corner of the page. Click the button now, and you'll see a form with all the fields for a `Musician`. Figure 5.6 shows the Add screen with the fields filled in to add Jimi Hendrix to the database. The Birth field has an optional date picker, although for 1942, that'd be a lot of clicking. Once you have filled in the form, you have three choices for saving: Save and Add Another saves the record and takes you back to this same page; Save and Continue Editing saves the record and keeps you editing Jimi; and Save saves the record and returns you to the listing.

Back on the listing screen, to edit a `Musician`, you click the link for its object. The text of this link is the result from `Musician.__str__()`. The Django Admin refers to edits as *changes*. The Change page is similar to the Add page, but it comes prepopulated with the `Musician` being edited.

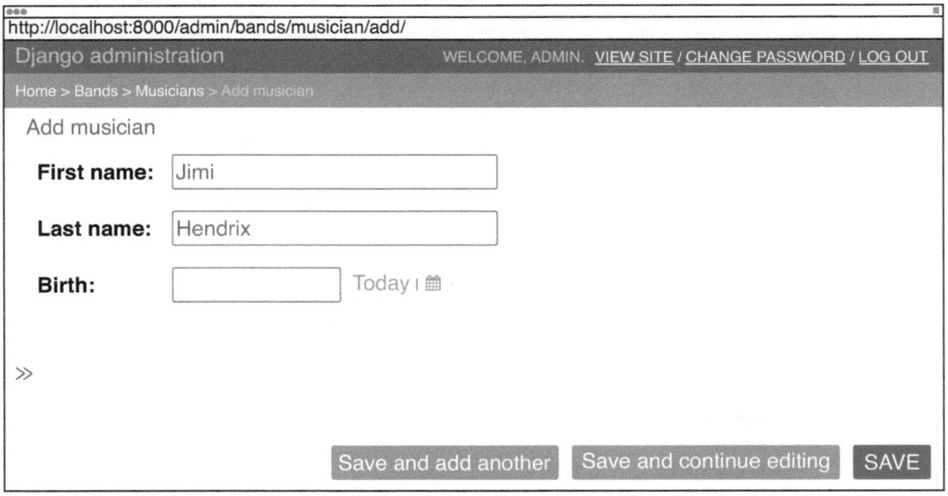

Figure 5.6 Add `Musician` page

To delete a `Musician`, you can either go to the Change screen and push the Delete button, or on the listing screen, you can select one or more `Musician` objects using the check boxes and then choose Delete Selected Musicians from the Action drop-down menu.

All these pages get created for you because you wrote a simple `admin.ModelAdmin` class. That's a lot of benefit for very little work, and what you've seen so far is merely the default. You can also customize the class to control the appearance and features of the page.

5.2 *Customizing a listing page*

The Django Admin's class listing page shows each of the objects in the database for the corresponding class. By default, each object gets represented using the class's `.__str__()` method. You can change this behavior by adding the `list_display` attribute to the `admin.ModelAdmin` class, which controls which columns are shown on the listing page. The attribute takes an iterable (usually a `tuple`) with an item for each desired column. Each item is a string: naming an object attribute, an argument-less object callable, or a callable on the `admin.ModelAdmin` class itself. In the case of a callable, the result returned from the method is the value for the column.

Let's replace the default display for the `MusicianAdmin` class. Add the `list_display` attribute to the `MusicianAdmin` class, setting it to a `tuple` containing (`"id"`, `"last_name"`, `"show_weekday"`). The first two items in this `tuple` result in a `Musician` object's ID and `last_name` fields being used as columns. The `"show_weekday"` value, in this case, is for a callable, which will be added to the class.

My `.show_weekday()` callable is a bit silly—it shows the day of the week the artist was born and can be implemented on either the `Musician` class or the `admin.Model-Admin` class. On the `Musician` class, it needs to be a method without any arguments. As I only want this "feature" in the Django Admin, it is a best practice to put it on the `MusicianAdmin` class instead. In this case, the method takes a single argument, the object to be displayed, and gets called once for each object in the listing. The return value of the method populates the row in the column.

The title of the column for a callable is based on the name of the callable. Underscores are turned into spaces, and words are displayed in small caps. You can separate the name of your callable from the title name with one unusual thing. You may have heard that everything in Python is an object, even functions—well, this goes for methods on objects as well. Like all objects, you can assign attributes to a method. To me, this feels sort of strange, and there aren't many use cases for it in the real world, but Django uses this language feature. The `.show_weekday()` method gets the optional string attribute `.short_description`, which, if present, gets used as the column title instead of the method name.

Listing 5.2 shows the new version of `MusicianAdmin` that defines the `list_display` attribute and the `.show_weekday()` method, including the `.short_description` attribute that renames the column title. Update your admin.py with this content.

Listing 5.2　Customized `MusicianAdmin` class with three columns

```python
# RiffMates/bands/admin.py
from django.contrib import admin
from bands.models import Musician

@admin.register(Musician)
class MusicianAdmin(admin.ModelAdmin):
    list_display = ('id', 'last_name', 'show_weekday')

    def show_weekday(self, obj):
        # Fetch weekday of artist's birth
        return obj.birth.strftime("%A")
    show_weekday.short_description = "Birth Weekday"
```

The listing page has three columns.

The date format "%A" is for the weekday.

Callable in list_display, invoked for each Musician object in the listing.

Customize the column title.

With these changes in place, start your development server, and visit the `Musician` class's listing page. It now looks like figure 5.7.

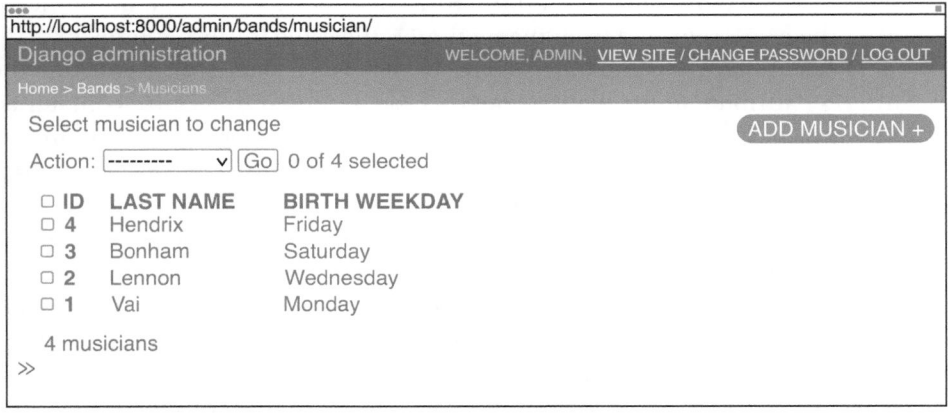

Figure 5.7　Customized `Musician` listing page

5.2.1　Sorting and searching

It isn't obvious unless you mouse over them, but the column headers in the listing page are clickable. Clicking a column sorts it, in ascending order. Once a column gets sorted, a mouse-over reveals a toggle to turn sorting off. You can sort by multiple columns, allowing "first sort-by then sort-by" ordering. A small number shown in the header indicates the sorting precedence. Sorted columns also feature a small triangle that changes from ascending to descending sort order when clicked.

Sorting is performed at the database level for efficiency. You haven't seen it yet, as you only have four objects, but the Django Admin supports pagination. If you have a lot of objects, Django doesn't load them all into memory to perform the sort but gets the database to do the work. This has a consequence: Your custom columns can't participate in the sort, as they aren't in the database. The Birth Weekday column created in the previous example is not clickable, as you can't sort by it.

The Django Admin also supports search. To enable this feature, you add a search_fields attribute to the admin.ModelAdmin class. Like list_display, this takes an iterable of field names—in this case, the fields to matched against a search term. When search_fields is present, the Django Admin adds a search box to the top of the page.

Different search behavior can be specified by adding a suffix to the name of the participating field. Without a suffix, the search term gets used as a substring for matches. For example, using last_name in search_fields and searching for *e*, results in listing Hendrix and Lennon because they have the letter *e* in their last names.

The __startswith suffix causes search terms to match the beginning of the field. Configuring first_name__startswith and searching for *j* returns Jimi Hendrix, John Bonham, and John Lennon. The __exact suffix requires search terms to be exact matches (case insensitive).

The search_fields attribute can take multiple fields, and you can mix and match the suffixes as you like within the values. The following listing modifies the list_display attribute of MusicianAdmin to add the first_name field as a column and makes the first and last names searchable.

> **Listing 5.3   Modified MusicianAdmin class to support search**

```
# RiffMates/bands/admin.py
...
class MusicianAdmin(admin.ModelAdmin):
    list_display = ("id", "last_name", "first_name", "show_weekday", )
    search_fields = ("last_name", "first_name", )
    ...
```

5.2.2   *Filtering*

In addition to searching, you can filter content as well. The way you implement this is similar: you add the list_filter attribute to your admin.ModelAdmin class. The simplest form of list_filter is the name of a field to filter by.

Filters are shown as widgets on the right-hand-side of the listing page. For fields in the list_filter configuration, all values for the field are shown as filter links—which can be problematic.

For a field that has a limited selection, like a BooleanField or anything restricted using the choices attribute, a complete list of values is fine. For a wide-open field, like last_name, this becomes both ugly and a performance limitation. For a large dataset, you do not want every single last name in your database showing on the right-hand side; in this case, you should use search capabilities instead.

The default filter for a DateField shows a small set of values to choose from: today, the last seven days, this month, and this year. For our musicians' birthdays, this isn't going to be helpful. You can define a custom filter list by extending the `SimpleList-Filter` class. This class has two methods: one that defines the values to show in the filter listing and another that determines the corresponding filter to run on the `QuerySet` used for the page.

Although I've been using some famous musicians as my examples, RiffMates is really about musicians seeking musicians. It is reasonable to assume anybody in the database actively looking for another musician is alive. Filtering by the last few decades is likely good enough.

A custom list filter class extends `admin.SimpleListFitler`, defines two attributes, and defines two methods. The attributes are `title` and `parameter_name`, specifying the title of the filter and the name of what is being filtered by. The methods are `.lookups()` and `.queryset()`, which are responsible for naming the filter choices and performing the filter query, respectively. Figure 5.8 shows a high-level version of this code.

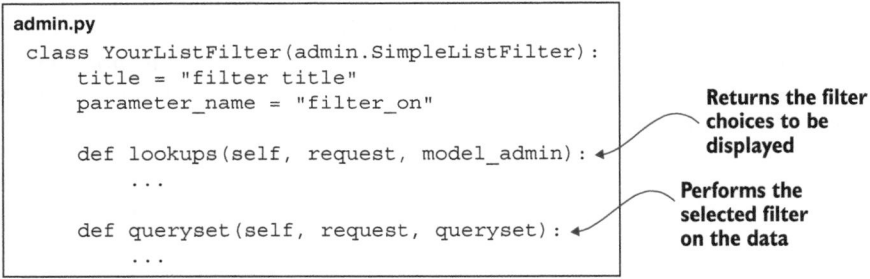

Figure 5.8   An overview of a custom list filter

The `.lookups()` method takes two arguments: the page's `request` object and a reference to the associated `admin.ModelAdmin` class. The method is responsible for returning an iterable of `tuples`, each containing a short- and long-form display of the filter choice. The choices are strings, and the short form is used in the URL as a query parameter to the filtered page. The long form is what is displayed to the user as the filter link. This structure is similar to what Django expects in the `choices` attribute of a field constructor.

The `.queryset()` method is responsible for doing the actual filtering. It takes two arguments: the page's `request` object, and a `QuerySet`. When Django Admin calls this method, it has already preformed a query, which was used to construct the page. The resulting `QuerySet` object gets passed into `.queryset()`, allowing you to further perform actions on it. This method returns the modified `QuerySet` object with filtered contents.

Let's define a custom filter that provides the last 10 decades as date groups to filter by, calling it `DecadeListFilter`. Its `.lookups()` method returns an iterable of decade ranges, and its `.queryset()` method filters the `QuerySet` argument by the decade chosen.

To calculate the range of decades, start with the current year, ignoring the current decade, and then count the 10 decades preceding it. The `.lookups()` method returns a `list` containing a series of `tuples`, with each `tuple` containing the beginning year of decade as a string and another string showing the year range of the decade. The first value gets used as a query parameter in the URL, and although it would be nice for it to be an integer, it has to be a string. When the `.queryset()` method uses it, it must convert it back to an integer to perform the filter.

The `.queryset()` method uses the query parameter argument to affect a filter by date range. The `QuerySet` argument will be the entire set of `Musician` objects, and the filtered version returned needs to be limited to just the chosen decade. This filtering is done by calling `.filter()` on the `QuerySet`, passing in two limiters on the `birth` field. Recall that the `.filter()` method supports the use of suffixes to do comparisons. A decade range is all the dates greater than or equal to January 1st of the first year of the decade, limited by dates less than or equal to December 31st of the last year in the decade. Applying the `__gte` and `__lte` suffixes on the `birth` field in the call to `.filter()` achieves this result.

When a user clicks a link in the filter widget, the same listing page gets reloaded but with a corresponding query parameter set. To save you from having to process the query parameter yourself, the class has a `.value()` convenience method that returns the chosen filter argument. As our filter argument is a number containing the chosen, you convert it back to an integer and then use this to construct the decade date ranges for your `.filter()` call.

The following listing shows the `list_filter` argument to the `MusicianAdmin` class that references the new `DecadeListFilter` and the class code for the filter itself. Modify your admin.py file with the changes shown, and you'll be able to filter your musicians by decade.

Listing 5.4   Custom list filter based on decades

```
# RiffMates/bands/admin.py
...
from datetime import datetime, date      # Import datetime and date for decade calculations.
...
class DecadeListFilter(admin.SimpleListFilter):      # Inherit from SimpleListFilter to define a new list filter.
    title = 'decade born'      # Define the list filter's title.
    parameter_name = 'decade'      # Define the list filter's query parameter name.

    def lookups(self, request, model_admin):
        result = []

        this_year = datetime.today().year      # Determine the current decade.
        this_decade = (this_year // 10) * 10
        start = this_decade - 10
        for year in range(start, start - 100, -10):      # Loop backward through the 10 previous decades.
```

```
        result.append( (str(year), f"{year}-{year+9}") )        ◄───┐

    return result                                           Add a tuple containing the base year
                                                              of the decade and a display string.
def queryset(self, request, queryset):
    start = self.value()                ◄───┐ Get the filtered value, checking
    if start is None:                         for None (meaning no filter).
        return queryset
                                            Run a subfilter on the QuerySet,
    start = int(start)                      restricting the birth field to the chosen
    result = queryset.filter(               decade, starting on January 1st and going
        birth__gte=date(start, 1, 1),   ◄──┘ through December 31, 9 years later.
        birth__lte=date(start + 9, 12, 31),
    )

    return result                                                  Add a birth
...                                                              field column to
class MusicianAdmin(admin.ModelAdmin):                             the listing.
    list_display = ("id", "last_name", "first_name", "birth",
        "show_weekday", )                         ◄───
    list_filter = (DecadeListFilter, )   ◄───┐ Add the new DecadeListFilter to
                                               the admin.ModelAdmin class.
```

To make it a little more obvious, the code in the preceding listing also adds `birth` to the `list_display` attribute, so you can see if the decade filter is working. With the code in place, start your development server and take a look at your new `Musician` listing page. Figure 5.9 shows a page filtered from 1940–1949.

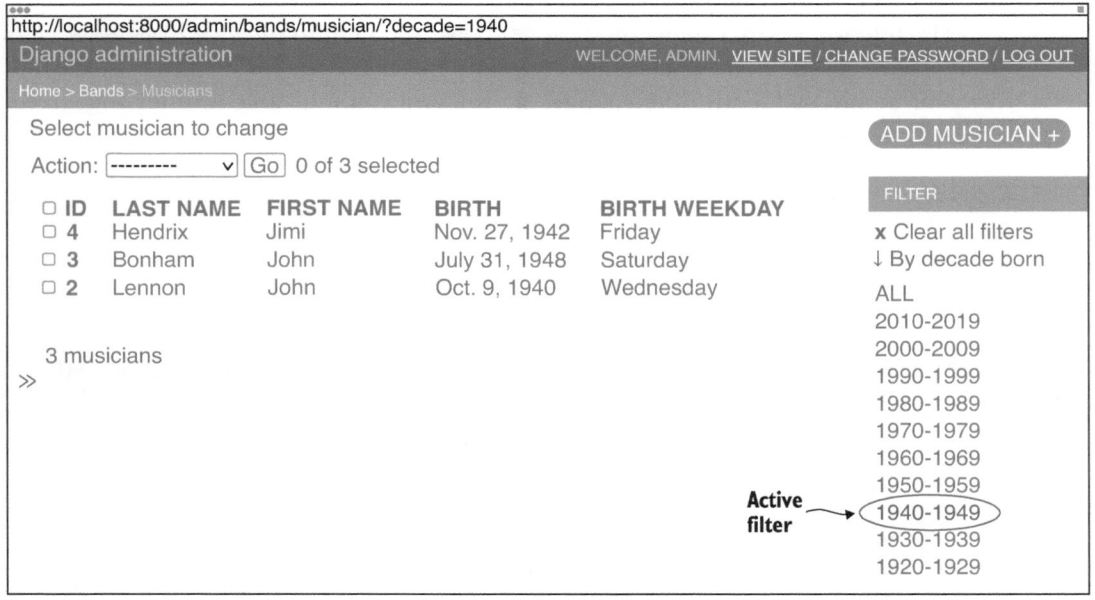

Figure 5.9 Listing page filtered by the 1940s

Django comes prepackaged with some other filters. You can dive deep into the documentation to see what is available or learn to further customize on your own: https://docs.djangoproject.com/en/dev/ref/contrib/admin/filters/.

When playing with your new list filter, take a look at the resulting URL. The first value in each `.lookups()` tuple gets used as the query parameter. The query parameter itself is defined through the `parameter_name` attribute. All of this is still a web application—Django is just doing many things on your behalf. Because the Django Admin uses query parameters to modify what is displayed on the page, you can take advantage of this and add features for yourself, you'll do just that in the next section.

5.2.3 New in Django 5: Facets

If you're using Django 5, you may have noticed another link in the filter control box on the right-hand side of the page: Show Counts. When you click this link, each filter choice has a counter appended, showing how many items are included in that filter. These counts are called *facets*. Clicking the link adds a `__facets=True` query parameter to the URL. When facets are being displayed, Show Counts becomes Hide Counts.

You can control whether facets are displayed by adding a `show_facets` member to your admin model. There are three possible settings:

- `show_facets = admin.ShowFacets.ALWAYS`—Always display the facet.
- `show_facets = admin.ShowFacets.ALLOW`—Use the Show and Hide links, displaying facets if the query parameter is present (this is the default).
- `show_facets = admin.ShowFacets.NEVER`—Disable facets.

Displaying the facet information means extra queries to the database because the Django Admin has to look up the count of each filter. This is why the NEVER option is available, so you can turn it off if the query is too expensive for your page.

5.3 Cross-linking between related objects

So far, you've only added `Musician` to the Django Admin. Adding a `Band` object is no different but has the added wrinkle of the `BandModel` including a relationship with the `Musician` class. To see how the Django Admin deals with inter-object relationships, create a bare minimum `BandAdmin` class, like the one in the following listing.

Listing 5.5 `BandAdmin` class

```
...
from bands.models import Musician, Band          ◁——— Add the Band class
...                                                     to the import.
@admin.register(Band)                             ◁——┐ Define and register
class BandAdmin(admin.ModelAdmin):                    │ a minimum BandAdmin class.
    pass
```

With your new class in place, run the development server, visit the Band Listing page, and then click on Wishful Thinking. Figure 5.10 shows the Change page for the object, including a multiselect widget for choosing the related `Musician` objects.

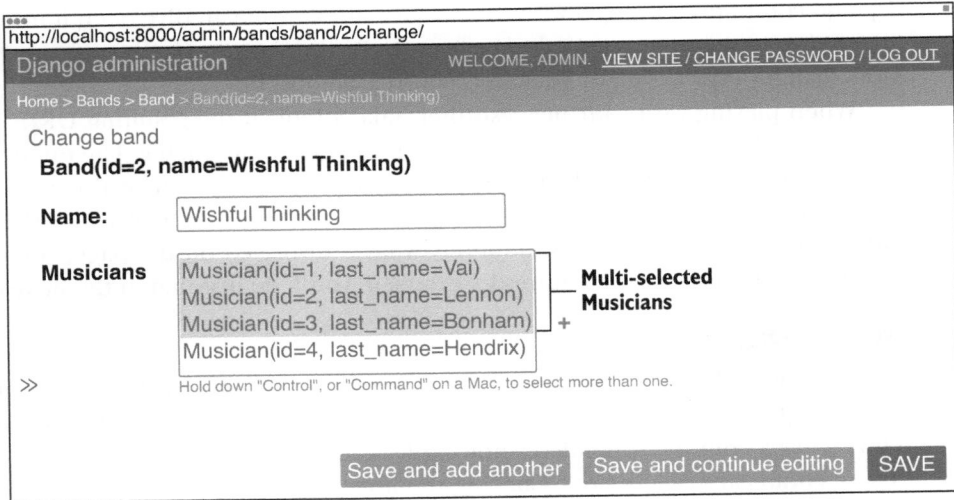

Figure 5.10   Band **Change screen with associated** `Musician` **objects**

For large datasets this screen can be rather slow to load. To populate the Musician Multiselect, every possible `Musician` object needs to be queried and shown. One way to improve the performance is to keep the `.__str__()` result as short and simple as possible.

You saw how the Django Admin uses query parameters to display a subset of the results on the listing page when you use filters. Whether or not you have a filter, you can take advantage of this feature in your own code. You can add query parameters to the URL and change what is shown on the screen. This is handy if you want to display a single object without using the Change page. For example, http://localhost:8000/admin/bands/band/?id=2 displays the listing page with only the `Band` with an ID of 2 in the list.

The filter query parameters also support the same field lookup modifiers as the ORM. The http://localhost:8000/admin/bands/musician/?id__gte=3 URL shows the Musician Listing page containing only those `Musician` objects with an ID greater than or equal to 3. A more useful field lookup modifier is `__in`; passing it a comma-separated list of numbers limits the content of a listing page to just those IDs.

Using this feature, you can add a column to the listing page with clickable links to related objects—for example, a column on the Musician page that links to the musician's bands. To do this, add another callable that returns a link. You don't want to hardcode the link to the Band Listing page; you want to look it up. Recall the `{% url %}` that does this kind of lookup in a template—the Python code equivalent is the `reverse()` function in the `django.urls` module. All the Django Admin URLs are named, so if you know the pattern, you can look up other Django Admin pages using `reverse()`.

The name of a Django Admin listing page is `admin:module_class_changelist`, where *module* and *class* get replaced with the module and class name of the `Model` object listed. Calling `reverse()` with the right argument gives you the URL of the listing page, which you augment with a query parameter to filter the page.

Let's add a band-membership link to the Musician Listing page. You need a new callable for the column—I've named mine `show_bands`. Inside the callable, use `reverse()` to look up the URL for the Band Listing page. This page is named `admin:bands_band_changelist` (`bands` for the app and `band` for the `Model`). To filter the listing by a musician's bands, you need the IDs of those bands. Query those IDs, and then construct an `?id__in` query parameter to append to your listing page URL.

Recall from the chapter on templates that Django escapes HTML, by default. You can't just return text with an `<a>` tag inside it; you need to mark it as safe for rendering. The `format_html()` function from the `django.utils.html` module lets you build safe HTML. This function uses paired braces (`{}`) as placeholders, allowing you to parameterize a string with an HTML link inside it. Like with `show_weekday`, add the `.short_description` attribute to change the column title. Make the changes shown in the following listing to your admin.py file, and then visit the Django Admin to see your new content.

Listing 5.6   The `MusicianAdmin` class with links to the `Band` listing page

```
# RiffMates/bands/admin.py
...
from django.utils.html import format_html       ◁──── Import format_html and
from django.urls import reverse                         reverse for use in the method.
...
@admin.register(Musician)
class MusicianAdmin(admin.ModelAdmin):
    list_display = ("id", "last_name", "first_name", "birth", "show_weekday",
        "show_bands")                    ◁──┐ Add the show_bands
        ...                                   callable to the columns.

    def show_bands(self, obj):                    ┌── Query all bands associated
        bands = obj.band_set.all()       ◁───┘    with this musician.
        if len(bands) == 0:                         ◁───┐
            return format_html("<i>None</i>")             If there are no bands, use format_html
                                                          to show an italicized None.
        plural = ""                       ◁──┐
        if len(bands) > 1:                      If there is more than
            plural = "s"                        one band, the output      Query parameter using the
                                                should say Bands.         __in suffix and a comma-
                                                                          separated list of Band IDs.
        parm = "?id__in=" + ",".join([str(b.id) for b in bands])         ◁──
        url = reverse("admin:bands_band_changelist") + parm
        return format_html('<a href="{}">Band{}</a>', url, plural)        ◁──
    show_bands.short_description = "Bands"
                                                    Create a safe <a> tag using the
                                                    URL and the pluralization of Band.
```

Look up the Band listing page, and then add the query parameter to the end. (annotation pointing to `parm`/`url` lines)

Start your development server, and then return to the Musician Listing page. You now have a Bands column with clickable links. Each link goes to a filtered version of the Band Listing page, showing only those bands the musician is a member of.

5.4   *Model Meta properties*

You've seen how the `.__str__()` method on a `Model` class changes the corresponding Django Admin listing page. Other properties of the `Model` can also effect the Django Admin. This is another one of those cases where Django takes advantage of a seldom used Python language feature. I heard you like classes—how about a class inside your class?

Django `Model` classes can optionally define a nested class named `Meta`. Django uses the attributes of this class to modify the default behavior of the resulting `Model` object. Some attributes are only used by the Django Admin, and others change the behavior of the `Model` itself, such as modifying the underlying database queries.

The following sections provide details on some of the most popular `Meta` attributes. For a full list, see https://docs.djangoproject.com/en/dev/ref/models/options/.

5.4.1   *Sort order*

The `ordering` `Meta` attribute specifies the default sort order in response to queries on the object. This impacts both the order of the objects in the Django Admin listing pages as well as any query you run in your code. The underlying SQL gets an `ORDER BY` clause attached automatically. This attribute takes a list of field names and supports a dash (-) prefix to indicate descending sort order, as shown in the following example:

```
class VenueStaff(models.Model):
    # first_name, last_name, employee ID number fields
    ...

    class Meta:
        ordering = ["last_name", "-employee_id"]
```
Sort by last_name and then by employee_id, in reverse order.

The default sort order is none. SQLite appears to return the `Musician` objects in reverse order by ID, but this should not be depended upon. Ordering costs overhead and requires the database to do additional work. It is handy though. To change the default sort order of the `Musician` class to be based on `last_name` and then `first_name`, make the following change in your RiffMates/bands/models.py file:

```
class Musician(models.Model):
    ...

    class Meta:
        ordering = ["last_name", "first_name"]
```

Once you've made the change, try running `Musician.objects.all()` in the REPL or visit the Django Admin `Musician` listing page to see the difference.

5.4.2   *Indexes*

In chapter 4, you learned about specifying an index in the field declaration of a `Model`. You can also declare indexes via `Meta` attributes. Using this mechanism allows you to have multiple fields participate in a single index.

The attribute name for this is `indexes`. It takes a list of `models.Index` objects, with each object instance specifying the participating fields, as shown in the following example:

```
class VenueStaff(models.Model):
    # first_name, last_name, employee ID number fields

    class Meta:
        indexes = [models.Index(fields=["last_name", "first_name"])]
```

NOTE Remember, indexes make a big performance difference on query results for the fields being searched. Without an index, the database needs to scan the entire table until it finds a matching result. The index works like a hash table, providing a shortcut to finding your values.

5.4.3 *Uniqueness*

The Django ORM automatically creates the ID field for you as a unique identifier for an object in the table. There may be situations where you want to ensure one or more other fields are also unique within a table. The `unique_together` attribute allows you to do just that.

This attribute takes a list of lists. The nested list contains the fields that are to be unique when combined, which are all in a list, as you can specify more than one set of fields. As a shortcut, you can specify this as a single list if you only have one set of fields that are to be unique together.

Consider the `Room` object, which defines a room in a `Venue`, discussed in chapter 4. You don't want two rooms to have the same name in the same venue. You can avoid this by making the `Room` name and the venue `ForeignKey` unique together:

```
class Room(models.Model):
    # name and venue field declaration

    class Meta:
        unique_together = [["name", "venue"]]

        # alternate short-cut version as there is only one "uniqueness"
        # unique_together = ["name", "venue"]
```

The enforcement of the `unique_together` clause is done at the database level. If you create an object that violates this in code, an exception will be raised. If you attempt to do the same in the Django Admin, you will get an error message. If you make these kinds of changes to your models, don't forget you'll need to run the `makemigrations` and `migrate` management commands to have them take effect.

More recent versions of Django have a general-purpose mechanisms for specifying constraints on your tables. Django has constraint classes—one for uniqueness and the other for enforcing values. There is also an abstract base class, so you can write your own. The `unique_together` attribute duplicates the constraint case. It hasn't been deprecated yet, but the documentation indicates it may be in the future. Writing your own constraints requires ORM features beyond the scope of this book (see: https://docs.djangoproject.com/en/dev/ref/models/constraints/ for more information).

5.4.4   *Object names*

Inside the Django Admin, the name of your `Model` is directly derived from the `Model` class name. For example, the `Musician` class appears as *musician, musicians, Musician,* and *Musicians,* depending on the context. Take a look at the Musician Listing page; on this page, you will find *Select musician to change* in the title and *Musicians* in the navigation breadcrumbs.

If your `Model` class consists of multiple words formatted in camel case, Django parses it into spearate words, capitalizing when necessary and appending the letter *s* to pluralize. For example, the `MusicianClassified` object is shown as *Musician classifieds* in its plural form. If you're not happy with how this is done, the `verbose_name` and `verbose_name_plural` attributes give you control. These two `Meta` attributes are available on the class, but I've only ever seen them used by the Django Admin.

A `verbose_name` containing capitals appears that way everywhere. If the attribute is lowercase, it is capitalized where Django sees fit. I don't like the mixed-case class name in the navigation bar, so I often set `verbose_name` to use the capitalization I want. Without `verbose_name`, `MusicianClassified` appears as *Musician classifieds* in the nav. I set `verbose_name` to `Musician Classified` to get *Musician Classifieds* in the nav. The downside is the title becomes *Select Musician Classified to change.* Pick your preference.

The most common use of `verbose_name_plural` is for words that don't pluralize in normal ways or that are already plural. Consider a model named `Box`:

```
class Box(models.Model):
    # field declarations
    ...

    class Meta:
        verbose_name_plural = "boxes"
```

Use of `verbose_name_plural` alone, or along with `verbose_name`, gets your `Model` names showing properly. My mother, the retired kindergarten teacher, thanks you for your proper grammar.

5.5   *Exercises*

1 Add search capabilities to the `BandAdmin` class.
2 Add default sorting by name to the `Band`, `Venue`, and `Room` classes.
3 Create `admin.ModelAdmin` classes for the `Venue` and `RoomModel` classes, including custom-linked column methods, like with `Musician` and `Band`, and searchable name fields.
4 Add a Members column to the Band Listing page, containing multiple links, one to each `Musician` in the `Band`. Note that appending to a string makes it unsafe again. Use `mark_safe` to fix that.

Summary

- The Django Admin is a built-in web interface for creating, editing, and deleting your `Model` objects.
- You create `admin.ModelAdmin` classes to register your `Model` classes with the Django Admin.
- Access to the Django Admin is restricted to special users only: staff and admins (aka superusers).
- A superuser account is created using the `createsuperuser` management command.
- The home page of the Django Admin lists all registered `Model` objects, grouped by their app.
- Each `admin.ModelAdmin` class generates a listing page and pages for adding, changing, and deleting objects.
- Columns on the listing page are determined by the `list_display` property of your `admin.ModelAdmin` object.
- The `list_display` attribute contains the names of `Model` fields, argument-less `Model` methods, or methods on the `admin.ModelAdmin` class.
- Columns based on `Model` fields are sortable by clicking the column header. Sorting by multiple columns as well as ascending and descending order are supported
- A callable used by `list_display` can return HTML, including links to other Django Admin pages, as long as it is a safe string.
- Django Admin listing pages support search using fields named in the `search_fields` attribute on the `admin.ModelAdmin` class.
- A filter on the listing page restricts what data is shown. Filters are enabled via the `list_filter` attribute on the `admin.ModelAdmin` class.
- Custom filters inherit from `SimpleListFilter` and define the filter choices and a method that modifies the listing page's `QuerySet`.
- Registered URL routes, including Django Admin's, can be looked up in Python, using the `reverse()` function.
- Listing pages support query parameters to show a subset of the page contents. These parameters can be mixed with a URL lookup to add links to related objects in a custom column.
- You can nest an inner `Meta` class inside a `Model` class to control the behavior of the objects. Commonly used parameters control indexes on the table, field uniqueness, and the name of the object in the Django Admin.

Part 2

Django building blocks

Part 1 was all about getting you going with the Django framework. This part builds on what you've learned, taking you from simpler single-user sites to full multiuser projects. You'll get started by learning how to manage user accounts and how to accept data and files from them. Once you have a multiuser site, you're going to want to maintain it, which means adding testing, using built-in management commands, writing your own commands, and understanding how changes to your ORM models get reflected in the database. When you're finished with this part of the book, you'll be familiar with what you need to build and maintain a multiuser website, using the Django framework.

User management 6

This chapter introduces you to the features of Django that enable multiuser websites. You'll learn how user authentication and authorization works, along with the ability to store data linked to a user's account.

6.1 Multiuser websites

By adding Django Admin functionality to RiffMates, you have already turned it into a multiuser site. At the moment, though, it is rather simplistic: you have administrators who use the Django Admin tools and everybody else. What if you want musicians to be able to edit their own profiles, create bands, and invite people to bands?

129

The primary idea behind RiffMates is to create a space for classified ads, where bands can seek musicians and musicians can seek bands. You could manage all this through email, having the musicians send a note to your admins, but that is a lot of work for your admins. Instead, you want your musicians and others to be able to serve themselves.

Self-service sounds great, but what if two bands are rivals? You can't have the Sharks and the Jets editing each other's profiles—that won't end well. Multiuser sites really are about being able to control who does what where. To provide this kind of control, you need two things: authentication and authorization. These are related concepts, and one sometimes implies the other. *Authentication* is proving who you are, while *authorization* is the system allowing you to perform an action. User accounts pair a login ID and password to provide the authentication part, while your code determines authorization.

As part of authentication, Django comes with a built-in ORM Model object for tracking users and passwords. It handles the encryption of the passwords for you and validation when a user enters a password to prove who they are. This is accomplished through middleware. *Middleware* is code that sits between the routing of the URL and the calling of the view and can affect what is sent to the view or whether the view gets called at all. Django provides some middleware out of the box, including session management. *Session management* is what determines whether a user gets logged in or not and when to log them out automatically, expiring the session. As with most things in Django, middleware is pluggable, and you can write your own, but doing so isn't covered in this book. In figure 6.1, you can see the middleware component in the framework part of the diagram. Additionally, the view in the diagram has a decorator: `@login_required`. This is the simplest form of authorization: the view can only be used by those who are authenticated.

A view may also contain further authorization logic. For example, a page might be a private area only band members can see. The URL for such a page has a `Band` ID, is wrapped with the `@login_required` decorator to ensure a musician attempting access gets authenticated, and validates that the user account belongs to a musician that is a member of the band. If authorization fails, the usual response is to raise an `Http404` error.

As soon as you have user accounts, you have a password management problem. People are forgetful, and the late-night, hard-living lifestyle of musicians makes them even more so. Django provides views and utilities for both user creation and password management, but as most of this needs to look like your site, it isn't quite ready out of the box; you have to do some customization to make it work.

This chapter is all about user accounts: how to create them, how to manage them, how to use them to authenticate and authorize users, and how to manage password resets.

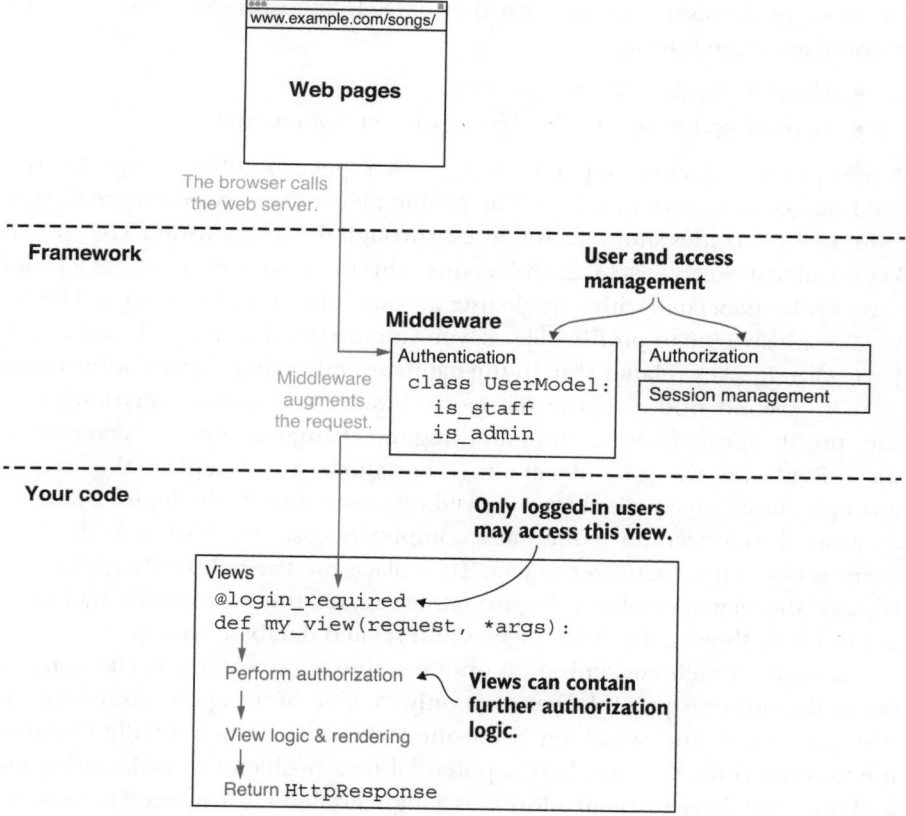

Figure 6.1   Session management and login control through middleware

6.2   *Storing user data*

In the previous chapter, you used the `createsuperuser` command to create an admin account to access the Django Admin. On the Django Admin home page, there is a listing of ORM objects registered with the site—one of which being the `User` object. Each user account in the system is represented by an entry in the database proxied by a `django.contrib.auth.models.User` object. The `User` object stores a username and password in the database. All of this is an oversimplification (read: lie); Django's user management system is quite flexible and allows you to customize heavily, but for the time being, the mental model of a plain `User` object is easier to consider.

6.2.1   *Choosing a user account mechanism*

Most of the time, you want to associate data with a user account. Consider a musician's account; you already have a `Musician` ORM object, and now, it would be nice to associate the user account with that data. Django provides two ways of defining account-associated storage:

- Using a profile ORM object
- Replacing the `User` ORM object with a custom model

A user profile object is a separate `Model` with a special kind of foreign key pointing to the Django `User` account object. The profile object stores your custom data, while the `User` `Model` provides shortcuts for access through the relationship. The special foreign key is called a `OneToOneField`, and it constrains the relationship so that a profile object can only be associated with a single user account object, and vice versa. The `OneToOne-Field` isn't specific to profile objects; you can use them in any code where you wish to have a foreign key relationship in the database with a single relation restriction.

The second option is the hardcore, I-want-to-customize-everything-option. The user profile approach locks you into using the Django `User` `Model`'s credential mechanism. Replacing the `User` object altogether allows you to replace the credentials, for example, using an email address instead of a username as the login. Django's flexibility around user accounts comes at a complexity cost: in addition to the `User` object, there is also a user manager object. To replace the `User` altogether, you also have to replace the manager object. Figure 6.2 compares the user profile and replacement approaches, showing both the objects and related database changes.

Choosing which customization option to use is important, as changing your project in the future is painful. Django is only capable of using one user account mechanism at a time, and switching from one style to the other usually requires custom migration scripts. You also have a potential data problem: consider using usernames and then switching to email address as a login credential. You need to make sure all of your users have email addresses in the system and that they are unique. This is a design decision you should make as close to the beginning of your project as possible—and that you should stick with.

As the hardcore option is, well, hardcore, this book will stick to the user profile case. If you're interested in more customization than is covered in this chapter, see https://mng.bz/RZZn.

> **Proxy models**
>
> Django allows a third option for customizing the user account if all you want is behavioral changes. An ORM model can be declared a *proxy model* by inheriting from the model being proxied and adding `proxy = True` to the model settings in the `Meta` subclass.
>
> A proxy model object uses the same table as its parent; the attributes and their corresponding columns are the same. Both the proxy and its parent abstract the same rows in the same table. What can change in a proxy is its behavior. For example, you can add a different `ordering` attribute to the `Meta` subclass, and your default sorting of the proxy will be different from its parent.

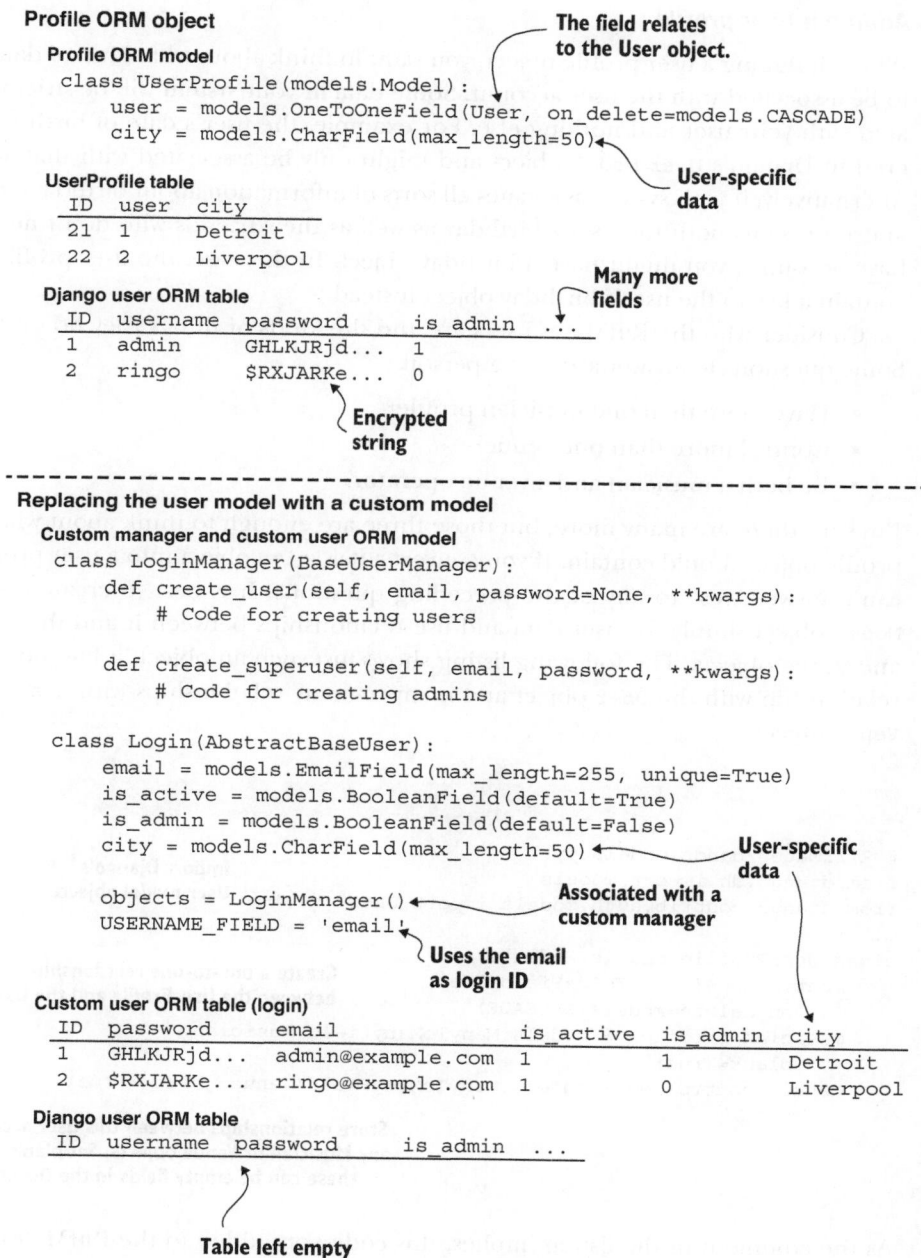

Figure 6.2   User profiles vs. replacing the User ORM object for user data storage

6.2.2 *Adding a user profile*

When designing a user profile object, you want to think about what kind of data needs to be associated with the user account. Some data in your system will be strictly associated with your user and nothing else. For example, the user's date of birth isn't covered in Django's User Model object and might only be associated with that account. Alternatively, if your system associates all sorts of information about birthdays together and represents both the user's birthday as well as their friends who don't necessarily have accounts, you might have a birthday object. In this case, the user profile would contain a key to the user's birthday object instead.

Consider who the RiffMates users are and the kinds of things they do on the site. Some questions to answer are, can a person

- Have more than one musician profile?
- Control more than one venue?
- Be both a musician and a venue operator?

I'm sure there are many more, but those three are enough to think about what a user profile object should contain. If you convert a Musician object into a user profile, you can't answer "yes" to any of the preceding questions. It is best to create a separate Model object simply for user data and use relationships between it and the Musician and Venue objects. The following listing shows just such an object; it has a one-to-one relationship with the User object and many-to-many relationships with Musician and Venue objects.

Listing 6.1 The UserProfile class

```
# RiffMates/bands/models.py
from django.db import models
from django.contrib.auth.models import User          ← Import Django's
...                                                     User model object.
class UserProfile(models.Model):
    user = models.OneToOneField(User,                 | Create a one-to-one relationship
        on_delete=models.CASCADE)                    ← | between the UserProfile and the User.
    musician_profiles = models.ManyToManyField(Musician,
        blank=True)
    venues_controlled = models.ManyToManyField(Venue, blank=True)
```

Store relationships between this user account and any Musician or Venue objects. Set blank=True, so these can be empty fields in the Django Admin.

As the comment in the listing implies, this code gets added to the RiffMates/bands/models.py file. To make user management easier, the Django Admin understands the relationship between a user profile object and the user account. It allows you to define a form to be used within the user account management screens to deal with the associated data. To use this feature you need to define a *stacked inline form* and tell the Django Admin to use it.

Django provides you a base class for defining stacked inline forms, called `admin.StackedInline`. After inheriting from this class and pointing at the associated user profile, Django Admin takes care of the rest. This new form gets associated with the `User` object admin form by creating a new class in your admin.py file. This `UserAdmin` class inherits from the built-in admin class for a `User` and adds the new stacked inline form to an attribute called `inlines`. Finally, you replace the default class by unregistering it and registering your new one. Add the code in the following listing to your RiffMates/bands/admin.py file.

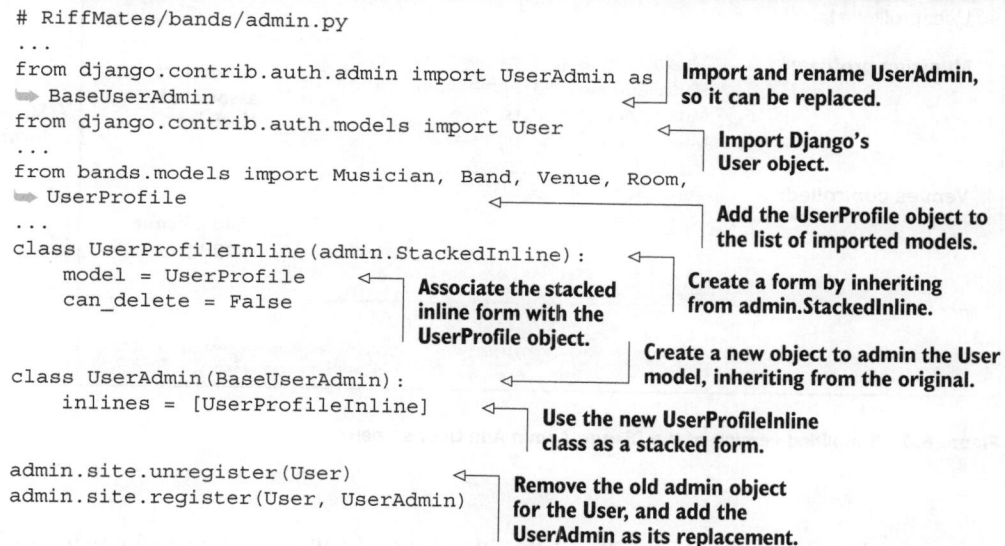

Listing 6.2 Code for managing your `UserProfile` class through the Django Admin

```
# RiffMates/bands/admin.py
...
from django.contrib.auth.admin import UserAdmin as          Import and rename UserAdmin,
    BaseUserAdmin                                            so it can be replaced.
from django.contrib.auth.models import User                 Import Django's
...                                                          User object.
from bands.models import Musician, Band, Venue, Room,
    UserProfile
...                                                          Add the UserProfile object to
                                                             the list of imported models.
class UserProfileInline(admin.StackedInline):
    model = UserProfile          Associate the stacked    Create a form by inheriting
    can_delete = False           inline form with the     from admin.StackedInline.
                                 UserProfile object.
                                                          Create a new object to admin the User
class UserAdmin(BaseUserAdmin):                            model, inheriting from the original.
    inlines = [UserProfileInline]        Use the new UserProfileInline
                                         class as a stacked form.

admin.site.unregister(User)          Remove the old admin object
admin.site.register(User, UserAdmin)  for the User, and add the
                                      UserAdmin as its replacement.
```

With the model and admin code changes done, you're ready to test it out. As the `User-Profile` object is a new ORM Model, you need to run the `makemigrations` and `migrate` management commands. Once you've done that, run the development server, and then log in to the Django Admin by visiting http://localhost:8000/admin/, using your superuser credentials.

Once you're on the Django Admin home page, click Add next to the Users object control in the left-hand nav. Let's create an account for your cousin Nicky. Figure 6.3 is a simplified representation of the Django Admin Add User screen. It is divided into two sections: one for account information and the stacked-inline form with your user profile data. The actual Add User screen has more details on it, including information about how to choose a proper password, how to multiselect Musicians, and more, but I've left that out in the diagram to reduce clutter.

You create Nicky's credentials by filling in the username field (*nicky*) and choosing a password. This is also where you can associate Nicky's account with one or more `Musician` or `Venue` objects. For our purposes, associate Nicky with the CBGB venue

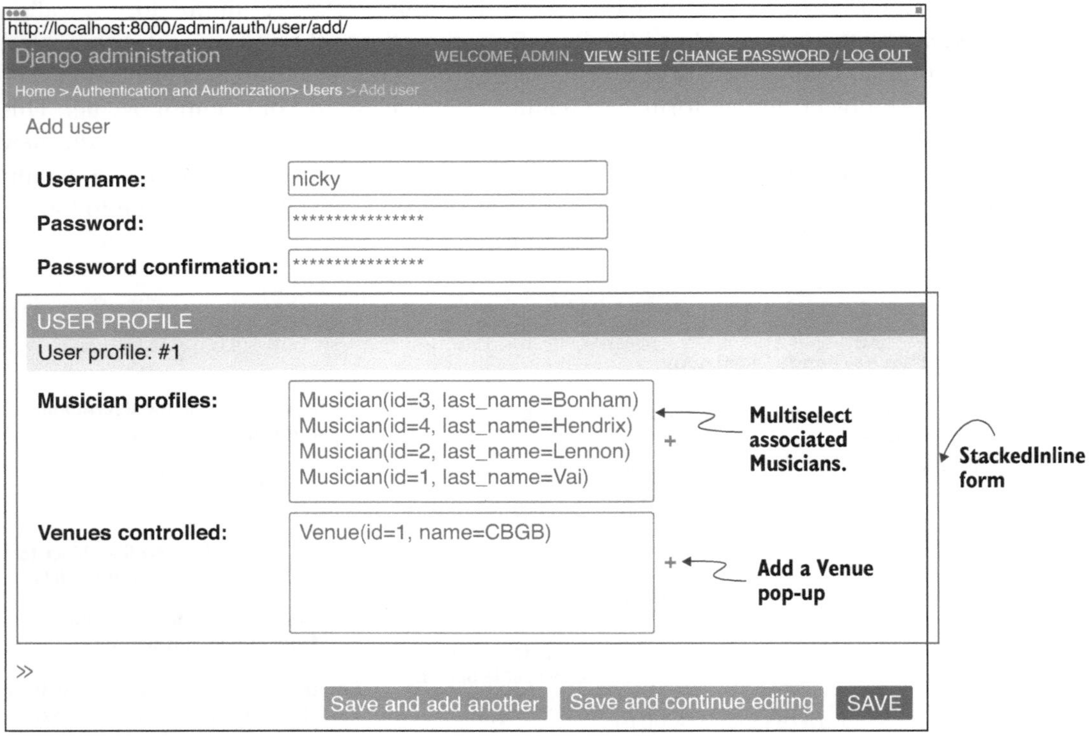

Figure 6.3   Simplified version of the Django Admin Add User screen

and nothing else. If you don't do this, some of the code later will crash. You'll learn why and how to prevent the problem before the end of the chapter.

When you click Save, you are taken to another version of the Add User screen with even more information on it. The Django Admin splits account creation into a two-step process. The first step creates the username and password, while the second step allows you to fill in more information about the user and manage their permissions. If you want to make Nicky an admin or staff member, this second page is where that is done. There are also fields for managing permissions. The chapter on the Django Admin introduced the idea of a staff member being someone with access to the Django Admin but not necessarily permissions to do everything. The permission fields on this second screen are where you control this access. This isn't a feature I ever take advantage of, personally. I tend to keep my sites simple: you're either an admin or not.

Now that Nicky's account has been created, you can do exactly nothing with it. The login you have been using so far is only for the Django Admin. If Nicky isn't a superuser, she can't log in. Before playing with nonsuperuser account logins, you'll need a view that has restricted access.

6.3 *Restricting access to views*

With a little configuration, Django handles the authentication of a user account (more on this in a bit); the authorization of an action is up to you. The simplest form of authorization is to allow anyone that has an active account to take an action. When you wrap a view with the built-in `@login_required` decorator, that view's authorization is restricted to only users with accounts.

Let's start by creating a new page that can only be viewed by authenticated users. As the view needs to show some content, you're going to need a new template. An all-purpose template can be handy for messaging the user; all it needs is a single variable displayed using the `| safe` filter, allowing you to write HTML content into the page. Create RiffMates/templates/general.html, and insert the content from the following listing.

Listing 6.3 A generic template that can be used by many views to message the user

```
<!-- RiffMates/templates/general.html -->
{% extends "base.html" %}                   ◁─┐  Inherit the base template for a
                                                 look and feel consistent with
{% block title %}                                the rest of your website.
  {{block.super}}: {{title}}        ◁─┐
{% endblock %}                           Alter the
                                         page's title.
{% block content %}
  {{content|safe}}          ◁─┐  Use the | safe filter to prevent HTML
{% endblock content %}           content being escaped by Django.
```

Any view using this template can show arbitrary HTML to the user by populating `content` in the context dictionary. The `restricted_page` view has very little logic; it simply renders an HTML message using the general.html template. Wrapping the view in the `@login_required` decorator takes care of the authorization. Add the code in the following listing to RiffMates/bands/views.py, creating your first view with authorization.

Listing 6.4 A view only visible to authenticated users

```
# RiffMates/bands/views.py
from django.contrib.auth.decorators import      │  Import the authorization
⮕ login_required                            ◁─┘  decorator.
...
@login_required                    ◁─┐  Wrap the view requiring
def restricted_page(request):           authentication.
    data = {
        'title': 'Restricted Page',
        'content': '<h1>You are logged in</h1>',   ◁─┐  The HTML message to display
    }                                                   in the rendered page

    return render(request, "general.html", data)   ◁─┐  Render content using
                                                         the generic template.
```

In addition to adding the view, you'll also need to register it. Add a `path` object defining `"restricted_page/"` to RiffMates/bands/urls.py. With the new view and route in place, load up the development server and visit http://localhost:8000/bands/ restricted _page/.

Did it work? Depending on what state you were in when you visited the page, you may have seen the expected message or an error. If you were still authenticated as the superuser, from using the Django Admin, you would be able to see the page. Any authenticated account sees You Are Logged In on the restricted page.

If you got an error message, go back to the Django Admin (http://localhost:8000/ admin/), log in, and then visit the page. To see the error message, go to the Django Admin, and in the top-right corner, click the Log Out link. When you click the link, the Django Admin informs you that you are successfully logged out. Once logged out, go back to the restricted page. This time, you will see a `404` message.

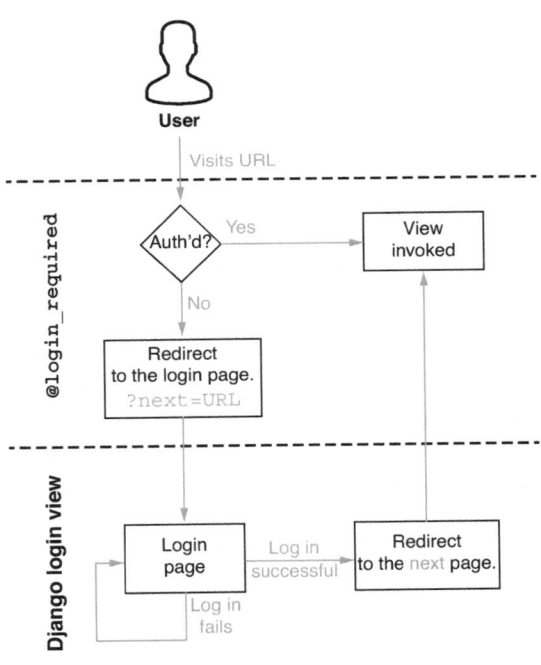

The `404` error is not generated because you aren't authenticated; it is because there is no login screen yet. The `@login_required` decorator checks your session to see if you are authenticated, and if you are not, it redirects to the login page. Django has a default value for the login page of /accounts/login/. If you look closely at the `404` message, you'll see this URL along with an extra query parameter called `next`. The value of `next` is where the login view will send you if you successfully authenticate. Figure 6.4 shows the steps involved in visiting a `@login_required` wrapped view.

Django treats the login for Django Admin as a special case and does its own authentication. This is because you may or may not use the Django Admin in your site, and your site's login page should look like your site, not the Django

Figure 6.4   Authentication verification steps for visiting a `@login_required` wrapped view

admin. Django provides a built-in view for authentication, but you have to write the template to go with it.

There are several views Django provides for authentication and user management; they are all in the `django.contrib.auth.urls` module and can be included directly into your site by adding them to your main urls.py file. Add the following to urlpatterns inside RiffMates/RiffMates/urls.py—I usually keep mine next to the admin route:

```
path('accounts/', include('django.contrib.auth.urls')),
```

The URL/view mappings defined in that module include a view for a login page, now registered under /accounts/login/. This view has all the login page logic, but it expects a template called registration/login.html. The view uses a Django Form that the user fills providing their username and password. Chapter 7 shows you how to write your own forms; for now, you need to know two things: first, an object called form has a method called .as_p() that renders the <input> tags of the login page, and second, there is a bit of "black magic" called a {% csrf_token %} tag used for security. The black magic bits will be explained in Chapter 7. Create a directory called *registration* under RiffMates/templates, and add the contents from the following listing to a file named login.html.

Listing 6.5   Login template for the built-in view

```
<!-- RiffMates/templates/registration/login.html -->
{% extends "base.html" %}

{% block content %}
<h1>Login</h1>

<form method="post">
  {% csrf_token %}
  {{form.as_p}}
  <button class="btn btn-dark" type="submit">Login</button>
</form>

{% endblock content %}
```

Your login view is registered, and you have written the corresponding template. You're all set to try it out. Revisit http://localhost:8000/bands/restricted_page/. Unfortunately, logging out is not a simple matter. You'll learn how to create a logout button shortly, but in the meantime, you have to visit the Django Admin and use their logout link. If you're playing around with accounts and you're logged in as *nicky* (or any other non-staff account), you'll have to log in with your admin account to log out altogether.

6.4   Authorization in views

The @login_required decorator quickly gives you the ability to restrict a view to only authenticated users. Often, though, you want finer-grained control than this. Your view can contain logic for authorization. For example, let's create a view that is limited to a musician and their bandmates: musician_restricted.

This view still uses @login_required, as you want to ensure users got authenticated first. The request object passed to a view includes information on the authentication state, including who the authenticated user is. The musician_restricted view takes a

Musician object ID as a parameter and checks if the authenticated user is either that musician or one of their bandmates. This relationship is found through the use of the user profile data object.

The steps for this view are as follows:

1 Use `get_object_or_404()` to turn the `musician_id` argument into a Musician object.
2 Check if the user profile object's `musician_profiles` field contains the argument musician (user is this musician).
3 If the user profile doesn't point to the argument musician, loop through all the bands associated with the argument musician and check if any of the user's musician profiles intersect with band membership.
4 If the user is neither the musician nor a bandmate, raise an error.

The code for these steps is provided in listing 6.6. Add it to the RiffMates/bands/views.py file, and then register a new `path` object in RiffMatest/bands/urls.py for the URL `musician_restricted`. Don't forget to add an expression for the `musician_id` argument, similar to how you did for the unrestricted version of this view in Chapter 4.

Listing 6.6   View with authorization code for musician profiles or band-mates

```
# RiffMates/bands/views.py
...
from django.http import Http404
...
@login_required
def musician_restricted(request, musician_id):
    musician = get_object_or_404(Musician, id=musician_id)
    profile = request.user.userprofile
    allowed = False

    if profile.musician_profiles.filter(
            id=musician_id).exists():
        allowed = True
    else:
        # User is not this musician, check if they're a band-mate
        musician_profiles = set(
            profile.musician_profiles.all()
        )
        for band in musician.band_set.all():
            band_musicians = set(band.musicians.all())
            if musician_profiles.intersection(
                    band_musicians):
                allowed = True
                break

    if not allowed:
        raise Http404("Permission denied")
```

Annotations: Raise the Http404 exception for disallowed access. request.user is the authenticated user, and .userprofile is the reverse relationship to the UserProfile ORM model. Set to True if authorization succeeds. Query the user's associated Musician objects for the argument musician_id. The .exists() query returns True if a matching relationship is found. Store all the band's associated Musician objects as a set, and then intersect it with the user's musicians. Store all the user's associated Musician objects as a set. A nonempty intersection between the sets means one of the user's Musician objects was in the band's musician list. If allowed is not True, authorization is denied. Raise an error.

```
content = f"""
    <h1>Musician Page: {musician.last_name}</h1>
"""
data = {
    'title': 'Musician Restricted',
    'content': content,
}

return render(request, "general.html", data)
```

You can start out your testing by trying the negative case: log in as Nicky, and then try to view any Musician. Visiting http://localhost:8000/bands/musician_restricted/1/ results in a 404 error, as Nicky is not Steve Vai, nor is she in his band.

To try the positive case, you need to make some changes to Nicky in the Django Admin. Log out of Nicky, and then log in to the Django Admin. Use the Admin to perform the following steps:

1 Add a new Musician object for Nicky (first name: Nicky, last name: Cousin, date of birth: 2001-01-13).
2 Edit Nicky's user account, and add the association for the newly created Musician object.
3 Edit the Wishful Thinking Band object, adding Nicky's Musician object as a member.

Once you've performed these steps, log out of the Django Admin, and then log back in as Nicky. Now, when you visit http://localhost:8000/bands/musician_restricted/1/, you can see Steve Vai's page. Try visiting using Jimi Hendrix (id = 4), instead. As Jimi isn't part of Wishful Thinking, you should, once again, see a 404 page.

6.4.1 Handling logouts

Before Django 5.0, logging the user out was fairly simple: there was a Logout link you could embed in your HTML. For security reasons, "simple" was deprecated in Django 4.1, and as of Django 5.0, you now need to have a logout form. Chapter 7 describes forms in detail, but waiting until then means you'd have to constantly be logging into the Django Admin just to log out.

It is common practice to have a header with the user's info and frequent actions at the top of your site's pages. Let's go on a bit of a tangent and build such a header, including a logout action. The following listing contains the code you need to add to RiffMates/templates/base.html to include Login and Logout links, depending on the user's state.

Listing 6.7 Something approximating a nav bar

```
<!-- RiffMates/templates/base.html -->
<!-- ... -->
<body>
```

```
<div style="float: right;">
    {% if user.is_authenticated %}
        Hello, {{user.username}}!  

    <form id="logout-form" method="post"
        action="{% url 'logout' %}"
        style="display: inline;">
        {% csrf_token %}
        <button type="submit"
            style="background: none; border: none; cursor: pointer;
                padding: 0; text-decoration: underline;"
            >Logout</button>
    </form>
    {% else %}
        <a href="{% url 'login' %}">Login</a>
    {% endif %}
</div>

<!-- ... -->
```

If the user is authenticated, greet them.

Style the nav so that it pulls to the right of the page.

The <form> tag needed to log a user out

A link to the login page

The `<form>` for logging out a user is a bit messy and includes some horrific inline CSS styling. Forms don't work with links; they require buttons. And buttons don't look like links; they look like buttons. That long, ugly style chunk is to make the button look more like a link.

You can configure Django to go where you want when a user logs out. A common choice is to send them to the home page. As you haven't built a home page yet, let's send them to the band listing page. Add the following snippet to your settings file:

```
# RiffMates/RiffMates/settings.py
...
# Account Management
LOGIN_REDIRECT_URL = '/bands/bands/'
LOGOUT_REDIRECT_URL = '/bands/bands/'
```

Where to redirect to if there is no next argument provided to the login page

Where to redirect to when the user logs out

6.5   *Using signals to automatically create a user profile*

The `musician_restricted` view has a dangerous assumption in it: it directly accesses the user's associated user profile object without validating it exists. If you log in as the admin account and visit the view, you see a 500 error `RelatedObjectDoesNotExist`, as the admin doesn't have a user profile.

At the moment, the user profile object only gets created if you create a `User` in the Django Admin and that user has either a `Musician` or `Venue` associated with it. There are two solutions to this problem; the simplest is to always check for the existence of a user profile before using it. In the previous example, you could raise a 404 error if the user profile does not exist.

Alternatively, you can write code that automatically creates a `UserProfile` object immediately after a `User` ORM object is made. This requires a bit more programming, but it makes your code safer, as forgetting to check for a user profile's existence won't crash your site.

Django has a signaling system that allows you to react to certain events as they occur. This mechanism is designed as if it were meant for bigger things, but for the most part, it is used to interact with the ORM. In practice, I've only ever used it to do exactly what is described in this section: creating a second Model object as a side effect to the creation of a first.

Signals use the *observer/observable* pattern, meaning you register interest in an action and are notified when that action takes place. Figure 6.5 shows an overview of the model, signal registry, and signal handler interactions. Most ORM actions have two signals associated with each, a *pre signal* and a *post signal*. Pre signals are emitted just before the action is to take place, and post signals indicate the action has happened. It is possible to prevent an action inside a pre handler. For example, when saving an object, there is both a pre_save and post_save signal. If you register for the pre_save signal, the return value of your handler indicates whether you want the save to take place.

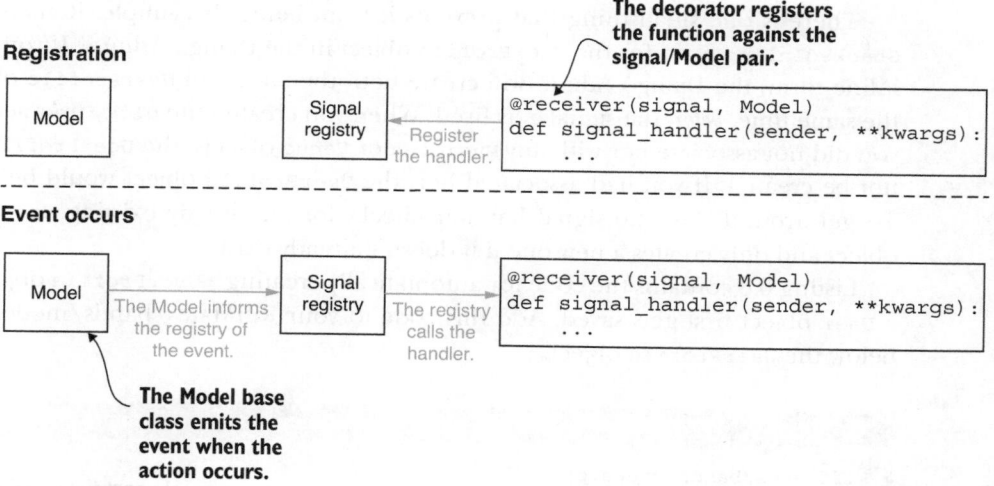

Figure 6.5   Registering and handling a signal from a Model

To create a UserProfile object as a side-effect to the User object being created, you trap the post_save signal, which is defined in django.db.models.signals. To register a signal handler, you use the @receiver decorator to wrap your handler function. The decorator connects a *sender* to a signal. The sender is the Model object whose actions you wish to receive.

There is no signal for a create action, only for save, which means your code needs to know the difference between a save for the first time and save for updating an object. To make it more complicated, there are also several ways to create a Model object:

- In your code
- In the Django Admin
- As a result of loading a fixture

All three of these cases need to be dealt with in your signal handler. Signal handlers take at least one argument: the sender of the signal. Specific signals may also send other parameters, so it is best practice to include `**kwargs` in your function signature. The `post_save` signal includes three additional arguments to the function:

- `created` is `True` if the save action created the object and `False` on object updates.
- `raw` is `True` if the save is from a fixture being loaded.
- `instance` contains the created object.

To write a signal that automatically creates a `UserProfile` object, you need a function registered as a signal handler for `post_save` against the `User` ORM object. If the function got called for (1) a newly created object that (2) wasn't created by loading a fixture, then you can create a corresponding `UserProfile` object.

There is one small thing that prevents it from being this simple. Remember the `StackedInline` form for the `UserProfile` object in the Django Admin? If you use this inline form, the Django Admin will create both the `User` and `UserProfile` objects at the same time, *before* the signal gets fired. When you created the `nicky` user account, if you did not associate her with any `Musician` or `Venue` objects, the `UserProfile` would not be created. If you had associated her, the `UserProfile` object would be created. To get around this, the signal handler checks for an already existing `UserProfile` object and only creates a new one if it doesn't already exist.

Listing 6.8 contains the code for automatically creating a `UserProfile` object when a `User` object first gets saved. Add this code to your RiffMates/bands/models.py file below the `UserProfile` object.

> **Listing 6.8   View with authorization code for musician profiles or bandmates**

```
# RiffMates/bands/views.py
...
from django.db.models.signals import post_save        Import the signal called
from django.dispatch import receiver                    when an ORM Model is saved.
...                                                    Import the @receiver decorator.
@receiver(post_save, sender=User)                      Register this function to be
def user_post_save(sender, **kwargs):                  called when a User object
    # Create UserProfile object if User object is new  emits the post_save signal.
    # and not loaded from fixture
    if kwargs['created'] and not kwargs['raw']:         Only take action if the User object is
        user = kwargs['instance']                       new and not created by a fixture.
        try:
            # Double check UserProfile doesn't exist already
            # (admin might create it before the signal fires)
            UserProfile.objects.get(user=user)          Attempt to get an existing
                                                        UserProfile object.
```

The newly created User object

```
except UserProfile.DoesNotExist:
    # No UserProfile exists for this user, create one
    UserProfile.objects.create(user=user)
```
◁──┐ **If no object existed,
    create one.**

With your signal defined, you can test it out by signing in to the Django Admin and creating a new user named *vinny*. Within the Django Admin, you won't be able to tell the difference, as the `StackedInline` form is there, whether or not the `UserProfile` object exists. Inside a terminal, run the `shell` management command, and do the following:

```
>>> from django.contrib.auth.models import User
>>> User.objects.all()
<QuerySet [<User: admin>, <User: nicky>, <User: vinny>]>
>>> v = User.objects.last()
>>> v.userprofile
<UserProfile: UserProfile object (2)>
```

If your signal code had not worked, the last line in the REPL session would have caused an exception. Speaking of exceptions, having the signal handler in place does not fix past problems. Your admin account does not have a `UserProfile` associated with it. There are two things you can do to solve this problem. The first is to use the REPL and create a `UserProfile` object there; alternatively, you can use the Django Admin. Edit the admin user account, and create an association with a Musician object. Save it, and then go back and remove the association. The process of adding a `Musician` causes the Django Admin to create the `UserProfile` object for you.

> **The trouble with signals**
>
> Remember that ORM objects are proxies to the database. Signals are part of the ORM mechanic and are not tied to the database itself. Direct operations on your database will not emit a signal. Opening the SQLite REPL and adding a `User` by hand will result in a missing `UserProfile`.
>
> Likewise, there are some bulk data operations available in Django that allow you to directly call SQL. These operations bypass the ORM layer and, therefore, also do not emit signals. Signals can be very handy, but you need to be cautious with the corner cases.

6.6 Password management

In addition to providing a view handling logging in, Django also provides views for dealing with password resets. This process emails the user an account reset link with a one-time token, and when the user clicks it, they are sent to a form to create a new password. Figure 6.6 shows the steps in the process.

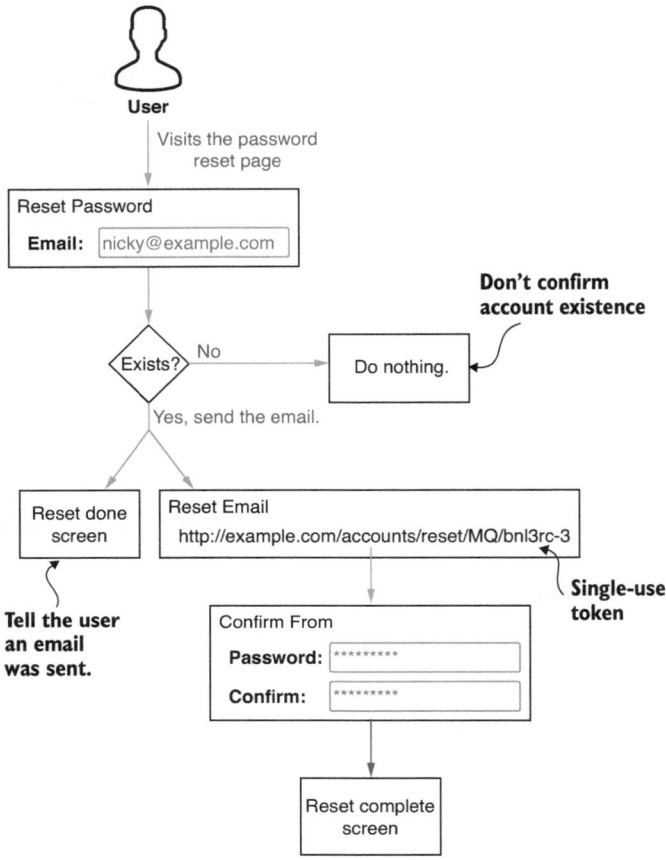

Figure 6.6 Steps involved in a password reset

Let's follow the flow, building each piece along the way. To start, add a password reset link to your login page. The link can be looked up using `password_reset` as a key to the `{% url %}` tag:

```
<!-- RiffMates/templates/registration/login.html -->
...
<br/>
<p>
  <a href="{% url 'password_reset' %}">Lost password?</a>
</p>
```

6.6.1   *Password reset page*

Clicking the reset link takes the user to a view asking for their email address. This view renders the `password_reset_form.html` template. Like the form in the login page, you need `{{ form.as_p }}` to render the `<input>` tags and `{% csrf_token %}` black magic (you'll learn this spell later). Create RiffMates/templates/registration/password _reset_form.html with the contents from the following listing.

Listing 6.9   Form asking for the user's email to send them a reset link

```
<!-- RiffMates/templates/registration/password_reset_form.html -->
{% extends "base.html" %}

{% block content %}
<p>
  Forgotten your password? Enter your email address below, and we'll
  email instructions for setting a new one.

</p>

<form method="post">
  {% csrf_token %}
  {{ form.as_p }}                          Renders the form's
                                           <input> tags

                                           A submit button
  <input type="submit" value="Reset Password">     for the form
</form>
{% endblock content %}
```

Filling this form starts the password reset process. Whatever the user submits, they get the same message. In olden times, websites would sometimes include helpful information like *we have no such email address*, but that is considered a security flaw. You're exposing to the black hats some information about accounts in your system. The more secure approach is to do the same thing regardless of whether the email matches an account in the system.

6.6.2   Password reset email

The message shown after submitting the reset form is stored in a template called password_reset_done.html. Create a new file in the registration directory with the others. Sample content is provided in the following listing.

Listing 6.10   Message shown after a reset has been requested

```
{% extends "base.html" %}

{% block content %}

<p>
  We've emailed you instructions for setting your password, if an
  account exists with the email you entered. You should receive them
  shortly.

</p>

<p>
  If you don't receive an email, please make sure you've entered the
  address you registered with and check your spam folder.
```

```
</p>

{% endblock content %}
```

While it shows the user this message, Django simultaneously determines whether there is a `User` object with the submitted email address. If so, an email gets sent to the address. If there is no match, Django does nothing. Configuring your system to send email correctly is a book in its own right. Django provides a variety of *email backends*, depending on how you communicate with your email server.

The most common email backend uses SMTP to communicate with an email server. There are many third-party providers for such a service, or if you're brave, you can run your own. Appendix B has more details on how to configure the `smtp.EmailBackend` for use in a production environment.

Thankfully, you don't need to setup SMPT if you're still developing or if you only want to test. My favorite email backend prints the email to the console instead of sending it; you see the results inline with the other output from the development server. To use the console backend, add the following to settings.py:

```
EMAIL_BACKEND = 'django.core.mail.backends.console.EmailBackend'
```

The email sent to the user is based on a template: password_reset_email.html. The message can say anything you want, as long as it includes the reset link. This link is accessible through the {% url %} tag, using `password_reset_confirm` as the argument. The view for this link takes two arguments that must be provided to the {% url %} tag: `uidb64=uid` and `token=token`. These values make up the one-time token in the reset link. A sample email message including the reset link is shown in the following listing. Add a new file called RiffMates/templates/registration/password_reset_email.html with the contents from the listing.

Listing 6.11   Template for the reset email sent to the user

```
{% autoescape off %}          ◁─┐ Turn off HTML escaping
                                │ throughout the template.
   You're receiving this email because you requested a password reset
   for your user account at Alexandria.

   Please go to the following page and choose a new password:

   {% block reset_link %}
      {{ protocol }}://{{ domain }}{% url 'password_reset_confirm'
➥ uidb64=uid token=token %}              ◁─┐ A fully qualified reset link
   {% endblock %}                            │ with a one-time token

   Your username, in case you've forgotten: {{ user.get_username }}

   Thanks for using our site!

{% endautoescape %}
```

Note that the {% url %} tag returns relative URLs. This isn't a problem on a website, as the browser takes care of sending you to the right site. In an email, this is problematic, though, so you must include the protocol and domain in the link. The view includes this information in the context dictionary; you just need to render it. Using the console backend for development, you get the following email info:

```
Content-Type: text/plain; charset="utf-8"
MIME-Version: 1.0
Content-Transfer-Encoding: 7bit
Subject: Password reset on 127.0.0.1:8000
From: webmaster@localhost
To: admin@example.com
Date: Tue, 02 May 2023 18:54:52 -0000


You're receiving this email because you requested a password reset
for your user account at RiffMates.

Please go to the following page and choose a new password:


  http://127.0.0.1:8000/accounts/reset/MQ/bn15vg-f639/


Your username, in case you've forgotten: admin

Thanks for using our site!
```

6.6.3 New password form

The next step in the reset process happens when the user clicks the one-time link in the email message. The link leads to a view that shows a form for entering a new password. This form uses the standard enter-it and then enter-it-to-confirm mechanism. The associated template is password_reset_confirm.html. Add the contents of the following listing to RiffMates/templates/registration/password_reset_confirm.html.

Listing 6.12 Template where the user chooses a new password

```
{% extends "base.html" %}

{% block content %}

{% if validlink %}
  <form method="post">
    {% csrf_token %}
    {{ form.as_p }}

    <input type="submit" value="Change password">
  </form>
{% else %}
  <p>
    Invalid password reset link!
```

```
   </p>
{% endif %}

{% endblock content %}
```

This template contains the by now familiar {{ form.as_p }} and black magic security token. The view passes a value in the context dictionary called validlink, which is True if the one-time token is valid. This allows you to use the same template for the view, even if the user has messed with the token. It does mean you need to have logic for handling the error case, though—not showing the <form> tag is good enough.

The final step in the process is telling the user that the reset process is complete. The password reset view expects this content to be in password_reset_complete.html. This can be a simple message, but it is often handy to include a link to the login page as well. Create RiffMates/templates/registration/password_reset_complete.html, using the contents of the following listing.

Listing 6.13 Template telling the user their password reset process is complete

```
{% extends "base.html" %}

{% block content %}
<h2>Your password has been set</h2>

<p><a href="{{ login_url }}">Login</a></p>
{% endblock content %}
```

The URL to the login page does not include the ?next argument, so if the user clicks it, they are sent to the default. If you added LOGIN_REDIRECT_URL = '/bands/bands/' to the configuration, as recommended earlier, that default is the bands listing page.

If you've done all that work, you're ready to test it out. Start the development server, and make sure to log out. Visit one of your new restricted view pages, and you will be redirected to the login page. On the login page, click the Lost Password? link. Unless you had the foresight to include an email address for the *nicky* account, the admin will be the only account with an email value. Use *admin@example.com* in the reset form, and then copy the reset link printed to your console. Paste the link in your browser, and complete the password reset process. And there you go! RiffMates is now a multiuser site, complete with restricted pages and password management.

6.7   *Exercises*

1 The @login_required decorator only checks if a user got authenticated. A more generic view restriction can be performed using the @user_passes_test decorator in the same module (https://mng.bz/2KKN). It takes one required argument: a reference to a function that takes the User object as an argument and returns True if the user should be allowed in. Write a new view venues_restricted() that is only visible by those users associated with a Venue object and displays a list of all venues. Hint: You can take advantage of other views in your code. They are just functions.

2 The auth system emits signals on login events. Capture the `django.contrib` `.auth.signals.user_login_failed` signal, and print a message displaying the username and path of the login attempt. See https://mng.bz/1GGZ for details on the arguments passed when receiving this signal. (Note that in production, you should use logging rather than `print()`. See appendix B for more details.)

Summary

- Django supports multiuser websites.
- Authentication proves who a user is, while authorization specifies what actions they can perform.
- User data can be stored in a profile object associated with the `User` account object through a `OneToOneField` relationship field.
- Django supports the use of a custom-defined `User` object as an alternative to a profile.
- The Django Admin supports the addition of inline forms to add user profile fields to the `User` object Add and Update screens.
- When placed on a view, the `@login_required` decorator redirects anonymous users to the login page, asking them to authenticate.
- Django provides a view handling user login but requires you to add a template to your site's look and feel to work properly.
- Login for the Django Admin is handled similarly to site login but using separate views. If you're only using the Django Admin and not otherwise providing user accounts, you avoid the need for a custom login page.
- Authorization code is typically view specific. You can add more detailed permission requirements, as needed.
- Django emits signals when it performs certain actions. These signals can be received in a function, allowing you to perform side effects.
- You can use a signal to automatically create a user profile object whenever a User ORM object gets created. Your signal handler traps the `post_save` signal and checks for a newly created `User` object that wasn't created by a fixture.
- Django provides built-in views for the password reset process but requires you to customize the corresponding templates.
- The password reset process prompts the user for their email, sends them a one-time link, displays a reset form, and then a confirmation message.
- Django provides features for sending email and uses different backends for implementation. The `console.EmailBackend` is used during development, printing the email's content to the console instead of sending it.

Forms, user data, static files, and uploads

This chapter covers

- Writing views that handle form submissions
- Using the `Form` class to write web forms
- Cross-site request forgery (CSRF) protection
- Using the `ModelForm` to create forms based on `Model` classes
- Writing views that handle file uploads
- Providing access to both uploaded and static files

This chapter covers content handled by your website over and above a simple view. It starts out by showing you how to receive user input data through web forms, and then it moves on to dealing with files. Files can be uploaded by your users, and if they are, those same files can be downloaded or shown on a page. There are also files you include in your site that aren't served by Django: CSS, images, JavaScript, and more. This chapter covers how to deal with user data and all kinds of file input and output as well as how to do it to manage it all securely.

7.1   Web forms

In the previous chapter, you took the first steps toward having self-serve user features in RiffMates. And although it wasn't explicitly called out, you started using *web forms*. The login page is a web form with two fields: Username and Password. Submitting this form gets handled by a built-in Django view, which adds data to the user's session, indicating they are authenticated. The mechanisms the login view uses are built on top of the tools available to you as a programmer. With them, you can build your own forms and have users submit data to your site.

The connection between a web form's HTML and Django is loosely coupled. Django provides utilities to reduce the amount of coding you need, but they are not required. The Django `Form` object provides a shortcut for creating web forms and their corresponding HTML, but the processing of data submitted through this form is generic, and it is up to you to code your view as you see fit.

An instance of a Django `Form` specifies a number of fields, with each field corresponding to an HTML tag. You can use a form instance in a template to render the HTML tags, but you don't have to. Figure 7.1 shows a form with a field for entering a person's name and email address along with the corresponding HTML.

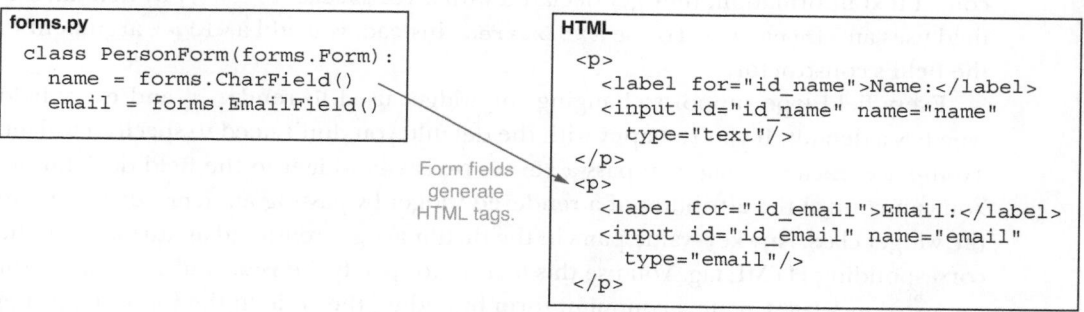

Figure 7.1   The relationship between a `Form` object and the HTML

Form fields get rendered through an associated widget object. The widget object is responsible for rendering the corresponding HTML tag. There are over 20 different widgets provided by Django, but most of them result in the `<input>` tag, with varying values of the `type` attribute. For example, the `CharField` renders as `<input type="text">`, while the `EmailField` renders as `<input type="email">`. Beyond the `<input>` tags, there are also widgets for drop-down selects, multiple selection boxes, radio buttons, dates, times, and file handling.

You have some control over the appearance of the widget, but you can't use template features, like conditional formatting. This limitation can be a little frustrating; a

`Form` object can save you from writing a lot of HTML, right up until you hit its limits, and then you're back to writing all the HTML. If your site uses a framework like Bootstrap, which requires wrapping `<div>` tags in forms for styling, you may have to write the HTML by hand.

Keeping the limitations in mind, let's start by building a simple form, so you can see what it can and can't do. The `Bands` app is getting a little full, so for this chapter, create a new app, called `Content`, using the `startapp` management command. Don't forget to add it to `INSTALLED_APPS` in settings.py as well. See Chapter 2 if you need a refresher on how to do this.

Inside your newly created RiffMates/content directory, create a file called forms.py to build your first `Form` class. *Form objects* are quite similar to `Model` objects: they contain fields that specify areas of input in the form. Like with a model, you inherit from a class and declare attributes to build the form. The class you inherit from is `django.forms.Form`. Inside the form class, you add attributes for each field you want, with a variety of fields provided in the `forms` module.

Your first form is for collecting comments from your site's visitors. It has a name field and a comment area. The corresponding HTML contains an `<input>` tag for the name and a `<textarea>` tag for the comment. As both the name and comment fields collect text information, they get declared with a `forms.CharField()`. By default, this field uses an `<input>` tag. To use a `<textarea>` instead, you add a `widget` argument to the field's constructor.

Every field type supports changing the widget used to render it, and every field type has a default. If you're happy with the default, you don't need to specify a widget. To use a `<textarea>` tag, you pass a `forms.Textarea` widget to the field declaration. You can control the attributes of a rendered widget by passing an `attrs` dictionary to the widget class. Any key–value pairs in the dictionary get rendered as attributes in the corresponding HTML tag. You use this feature to specify the `rows` and `cols` values for a `<textarea>` tag. Create a comment form by adding the code in the following listing to your newly created file.

Listing 7.1   A form class for accepting comments

```
# RiffMates/content/forms.py
from django import forms
```
← The forms module contains the form base class, fields, and widgets.

```
class CommentForm(forms.Form):
    name = forms.CharField()
    comment = forms.CharField(
        widget=forms.Textarea(
            attrs={"rows": "6", "cols": "50"}
        )
    )
```

Inherit from forms.Form to create a Form object.

forms.CharField is used to collect text and uses an `<input>` tag by default.

Specify the widget attribute to change what tag gets used to collect data.

You can pass additional attributes to the tag using the attrs dictionary argument in the widget object constructor.

Form objects provide a method called `.as_p()` that outputs the form fields surrounded in paragraph (`<p>`) tags. Recall using `{{form.as_p}}` inside the login page, which is what rendered the fields in the form. To quickly test your new creation, open the REPL using the `shell` management command, create an instance of the `CommentForm`, and then print the results of `.as_p()`:

```
>>> from content.forms import CommentForm
>>> f = CommentForm()
>>> print(f.as_p())
<p>
    <label for="id_name">Name:</label>
    <input type="text" name="name" required id="id_name">
</p>
<p>
    <label for="id_comment">Comment:</label>
    <textarea name="comment" cols="50" rows="6" required
        id="id_comment"></textarea>
</p>
```

The results in the previous example were reformatted for readability. The actual content has more whitespace and newlines—Django forms are a bit messy with their indentation, but HTML doesn't care.

The `"name"` field in the `CommentForm` gets rendered as a `<label>` and `<input>` tag, while the `"comment"` field gets rendered as a `<label>` and `<textarea>`. Both fields have the `required` attribute, as this is the default. You can pass `required=False` to a field to turn this behavior off. Both fields also provide `id` and `name` attributes. This is important if you are planning on hand-tooling a form; you need to provide both of these attributes to process the form properly. More on this later. Finally, the `<textarea>` tag has the additional `rows` and `cols` attributes from the `attrs` dictionary provided.

With a form in place, you're all set to collect some data. You'll need a view for that.

7.1.1 Handling GET and POST in views

Up until now, your views have all been one-way: the user visits your URL, and your code provides some output. Recall that HTTP has multiple methods; the one you've been using is GET. When a form gets submitted by a web browser, the HTTP method is POST. The POST method almost never gets used on its own; typically, you perform a GET to fetch the page and its form, and then the browser submits the data back to you through a POST. The website validates the contents of the form, and if that validation fails, the same page gets displayed but with error information. If the validation passes, a different page gets displayed.

At first glance, this process sounds like you need multiple views. You can construct it that way, but the usual pattern is to use a single view and a redirect. With a single view handling both the GET and POST case, the rendered HTML doesn't need extra code in the `<form>` tag to tell it where to POST. It POSTs to the same place as the GET that rendered the page.

The view function first determines whether it was invoked through a GET or a POST call, displaying the form in the first case and handling the submission in the second. If the form validates, the view redirects the user to another page. If the form doesn't validate, error information gets added to the form, and the GET code gets called again. Figure 7.2 details this process.

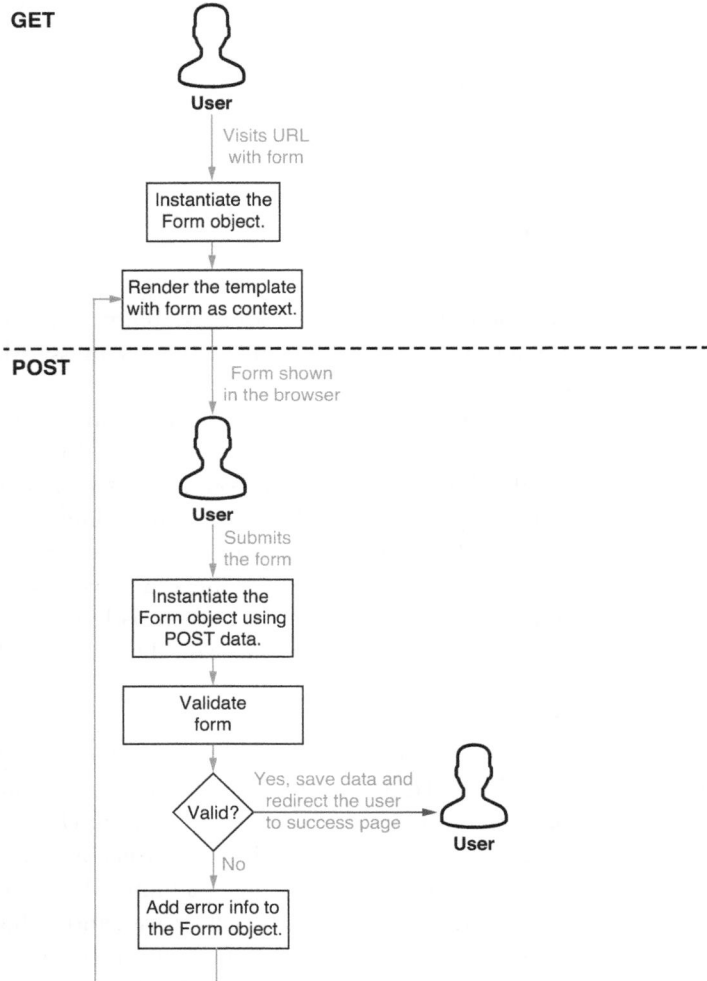

Figure 7.2   Logic flow for a view that handles form submission

Let's put this into practice by writing a view that uses your `CommentForm`. The `comment()` view is divided into three parts: a GET handler, a POST handler, and the form renderer. The view first checks if the HTTP method was GET, and if so, it instantiates a new

`CommentForm` instance. If the method wasn't GET, it must have been POST. In the POST case, the user submitted a form, and the data from the submission is contained in `request.POST`. You pass this data into your form's initializer to populate it.

The Form base class provides the `.is_valid()` method for validating the data sent by the user. The validation process is based on the fields in the form and their configuration. In the `CommentForm` case, the data is all text. As data submitted by HTTP is all text, there is very little validation done here. The fields are required, which the validator enforces, but if the user used the browser to submit the form, the browser would have enforced this anyhow.

Tricky, tricky users

Never trust your users. That last paragraph had an important caveat in it: "if the user used the browser to submit the form." Although well-behaved users will do this, your site openly accepts requests from HTTP. There are ways of issuing an HTTP POST without using the browser or, in the browser, using development tools that don't enforce the form's rules.

Always (it bears repeating: *always*) assume your users are malicious. Browser-side JavaScript validation is helpful to users, giving them a quick response on errors, but it should never be the only enforcement. Always validate your data in your views.

If the form is valid, you have a comment. Now what? Let's inform the admin through email. The `send_mail()` function in `django.core.mail` is a quick way to send an email using the currently configured email backend. In the previous chapter, you configured Django to print email messages to the console using the `console.EmailBackend` class. Using `send_mail()`, you can send a note with the contents of the comment. The note will be from the admin, and to the admin, you're sort of talking to yourself.

The `.is_valid()` method on a form sets up a dictionary in the form named `cleaned_data`. This dictionary has a key–value pair for each field named in the form and its contents. Using `cleaned_data`, you construct an email message and then send it. By default, the `send_mail()` function fails silently; this is not usually the best choice, so add `fail_silently=False` to the call, causing an exception if there is a problem. With the development server, this kind of problem shows up in the console as a `500` error, while in a production environment, this shows in your logs.

Once the form gets processed, you need to send the user somewhere new. A second view, called `comment_accepted()`, displays a thank-you note. This view can take advantage of the general.html template created in the previous chapter. To send the user to another view, you use the `redirect()` function from the `django.shortcuts` module. This function takes at least one argument which indicates where to redirect the user to. The argument can be a string containing a named URL path, a string containing a URL, or a reference to a view function. If you are using the name of a path or a view and the associated view takes arguments, you also pass those to `redirect()`.

The third part of the `comment()` view is the *form renderer*. This is like the final part of most views, creating a context dictionary and calling the `render()` shortcut. Note that this code can be reached for two reasons: because the HTTP method was GET or because the method was POST and the form was not valid. In the latter case, the form object contains error information that can be displayed to the user.

Add the code in listing 7.2 to RiffMates/content/views.py. You also need to create RiffMates/content/urls.py with a `path` object for the view, similar to RiffMates/bands/urls.py. To register all the paths in content/urls.py, make sure to add an `include` line inside RiffMates/RiffMates/urls.py for the new file. Review chapter 4 if you need a refresher on using app-based URL routing files.

Listing 7.2   A view accepting both HTTP GET and POST to handle comment form data

```
# RiffMates/content/views.py
from django.core.mail import send_mail
from django.shortcuts import render, redirect                    The CommentForm
                                                                  class with name and
from content.forms import CommentForm          ◄─                comment fields

def comment(request):                           In the GET handler portion
    if request.method == 'GET':                 of the code, create an
        form = CommentForm()       ◄─           empty form object.          The POST handler
                                                                             portion of the code,
    else: # POST          ◄─                                                 reached on form submit
        form = CommentForm(request.POST)    ◄─   Create a form object, populating
                                                 it with the data from the submit.
        if form.is_valid():
Validate          name = form.cleaned_data["name"]          ◄─   The cleaned_data dictionary
the form.         comment = form.cleaned_data["comment"]         contains the form contents.

            message = f"""\
                Received comment from {name}\n\n
                {comment}
                """                                              Use send_mail() to
                                                                 send an email from the
            send_mail("Received comment", message,    ◄─        admin to the admin.
                "admin@example.com", ["admin@example.com"],
   Turn           fail_silently=False)
fail_silently off.  return redirect("comment_accepted")    ◄─   Redirect the user to the comment_
                                                                accepted view, using its path name.

    # Was a GET, or Form was not valid    ◄─     The rendering part of the view, used
    data = {                                     in both the GET case and the POST
        "form": form,                            case if the form wasn't valid
    }

    return render(request, "comment.html", data)
```

You're not quite done yet. The `comment()` view redirects to a view named `comment_accepted()`, which someone has to write. Luckily, you're someone! Add the code from the following listing to RiffMates/content/views.py. Don't forget to register this route as well, and make sure to name the path `"comment_accepted"`, as that is what the `redirect()` shortcut looks for in the `comment()` view.

Listing 7.3 A view saying Thank You when a user submits a comment

```python
# RiffMates/content/views.py
...
def comment_accepted(request):
    data = {
        "content": """
            <h1> Comment Accepted </h1>

            <p> Thanks for submitting a comment to <i>RiffMates</i> </p>
        """
    }
    return render(request, "general.html", data)
```

> Reuse the general.html template from the previous chapter.

There is one last step: you need the template that renders the comment form. Create RiffMates/templates/comment.html, and add the code in the following listing. This template is quite similar to the login page, using a `<form>` tag and rendering the form field using `{{form.as_p}}`.

Listing 7.4 The comment form template

```html
<!-- RiffMates/templates/comment.html -->
{% extends "base.html" %}

{% block content %}
<h1>Comment</h1>

<form method="post">
  {% csrf_token %}
  {{form.as_p}}
  <button class="btn btn-dark" type="submit">Send</button>
</form>

{% endblock content %}
```

> The security black magic, once again

> The .as_p() method renders the fields within <p> tags.

The content template includes the `{% csrf_token %}` black magic mentioned in the previous chapter. The next section dispels the spell; for now, just make sure to include it. With all those pieces in place, you should be able to fire up your development server and visit http://localhost:8000/content/comment/. Figure 7.3 shows the resulting form.

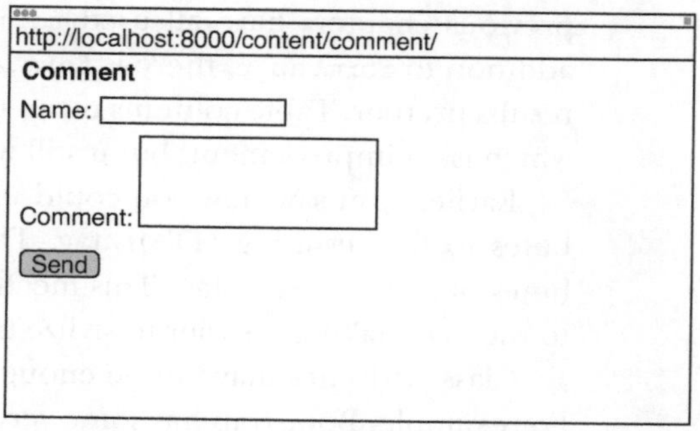

Figure 7.3 Leave a comment—we're interested, honest!

Without styling, it is rather jumbled, but your users can now complain about that with your new comment form.

Test your form out by leaving your name and comment. As you're using the `console.EmailBackend`, the resulting email will display in the terminal.

7.1.2 CSRF

You've been patient with my hand-waving and references to black magic, so just what is the `{% csrf_token %}`? *Cross-site request forgery* (CSRF) is an attack that tricks a user into doing something on your site that they didn't intend. A malicious site can be designed to look exactly like your site and use a form that looks like an innocuous task but actually causes a change on the real site. For example, the malicious site might have a form that looks just like your comment form but contains hidden fields for doing a password change. When the user hits Submit, the malicious form communicates with your real site, causing the user's password to change. The bad hats can then use the changed password to access the user's account.

To prevent this attack, Django uses the `{% csrf_token %}`. It works through a piece of Django Middleware called `CsrfViewMiddleware`, which creates a session cookie containing a random value. A variation on this value gets included as a hidden form field when you use `{% csrf_token %}`. When your form gets submitted, the value gets included in the POST. Django looks for this token, and if it isn't there or doesn't match the one in the session, the POST gets rejected.

The malicious site has no way of knowing the value of the CSRF token, so a fake form will not be able to include it. For more information on CSRF attacks in general, see the Open Worldwide Application Security Project's (OWASP) "Cross Site Request Forgery" article (https://owasp.org/www-community/attacks/csrf). For specifics on how Django prevents the attack, see the CSRF documentation: https://docs.django project.com/en/dev/ref/csrf/.

7.1.3 Beautifying web forms

I haven't seen a web page without CSS since the 1990s. It sounds like a bad joke: the author's so old he used the web before it was stylized! The form examples in this and previous chapters have all used `form.as_p` to render the necessary HTML tags. In addition to `form.as_p`, there is `form.as_table`, but this doesn't do much to make the results prettier. Table columns mean the labels in the forms all end up the same width, which is an improvement, but it still won't win any design awards.

Earlier, you saw how you could use the `attrs` argument to a widget to add attributes to the resulting HTML tag. The example populated the `rows` and `cols` attributes of a `<textarea>` tag. This mechanism can also be used to add a `class` attribute to the tag, making it easier to stylize the result with CSS.

Class attributes may not be enough, depending on what you are trying to achieve. For example, Bootstrap has some very pretty forms, but to get them, you need to wrap the tags in other tags. At this point, you're beyond the limit of what the Django forms will render for you. You can still use Form objects, but you need to write the corresponding HTML in full. The key to getting this to work is the correct use of id and name attributes on the tags. Django expects the field name to show up as the tag's name attribute and the tag's ID attribute to contain id-underscore-field.

The form object in the template provides access to each individual field via dot-notation. Each field has attributes for the value of the field, corresponding help text, and any associated error message. Each of these pieces can be accessed in your template to help you render beautiful content.

The following code is a sample Bootstrap field for entering a first name:

```
<div class="form-group">
    <label for="first_name">First name</label>

    <input type="text" class="form-control"
        id="id_first_name" name="first_name"
        aria-describedby="first_name_help"
        placeholder="First name"
        {% if form.first_name.value %}
            value="{{ form.first_name.value }}"
        {% endif %}
    >

    <small id="first_name_help"
        class="form-text text-muted">
            If you are Cher or Madonna, enter your name
            in the last name field
    </small>

    {% if form.errors.first_name %}
        <small class="text-danger">
            {{ form.errors.first_name }}
        </small>
    {% endif %}
</div>
```

That's a lot of code, isn't it? The Form does so much for you: properly populating the field, showing help text, and errors when they occur. If you can get your forms to be beautiful enough through CSS alone, you can write a lot less HTML. Depending on your style toolkit, there may be third-party libraries that build on top of Form, doing the work for you. They're worth checking out before writing all that HTML.

7.1.4 *New in Django 5: Reusable field group templates*

Having to write HTML by hand due to styling is a step backward. Django 5 recognizes this and adds a new feature: reusable field group templates. In Django 5, the structure of a form field is determined by a template. This template contains the tags for labels and inputs along with if clauses that display help text if it is associated with the field. The provided template uses <div> tags for structure. You can override the template

used to display a field by adding a `template_name` argument to any field object in your
`Form` class:

```
class CommentForm(forms.Form):
    name = forms.CharField(template_name="custom_input_field.html")    ◁─────┐
    ...
```
Specify the use of a custom template to render your field.

This means you can build Bootstrap-style widgets as field templates and reuse them in
your forms. If you're going to customize a field, it is best to start with Django's own
template as a base. You can find it in the Django package under forms/templates/
django/forms/field.html.

7.2   *Django ModelForm*

It is quite common for there to be a link between the data you ask your users to submit
and the information you store in your database. To reduce the amount of code you
write, Django includes the `ModelForm` class. This class extends from `Form` and automatically creates fields based on the structure of an associated model class.

It is finally time to implement Nicky's original idea: ads for musicians seeking
bands and bands seeking musicians. Ultimately, the goal is to use a `ModelForm` to get
your user's input, but there is a bit of a journey to get there. First off, you'll need
somewhere to store the ad, which means a new model class. Along the way to implementing the `ModelForm`, you'll learn some more about ORM fields, how to validate
multifield interdependencies, and how to use the undocumented `Truncate` class to
show part of some text.

7.2.1   *Validating fields in a model*

Before providing a self-service feature for your users, like writing a classified ad, it is
good practice to get any new model working in the Admin first. This provides a way
for you to test out your thoughts before exposing it to your users.

The `SeekingAd` model stores a classified ad written by a user, and its key component is a `TextField` containing the ad's content. Ads can be either written by musicians seeking a band or bands seeking musicians. To capture that, you need a foreign
relationship to a `Musician` object and a second one to a `Band` object. You also need to
store which kind of ad it is; you can do this in several ways. A `BooleanField` could be
used, where `True` means *musician seeking band*, and `False` means *band seeking musician*,
but then, you have to remember what `True` means. A better choice is to use a `Char-`
`Field` and store `"M"` when seeking a musician, or `"B"` when seeking a band.

The `CharField` takes an optional argument called `choices` that restricts the values
allowed in the field. By using `choices`, you can guarantee that only an `"M"` or `"B"` is
stored. The `choices` argument takes a tuple-of-tuples structure, where each `tuple`
defines a choice, and the `tuple` within the choice pairs a value with a human-readable
label, as shown in the following example:

7.2 Django ModelForm **163**

```
SEEKING_CHOICES = (
    ("M", "Musician"),
    ("B", "Band"),
)
```

Django also provides utility classes for building these kinds of structures. The
`django.db.models.TextChoices` class allows you to achieve the same result by coding
an enumeration-like class:

```
class SeekingChoice(models.TextChoices):
    MUSICIAN = "M"
    BAND = "B"
```

`TextChoices` classes use attribute names as labels with attribute values as the value in
the database. All-capital attribute names get converted into sentence-case labels: the
`MUSICIAN` attribute becomes the `"Musician"` label. The `.choices` attribute of this class
contains the tuple-of-tuples structure required by the `choices` argument to `CharField`.
There isn't much difference in the amount of code here, but the `TextChoices` class is
more explicit about its purpose, and personally, I find it easier to read.

> **Nesting your choices**
>
> Some programmers prefer to make their choices structure a member of the model
> class that uses it. For example, `MusicianBandChoice` could be an inner class of
> `SeekingAd`. This is a matter of preference. Scoping it this way makes it clear where
> it gets used, but accessing it requires writing out the whole thing. Personally, I find
> `MusicianBandChoice.MUSICIAN` lengthy enough, and having to type `SeekingAd`
> `.MusicianBandChoice.MUSICIAN` feels like overkill.

When a band is seeking a musician, the `seeking` field is `"M"`, and you want to track
which band is seeking a musician. You do this by populating the `band` foreign key. Likewise, when a musician is seeking a band, the `seeking` field is `"B"` and the `musician` foreign key should be populated with the musician seeking a band. This introduces a new
wrinkle: the validation of the fields in your model are interdependent.

In chapter 4, you learned about basic ORM field validation, like disallowing empty
values and constraints limiting what could be in a field. Most validation and constraints are field level, meaning inter-field dependencies don't come out of the box.
The `Model` base class has a series of methods that are called to validate an object. One
of them is called `.clean()`, and it can be overridden to verify inter-field relationships.
The base class's `.clean()` method is empty, but you can add code to check for problems and raise a `ValidationError` if one is found. The following code is part of just
such a validation process:

```
def clean(self):
    if self.seeking == MusicianBandChoice.MUSICIAN:
        if self.band is None:
```

```
        raise ValidationError(
            "Band field required when seeking a musician")
    ...
```

The `SeekingAd` model needs two more fields: an `owner` and a `date`. The `owner` field is a foreign key to a `User` account to track who created the ad. This is especially important if you want to provide the ability to edit ads, as only the owner should be able to edit it. The `date` field tracks when the ad got created. Conveniently, `DateField` has an optional argument called `auto_now_add` that, when set to `True`, automatically populates the field with the current date. (There is also another option, `auto_now`, that gets populated whenever the object gets saved.) The Django Admin is aware of this and won't even prompt you for the field—it lets the model set it for you. The following listing puts all these pieces together. You'll need a new models.py file in the RiffMates/content app directory.

Listing 7.5   The `SeekingAd` model stores a RiffMates classified ad

```
# RiffMates/content/models.py
from django.contrib.auth.models import User
from django.core.exceptions import ValidationError
from django.db import models

from bands.models import Musician, Band          Extending TextChoices allows
                                                  you to write a choices object,
class MusicianBandChoice(models.TextChoices):  ◁──┘ like an enumeration class.
    MUSICIAN = "M"
    BAND = "B"                                 Using auto_now_add=True means this field
                                               gets automatically populated with the
                                               current date when the object gets created.
class SeekingAd(models.Model):
    date = models.DateField(auto_now_add=True)  ◁──
    owner = models.ForeignKey(User,             A CharField using the choices
A foreign key   ┌─▷  on_delete=models.CASCADE)  argument, so seeking can only contain
to the user who │    seeking = models.CharField(max_length=1,  "M" or "B", indicating whether a
owns the ad     │        choices=MusicianBandChoice.choices)  ◁── musician or band is being sought.
                │    musician = models.ForeignKey(Musician, on_delete=models.SET_NULL,
                │        blank=True, null=True)             ◁──
                     band = models.ForeignKey(Band, on_delete=models.SET_NULL,
A foreign key    ┌─▷     blank=True, null=True)             A foreign key
relationship to  │   content = models.TextField()   ◁────  relationship to the musician seeking
the band seeking │                                  Storage band. The arguments blank=True and
a musician       │   class Meta:                    for the text  null=True ensure this can be empty in
                 └─▷     ordering = ["date", ]      of the ad both the Django Admin and the database.

Default query                                       Validation for inter-field
order is by the                                     dependencies gets done in
date field           def __str__(self):             the .clean()
                         return f"SeekingAd(id={self.id}, seeking={self.seeking})"  method.

                     def clean(self):               ◁──
                         if self.seeking == MusicianBandChoice.MUSICIAN:
                             # Validate seeking musician case   ◁──  When seeking a musician, ensure
                             if self.band is None:                   the band field gets populated
                                                                     and the musician field is empty.
```

```
        raise ValidationError(
            "Band field required when seeking a musician")
    if self.musician is not None:
        raise ValidationError(
            ("Musician field should be empty for a band "
            "seeking a musician"))
else:
    # Validate seeking band case
    if self.musician is None:
        raise ValidationError(
            "Musician field required when seeking a band")
    if self.band is not None:
        raise ValidationError(
            ("Band field should be empty for a musician "
            "seeking a band"))

super().clean()
```

When seeking a band, ensure the musician field gets populated and the band field is empty.

WARNING `.clean()` is not called automatically!

Early versions of Django did not include object validation methods, like `.clean()`, and to maintain backward compatibility, it was decided not call it automatically. It is possible to create an object programmatically that violates your validation code. The `.clean()` method gets called when you use the Django Admin, but if you open up the REPL and create an object by hand, `.clean()` is not called. One work around for this is to override the model's `.save()` method and force a call to `.clean()` inside it. The downside of this approach is `.save()` doesn't know what to do with a `ValidationError`, and if your code doesn't catch it, the error will show as a `500` error in your logs. If you do decide to override `.save()`, make sure you use a `try` block in your code to properly handle any `ValidationError` that gets raised.

7.2.2 *A ModelAdmin for SeekingAd using Truncate*

To test your new `SeekingAd` model out, you need an Admin class to go with it. Inside RiffMates/content/admin.py, add a `SeekingAdAdmin` class similar to those you wrote for the `bands` app. The Django Admin automatically uses the labels from the `seeking` field, so when you include it in `list_display`, it will show `"Musician"` rather than `"M"`.

The ad text from the object might be quite long; displaying it on the Django Admin summary page could be unwieldy. There are several template filters that perform *truncation* on strings. The `{{ |truncatewords }}` filter truncates a string on word boundaries. It would be nice to use this functionality outside of templates. If you go digging through the Django source code, you will find the `Truncator` class inside `django.utils.text`. This undocumented feature is what the truncation filters got built on top of. It is unclear to me why this isn't documented; it is a handy class to take advantage of outside a template. The `SeekingAdAdmin` class uses `Truncate` to show a short version of the ad description in the Django Admin listing page. The complete code for RiffMates/content/admin.py is shown in the following listing.

Listing 7.6   Register `SeekingAdAdmin` in the Django Admin

```
# RiffMates/content/admin.py
from django.contrib import admin
from django.utils.text import Truncator          ◄─┐  The hidden gem Truncator
                                                     makes readable shortened text.

from content.models import SeekingAd

                                        ┐  Register SeekingAd for
@admin.register(SeekingAd)          ◄─┘  use in the Django Admin.
class SeekingAdAdmin(admin.ModelAdmin):
    list_display = ("id", "date", "owner", "seeking",
        "show_ad", )                    ◄─┐  A list of the fields to display, including one
                                             calling the custom .show_ad() method
    def show_ad(self, obj):
        return Truncator(obj.content).words(5,
            truncate=' ...')            ◄─┐  Pass Truncator the ad's content
    show_ad.short_description = "Ad"  ◄──    field, restricting the result to 5
                                             words in length, appending " ..."
                                             if content got truncated.
            The short_description attribute
            for the method changes the title
            in the Django Admin listing page.
```

You've got a new model class, so you need to run the `makemigrations` and `migrate` management commands to perform the necessary database actions. Once you've done that, you can load your development server and add a new classified ad. Play with the various combinations of values for the `seeking`, `musician`, and `band` fields to verify your validation code works.

7.2.3   *Writing a ModelForm*

It was a bit of a winding road, but you're at your destination. It is time to write the self-serve code allowing users to create a classified ad. `SeekingAd` stores the classified ad, and any web form you write would map almost directly to the storage class. The web form needs an ad type selection widget, musician and band selection widgets, and a place to write the text of the ad. You could write a `Form` class that does all this, but Django's `ModelForm` means you don't have to. A `ModelForm` inherits from the `Form` class and automatically creates the form's fields, based on an associated model.

The `ModelForm` works a bit like a `ModelAdmin`: you create a class and associate it with a model. Unlike `ModelAdmin`, the `ModelForm` uses an inner class called `Meta` to specify its behavior. Inside the inner class, the `model` attribute links the `ModelForm` to an ORM model. The `fields` attribute indicates which fields in the ORM model participate in the form.

If you don't require further customization, then that's all you need. Simply inherit from `ModelForm`, point the inner `Meta` class's `model` attribute at a model, and specify which fields participate. You've got a form. Figure 7.4 shows the equivalent `Form` object that a `ModelForm` represents.

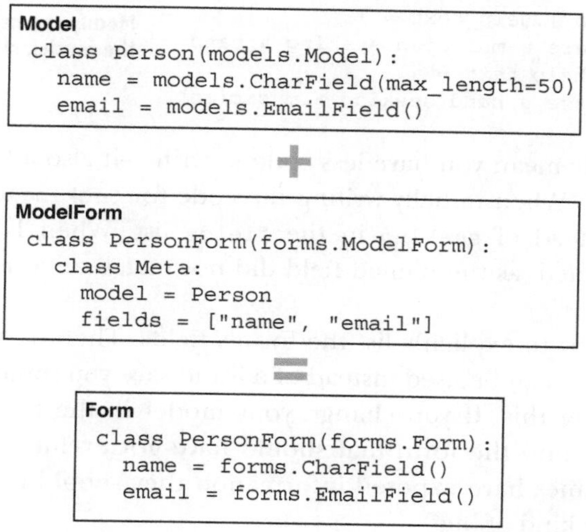

```
Model
 class Person(models.Model):
   name = models.CharField(max_length=50)
   email = models.EmailField()
```

➕

```
ModelForm
 class PersonForm(forms.ModelForm):
   class Meta:
     model = Person
     fields = ["name", "email"]
```

➖

```
Form
 class PersonForm(forms.Form):
   name = forms.CharField()
   email = forms.EmailField()
```

Figure 7.4   A `ModelForm`
generates a `Form` **equivalent for**
you based on a model class

You can customize things further, though, if you wish. When you use a `Form` class to build a form, you can modify each field as part of their declaration. You can change the field's label, help text, or which widget renders the result. A `ModelForm` declares the fields for you, so you don't have the opportunity to change these attributes at declaration time. Instead, you can override the .`__init__`() method.

Both the `Form` and `ModelForm` classes have an attribute called `fields`, which is a dictionary containing the fields on the form. By overriding .`__init__`(), you can modify any field after it has been constructed through the use of this dictionary. This means you can change the label, the help text, or the widget that renders the tag.

Open RiffMates/content/forms., and add the `SeekingAdForm` class found in the following listing. This class creates a form based on the `SeekingAd` model and modifies some of the labels and help text of the corresponding fields.

Listing 7.7   Django `ModelForm` **for the** `SeekingAd` **ORM model**

```
# RiffMates/content/forms.py
...
from content.models import SeekingAd
...

class SeekingAdForm(forms.ModelForm):
    class Meta:                          Associate SeekingAdForm with
        model = SeekingAd          ◁─── the SeekingAd ORM model.
        fields = ["seeking", "musician", "band",
            "content", ]                 ◁───  A list of the fields from SeekingAd
                                               that should appear in the form
    def __init__(self, *args, **kwargs):
        super().__init__(*args, **kwargs)              Modify the label for
        self.fields["seeking"].label = "I am seeking a"  ◁─── the seeking field.
```

```
self.fields["musician"].help_text = \
    "Fill in if you are a musician seeking a band"
self.fields["band"].help_text = \
    "Fill in if you are a band seeking a musician"
```
Modify the help text for the musician field.

Using a `ModelForm` doesn't only mean you have less code to write—it also adds some verification in the background. When initially writing the code for `SeekingAdForm`, I accidentally wrote `seeing` instead of `seeking` in the `fields` list. When I ran the Django server, an error got issued, as the named field did not match an attribute of the `SeekingAd` model.

It is generally recommended to explicitly list the form's fields. There is a special value, `fields = "__all__"`, that can be used instead of a list to save you some typing, but I recommend against using this. If you change your model in the future, you might accidentally add a field into the form that should have got excluded. There have been cases where companies have exposed information they shouldn't have to the public through exactly this kind of bug.

An alternative to using the `fields` attribute is `except`. This is also a list, but here you list the fields that don't participate in the form. This has the same danger as `__all__`, where additions to the model automatically show up in the form, so again, this is probably not the best choice.

A shorter shortcut

If the only thing you need to do with your `ModelForm` is associate it with a `Model` class and specify the `fields` attribute, you can get there with even less code. The `modelform_factory` function is a factory that creates `ModelForm` classes. The typical use takes two arguments: a reference to the `Model` and a list of fields:

```
from django import forms

SeekingAdForm = forms.modelform_factory(SeekingAd, fields = ["seeking",
    "musician", "band", "content", ]
```

The factory takes other arguments as well. Like with the class, you can use `except` instead of `fields`; specify the labels, widgets, help text, and error messages; and more. For more information, see https://docs.djangoproject.com/en/dev/ref/forms/models/.

Instead of overriding the `.__init__()` method, there are several dictionaries you can use inside the `Meta` inner class. The `labels`, `help_texts`, `widgets`, and `error_messages` attributes all override the corresponding item for a field. For example, the following is an alternate way of overriding the label for the `seeking` field:

```
class SeekingAdForm(forms.ModelForm):
    class Meta:
        model = SeekingAd
        fields = ["seeking", "musician", "band", "content", ]
```

```
        labels = {
            "seeking": 'I am seeking a'
        }
```

7.2.4   Using SeekingAdForm in a view

For the sake of completeness, let's write out the view and templates for the classified submission. You need two views: one that handles the form and one to redirect the user to when the form is complete. The latter can be the classified ad listing page. The listing page can be public, but the form submission view should be restricted to users.

Recall that the `date` and `owner` fields from the `SeekingAd` model are not included in the form. The `date` field's exclusion is OK because the `auto_now_add` attribute populates it automatically the first time the model gets saved. The `owner` field gets excluded, as this isn't something the user should be filling in. The owner field should be populated by the view, ensuring the value contains the user that created the ad.

Let's start with the classifieds listing page. It is a short view that contains two pieces of data: all of the ads for musicians seeking bands and all the ads for bands seeking musicians. Both of these are queries on the `SeekingAd` class but with different `.filter()` parameters. The following listing contains code for RiffMates/content/views.py.

```
# RiffMates/content/views.py
...
from content.models import MusicianBandChoice, SeekingAd
...
def list_ads(request):
    data = {
        'seeking_musician':SeekingAd.objects.filter(        Band-seeking-musician
            seeking=MusicianBandChoice.MUSICIAN),    ◁──┘  query
        'seeking_band':SeekingAd.objects.filter(
            seeking=MusicianBandChoice.BAND),    ◁──┐
    }                                                 Musician-seeking-band
                                                      query

    return render(request, "list_ads.html", data)
```

Don't forget to add a `path` object to RiffMates/content/urls.py to register this view, and make sure you name the URL, so it can be used in a `redirect()` call in the form view. The following listing contains a simple template for this view. Create RiffMates/templates/list_ads.html, and add the code there.

```
<!-- RiffMates/templates/list_ads.html -->
{% extends "base.html" %}

{% block content %}
```

```
<h1>Musicians Seeking Bands </h1>

{% for ad in seeking_band %}          ←┐  Loop through the ads for
  <p>                                   └  musicians seeking bands.
    {{ad.date}} &mdash;
    {{ad.musician.first_name}} {{ad.musician.last_name}}  ←┐  Show the ad date
    <br/>                                                   │  and the name of the
    <i>{{ad.content}}</i>        ←┤  Text content of the ad  └─ seeking musician.
  </p>
{% empty %}                      ←┐  Alternate text copy if there
  <p> <i>No ads at this time</i> </p>  │  are no ads in the query
{% endfor %}

<h1>Bands Seeking Musicians </h1>

{% for ad in seeking_musician %}   ←┐  Similar structure for
  <p>                               └  bands seeking musicians
    {{ad.date}} &mdash; {{ad.band.name}}
    <br/>
    <i>{{ad.content}}</i>
  </p>
{% empty %}
  <p> <i>No ads at this time</i> </p>
{% endfor %}

{% endblock content %}
```

When playing with `SeekingAd` in the Django Admin before, you likely created one or more ads. If you did, you should be able to see them in your new view. Figure 7.5 shows my version of the content with an ad from Nicky.

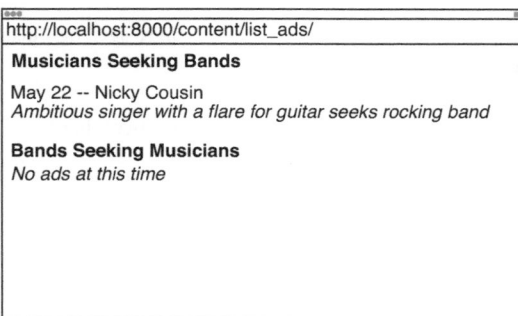

Figure 7.5   The ad listing page with a single lonely ad

The view for submitting an ad is similar to the view you wrote to submit comments earlier. The only thing you need to learn when using the `SeekingAdForm` is how to create the corresponding `SeekingAd` model object. Once you have verified that the form is valid, you call `.save()` on the form to get an instance of the corresponding model. The `.save()` method on a `ModelForm` has an optional parameter `commit`, which determines whether the returned instance object gets saved or not.

In the `SeekingAd` case, there is no `owner` field in the form, and as it is a required field on the ORM object, attempting to save without it results in an exception. Using `commit=False`, you get an instance of the object before it is saved, so you can modify it before storing it in the database. Add the form handling view code from the following listing to RiffMates/content/views.py.

Listing 7.10   View for displaying and submitting `SeekingAdForm`

```
# RiffMates/content/views.py
from django.contrib.auth.decorators import login_required
...
from content.forms import CommentForm, SeekingAdForm
from content.models import MusicianBandChoice, SeekingAd


@login_required          ←┘  Ads belong to users and enforce
def seeking_ad(request):     that they are logged in.
    if request.method == 'GET':       The GET mode displays
        form = SeekingAdForm()    ←┘  an empty form.

    else: # POST                                      The POST mode populates the form
        form = SeekingAdForm(request.POST)      ←    based on the user's submitted data.

        if form.is_valid():                        Save the form, creating a SeekingAd
            ad = form.save(commit=False)    ←      object without saving the model.
            ad.owner = request.user    ←
            ad.save()                      Add the user's account object
                                           to the SeekingAd object.

            return redirect("list_ads")    ←   Redirect to the
                                               classified listing page.
    # Was a GET, or Form was not valid    ←
    data = {
        "form": form,               Handle the GET and invalid form
    }                               cases by displaying the form.

    return render(request, "seeking_ad.html", data)
```

Verify the form's contents. (annotation pointing to `if form.is_valid():`)

Save the SeekingAd model. (annotation pointing to `ad.save()`)

To go along with your new view, you'll need a template. Add the code from the following listing to RiffMates/templates/seeking_ad.html.

Listing 7.11   Template for the classified ad submission form

```
<!-- RiffMates/templates/seeking_ad.html -->
{% extends "base.html" %}

{% block content %}
<h1>Seeking Ad</h1>

<form method="post">
  {% csrf_token %}
  {{form.as_p}}
```

```
    <button class="btn btn-dark" type="submit">Save</button>
</form>

{% endblock content %}
```

This template doesn't have anything you haven't seen before, except you have fresh eyes on {% csrf_token %}. Now, you should see it as an important piece of security technology rather than scary-sounding black magic.

7.2.5   *Editing existing data with forms*

You've got a form, and you've got a corresponding model in the database—all is good! Now, what if your user wants to make an edit? If they own the ad, they should be able to update its contents. With a few small changes to your code, you can handle this situation.

This scenario is commonplace. Most times when you have user driven input, you want the user to be able to edit the input. You could write two views, one for adding new content and one for editing existing content, but most of the code will be similar. Instead, you can write one view that works in two different modes.

Views are just functions, and like all functions, they can take default arguments. When in Edit mode, you need the view to take the ID of the item being edited. When in Add mode, you don't need an ID, but you do need some indication that you're adding instead of editing. ORM object IDs start counting at 1, which means you can take advantage of this and use an ID of 0 to indicate Add mode. By setting the item ID's default value to 0, you have two different ways of calling your view.

URLs aren't quite as flexible as Python functions. To go with your two-mode view, you can either use an optional query parameter for the item ID or register two different routes. The first route is for adding a new object, and the URL path contains no arguments. The Add route calls the view without any arguments, and the default ID of 0 gets used. The second route is for editing, and that URL takes the ID of the object to be edited.

The URL query parameter and two-route designs are equally effective. The latter is more Django-esque, though. Once you start using path arguments in a URL, going back to query parameters seems inelegant. This could just be my personal bias, though.

Let's put this into practice by adding the ability to edit ads in the seeking_ad() view. In this case, the object being edited is a SeekingAd model, which when you're in Edit mode, you'll need to fetch from the database. You've done this before, using the get_object_or_404() shortcut. With the object in hand, use the instance argument to prepopulate the ModelForm with the model's contents. This happens in both the GET and POST sections of the view when in Edit mode. Figure 7.6 shows how the original flow of GET and POST change now that the view handles both adding and editing objects. The code in listing 7.12 shows the changes to the view necessary for supporting both Add and Edit modes.

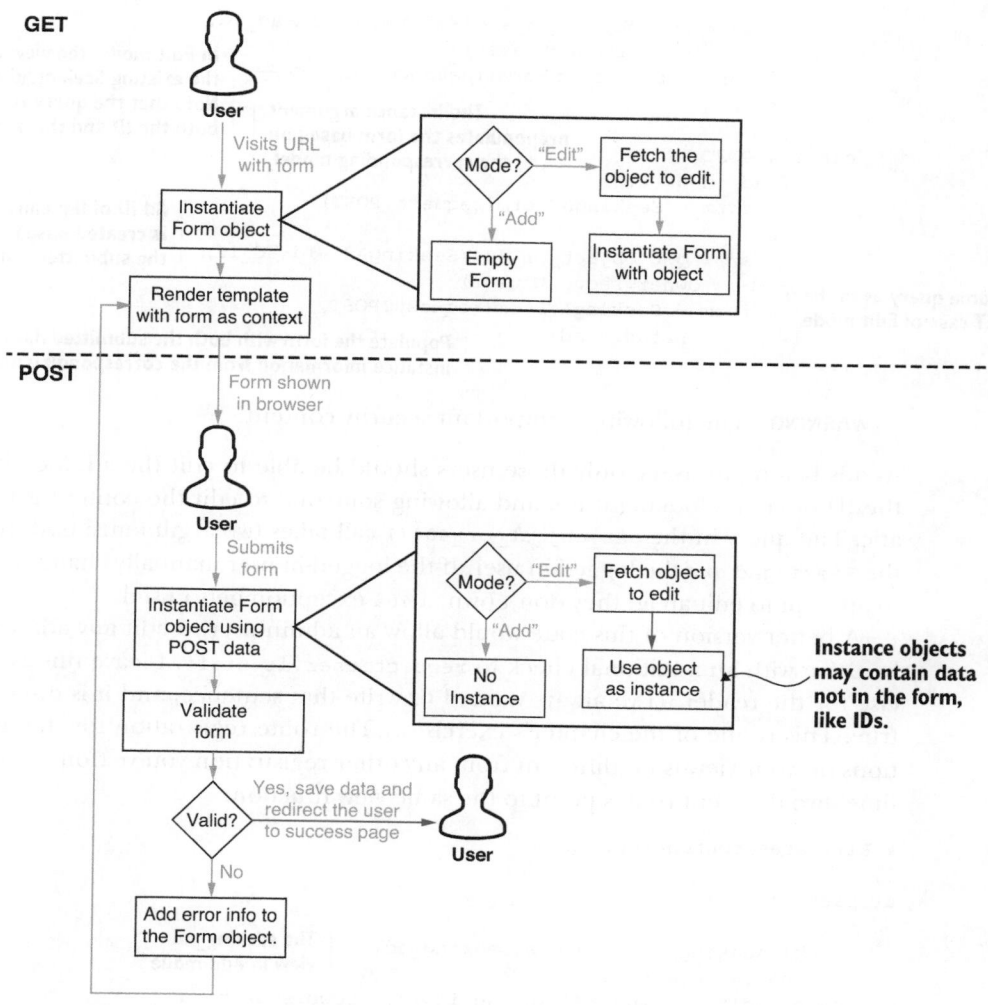

Figure 7.6   Prepopulating the form with an existing object for Edit mode

---

Listing 7.12   View for displaying and submitting `SeekingAdForm`

```
# RiffMates/content/views.py
...
from django.shortcuts import render, redirect, get_object_or_404
...
@login_required
def seeking_ad(request, ad_id=0):
    if request.method == 'GET':
        if ad_id == 0:
            form = SeekingAdForm()
        else:
```

The view now takes the ID of a model object to edit as an argument.

An ID of 0 indicates a new model object should be created.

```
        ad = get_object_or_404(SeekingAd, id=ad_id,
            owner=request.user)
        form = SeekingAdForm(instance=ad)


    else: # POST
        if ad_id == 0:
            form = SeekingAdForm(request.POST)
        else:
            ad = get_object_or_404(SeekingAd, id=ad_id,
                owner=request.user)
            form = SeekingAdForm(request.POST,
                instance=ad)
        ...
```

In Edit mode, the view looks up the existing SeekingAd object. Note that the query requires both the ID and the owner.

The **instance** argument prepopulates the form based on the corresponding model.

Ad ID of 0 means the form is created based solely on the submitted data.

The same query as in the GET case of Edit mode

Populate the form with both the submitted data and the instance information from the corresponding model.

WARNING The following is important security content!

As ads belong to users, only those users should be able to edit the ad. Merely taking the ID of an ad, looking it up, and allowing someone to edit the content is problematic. The query in the `get_object_or_404()` call takes two arguments: both the ID of the `SeekingAd` *and* the logged-in user. If the logged-in user manually changes the URL to attempt to edit an ad they don't own, a `404` exception gets raised.

A better version of this code would allow an admin user to edit any ad, which can be done with an additional check to `request.user.is_staff`. I leave this as an exercise for the reader. (I've always wanted to write that sentence, and it is quite literally true. This is one of the chapter's exercises.) The route registration for the two variations on your view is no different from any other registration you've done, except this time, two different routes point to the same view function:

```
# RiffMates/content/urls.py
...
urlpatterns = [
    ...
    path("seeking_ad/", views.seeking_ad,
        name="seeking_ad"),
    path("edit_seeking_ad/<int:ad_id>/", views.seeking_ad,
        name="edit_seeking_ad"),
]
```

The **seeking_ad** view in Add mode

The **seeking_ad** view in Edit mode with its required ad_id argument

The list_ads.html file needs a small tweak: it needs Edit links for ads owned by the logged-in user. When you call `render()` from a view, the `request` object you pass in gets included in the template's context dictionary. That means anything in the `request` can be accessed within your template. The following code goes inside the `{% for %}` loop where an ad gets rendered, displaying a link if the ad's owner is the `request.user`:

```
<!-- RiffMates/templates/list_ads.html -->
<!-- ... -->
{% if ad.owner == request.user %}
    <a href="{% url 'edit_seeking_ad' ad.id %}">Edit</a>
{% endif %}
```

Remember that list_ads.html divides the ads into two sections: one for musicians seeking bands and the other for bands seeking musicians. In both these cases, the Edit links need to be added in the template.

Another worthwhile change to this template is to add a link for new ads, but only if the user is authenticated. Put this near the top of the file:

```
{% if request.user.is_authenticated %}
   <a href="{% url 'seeking_ad' %}">New Ad</a>
{% endif %}
```

Although `is_authenticated()` is a method on the User object, remember that templates can call methods if they take no arguments.

With the changes to the view, the new route registered, and the tweak to your template, you're ready to go. Run your development server, and visit the ad listing page. You should now have Edit links for ads owned by the authenticated user, which take you to the Edit mode of the ad view.

7.3 Serving static files

All the content so far was from dynamic web pages output from Django views. There are two more types of content that your project may include: static files and user uploaded files. *Static files* are those that don't change and are typically related to the presentation layer. CSS, JavaScript, and images on the site are common examples of static files. Django has not been optimized to serve this kind of content, so in production, it should be delegated to a web server. The Django development server does have an inefficient static serving mechanism, so you don't have to use a separate web server when testing your site. The details about static file serving in production get covered, with all the other bits about production, in appendix B.

Because of the minimal understanding of technology (MUT; patent pending, offer may not be valid in your area) approach taken so far, a core piece of RiffMates is missing: a home page. Let's throw together a basic home page that has an image file: the RiffMates logo.

I'll leave it to you to create a view for the home page; it should go in the RiffMates/home/views.py file and really only needs to contain a single call to `render()`. There is one small thing to be aware of when registering a home page view: the relative URL portion of the `path` is an empty string. Modify your RiffMates/RiffMates/urls.py file to include the following route:

```
# RiffMates/RiffMates/urls.py
...
urlpatterns = [
    ...
    path("", home_views.home, name="home"),          ⟵— An empty path string registers
]                                                        a view against the base URL.
```

The logo image is a static file. The location of static files is typically different in development and production. Both the URL and the absolute path to the file are usually different, depending on environments. To help with this, Django provides the `{% static %}` template tag, which sets the base URL and handles the full file name.

The tags you encountered in chapter 3 were all part of the default tag library. Although `{% static %}` comes with Django, it isn't part of the main module, you have to load it separately. The `{% load %}` tag works like the `import` statement in Python, adding tags from the loaded module into the template's namespace. Somewhat confusingly, the name of the module and the name of the tag are the same. This is similar to some functions found in the Python standard library, like `from pprint import pprint`.

The `{% static %}` tag returns a URL and gets used inside `<img>` and `<link>` HTML tags, similar to how the `{% url %}` tag gets used in an HTML anchor (`<a>`). The argument to `{% static %}` is the name of the static file, relative to the static directory.

The static directory is where you keep your static files in your project. This may be different from where they are deployed in production. Common practice is to create a directory called *static* in your project folder, which you point at by adding a configuration to settings.py. As there are several kinds of static files, I usually create separate subdirectories for images, JavaScript, and CSS to keep them organized. Create a directory in your project for your static files and one under that for the images:

```
(venv) RiffMates$ mkdir static
(venv) RiffMates$ mkdir static/img
```

The RiffMates logo file goes in RiffMates/static/img. To tell Django about your new static directory, edit RiffMates/RiffMates/settings.py, and look for the existing setting named `STATIC_URL`. Underneath that, add the following configuration:

```
# RiffMates/RiffMates/settings.py
...
STATIC_URL = '/static/'
STATICFILES_DIRS = (
    BASE_DIR / 'static',
)
```

Static files have a base URL of /static/. This is the default value provided when Django created settings.py.

Your static files are in the static directory underneath your project directory. Remember that BASE_DIR is a pathlib.Path object, so the / operator creates a new Path.

For production, there are a couple more steps you can learn about in appendix B. The development server knows all about `STATICFILES_DIR`, and with the configuration done, it will serve your logo.

With all that in place, it is time to write the home page. The following listing contains an example—feel free to be more creative. The content goes in RiffMates/templates/home.html.

> **Listing 7.13   Template for the home page that includes a static file**

```
<!-- RiffMates/templates/home.html -->
{% extends "base.html" %}
{% load static %}
```

Load the tag module that includes the {% static %} tag.

```
{% block content %}
  <img src="{% static 'img/logo.png' %}" height="100">
  <h1>Welcome to RiffMates!</h1>

  <ul>
    <li> <a href="{% url 'news' %}">News</a> </li>
    <li> <a href="{% url 'musicians' %}">Musicians</a> </li>
    <li> <a href="{% url 'bands' %}">Bands</a> </li>
    <li> <a href="{% url 'venues' %}">Venues</a> </li>
    <li> <a href="{% url 'list_ads' %}">Classified Ads</a> </li>
    <li> <a href="{% url 'comment' %}">Leave a comment</a> </li>
  </ul>

{% endblock content %}
```

Use the {% static %} tag to get the URL for the logo file. The argument is the name of the file relative to the **STATICFILES_DIR** base configuration.

For convenience, some links to the pages you've written so far

Of course, you'll need an actual logo file to make all this work. The sample code includes a simple image, but any image file named logo.png inside RiffMates/static/img will work.

While you're doing some cosmetic work, add a link to the home page into the nav header you created in chapter 6. The following listing shows the modification you need to make to RiffMates/templates/base.html.

Listing 7.14   Adding a Home link to that thing approximating a nav bar

```
<!-- RiffMates/templates/base.html -->
<!-- ... -->
<body>
  <div style="float: right;">
    <a href="{% url 'home' %}">Home</a>   

  <!-- ... -->
```

The new Home link in the nav header of the base template

You're all set! Fire up the development server, and take a look at the results. It should be something like figure 7.7.

We need to make one other small change, now that you have a home page. Inside RiffMates/RiffMates/settings.py, change the values of LOGIN_REDIRECT_URL and LOGOUT_REDIRECT_URL to /. This is a more logical place to send the user when they log in or out without a destination page:

```
# RiffMates/RiffMates/settings.py
...
LOGOUT_REDIRECT_URL = '/'
LOGIN_REDIRECT_URL = '/'
```

With static files working, there is only one content type left: user-uploaded files. That's what's next.

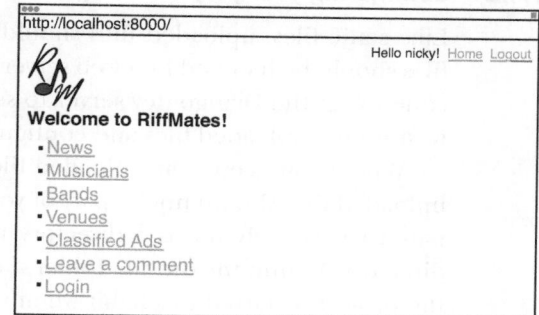

Figure 7.7   Finally, a home page for RiffMates

Loading by default

If you are frequently loading other template libraries using the `{% load %}` tag, there is a shortcut. Inside the `TEMPLATES` configuration setting, there is a section called `OPTIONS`. Inside `OPTIONS`, you can add a key called `builtins` with a list as its value. Whatever tag modules are named in this list are automatically loaded across all your templates. For example, to use the `static` template tag library throughout your system, modify `TEMPLATES` in settings.py as follows:

```
TEMPLATES = [
    {
        ...
        "OPTIONS": {
            "builtins": ["django.templatetags.static"],
            ...
        },
    },
]
```

7.4   *Uploads*

HTML forms allow your users to attach files, submitting them to your site. Unlike other submitted data, files generally shouldn't go in a database; it is far more efficient to store them as files on the server. Files often get associated with data, though, so you need database columns to reference them. Django handles this through the `FileField` model field.

I've mentioned before that you should never trust your users; for file uploads, this goes double. Just because the user says they're uploading an image doesn't mean what they're uploading is an image. At least for the case of images, Django can help you here. The `ImageField` inherits from the `FileField` and validates that the associated file is an image. To do this, it uses the Pillow image library (https://pillow.readthedocs .io/en/latest/), which has to be installed separately:

```
(venv) RiffMates$ python -m pip install pillow
```

7.4.1   *Configuring your project for uploads*

Like static files, uploaded files shouldn't be served by Django. In production, these files should be handled by a web server. In development, you can add a couple lines of code to get the Django dev server to serve files. Also like static files, you need a place to store the uploaded files and configuration to tell Django where that is.

Where you keep your uploaded files is a matter of preference. Unlike static files, uploaded files should not be part of your project. For smaller projects and testing, the pattern I typically use is a directory named *outside* at the same level as the project directory. Within the outside folder, I create another directory with the same name as the project. I started this habit when working with smaller customers, who ran multiple Django projects from the same server. Having the project name inside the outside directory created a separate upload location for each project.

This outside directory can be used for other things as well, so I typically create an *uploads* directory inside the project folder. Here is a sample file tree for the RiffMates project, its associated outside folder, and a hypothetical second project called *Beat-Bosses*:

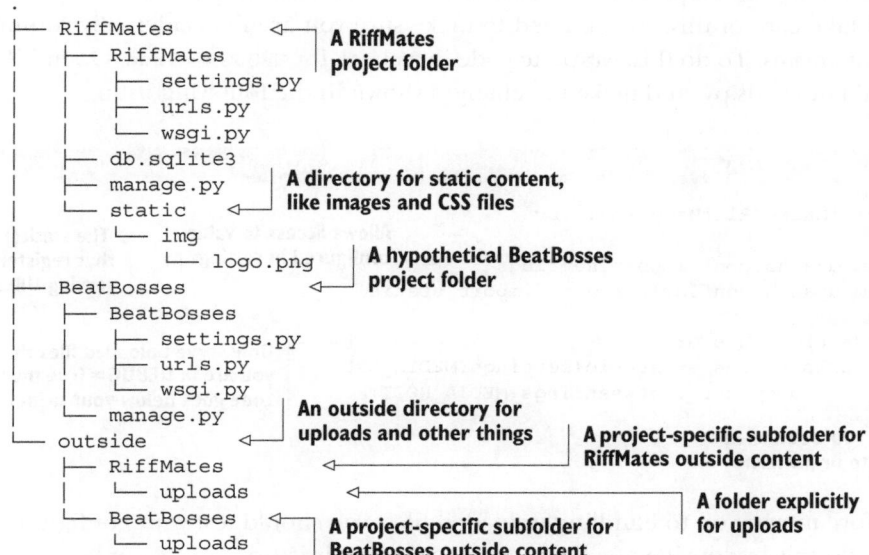

This file structure might be overkill for simpler projects, but I'm a fan of consistency and stick with the structure all the time. This means I don't have to think about it; I know exactly where everything is from project to project. Go ahead and create the necessary directories on your system.

Once you've got the directories in place, it is time to tell Django where they are. There are two configuration items you'll need: MEDIA_URL and MEDIA_ROOT. The first defines the base URL used to serve uploaded files—by convention, this is /media/. The second is the base file path of those files on your server. Add the following to your RiffMates/RiffMates/settings.py file:

BASE_DIR.parent is the parent of the project directory. Everything after the / is the folder for RiffMates uploads.

```
# RiffMates/RiffMates/settings.py
...
MEDIA_ROOT = BASE_DIR.parent / 'outside/RiffMates/uploads'
MEDIA_URL = '/media/'
```
The base URL for serving uploads

The Django development server does not serve these files by default, but you can add the capability. In the previous section, you learned about static files and how the development server can serve them. Under the covers, the dev server does this using the static() function. Yep, for those keeping track, that's a third thing with the same name. The function takes two arguments: the base URL to serve from and the location of the files; it returns a URL configuration that can be used to serve files in DEBUG mode. Although your uploaded files aren't static, in development, you can pretend they are and essentially add them to the list of things the development server serves up.

This is a little bit "hackish," but the only alternative is to run your own web server when doing development, and that's a lot of extra work. In production, the web server will take care of this, so you need to make sure you aren't accidentally running both mechanisms. To do this, wrap the code in a check for DEBUG == True. Open RiffMates/ RiffMates/urls.py, and make the changes shown in the following listing.

Listing 7.15   Serve uploaded files as if they were static files, in development mode

```
# RiffMates/RiffMates/urls.py
...
from django.conf import settings
from django.conf.urls.static import static
...
if settings.DEBUG:
    urlpatterns += static(settings.MEDIA_URL,
        document_root=settings.MEDIA_ROOT)
```

Allows access to values configured in settings.py

The static() function that registers static serving URLs

Only serve uploaded files this way if you are in DEBUG=True mode. This code goes below your urlpatterns list.

Add the new route returned by static() into urlpatterns.

Before moving on to handling uploaded files, you should test your configuration. You can do this by copying any file into the uploads directory. For example, copy the RiffMates logo into ../outside/RiffMates/uploads. With the development server running, visit http://localhost:8000/media/logo.png to verify your upload directory is working. Don't forget to remove the file when you're done.

7.4.2   *Storing and referencing uploaded files*

To allow a user to upload a file, you need a form and a view. Before doing that, though, let's start by creating the associated model changes and using the Django Admin to verify that it works.

You store a reference to an uploaded file in the database using either a FileField or an ImageField. Both hold a path to the file on the server, while the ImageField also validates that the uploaded file is an image. The ImageField uses the Pillow library to process the uploaded file, so a valid image is any format that Pillow handles. This includes the most common bitmap based image formats found on the web, including GIF, JPG, PNG, and WebP. Note that Pillow does not support vector-based image formats—SVG files cannot be stored in an ImageField. If you're playing with SVG files, you'll have to use the more generic FileField instead.

In chapter 4, you added the Venue model to store information about the clubs hosting bands. At the moment, the venue listing page only has the names of the venues; let's extend that, so each venue can have a description and an optional image. The first step in this direction is to add fields to the Venue model object: a TextField for the description and an `ImageField` for the picture. The following listing contains the new fields to be added inside the `Venue` model within RiffMates/bands/models.py.

Listing 7.16   Adding description and picture fields to the `Venue` model

```
# RiffMates/bands/models.py
...
class Venue(models.Model):
    name = models.CharField(max_length=20)
    description = models.TextField(blank=True)          ⟵   A new description field,
    picture = models.ImageField(blank=True, null=True)  ⟵   which can be empty in the
    ...                                                      Django Admin (blank=True)

                                                            A new picture field,
                                                            which can be NULL in
                                                            the database and empty
                                                            in the Django Admin
```

These changes impact the database: two new columns need to be added to the `Venue` model's corresponding table. Run the `makemigrations` and `migrate` management commands to update the database.

NOTE   If you forgot to install Pillow, don't worry. Django will remind you when you attempt to make a migration that has an `ImageField`.

Once that's done, you're set to go, since you've already got an Admin class for the Venue. Run the development server, go to the Django Admin, and edit a Venue. You'll now get `description` and `picture` fields, like in figure 7.8.

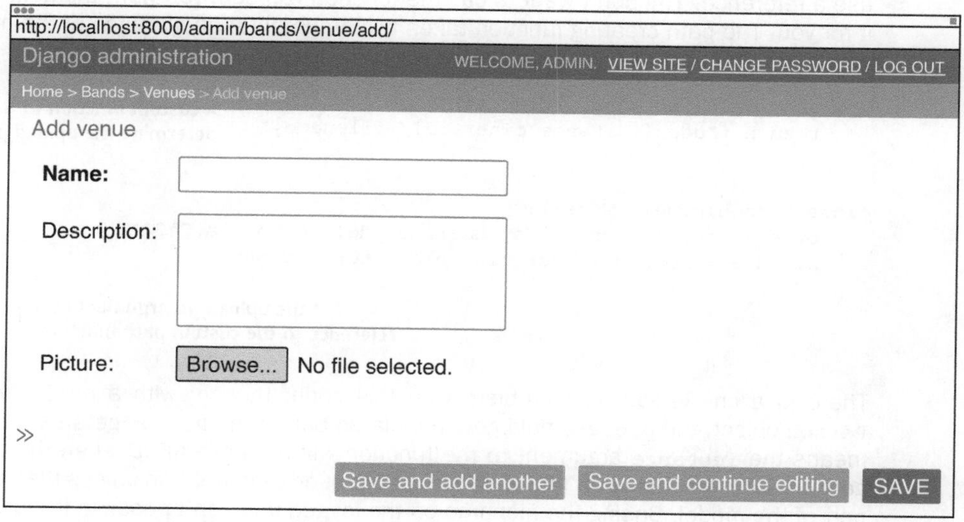

Figure 7.8   Django Admin screen with a file upload field

Edit the venue, add a description, upload an image, and save the changes. If you check out your uploads directory, you'll find the image you uploaded. Wait a second—what if you upload another file with the same name? What happens? Django takes care of that for you: when it saves a file to the uploads folder, it checks for naming conflicts, renaming the file with a random ending when necessary. It even makes sure the resulting filename is shorter than the maximum allowed by the field.

> **NOTE** By default, `FileField` and `ImageField` use a 100-character varchar to store your filename. You can change this with the `max_length` argument, similarly to `CharField`.

Dynamically changing the upload directory

Both the `FileField` and `ImageField` have an optional argument called `upload_to`, which you can use to alter the name of the directory a file gets uploaded into. This argument supports the string notation of the `strftime()` function, allowing you to set the upload directory based on the current date, as shown in the following example:

```
class Person(models.Model):
    picture = models.ImageField(upload_to="%Y/%m/%d/")
```

The upload is always relative to the `MEDIA_ROOT` value. Using a date stamp can make your upload directory cleaner, with fewer files in the root.

Instead of using a string, `upload_to` also supports calling a function. You pass a reference to the function, which the field then invokes when it needs to create a path. Your code is responsible for providing the path for the uploaded file. Remember to use a reference. You don't want to call the function yourself; you want the field to do it for you. The path creating function takes two arguments: an instance of the model object and the name of the file being saved.

```
def user_path(instance, filename):          ◁———  A custom function to
    return f"user{instance.owner.id}/{filename}"     determine the upload path
```

```
class Person(models.Model):
    owner = models.ForeignKey(user, on_delete=models.CASCADE)
    picture = models.ImageField(upload_to=user_path)      ◁———┐
```

Set the upload_to argument to a
reference to the custom path function.

There is a chicken-and-egg problem with this code, though: with a newly created `Person` object, the `picture` field gets populated before the `Person` gets saved. This means the `instance` argument to the function will not have an ID when the object gets created. You also don't have access to the user's information unless that is also part of the model. Basing the filename on the logged user isn't possible through this mechanism, unless that information is stored in the model.

7.4.3   File upload forms and views

You've added an `ImageField` to the `Venue` model and, through the Django Admin, have uploaded a picture. The Django Admin is for, well, admins, so to create a self-service version of this, you need a new view. Since the data getting filled in is for a model, it makes sense to use a `ModelForm`. The `Venue` object is in the `bands` app, which means you'll need a new file: RiffMates/bands/forms.py. Inside this file, add the code in the following listing, which uses the `modelform_factory` shortcut to quickly build a form based on the `Venue` model.

Listing 7.17   Create a form for a `Venue` using `modelform_factory`

```
# RiffMates/bands/forms.py
from django import forms
from bands.models import Venue

VenueForm = forms.modelform_factory(Venue,
    fields=["name", "description", "picture"])
```

The factory function returns a ModelForm class and takes the associated model class as well as a list of fields as arguments.

The VenueForm contains name, description, and picture fields.

Aren't `ModelForm`s wonderful? Two lines of code (one if you aren't old school like me and insist files are restricted to 80 columns), and you're ready to take data from the user and populate your model.

The view for this form is very similar to the one you wrote to input a classified ad, but in this case the security check is a little different. Recall that users get associated with venues through the `venues_controlled` many-to-many relationship inside the `UserProfile` object. To keep things simple, anyone who is logged in can add a `Venue`, but only those with a corresponding `venues_controlled` entry can edit one.

Like with the classified view, this view does double duty: a venue ID of 0 results in adding a new venue, while a larger venue ID performs an edit. The code after the security check is almost identical. The HTTP mechanism for uploading files is slightly different from regular form fields, and the associated file isn't in the `request.POST` attribute but in `request.FILES`. The form constructor knows how to handle this, and you simply pass it in with the other arguments.

This time around, you don't need to modify the contents of `VenueForm` before creating the associated `Venue` object, so the form's `save()` method no longer needs the `commit=False` argument. One last step is to add the newly created `Venue` object to the user's `venues_controlled` relationship. The `add()` method on a `ManyToManyField` is smart enough to disallow adding something twice, so you don't even have to check if the relationship already exists.

Add the code in the following listing to RiffMates/bands/views.py, and then afterward, register a route for both adding and editing a venue. You can register the route twice with two different names: the first for adding a venue using the default value for `venue_id` (and thus not requiring a URL argument) and the second for editing the venue (which does require a URL argument). Don't forget to name the routes, as you'll want to link to them later.

Listing 7.18   The self-service view for adding and editing venues

```
# RiffMates/bands/views.py
...
from django.shortcuts import render, get_object_or_404, redirect

from bands.models import Musician, Band, Venue, Room
from bands.forms import VenueForm
...
@login_required
def edit_venue(request, venue_id=0):
    if venue_id != 0:
        venue = get_object_or_404(Venue,
            id=venue_id)
        if not request.user.userprofile.venues_controlled.filter(
                id=venue_id).exists():
            raise Http404("Can only edit controlled venues")

    if request.method == 'GET':
        if venue_id == 0:
            form = VenueForm()
        else:
            form = VenueForm(instance=venue)

    else: # POST
        if venue_id == 0:
            venue = Venue.objects.create()

        form = VenueForm(request.POST, request.FILES,
            instance=venue)

        if form.is_valid():
            venue = form.save()

            # Add the venue to the user's profile
            request.user.userprofile.venues_controlled.add(venue)
            return redirect("venues")

    # Was a GET, or Form was not valid
    data = {
        "form": form,
    }

    return render(request, "edit_venue.html", data)
```

- This is the edit case. → `def edit_venue(request, venue_id=0):`
- Check if the requested Venue object is part of the user's venues_controlled relationship. If not, raise a 404 error.
- Fetch the requested Venue object.
- The GET portion is the same as other form processing views.
- In the add case, create a new, empty Venue object to associate with the form.
- Include request.FILES in form creation to get both the form's fields and the uploaded file.
- Add the (possibly new) venue to the user's venues_controlled relationship. The .add() method handles the case where the relationship already exists.

Of course, you'll need a template to go with this view. Listing 7.19 shows the contents of the new RiffMates/templates/edit_venue.html file. This file is almost identical to the classified ad form-handling template, with one exception. To handle files, the `<form>` tag needs an additional argument: `enctype="multipart/form-data"`. Without this, the upload won't work properly, and this can be a painful bug to find.

Listing 7.19 Template for adding or editing a `Venue` object

```
<!-- RiffMates/templates/edit_venue.html -->
{% extends "base.html" %}

{% block content %}
<h1>Venue Details</h1>

<form enctype="multipart/form-data" method="post">
  {% csrf_token %}
  {{form.as_p}}
  <button class="btn btn-dark" type="submit">Save</button>
</form>

{% endblock content %}
```

> **Make sure to include the enctype argument, or file uploads won't work.**

You're more or less there, but for ease of use, it would be nice to provide links for the user. Inserting an Add Venue link in the venues.html template is just a single line of HTML. Providing Edit links that only show up if the user is associated with the venue means a bit more work.

Inside the existing `venues()` view, you can annotate each `Venue` object with an attribute indicating whether the user is associated with the venue. This might seem a little weird, as you're inserting an attribute on a model, but models are just objects, and Python lets you add attributes to objects dynamically. This has no effect on the database, and the lifetime of the attribute is only the lifetime of the view. Inside Riff-Mates/bands/views.py, modify the `venues()` view to include the code in the following listing.

Listing 7.20 Adding info about user's logged-in status to `Venue`

```
# RiffMates/bands/views.py
...

def venues(request):
    all_venues = Venue.objects.all().order_by("name")
    for venue in all_venues:
        # Mark the venue as "controlled" if the logged in user is
        # associated with the venue
        profile = request.user.userprofile
        venue.controlled = \
            profile.venues_controlled.filter(\
            id=venue.id).exists()
        ...
```

> **A previously existing line in the view querying all Venue objects**

> **New code that loops through each of the Venue objects to add a new attribute**

> **A quick reference to shorten the following line**

> **Even with the previous reference, this line is unwieldy. The .exists() query returns True if the Venue object is in the user's venues_controlled relationship.**

Inside the template, the short-lived `.controlled` attribute is used to determine whether an edit link should be shown. The changes to the venue listing template are shown in the following listing. Open and edit RiffMates/templates/venues.html.

Listing 7.21   Modifications to the venue listing template

```
<!-- RiffMates/templates/venues.html -->
<!-- ... -->

  <h1>Venues</h1>
                                              If the user is logged in, provide
  {% if user.is_authenticated %}   ◁──┘  a link for adding a venue.
    <a href="{% url 'add_venue' %}">Add Venue</a>   ◁──   Reference the named route
  {% endif %}                                              for adding a venue, which
                                                           points at the edit_venue()
<!-- ... -->                                               function but uses the default
    <li>                                                   argument of venue_id=0.
      <b> {{venue.name}} </b>
      {% if venue.controlled %}   ◁──   If the venue is controlled by
        <br/>                            the user, provide an Edit link.
             
        <a href="{% url 'edit_venue' venue.id %}"
          >Edit</a>   ◁──   Reference the named
        <br/>              route for editing a venue.
      {% endif %}
      {% if venue.picture %}   ◁──   If the venue has
        <br/>                         a picture, display it.
             
        <img src="{{venue.picture.url}}" height="50"/>
        <br/>                          If the venue has a
      {% endif %}                       description, display it.
      {% if venue.description %}   ◁──┘
        <br/>
        <i>       {{venue.description }} </i>
        <br/>
      {% endif %}
      Rooms:
    </li>
```

You're all set. Fire up your development server, and go to the venue listing page. If you're logged in, you'll now have the Add Venue link. Use that link to add a new venue, including a picture and a description. Log in as someone else, and do it again. On the Venue listing page, you should only see Edit Venue for those venues associated with the current user account. Test out the editing feature by clicking the link and changing the form.

Bug alert!

The changes to `venues()` in chapter 7 work if you are logged in. If you're not logged in, the code crashes. The view accesses the user's associated profile object, which only exists for authenticated users. Recall that Django refers to unauthenticated users as anonymous. These users are represented in a `request` object with an instance of an `AnonymousUser` class, whose `.is_authenticated` attribute is always `False`. This class has no related `UserProfile` object, and attempting to fetch one will result in an error.

To fix `venues()`, you need to make a decision. If you don't want anonymous users to be able to access the venue information, you can wrap the view with

@login_required (see chapter 6 for more on this). Alternatively, if you want the venue information to be public, the view code needs to properly handle the possible lack of an associated profile. The following listing contains code for this latter approach.

Listing 7.22 A venues() view that handles unauthenticated visitors

```
# RiffMates/bands/views.py
...

def venues(request):
    all_venues = Venue.objects.all().order_by("name")
    profile = getattr(request.user, "userprofile", None)
    if profile:
        for venue in all_venues:
            # Mark the venue is "controlled" if the logged in user is
            # associated with the venue
            venue.controlled = profile.venues_controlled.filter(\
                id=venue.id).exists()
    else:
        # Anonymous user, can't be associated with the venue
        for venue in all_venues:
            venue.controlled = False
    ...
```

Don't assume that the .user attribute has a profile; use None if the user is anonymous.

If there is a profile, loop through the venues like before.

If there isn't a profile, the user can't control any venues. Set all attributes to False.

How paranoid should you be with files?

A lot happens behind the scenes for an image file to be uploaded and then presented to a user. A form gets used to submit a file, the file is stored on the server, and then the server serves the file in other pages. In the case of an image, the web server will set an appropriate mimetype for the file, giving the browser a hint about what is being served. Depending on the browser, that MIME type may be redundant, and anything pointed to by an `<img>` tag might get treated as an image.

There is a lot of *depending on* and *might* in that previous paragraph. A web server's features and configuration determine how it decides on a file's MIME type. By default, most web servers use the file extension as a hint. In theory, a user can upload a valid image file without the right file extension or with none at all. Django and your web browser try to help with this, but there are ways around it: never trust your users! In the case of an image file, the worst case is the image isn't interpreted as an image. Instead, you'll get the broken-picture symbol on the page. You could put extra code in the view handling the upload to ensure this doesn't happen, but this is a thin edge case with little consequences, so it likely isn't worth the extra work.

If you're allowing the user to upload files other than images, you might want to be more careful. A lot depends (there is that word again) on what you're doing with the uploaded file. If your service simply allows the file to be downloaded again, you may be able to get away with doing nothing with it. If you're doing data processing on the file, be very careful to check the file is what you expect. Good practice is to use third-party parsing libraries: someone else who is an expert in the file format is more likely to understand the corner cases than you are.

7.4.4 *Restricted file downloads*

So far, all the work with uploaded files has resulted in files that can be downloaded without any restrictions. Everything at /media/ (or wherever your MEDIA_URL points) is available to all users, even those that aren't logged in. If you need to restrict downloads to logged-in users or wish to write complex logic for which users can see which files, you have two choices: a custom view or a hand-off view.

In either case, the uploaded file does not get stored in MEDIA_ROOT but somewhere else. Only Django and the web server have access to these kinds of files, and they aren't served under /media/, giving you control over who can access them.

The custom view choice is quick, dirty, and goes against recommended best practices. FileResponse, in django.http, works similar to HttpReponse, but it allows you to return a binary file object. It has both a streaming mode to return files inline (90s-style custom-GIF visitor counters anyone?) and an attachment mode to prompt the user for a download.

Django isn't optimized for dealing with binary files, and the quick-and-dirty choice doesn't handle caching or other optimization goodness unless you code it yourself. Even with fine-tuning, you're unlikely to be able to beat the performance of a web server.

The second choice is to take advantage of web server features. The two most popular web servers, Apache and Nginx, both support HTTP headers allowing you to hand off a download request. In this case, you still write a view, but the view returns HTTP headers that point to the file. With the right header in place, the web server does the rest of the work for you. The challenge with this approach is the headers are nonstandard and are different on different web servers. If you want to search the web for examples of how to do this, the header for Apache is X-Sendfile and the header for Nginx is X-Accel-Redirect.

Alternatively, you can skip all the hard work and use a third-party library. Both django-private-storage and django-sendfile2 provide tools for serving uploaded files from a restricted folder.

7.5 *Exercises*

1 Modify the musician() view to display an optional description and bio-pic. Add an edit_musician() view, so users can self-serve the creation and editing of their musician profiles. Insert an Add Musician Profile link to the home page and an Edit link to the musician details page if the logged-in user is the owner. Allow staff members to edit Musician objects as well.

2 Modify the seeking_ad() view so that staff and administrators are allowed to edit an ad. Don't forget to change list_ads.html, so the edit links show up as well.

Summary

- A Django Form class helps you process HTML <form> submissions, using form field attributes to describe each input.

- Form fields are rendered by widgets, with each field having a default widget that renders the corresponding HTML.

- The choice of a widget for a field can be overridden, like in the case of a `forms.CharField` using a `forms.Textarea` widget to be rendered as a `<textarea>` instead of an `<input>`.

- The `request.method` attribute contains the HTTP method.

- A view that handles forms typically has two modes: GET for displaying the form and POST for handling the submission.

- A `Form` object can be filled with the user's submitted data by passing in the `request.POST` value.

- The `django.core.mail` module contains the `send_mail()` function, which can be used to send email using the currently configured email backend.

- When processing a form, the `.is_valid()` method must be called. This method returns `True` if the data is compliant with the form's definition.

- When `.is_valid()` returns `True`, a dictionary called `.cleaned_data` is defined on the form containing the user's submitted input. The keys in the dictionary correspond to the names of the fields.

- A cross-site request forgery is an attack that tricks the user into doing something on your site they didn't intend. The `{% csrf_token %}` tag adds a special key to every form to help prevent this kind of attack.

- The `.clean()` method on a `Model` class can be used to do validation. It is typically used when there are interdependencies between the fields and field-level validation arguments are insufficient.

- The `.clean()` method is not called automatically when an ORM class is saved.

- The undocumented `Truncator` class is a utility that returns a shortened version of a string, truncating on word boundaries.

- The `ModelForm` class provides a shortcut for creating forms that correspond to Model definitions.

- A `ModelForm` uses an inner `Meta` class to indicate the configuration of the form, including which model is related and which fields on the model participate in the form.

- The `.save()` method on a `ModelForm` saves the corresponding model object. This method can be called with `commit=False` to return an unsaved copy of the model instance if you need to perform actions before invoking save.

- The `instance` argument to a `ModelForm` allows you to prepopulate the field contents based on a model object.

- You can register multiple routes against the same view. This is handy if your view uses default arguments. A common pattern is to have a view for editing be able to create new objects as well using an ID of zero to indicate creation.

- Web pages reference files that aren't produced by views, such as images, CSS, and JavaScript. These are known as static files.

- Static files should be served by the web server rather than Django, but Django provides utilities for managing them and their URLs. The `{% static %}` tag dereferences the URL for a static file.

- Django has the ability to deal with uploaded files, storing them in a directory defined by the `MEDIA_ROOT` configuration value.

- The `FileField` and `ImageField` ORM fields store references to a file on the disk.

- A model with file fields can be used with a `ModelForm`, producing an upload button in the HTML.

- The `<form>` tag for a form including file uploads must include the `enctype ="multipart/form-data"` argument.

- When using a `ModelForm` with uploaded files, the `request.FILES` argument needs to be passed in addition to `request.POST`.

Testing your project

This chapter covers

- Reasons to write automated tests
- Writing and running unit tests in Django
- Authenticating a user during a test
- Posting data and uploading files during a test

How do you know that a change in your code isn't going to break existing functionality? Automated testing is the answer. This chapter shows you how to write tests to check that your project continues to work even while you're making changes and adding features.

8.1 Automated testing

If you've been coding along as you've been reading, you have written more than 20 views and likely have over a thousand lines of code. It doesn't take long before manually testing everything in your project becomes a time-consuming endeavor. This becomes more complicated with a multiuser website: you need to test some views several times, using different credentials to ensure the right people can get where they're supposed to and the wrong people can't.

This section's header gives away the solution: automated testing. You write code to test your code. Learning how to write good, automated tests is a skill in itself and an important part of working as a developer. It isn't uncommon to find a 1:1 relationship between lines of code and lines of tests in larger organizations with a high degree of automation. That means you'll be spending half your time writing tests.

8.1.1   *The scope of tests*

Let's touch on a bit of background before diving into how Python and Django structure automated tests. Automated testing is usually broken down into categories. The category definitions are a little loose, and you'll find different developers split them at different points. Figure 8.1 shows a four-category version of the testing pyramid.

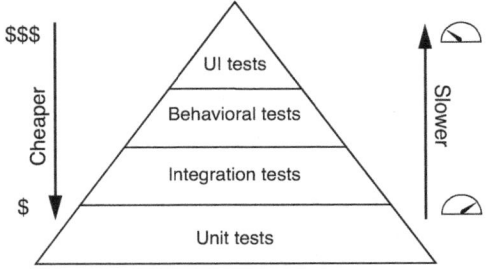

Figure 8.1   Hierarchy of testing categories

If you search around on the internet, you'll find several versions of this diagram, ranging from three levels to seven levels and with different names for each category. The most well-defined category is the one on the bottom: unit tests. A *unit test* is a test performed on a single component of software. This can be vague though, as two people might not agree on the definition of "component." Typically, a unit test is at the level of a single function.

You want your unit level to be as independent of other parts of your software as possible and with as few side effects as possible. If a series of tests gets done at the unit level, it shouldn't matter what order they run in; you should always get the same result. This can get tricky because writing to the database is a side effect. I'll cover this in more detail later in the chapter.

The next level up in the testing pyramid is *integration tests*. These are tests that operate over several units. The purpose here is to ensure that when the different pieces work together, you still get the desired result. This level is sometimes also known as *system tests*. In software, that has a graphical component: the integration typically is still only at the business logic or server level, not the GUI.

Behavioral tests are those that map to the requirements. You, or someone on your software team, has decided that a certain feature should exist and perform some action. A behavioral test ensures the feature is working as designed. These are also known as *acceptance tests*, named after Acceptance Criteria, which are part of a User Story, a common way of writing requirements in Agile development methodologies. This category of testing has become quite popular, as there are frameworks out there which specifically test at this level. One of the most popular is Cucumber (https://cucumber.io/).

At the top level of the pyramid, where you might be expecting an ominous looking eye, are *UI tests*. The name more or less gives it away: these are tests on the user interface. The line between this and behavioral tests can be rather blurry, as it is often hard to prove a feature works without interacting with the UI. At this level, you typically need custom tools that act like a user, interacting with the UI and clicking things.

The further up the test pyramid you travel, the slower and more expensive your tests become. Consider a web page where the user inputs their address and sees their cost of shipping calculated. To properly test this, you need all the variations on types of address (houses, apartments, rural routes, PO boxes, etc.) and all the variations on shipping zones. This could result in hundreds of test executions. If you test at the UI level, every single test execution requires the information to be entered in the browser; the data sent to the server; the server to do work; a look-up to happen in the database; the server to formulate a result; and, finally, the result to be displayed in the browser. This round trip is slow and requires you to run both a server and a browser. The vast majority of the logic in this example is in the backend, where the shipping cost gets calculated. By moving the testing down to the unit level, you skip most of the steps, making the test run significantly faster.

When you design tests, you want to appropriately select the level of testing. The vast majority of your tests should be at the unit test level. UI tests should focus on UI features, rather than using the UI as the testing interface. As much as possible, push your tests as far down the pyramid as they can go.

Speedy tests are important. If you test once a week, and something fails, it is hard to remember what you did to the code a week ago that caused the problem. If you test on every check-in of your code, possibly several times a day, you'll be more likely to remember what you were doing that caused the failure. Testing more frequently is good; slow tests make you not want to do this. One reason for using a hierarchy of test categories is to set different test frequencies at different levels. Unit tests are small and fast and done at every check-in. Integration tests might get done once or twice a day, and behavioral and UI tests could be part of a nightly process.

Most of this chapter focuses on unit tests. Behavioral and UI tests require additional tools that are beyond the scope of this book. The line between unit tests and integration test is fuzzy in the Django world, as bigger views likely call several functions. A common unit-test point for Django code is the view itself.

Test-driven development and behavior-driven development

Two testing philosophies have become quite popular in the software world: *test-driven development* (TDD) and *behavior-driven development* (BDD). These ideas are based more around when you write your tests than how. TDD and BDD state that you should write your tests before you write your code. The idea is to decide on a function's interface, write the tests for it, and then write the function. When all a function's tests pass, you are done writing the function. BDD is similar to TDD, with the focus being at the behavioral level, writing requirements-level tests rather than function-level tests.

I am a huge proponent of automated testing and think it is a really important part of modern development. Software teams should set standards for their testing and not

(continued)

accept code as being complete unless there are enough tests to go with it. I'm indifferent regarding whether the tests should be written first. You could say I'm a fan of TDD and BDD but a little flexible about the implementation.

8.1.2 *Automated testing in Python*

The Python standard library includes the `unittest` module to help you write automated tests. (You can write other categories of tests using it as well— don't let the name confuse you). The library is based on four concepts:

- Fixtures
- Test cases
- Test suites
- Test runners

A *fixture*, in this case, is the preparation needed to run a test and any clean-up needed when the test is finished. This terminology overlaps Django's use of the word *fixture*, which is data you can load into the database. The ideas are related, though: most of the time, test preparation is about getting your data set up.

A *test case* is the code that runs to perform your test. In the `unittest` module, these are defined as classes. A *test suite* is a collection of test cases, and a *test runner* is a program that determines which tests to run. Python's default test runner looks for files whose name begins with "test_" and runs any test cases found inside.

Django builds on top of the Python `unittest` module. It uses the same structure but provides its own test class and runner. Django's runner knows how to deal with the Django ORM, and each time you run a set of tests, it creates a new copy of a database, which you can populate for your tests. Django also subclasses the test case class providing additional methods that specialize in testing Django views.

Other test frameworks

There are several third-party libraries that are alternatives to Python's `unittest` framework. Two of the most popular are pytest (https://docs.pytest.org) and nose (https://nose.readthedocs.io/). Both of these have plugins for interacting with Django. If you're already a user of either of these, you can write your Django tests in your favorite flavor, if you wish.

8.2 *Your first Django test*

Django thinks tests are important. You can tell, as it automatically creates a tests.py file when a new app gets added. The skeleton version of this file contains a single import: the `django.test.TestCase` class. This class inherits from the Python class of the same name. To write a unit test, you inherit from this class and add methods with names that begin with "test_".

Way back in chapter 2 (it seems like so long ago, before we were friends), you wrote your first view: `credits()`. It is only appropriate that your first test should be for that very same view. The purpose of your test is to exercise the view and validate the results returned from it. Figure 8.2 shows the interleaved execution of a test for `credits()` and the view itself.

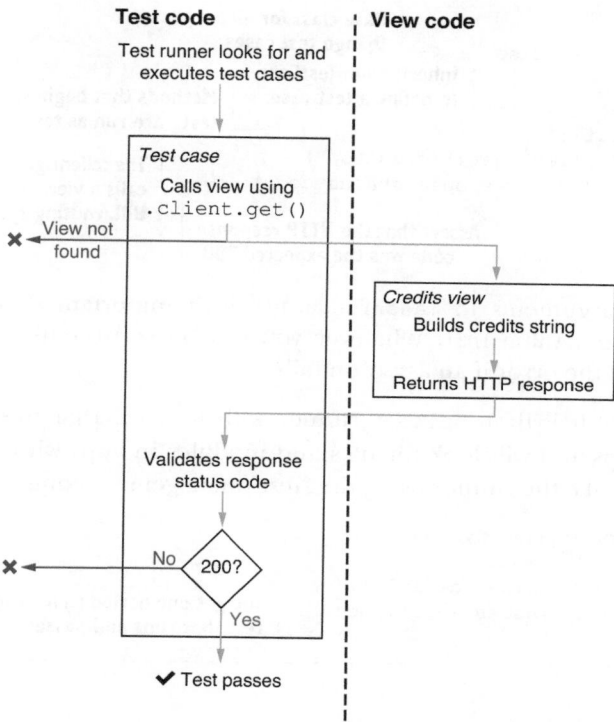

Test code

Test runner looks for and
executes test cases

Test case

Calls view using
`.client.get()`

✖ ◄─ View not
found

Credits view

Builds credits string

Returns HTTP response

Validates response
status code

No ◄─── 200?

Yes

✔ Test passes

View code

Figure 8.2   Testing the
`credits()` **view**

As the `credits()` view and its corresponding test case are both in the home app, a decent name for the test case is `TestHome`. Inside this class, you write a method called `.test_credits()`, which is the code that tests the view.

Django's version of the `TestCase` class includes an object called `.client` that you use to interact with the website. The `.client` object has both `.get()` and `.post()` methods, emulating a browser interaction. Note that it only emulates it, so the template gets rendered, but no browser is involved. If there is JavaScript on the page, it doesn't get run. Using `.client.get()` is almost like calling a view function directly, except it does it through the URL routing system.

Once you've invoked a view, you want to make sure it works properly. For a simple view, like `credits()`, there isn't much to test besides getting back the right HTTP status code. In this case, the expected value is `200`, the HTTP response code for "all good." To ensure you received this value, you call `.assertEqual()`. This is one of many assertion methods in the Python `TestCase` class that raises an exception if its stated condition isn't met. For a full list of the assertion methods, see https://mng.bz/PZZ2. The following listing shows the new contents of home/tests.py. Update your own copy to match.

Listing 8.1 A test case for the `credits()` view

```
# home/tests.py
from django.test import TestCase          ←┘ Base class for all
                                              Django test cases
                                           Inherit from TestCase
class TestHome(TestCase):               ←┘ to define a test case.     Methods that begin with
    def test_credits(self):                                         ←┘ test_ are run as tests.
        response = self.client.get("/credits/")            ←┐
        self.assertEqual(200, response.status_code)    ←┐    The .client.get() method
                                                          calls a view through the
                         Assert that the HTTP response    URL routing system.
                         code was the expected 200.
```

> **NOTE** The order of arguments to `.assertEqual()` isn't important, but I always put the expected value first. Whatever you do, be consistent—this makes it easier to read the error if an assertion fails.

Django extends the default Python `unitest` runner with its own. Django's runner knows about Django apps and will look for files and modules in apps whose names begin with "test". You invoke the runner using the "test" management command:

```
(venv) RiffMates$ python manage.py test
Found 1 test(s).
Creating test database for alias 'default'...
System check identified no issues (0 silenced).      ┐ You get one period (.) for each
.                                                  ←┘ test that runs and passes.
----------------------------------------------------------------------
Ran 1 test in 0.003s

OK
Destroying test database for alias 'default'...
```

The output from the `test` command tells you how many tests got run and alerts you if any failed. To see what failure looks like, change the `200` to `42` in the `.assertEqual()` call, and then run the test again. The results are as follows:

```
(venv) RiffMates$ python manage.py test
Found 1 test(s).                                     ┐ A failed assertion gets shown as F
Creating test database for alias 'default'...          instead of a period (.). An E gets
System check identified no issues (0 silenced).        shown if your code raises an
F                                                  ←┘ exception not caused by an assertion.
======================================================================
FAIL: test_credits (home.tests.TestHome.test_credits)
----------------------------------------------------------------------
Traceback (most recent call last):
  File "RiffMates/home/tests.py", line 8, in test_credits
    self.assertEqual(42, response.status_code)
```

```
AssertionError: 42 != 200

-------------------------------------------------------------------
Ran 1 test in 0.005s

FAILED (failures=1)
Destroying test database for alias 'default'...
```

Test assert methods raise exceptions if their conditions don't get met. In this case, .assertEqual() has decided that 42 != 200. Who am I to argue? Since assertions raise exceptions, you get a stack trace indicating where the failure happened. At the bottom of the output, you still see how many tests got run but also how many tests failed.

> **Django likes trailing slashes**
>
> Django expects a URL to end with a slash (/). If a URL does not end in a slash, Django issues a permanent redirect (HTTP 301) with the correction. Users don't notice this, as the browser takes care of it. If you forget the trailing slash in your test code, you'll get the wrong status code in response. Make sure all your URLs in your test suite end in a slash, and you'll be fine.

That's your first unit test for a view. One down, a little over 20 more to go. Don't forget to change 42 back to 200.

8.3   *Testing with the database*

The credits() view is pretty much the simplest view you can write. Testing more complex views requires a bit more effort, especially if you're interacting with the ORM. The Django test runner creates a new test database each time it starts up. The good news is you don't have to worry about your tests modifying your site's data. The bad news is your test environment has an empty database.

When run, each test gets wrapped in a database transaction, which is a way of atomically grouping a series of actions. When the test method completes, Django rolls back the transaction, undoing anything you did in the test method. This might sound like a problem, but it is actually a good thing: the tests can be run in any order, each starting with the exact same state.

You likely want some things in your database to use with the tests, and fortunately, you don't have to do this for every single test call. The Python unittest class has a method called .setUp() that gets invoked just before each test gets run. This is the perfect place to create your ORM objects as class members.

Let's write a test for the musician() view in the Bands app. You'll recall this view displays details for the Musician Model passed in as an argument. Figure 8.3 shows the setting up and testing of this view.

In the diagram, you see the first thing the test needs to do is create a Musician object in the test database; it does this inside the .setUp() method, keeping it as an attribute of the test case. This makes your Musician object available in all tests. Next,

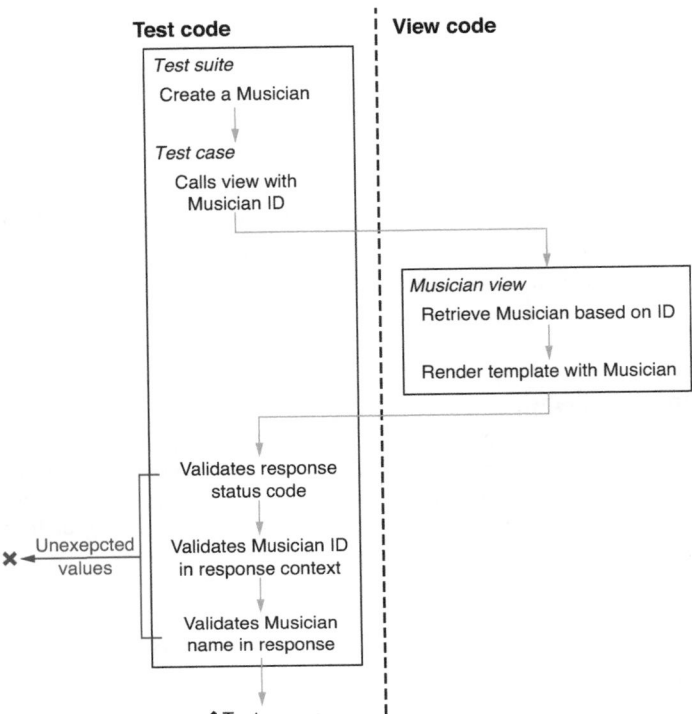

Figure 8.3   Testing the
`musician()` **view**

like with the `credits()` view, you visit the musician view using the `.client.get()` method. There are two schools of thought here: you can look the URL up, or you can hardcode it. Looking the URL up makes your test more bulletproof. Hardcoding it catches a problem if you've accidentally moved the URL route. I tend to hard code my URLs in my tests, but that means if I do want to move a URL, I have to make changes to all my tests.

The musician view takes a `Musician` ID, which is sent in through the URL. The view looks up the corresponding `Musician` object and then renders a template, displaying the musician information. To test this view, you want to validate the HTTP response code, check the `Musician` in the view is the correct one, and possibly verify some of the HTML. You already saw how to check the `200` status code in the `credits()` view test. The other two things get checked by examining the response object returned by `.client.get()`. It contains a couple useful attributes: `.context` is the context object passed to the template rendering engine, and `.content` contains the actual rendered response. You can assert that the `Musician` object in the view's context is the same as the one created by the test, and you can also check for values rendered in the HTML.

NOTE `response.content` is stored as a binary object, so you need to convert it to a string to do a comparison.

The following listing contains the test code for the musician view, including the database setup. Add the code to bands/tests.py to try the test out.

Listing 8.2 A test case for the musician view

```python
# bands/tests.py
from datetime import date
from django.test import TestCase
from bands.models import Musician

class TestBands(TestCase):
    def setUp(self):
        self.musician = Musician.objects.create(first_name="First",
            last_name="Last", birth=date(1900, 1, 1))

    def test_musician_view(self):
        url = f"/bands/musician/{self.musician.id}/"
        response = self.client.get(url)

        self.assertEqual(200, response.status_code)
        self.assertEqual(response.context['musician'].id,
            self.musician.id)
        self.assertIn(self.musician.first_name,
            str(response.content))
```

The .setUp() method is called at class creation and is typically used to create database entries.

Fetch the response for the musician view.

Validate that the musician in the view's context is the one in our test.

Validate that the musician's name shows up somewhere in the rendered HTML.

With your new test in place, use the test management command to execute it. I have a funny story for you. Ok, not funny "haha," more like funny "what's that smell." Writing this example test actually helped me find a bug. The exercise in chapter 7 adds features to the musician view that require use of the UserProfile object. This view doesn't require a user to be logged in, though, and the anonymous user doesn't have an associated UserProfile object. Writing this test caused my initial version of the view to crash, and I had to go back and put a check for the profile's existence in the code. See? Tests are important.

In addition to the .setUp() method, there is also a .setUpClass() class method. This gets called once when the TestClass is created. It may be more efficient to do your initial configuration there. If you're using the .setUpClass() method, it is important to remember two things: it must be wrapped with the @classmethod decorator, as it is a class method, and you must call the parent's method using super().setUpClass(), or you will get an error.

Going along with .setUp() and .setUpClass() are .tearDown() and .tearDownClass(). The first gets called each time a test method completes, and the second gets called when the class finishes. The same rules about the decorator and call to super() apply to .tearDownClass(). The tear-down methods are useful in Python to do things like database clean-up. As Django already does this for you, you won't find you need them as often when writing tests for Django code. The complete flow of creating a test class and running the setup and tear-down for each test is shown in figure 8.4.

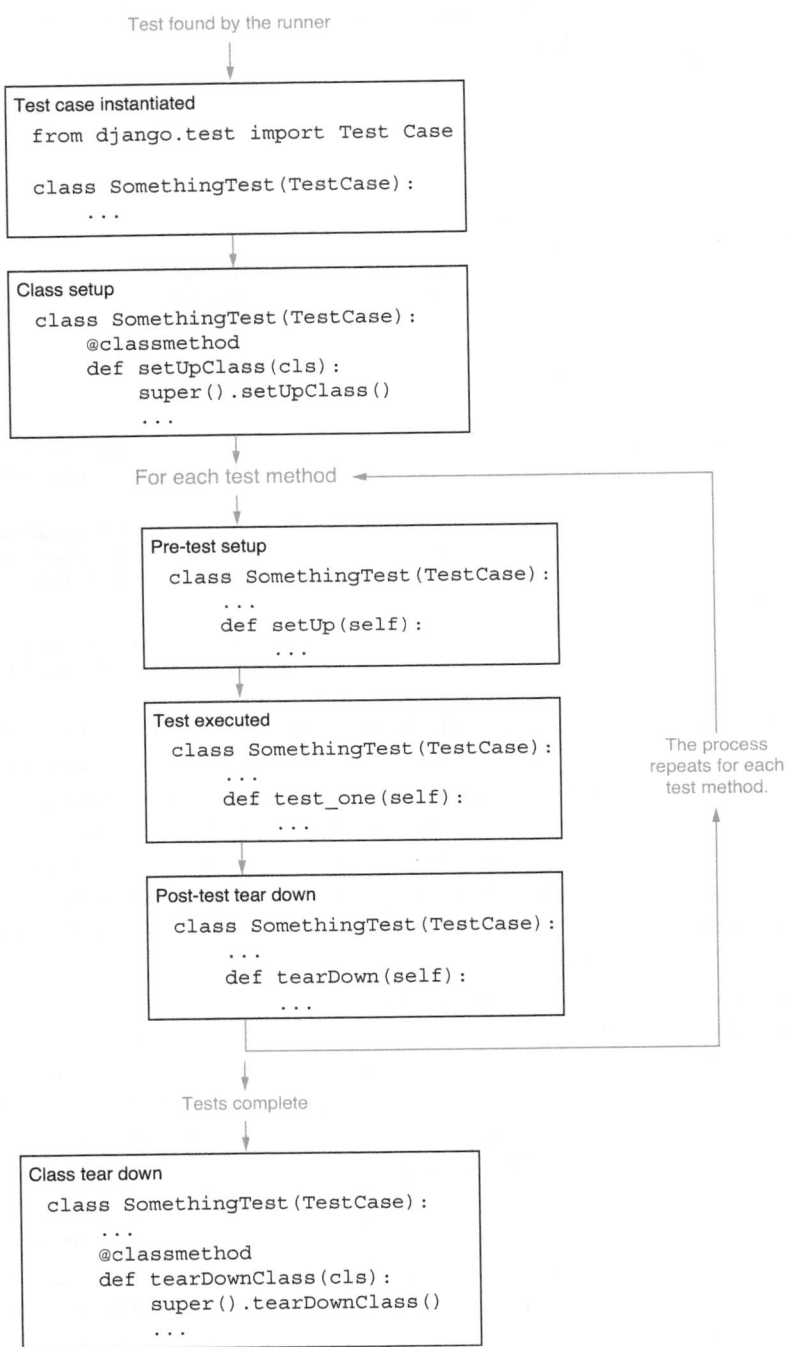

Figure 8.4   Order of method invocation of a `TestCase` class

> ### Using fixtures instead
>
> The Django `TestCase` class has an attribute named `fixtures` that takes a list of fixture filenames to load. You can use this instead of explicitly creating content. Fixture data gets loaded into the database once, at class creation time. Django will look for fixtures in your app directories as well as anywhere named in the `FIXTURE_DIRS` list in settings.py.
>
> I prefer not to use fixtures in my tests; explicitly creating the objects in the test feels clearer to me. I also don't like that there is no way of separating test fixtures from app fixtures and that it is easy to accidentally load your test data into the real database.

8.4 Expecting errors

You might be feeling pretty good about your test for the musician view, but you still haven't covered all possible scenarios. The view does a look-up of a `Musician` object by ID and is supposed to raise a `404` error if the `Musician` does not exist. You want to test that this code works as well. A good test ensures that negative cases get handled properly, instead of crashing the code.

Typically in a Python script, if an exception is raised, the program exits and a stack trace is displayed, unless the code catches the exception. The musician view raises an `Http404` error, but that doesn't exit the program because Django catches it. Django's error handling for this situation results in a `404` error page being presented to the user. A `404` error page sets the HTTP status code to `404`, hence the name.

Testing that a view raises an `Http404` error is a matter of validating that a status code of `404` is returned from the call. This is rather similar to checking a normal case, with a different expected return value. Listing 8.3 adds the new scenario to the test class, using an ID of `10` for the call, which doesn't exist in the database. Since a new test database is created each time you run your test suite, you know an ID of `10` doesn't exist as long as you have created fewer than 10 musicians in the test scenario. If you wanted to be really sure, you could query the ID of the last `Musician` (`Musician.objects.last().id`) and add `1` to its value, but I've simply hardcoded a bigger number instead.

Listing 8.3 Testing that an error gets handled properly

```
# bands/tests.py
...

class TestBands(TestCase):
    ...
    def test_musician_404(self):
        url = "/bands/musician/10/"          Look up the non-existent
        response = self.client.get(url)       musician with ID 10.
        self.assertEqual(404, response.status_code)    Check for the 404
                                                       response code.
```

Although Django wraps a `404` exception, there are scenarios in which you want to test uncaught exceptions. You likely won't need to do this in a view, but you may want to when testing a utility function. To test that an exception *is* raised, you need to catch the exception, verify it is the right kind of exception, and fail if an exception wasn't raised. Alternatively, you can use a utility that does that for you.

The Python `unittest` module has a special assertion called `.assertRaises()`, which validates that an exception is raised within a code context block. If your code reaches the end of the block without raising an exception, the test case fails (by raising a different exception). The following listing shows code that adds an example function intended to raise a `ValueError` as well as a test to verify that it did so.

Listing 8.4   Testing an exception got caused

```
# bands/tests.py
...
def raises_an_error():         ◁──┐  A sample function
    raise ValueError()                that raises ValueError

class TestBands(TestCase):
    ...
    def test_raises_an_error(self):              Asserts that a ValueError is raised
        with self.assertRaises(ValueError):   ◁─┘ before the context block exits
            raises_an_error()
```

8.5   *Authenticating and posting data*

Let's tackle a view with a little more complexity. The `edit_venue()` view from chapter 7 creates or edits a `Venue` object and ensures only users associated with the `Venue` are allowed to make changes. To fully test this view, you need two users: a user that owns the `Venue` and a user that doesn't. As the view is responsible for both creating and editing the `Venue`, you don't need to create a `Venue` object to test with, as creating it will be part of the test. The structure of the view and the test are visualized in figure 8.5.

Recall that this view uses both GET and POST HTTP methods, with GET fetching the form and POST submitting it. You've already seen `.client.get()`; unsurprisingly, there is a corresponding `.client.post()`. This method takes a dictionary containing the form values that the post submits.

The first code you need to add for this scenario is to create test users. The following listing shows the creation of an owner and nonowner account in the `.setUp()` method. Django's `User` Model object has a special method on its query manager for creating users; this is done rather than just creating the object normally, as the password needs to be encrypted before it is stored in the database.

Listing 8.5   Add users for testing

```
# bands/tests.py
...
from django.contrib.auth.models import User   ◁──┐  Import Django's
...                                                   user model.
class TestBands(TestCase):
    def setUp(self):
```

```
    ...
    self.PASSWORD = "notsecure"
    self.owner = User.objects.create_user("owner",
        password=self.PASSWORD)
    self.member = User.objects.create_user("member",
        password=self.PASSWORD)
```

Use a common password everywhere; it is only a test suite. →

← **Create owner and nonowner users using the .create_user() method.**

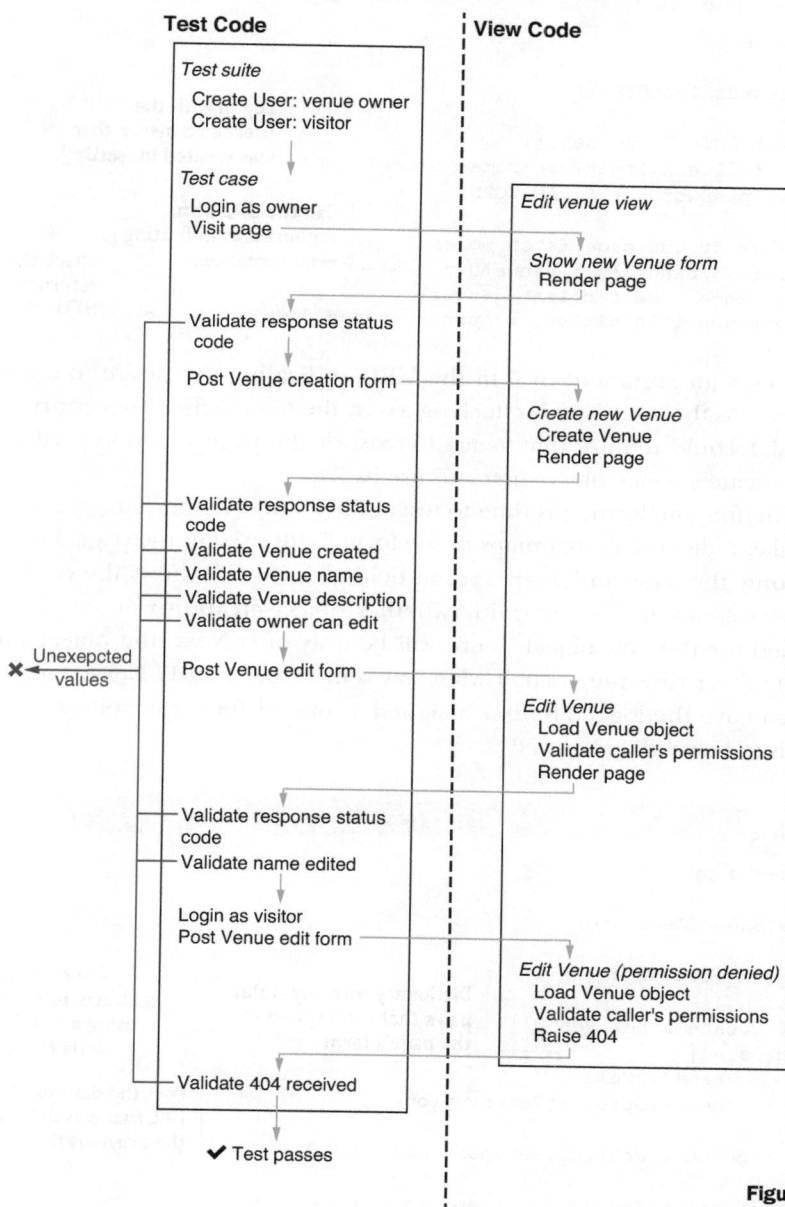

Figure 8.5 Testing the `edit_venue()` **view**

With the users added to `.setUp()`, it is time to start writing the test. This view expects a logged-in user, which you do in a test by calling `.client.login()`. The following listing logs in the user that will be the owner, does a GET, and validates the resulting HTTP 200 status code.

Listing 8.6   Verify the form can be fetched using GET

```
# bands/tests.py
...
class TestBands(TestCase):
    ...
    def test_edit_venue(self):
        self.client.login(username="owner",
            password=self.PASSWORD)

        # Verify the page fetch works
        url = "/bands/edit_venue/0/"
        response = self.client.get(url)
        self.assertEqual(200, response.status_code)
```

Log in with the username owner that was created in .setUp().

Call the URL with argument 0, indicating venue creation.

Check the view returned the right HTTP status.

This code uses an argument of 0 in the URL, indicating the desire to create a new Venue object. As the code is only checking a GET, the 0 isn't strictly necessary, but using any other ID would require that Venue to exist or the page would 404. Alternatively, you could create a Venue object first and use its ID.

After fetching the form, it is time to test adding a new venue. The `.client.post()` method takes a dictionary that maps to the form fields used in the page. For now, let's populate only the `name` and `description` fields. Listing 8.7 shows the code that tests Venue object creation. To determine whether object creation worked, the database gets queried for the new object; there will be only one. Next, the object's fields get checked, making sure they match what was sent in the POST. Newly created Venue objects also have the logged-in user assigned as one of their controllers, so this attribute needs to be validated as well.

Listing 8.7   Test creating a Venue

```
# bands/tests.py
...
class TestBands(TestCase):
    ...
    def test_edit_venue(self):
        ...
        # Create a new Venue
        data = {
            "name":"Name",
            "description":"Description",
        }
        response = self.client.post(url, data)

        self.assertEqual(302, response.status_code)
```

Dictionary with key–value pairs that correspond to the page's form

A successful creation redirects to another page, using a 302 HTTP status code for redirection.

Post the data to the URL that was defined in the previous listing.

Fetch the newly created Venue from the database.

```
# Validate the Venue was created
venue = Venue.objects.first()
self.assertEqual(data['name'], venue.name)
self.assertEqual(data['description'], venue.description)
self.assertTrue(
    self.owner.userprofile.venues_controlled.filter(
        id=venue.id).exists()
)
```

Validate the Venue object's attributes against the expected data.

Verify that the owner's UserProfile indicates they own the new Venue.

The `edit_venue()` view is used for both creating and editing a `Venue`, so now, it is time to add code testing `Venue` object edits. This situation is similar to creation, but instead, the URL contains the `Venue` object's ID and the data is set to change a field. The following listing shows the code that needs to be added to the test.

Listing 8.8 Test editing a Venue

```
# bands/tests.py
...
class TestBands(TestCase):
    ...
    def test_edit_venue(self):
        ...
        # Now edit that Venue
        url = f"/bands/edit_venue/{venue.id}/"
        data['name'] = "Edited Name"
        response = self.client.post(url, data)

        self.assertEqual(302, response.status_code)
        venue = Venue.objects.first()
        self.assertEqual(data['name'], venue.name)
```

Change the URL to point to the Venue getting edited.

Set a new value for the Venue's name.

Post the change request.

Check that the Venue content has changed.

WARNING Remember, `Model` objects are proxies; they won't update automatically. When your view changes the database, you need to refetch the `Model` object.

The last thing to test is the permission check. Re-attempt the edit with another user, and verify their attempt to edit gets denied. Listing 8.9 shows this new code; it is similar to the previous code, except this time the logged-in user is *member*.

Listing 8.9 Test Venue editing permissions

```
# bands/tests.py
...
class TestBands(TestCase):
    ...
    def test_edit_venue(self):
        ...
        # Verify that a non-owner can't edit
        self.client.login(username="member", password=self.PASSWORD)
        response = self.client.post(url, data)
        self.assertEqual(404, response.status_code)
```

Edit requests from users without permission cause an HTTP 404 error.

All told, that's over 40 lines of code to test a 32-line view. That's kind of typical. Writing tests that check all the conditions of your code tends to take about the same number of lines of code as the code under test. If writing automated tests isn't something you do at work, changing to this habit can be startling to your schedule. Suddenly, you're writing half the number of features in the same time because half the time you're writing tests. This can make management cranky. Long term, though, this is a far more efficient way of coding. What you're really doing is reducing the future test time, time that wasn't originally accounted for in the development portion of your schedule. With tests in place, you can quickly test the entire system as frequently as you like, something you can't do if you stick with a manual testing approach.

8.6   *Testing with file uploads*

There is one more scenario that the test for `edit_venue()` still doesn't cover: associating an image with the venue. This makes life a little more complicated than just having some text values in the POST dictionary. There are a couple of ways to handle this. First, you could keep a file with your tests, read it, and upload its contents as part of your test. Alternatively, you can create the file on the fly.

Django provides the `SimpleUploadedFile` class as a way to build files. The class gets used if you're writing a custom file handler, but is equally useful when testing. `SimpleUploadedFile` takes two arguments when constructed: the name of the file and its binary contents. As the `Venue` object's associated file is a picture, the binary contents need to pass the is-an-image validation performed by the underlying `Image-Field`. To save you some time (this is a full service book!) I created a 1-pixel GIF, JPG, and PNG and discovered that the GIF is the smallest. Using Python's `base64` library, I encoded the GIF into a string, which gets hardcoded in the test. When the `Simple-UploadedFile` gets created, the base64 string gets decoded into a binary representation of the GIF. I put this code in the `.setUp()` method, as it may be useful in another test (spoiler alert: it gets used in the excercises).

> **WARNING** `SimpleUploadedFile` gets accessed like a stream. If you are testing the same value more than once in a method, re-create it to reset its starting point to the beginning.

If you were actually doing an HTTP call in your test, you would have to treat the file data specially. This is the same as the need to specify `encytype="multipart/form-data"` in the `<form>` tag. The Django test utilities are smart, though, and take care of this situation for you. They automatically recognize file handles in the `.client.post()` dictionary and put them in the right part of the request.

One last tricky little thing: uploaded files go somewhere. You probably don't want your test file to end up in your uploads folder. If you're as anal- retentive as I am, you want to remove any files after the test. There is a better solution though: Django provides a decorator that modifies a configuration value for the duration of a test. The decorator is named `@override_settings`, and it takes one or more keyword arguments, corresponding to the name and value of the configuration value you wish to change. A cleaner approach than dealing with the uploaded file yourself is to let your operating system do it by using its temp directory for uploads. The Python `tempfiles` module has a function that returns the path of your system's temp directory, so you don't have to figure that out yourself.

The following listing contains a new test method that creates a `Venue Model`, this time including an uploaded file. In real life (as opposed to "book life"), this code would be included as the creation part of `test_edit_venue()`, as it also tests the other fields, but for learning purposes, I've separated it out into its own thing.

Listing 8.10 Test Venue creation, including a file upload

```python
# bands/tests.py
from base64 import b64decode
from django.core.files.uploadedfile import SimpleUploadedFile
...
class TestBands(TestCase):
    ...
    def setUp(self):
        ...
        # Base64 encoded version of a single pixel
        # GIF image
        self.image = "R0lGODdhAQABAIABAP///wAAACwAAAAAQABAAACAkQBADs="
        self.image = b64decode(image)

    @override_settings(
        MEDIA_ROOT=tempfile.gettempdir())
    def test_edit_venue_picture(self):

        file = SimpleUploadedFile("test.gif", self.image)
        data = {
            "name": "Name",
            "description": "Description",
            "picture": file,
        }

        self.client.login(username="owner", password=self.PASSWORD)
        url = "/bands/edit_venue/0/"
        response = self.client.post(url, data)

        self.assertEqual(302, response.status_code)
        venue = Venue.objects.first()
        self.assertIsNotNone(venue.picture)
```

Decode the binary representation of a GIF from the preceding base64-encoded string.

Override the MEDIA_ROOT configuration value to point to the operating system's temp directory, so any uploaded files get cleaned up.

Create an in-memory file for testing based on the GIF binary data.

Like in previous tests, check the object got created, this time validating the .picture attribute.

There it is—that's the complete picture (OK, there are bad puns, and then there are bad puns I shouldn't be allowed to get away with). You've got the tools now to create tests for all the views you've written so far.

8.7 *More testing techniques*

The start of this chapter introduced the testing pyramid and some terms used in the programming industry. Everything so far falls into the unit test and integration test levels. You can test Django projects at the UI level as well, but it requires a bit more work.

8.7.1   *LiveServerTestCase for Selenium*

There are several UI testing tools out there for websites, with one of the most popular being Selenium (https://www.selenium.dev/). There are entire books on using Selenium; here, I'll just give you a quick taste. Selenium integrates with web browsers and drives them the same way a user does. There are two general modes: click-and-record and API-based. Click-and-record uses a tool that tracks what you do to a web page, allowing you to play it back again as part of your tests. Or you can write scripts that use the API instead. These scripts include code that searches for tags in the HTML and interacts with them, by, for example, clicking links.

Click-and-record is faster to get going and requires less training. If you can learn to hit the Record button and use the web page you want to test, you're pretty much there. This method does tend to be a little more fragile. Small changes to the page may cause the script to break.

The API method requires more work and a bit of careful planning when you write your HTML. The easiest way to find an item in a web page is to search by its ID. Of course, you may not have put IDs on all of your tags. There are other ways to search, but they tend to suffer from the same fragility as the click-and-record method. I generally prefer to use the API and write a testable web page with IDs in all the tags.

Django's `TestCase` class calls views directly, meaning any JavaScript doesn't get called. If you want to test the page the way a browser sees it, you need a server. You could use the development server, but then, you have to make sure the state of your site is correct before running the Selenium script. Instead, you use `django.test` `.LiveServerTestCase` or its sibling `StaticLiveServerTestCase`. These test classes cause Django to run the development server during testing. As both classes inherit from `TestCase`, you can still use `.setUp()` to create any required data and then call the Selenium API from the test methods. As the name implies, the `StaticLive-ServerTestCase` also runs a static server, so your static files, like CSS and JavaScript, get served by the test harness. For more information on writing a Selenium test with Django, see the sample script in the documentation: https://mng.bz/wxx7.

8.7.2   *Third-party helpers*

This section could also be titled *Shameless Plug*. I'd like to point you at one of my own third-party libraries: Django Awl (https://github.com/cltrudeau/django-awl). This library is an odds-and-ends collection of stuff I tend to use in every Django project. I kept rewriting the same code for each new project and figured it was better to have a library instead. The `awl.waelsteng` module contains helpers for testing. There are tools for testing your Django Admin customizations, a class that acts like a request object in case you want to call a view without using the URL routing feature, and a custom test runner.

The Python `unittest` test runner (and its Django child) accepts arguments on the command line, allowing you to run a subset of the tests. For example, if you wished to run only the `test_musician_view()` method you could:

```
(venv) RiffMates$ python manage.py test
➥ bands.tests.TestBands.test_musician_view
```

Man, is that a lot of typing. The main reason I wrote `WRunner` was to provide a shortcut for calling a single test. `WRunner` treats an equal sign (=) prefix as shortcut and looks for any test in your suite that matches what comes after the sign. The previous test could be found with

```
(venv) RiffMates$ python manage.py test =music
```

It doesn't stop at the first match, so if you have several tests with the word *music* in their names, they'd all get invoked. As I'm already doing self-promotion, here is one more: `context_temp` (https://github.com/cltrudeau/context_temp). This library has two context managers, one that creates a temporary directory and another that creates a temporary file. The temp file or directory gets created when the context block gets entered and removed when it exits. If you need a temporary file or directory and don't want to worry about cleaning them up, this context manager tool could be for you.

8.8 *Measuring tests and code quality*

How do you know if you've tested everything? You can never be 100% sure, but there are things you can measure. Coverage (https://pypi.org/project/coverage/) is a third-party library you use when running your tests to track what project code got executed. After your tests complete, you get a summary showing the percentage of your code that ran under the test.

Measuring coverage gives you a sense of how much of your code has been tested, but it isn't perfect. Just because a line executed doesn't mean all possible conditions for that line got checked. Also, your code might have flaws that your tests don't trigger. In certain cases, failing to check for `None` may cause your code to crash, but if you don't have a test that checks it, your 100% coverage statement is a fake safety blanket. It isn't a silver bullet, but you can't improve what you can't measure, so it is still a good idea.

In addition to checking your code's functionality, you may want to check its quality. This is another deep subject, complete with fun phrases like *code smell*. There are dozens of tools out there that give feedback on your code. I typically have a shell script in my projects that runs the tests, measures the coverage, and runs a quality measure. If anything complains, I try to fix it immediately.

The following are some code quality tools you might be interested:

- *Linters*—These check for logical and stylistic problems. Popular Python linters are PyFlakes (https://github.com/PyCQA/pyflakes), Pylint (https://pypi.org/project/pylint/), ruff (https://pypi.org/project/ruff/), and MyPy for type enforcement (http://mypy-lang.org/).
- *Reformatting tools*—These make your code compliant with common style recommendations. Popular Python reformatting tools are Black (https://github.com/ambv/black), ruff (https://pypi.org/project/ruff/), and isort for import sorting (https://github.com/timothycrosley/isort).

- *Static analysis tools*—These check the logic in your code and alert on common fail points and security weaknesses. Popular Python static analysis tools are SonarQube (https://www.sonarqube.org/) and Codacy (http://codacy.com/). Note that both of these are commercial products with free and open source plans.

> ### ... not as I do
> When writing the book, I added new features to RiffMates as I went along, chapter by chapter. As testing wasn't covered until this chapter, I was lazy and didn't write unit tests for the project. This is bad practice, and it bit me. I found all sorts of problems in the sample code when I started writing tests. Writing automated tests should be treated as part of coding, not an "after task," as not having them piles up and becomes problematic.
>
> All the code in this chapter is in RiffMates/bands/tests.py, but that doesn't give good coverage of the project—it doesn't even cover all the views in the Bands app. To help catch problems, the sample code also contains RiffMates/tests/test_all.py. The name is a bit misleading, as it doesn't quite test everything, but it brings the coverage number up above 80%, which is a common threshold for being "good enough."

8.9   *Exercises*

1   In chapter 7's exercises, you added a view called `edit_musician()`, where users could create and manage their own musician profile page. Add a test for that view. Include testing for fetching the form, submitting the form, and adding a musician with a picture. A user can edit the musician profile they created, and so can staff and superusers. Test that those types of users can edit, while a non-owner cannot. Note that you can create a superuser with the `User.objects.create_superuser()` method.

2   Write a test for the `musicians()` view that validates that pagination is working. The view needs to be called multiple times with a variety of query parameters to test different settings for the number of items per page as well as the next and previous arguments. Note that the paginator's `.has_previous()` and `.has_next()` are methods, not attributes; you didn't need the parenthesis in the template, but you do when calling them in code.

Summary

- Automated testing is typically approached hierarchically, with each level of tests having a separate purpose and possibly approach.
- A unit test is the lowest level in the hierarchy and is performed on a single component of software, typically a function or class method.
- Integration tests verify that components interact well together and operate across several units.

- Behavioral tests, sometimes known as *acceptance tests,* specify a feature within your program and are often a user-facing process.
- UI tests focus on the user interface. These usually require specialty tools that simulate human interaction with your software.
- Testing your software from the top down is expensive: every UI interaction interacts with the entire stack. This slows your testing down and causes low-level components to be tested redundantly. The automated testing hierarchy is often visualized as a pyramid, with the majority of tests being at the bottom of the hierarchy, at the unit test level.
- Python's standard library includes the `unittest` module that defines the structure of automated testing.
- The `unittest` module searches for `TestCase` classes, running methods that begin with `test_`. The `TestCase` class also has methods for common setup and tear-down activities required for the test.
- A test runner is responsible for finding tests, executing them, and reporting on whether they have passed.
- Django inherits from Python's `TestCase`, providing additional features specific to the web framework.
- Django's test runner looks for `tests.py` files in the app directories and runs all methods that begin with `test_` inside a class that inherits from `TestCase`.
- You invoke the Django test runner using the `test` management command.
- The `TestCase` class provides a number of "assert" methods that raise an exception if their test condition isn't met. The most commonly used one is `.assert-Equal()`.
- The Django `TestCase` class creates a test copy of a database, setting up everything the ORM needs to work with your apps. The database begins empty, so you need to populate Model objects for your tests.
- Each test method gets wrapped in a database transaction, so the actions your test performs on the database get undone after the method completes. This ensures tests start in a known environment and can be run in any order.
- The `.setUp()` and `.setUpClass()` methods get used to create the environment needed for your tests, including populating any ORM Models.
- Django's `TestCase` class has a `.client` object that allows you to authenticate to the system and invoke both GET and POST methods through the URL router.
- The `.client.get()` and `.client.post()` methods return a response object that contains the context dictionary sent to the template engine, the resulting rendered content, and the HTTP status code for the call.
- Your tests should cover as many of the scenarios in your view as possible, including negative cases where errors should be displayed. For example, you can verify a `404` page was displayed by checking the `status_code` field of the response object.

- The `.client.post()` method takes a dictionary representing the form data included for an HTTP POST call. It recognizes file handles and puts them in the appropriate part of the request object.
- To test pages that require authentication, your `TestCase` class needs to create at least one user account in the test database. The `.client.login()` method allows you to log in as a user before visiting a page.
- `SimpleFileUpload` allows you to create an in-memory representation of a file that can be used to test views that handle file uploads.
- `LiveServerTestCase` and `StaticLiveServerTestCase` run the Django development server, so you can test with click-and-record tools, such as Selenium.
- There are many third-party libraries that can help both your testing and ensuring your code meets common quality conventions.

Management commands

This chapter covers

- Management commands built into Django
- Writing your own management commands
- Passing command-line arguments to management commands
- Creating unit tests for management commands

Management commands are Python scripts that allow you to control your Django project from the command line. Over two dozen commands are included with Django, and you can also write your own. This chapter covers management commands you haven't seen so far, along with details on how to build and test custom commands.

9.1 Management commands in practice

You've already used a number of management commands throughout this book. You've seen how to create a Django project, create a Django app, create a superuser, create and migrate ORM tables, launch a Django-aware REPL, launch your database's command-line tool, save and load fixtures, and run your unit tests. The common thread here is producing a change in your project without a web interface. A significant percentage of Django commands are about bootstrapping, deploying, testing, and debugging your software.

The other common use for commands is to execute offline operations, such as cleaning up old files. As Django doesn't really run on its own but is activated through a web server, running an operation periodically can be problematic. There are tools out there that act as separate services to do this, but a quick way is to write a management command and then use your operating system's periodic execution mechanisms. On a Unix-based system, this would be `cron`, but other operating systems have equivalent services.

Say you wanted to use musician data from RiffMates in a utility script. You could write some raw SQL and access the database directly, but if the database changed, you'd have to change your script. Instead, you could write a management command that provided a querying mechanism for the musician data, which you could then call in your utility script. Your management command works within the context of your project, so you can use the same `Musician Model` you use in your views to perform your queries. In this chapter, you'll be writing a management command that does just that.

As for cleaning up, recall how `ImageField` and `FileField` in a Model point to uploaded files. Removing an object with these fields does not remove the corresponding files. Occasionally, you'll want to check for any orphaned files to save on disk space. A short management command is all that is needed to compare the contents of the uploads directory with the database. Writing such a management command is part of the exercises in this chapter. You'll have everything you need to try it yourself by the time you get there.

9.1.1 Built-in management commands

You can see all the available management commands for your project by running the `manage.py` script without any arguments. Its output is organized by Django app. When you write your own later, a new section will appear. Django has several of its own apps built in, so in addition to the `django` section, you'll see commands grouped under `auth`, `contenttypes`, `session`, and `staticfiles`.

> **NOTE** Django's terminology is a bit inconsistent; the `manage.py` script refers to these as "subcommands," while the documentation simply calls them "commands." Don't be confused; they're the same thing. Table 9.1 contains a summary of the built-in management commands and their purpose.

Table 9.1 Common management commands that are built into Django

Command	App	Description
changepassword	auth	Change a user's password. Doesn't require authentication.
check	django	Runs a check on the project. This is the same check the development server runs on startup.

Table 9.1 Common management commands that are built into Django *(continued)*

Command	App	Description
clearsessions	sessions	Removes expired sessions from the database
collectstatic	staticfiles	Copies static files to the configured
compilemessages	django	Used to create translation files
createcachetable	django	Creates a database table to be used for page caching
createsuperuser	auth	Creates a superuser (admin) account in the database
dbshell	django	Opens your database's command-line tool
diffsettings	django	Displays differences between your settings and the defaults
dumpdata	django	Exports data from the database into a fixture
findstatic	staticfiles	Searches for a named static file and prints its details
flush	django	Removes all data from the database except migration state
inspectdb	django	Outputs a models.py file based on an existing table
loaddata	django	Imports a fixture into the database
makemessages	django	Builds translation files based on strings in the source
makemigrations	django	Creates migration files based on changes to Models
migrate	django	Performs migrations on the database
optimizemigration	django	Optimizes a migration file
remove_stale_contenttypes	contenttypes	Removes unused content type entries if the contenttypes app is in use
runserver	django	Runs the development server
sendtestemail	django	Sends a test email
shell	django	Runs a Django-aware REPL
showmigrations	django	Shows migrations in a project
sqlflush	django	Prints the SQL commands that are run when the flush management command executes
sqlmigrate	django	Prints the SQL for a named migration
sqlsequencereset	django	Prints the SQL for resetting an index sequence
squashmigrations	django	Squishes multiple migrations into a single file
startapp	django	Creates a new Django app directory
startproject	django	Creates a new Django project
test	django	Runs unit tests
testserver	django	Runs a development server but using a test database populated with the named fixture's deployment destination

NOTE The `staticfiles` app has its own version of `runserver`, which is a development server that also hosts static content. If `staticfiles` is configured in your system, `runserver` will show in that grouping instead.

The rest of this section covers a few of the most commonly used management commands that aren't already discussed in detail in the appropriate part of the book. For example, the `test` management command got covered in chapter 8 along with other content on testing. For a full list of the built-in Django management commands, see https://mng.bz/qOOK.

9.1.2 *Changing a password*

Django assumes that if you have access to management commands, you have administrative powers. Nobody but your system administrators should be allowed in the server account that hosts your Django project. This makes sense: if they're in there, they can tamper with your settings.py file and turn off all the security checks anyhow.

If you are an admin, one of the things you might want to do is reset a user's password. The Django Admin provides a mechanism for this, but if you are locked out of the admin account, you need another way. The `changepassword` management command lets you change any user's password from the command line. It's pretty straightforward; run the command giving the username to reset, and then follow the prompts:

```
(venv) RiffMates$ python manage.py changepassword nicky
Changing password for user 'nicky'
Password:
Password (again):
Password changed successfully for user 'nicky'
```

In chapter 2, you used the `createsuperuser` management command to create an admin account. If you tried to use a password that wasn't particularly secure, Django warned you and gave you the option to bypass password validation. The `changepassword` command does no such thing: you are bound by the current password security level.

Password validation

If you've been snooping around in your settings.py file, you may have noticed the AUTH_PASSWORD_VALIDATORS configuration value. This list of dictionaries specifies which password validation code gets executed when a new password gets created. By default, there are four validators; they check for similarity to the username, minimum length, common passwords, and requiring a password to contain a number.

Like most configurable things in Django, you can write your own validator, which you'd then register in AUTH_PASSWORD_VALIDATORS. Details can be found in the documentation: http://mng.bz/Xq6l.

9.1.3   Configuration

At this point in the book, I've written *settings.py* 39 times. Django is very configurable, and all that happens in your settings.py file (40). If you're trying to understand how your system is configured, it can be useful to see the difference between your current settings and the defaults. The `diffsettings` management command does just that:

```
(venv) RiffMates$ python manage.py diffsettings
DEBUG = True
DEFAULT_AUTO_FIELD = 'django.db.models.BigAutoField'
EMAIL_BACKEND = 'django.core.mail.backends.console.EmailBackend'
INSTALLED_APPS = ['django.contrib.admin', 'django.contrib.auth',
    'django.contrib.contenttypes', 'django.contrib.sessions',
    'django.contrib.messages', 'django.contrib.staticfiles', 'home',
    'bands', 'content']
LOGIN_REDIRECT_URL = '/'
LOGOUT_REDIRECT_URL = '/'
ROOT_URLCONF = 'RiffMates.urls'   ###
```

This output is truncated; the full list can be quite long. In chapter 6 you added LOGIN _REDIRECT_URL, LOGOUT_REDIRECT_URL, and EMAIL_BACKEND to settings.py, so it might not be a surprise to see them. A little less obvious is DEFAULT_AUTO_FIELD. Although you haven't set it yourself, the skeleton settings.py file created by the `createproject` command sets this value. It shows up in the output because it is different from the default, even if that difference got created by Django.

Likewise, for the INSTALLED_APPS value; it shows here that you've added your own apps, but even if you hadn't, the various `django` apps included by `createproject` aren't in the underlying default configuration. This is where `diffsettings` can get a little noisy, even things you haven't changed yourself might not match the base configuration. This means you have to go wading through some values set by `createproject` to see what you actually changed.

Note the ### on the end of the ROOT_URLCONF value; this is how `diffsettings` indicates a value that has no default. Your project won't work without a ROOT_URLCONF, but there is no default. Any custom values you add yourself will also appear with the ### suffix. If you'd like to see all the default configuration values, the global_settings.py file in the Django source code is the place to look: http://mng.bz/yZn7.

9.1.4   Flushing the database

One of the many wonderful experiences in writing a book is learning something new yourself. Until playing around with a few management commands to write this chapter, I wasn't aware that `flush` even existed. This command wipes your database, except without resetting your migrations. Obviously, this is a drastic move, but when you're developing a new project that hasn't gone into production yet, you likely have a bunch of sample data kicking around from your manual testing. Using the `flush` command clears all database tables, keeping the structure and migration state. As you might hope, it asks if you're sure:

```
(venv) RiffMates$ python manage.py flush

You have requested a flush of the database.

This will IRREVERSIBLY DESTROY all data currently in the
"RiffMates/db.sqlite3" database, and return each table to
an empty state.

Are you sure you want to do this?

    Type 'yes' to continue, or 'no' to cancel: yes
```

Before knowing about `flush`, I accomplished the same thing by removing the database file and running migrations once again. Using `flush` instead allows you to skip the second step.

There are times when `flush` isn't good enough, though. If you haven't released anything into production yet, there isn't much value in maintaining every step it took to get to your current state. Often, with a new project, I wipe the database as well as all the migration folders and create a new "initial" state based on my current Models. Once something has been released in production, you can't do this anymore: you need to track all changes, so they can be applied to the production system.

9.1.5 *SQL commands*

The ORM is a beautiful thing; it saves you from writing a lot of SQL. Abstractions can be dangerous, though, and there are times when you want to know what is happening underneath. There are two management commands that help you peek under the covers: `sqlflush` and `sqlmigrate`. These commands correspond to the `flush` and `migrate` commands but print out the equivalent SQL. The `sqlflush` management command doesn't require any arguments:

```
(venv) RiffMates$ python manage.py sqlflush
BEGIN;
DELETE FROM "bands_band_musicians";
DELETE FROM "django_session";
DELETE FROM "bands_room";
DELETE FROM "content_seekingad";
DELETE FROM "auth_group_permissions";
DELETE FROM "auth_user_user_permissions";
DELETE FROM "bands_musician";
DELETE FROM "auth_group";
DELETE FROM "auth_user_groups";
DELETE FROM "bands_userprofile";
DELETE FROM "bands_userprofile_venues_controlled";
DELETE FROM "bands_venue";
DELETE FROM "django_admin_log";
DELETE FROM "bands_userprofile_musician_profiles";
DELETE FROM "auth_user";
DELETE FROM "auth_permission";
DELETE FROM "bands_band";
DELETE FROM "django_content_type";
```

```
UPDATE "sqlite_sequence" SET "seq" = 0 WHERE "name" IN
    ('bands_band_musicians', 'django_session', 'bands_room',
    'content_seekingad', 'auth_group_permissions',
    'auth_user_user_permissions', 'bands_musician', 'auth_group',
    'auth_user_groups', 'bands_userprofile',
    'bands_userprofile_venues_controlled', 'bands_venue',
    'django_admin_log', 'bands_userprofile_musician_profiles',
    'auth_user', 'auth_permission', 'bands_band',
    'django_content_type');
COMMIT;
```

As you might expect from `flush`, all rows from almost all the tables get deleted. The ID key also gets reset to start over again, hence the `SET "seq" = 0` part of the `UPDATE` statement.

The `sqlmigrate` command is a little more complex. It requires the name of an app and the name of the migration in question. To see the first change made to the bands app after it was initially created, you specify `bands` and `0002` (you only need to provide enough of the migration file name for it to be uniquely found—you don't have to type the whole thing):

```
(venv) RiffMates$ python manage.py sqlmigrate bands 0002
BEGIN;
--
-- Create model Venue
--
CREATE TABLE "bands_venue" ("id" integer NOT NULL PRIMARY KEY
    AUTOINCREMENT, "name" varchar(20) NOT NULL);
--
-- Create model Room
--
CREATE TABLE "bands_room" ("id" integer NOT NULL PRIMARY KEY
    AUTOINCREMENT, "name" varchar(20) NOT NULL, "venue_id"
    bigint NOT NULL REFERENCES "bands_venue" ("id")
    DEFERRABLE INITIALLY DEFERRED);
CREATE INDEX "bands_room_venue_id_16903c8e" ON "bands_room" ("venue_id");
COMMIT;
```

The result, in this case, is the SQL that got run to create the tables for the Venue and Room Models as well as the database index on the column that relates the two. As everything you do to your models gets done through the migration mechanism, you can always see the underlying SQL with this command.

9.2 *Writing your own management command*

When you run manage.py on its own and get the list of all the installed management commands, the result is grouped by Django app. As you might guess from this, you can write your own management command. This can be useful to interact with your project data from the command line, for example running batch jobs or doing the occasional bit of clean-up.

To write a command, you simply need to put the right thing in the right place in your app. The "right thing" is a class in a file, with the file name dictating the name of the management command. The "right place" is a bit weird. Django looks for management command files in your app directory inside nested subdirectories, called *management/commands*. I've always figured that this was part of some deeper long-term plan, that there were going to be other kinds of "management" tools, and thus a nested directory would be needed. Whatever the reason for this otherwise empty structure, that's what Django expects.

Let's start by writing a management command that outputs all Musician objects in the database to the terminal. As the Musician Model lives in the bands app, it makes sense to put the command in there as well. The first thing you need to do is create the nested management/commands directory structure. And as commands are Python files, you also need to create empty __init__.py files to mark the directories as modules. The terminal session in the following listing shows you how to do just that.

Listing 9.1   The shell commands used to create command directories

```
(venv) RiffMates$ mkdir bands/management
(venv) RiffMates$ mkdir bands/management/commands
(venv) RiffMates$ touch bands/__init__.py
(venv) RiffMates$ touch bands/commands/__init__.py
```

Having performed these actions, you'll now have the following contents in the bands app directory:

```
RiffMates/
└── bands
    ├── __init__.py
    ├── admin.py
    ├── apps.py
    ├── fixtures
    ├── forms.py
    ├── management          ◁── Management directory
    │   ├── __init__.py     ◁── __init__.py file to make the directory a module
    │   └── commands        ◁── Nested commands directory
    │       └── __init__.py ◁── __init__.py file to make the directory a module
    ├── migrations/
    ├── models.py
    ├── tests.py
    ├── urls.py
    └── views.py
```

With the structure in place, it is time to create the file. To make a management command called musicians, you need a file in the commands directory called musicians.py. Inside that file, you create a class that inherits from django.core .management.base.BaseCommand (another unnecessary level of nesting—the Django developers must have been on an organizational bender). Django doesn't care what you call your class, as long as you inherit from BaseCommand. As the file name is what determines the command name, you only ever end up with one class in the file. I typically get creative and call my class Command.

The key part of your Command class is the .handle() method, which Django calls when your management command gets run. It is best practice to use *args and **options in the signature of .handle(). For the first version of the musicians command, it isn't necessary, but stick with it for now, and you'll use these pieces in the next section when you add command-line arguments.

By inheriting from BaseCommand, you automatically get some features, like help. If you include a help attribute on your class, Django uses its value to populate the command-line help information.

Our musicians command lists all the Musician objects in the database, so the command imports the MusicianModel, performs a query on it, and outputs the result. It is recommended to use self.stdout.write() for output inside of a management command instead of print(). The print() function will work, but by using self.stdout, you can take advantage of the testing capabilities for commands, covered later. The following listing contains the code for the first version of the musicians command.

Listing 9.2 A management command that displays the Musician objects in the database

```
# RiffMates/bands/management/commands/musicians.py
from django.core.management.base import BaseCommand
from bands.models import Musician
                                          Management commands are classes
                                          that inherit from BaseCommand.
class Command(BaseCommand):
    help = "Lists registered musicians"          Provide a help string for the
                                                 --help command-line flag.
    def handle(self, *args, **options):
        for musician in Musician.objects.all():           Query and loop
            self.stdout.write(                            through all
                f"{musician.last_name}, {musician.first_name}"   Musician objects.
            )
```

The .handle() method is the command's invocation point.

Output each Musician, using self.stdout.write() instead of print().

With the file in place, you're ready to go. First off, run manage.py without any arguments, and notice you now have a bands section with the musicians command inside of it:

```
(venv) RiffMates$ python manage.py

Type 'manage.py help <subcommand>' for help on a specific subcommand.

Available subcommands:

[auth]
    changepassword
    createsuperuser

[bands]
    musicians

...
```

If you aren't seeing the `bands` grouping or the `musicians` command, double-check that you created the bands/management/commands structure correctly and remembered each of the required __init__.py scripts. If the command is there, then run it:

```
(venv) RiffMates$ python manage.py musicians
Bonham, John
Cousin, Nicky
Hendrix, Jimi
Lennon, John
Star, Ringo
Vai, Steve
```

You should see each of the `Musician` objects in your database output to the screen. I mentioned that Django automatically provides a help interface:

```
(venv) RiffMates$ python manage.py musicians --help
usage: manage.py musicians [-h] [--version] [-v {0,1,2,3}]
                           [--settings SETTINGS]
                           [--pythonpath PYTHONPATH] [--traceback]
                           [--no-color] [--force-color] [--skip-checks]

Lists registered musicians          ◁─┐ The help string from
                                       │ your command class
options:
  -h, --help            show this help message and exit
  --version             Show program's version number and exit.
  -v {0,1,2,3}, --verbosity {0,1,2,3}
                        Verbosity level; 0=minimal output,
                        1=normal output, 2=verbose output,
                        3=very verbose output
  --settings SETTINGS   The Python path to a settings module, e.g.
                        "myproject.settings.main". If this isn't
                        provided, the DJANGO_SETTINGS_MODULE environment
                        variable will be used.
  --pythonpath PYTHONPATH
                        A directory to add to the Python path, e.g.
                        "/home/djangoprojects/myproject".
  --traceback           Raise on CommandError exceptions.
  --no-color            Don't colorize the command output.
  --force-color         Force colorization of the command output.
  --skip-checks         Skip system checks.
```

There is a lot buried in there. For now, just note that your help string is showing up. The rest of the options get covered in the next section when command-line arguments get discussed.

9.3   *Handling arguments*

When you write a program, you often need to pass in a some configuration information or data that changes the behavior of the script. Consider the `musicians` management command; it would be great to be able to filter the musicians based on name or date of birth, especially if you have a lot in your database. The kinds of arguments you pass to a command-line script are divided into two categories: positional arguments and flags. A positional argument is a value provided based on its spot on the command-line and is typically a piece of data or a filter on data. A flag is an optional argument that changes the behavior of the command.

For example, in Unix, the `zip` command creates a compressed archive. It takes two or more positional arguments. The first argument is the name of the archive to be created, the second and any subsequent arguments are the names of the files to put in the archive. If you want to know more about what `zip` is doing, you can add the `--verbose` flag, and it will print out more information. Figure 9.1 shows the parts of the `zip` command and its arguments.

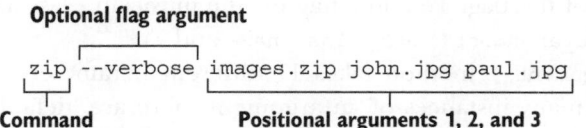

Figure 9.1 Positional and flag arguments to the `zip` command

In Unix systems, flags begin with either a dash (`-`) or a double-dash (`--`). Typically, the double-dash format is a readable word, while the single dash is an abbreviation. For example, most Unix commands support `-h` and `--help` as optional flags, both causing the command's help information to be printed to the terminal. With the `zip` command, `--verbose` can be shortened to `-v`. The `BaseCommand` class implements this flag for you out of the box.

NOTE Normally, I'd write about a function's arguments, but when you're writing about command-line arguments and function arguments in the same sentence, that can be confusing. For the rest of this chapter, a function's arguments will be referred to as *parameters* to help differentiate.

All your script's arguments get passed as strings by the operating system to your program. The Python standard library has a module called `argparse`, which parses these strings and turns them into positional arguments and flags. Django's management commands wrap this very same library, so you have less code to write.

`argparse` **references**

The examples in this chapter don't require familiarity with `argparse`; you'll be fine if you haven't used it before. It's a quite complex library, with a lot of choices. To take full advantage of its power, you'll want to dig in a little deeper:

- Python's documentation: http://mng.bz/M9jE
- Python's `argparse` how-to: http://mng.bz/amax
- An in-depth tutorial: http://mng.bz/g7GZ

Normally, when using `argparse`, you are responsible for instantiating a parser, but the `BaseCommand` class does this for you. When working with a Django management command, you override the `.add_arguments()` method, which gets the parser as parameter. Inside your `.add_arguments()` method, you register any command-line positional arguments and flags you want for your management command.

Consider adding three filter flags to our `musicians` management command: one for the birth year and one for each the first and last name. To do this, you need to call the parser object's `.add_argument()` method three times: once for each flag. The first parameter to `.add_argument()` is the name of the argument you're registering. You indicate it is a flag by naming it with leading dashes (as opposed to a positional argument, which has no dashes). For flags, you can optionally provide a second parameter with the short-form name of the flag. To add a flag for the musician's last name, the first two parameters to `.add_argument()` are `--last_name` and `-l`.

The parser's `.add_argument()` method takes 11 different parameters, allowing you to finely control how many instances of an argument there are, default values, what type the string should be converted into, and much more. For our `musicians` example, let's keep it simple and just add the `help` parameter. The string value of `help` gets included in the help screen for the management command, explaining how your flag gets used.

If the only parameters you pass to `.add_argument()` are the name of the flag and the `help` option, your flag gets configured to expect a string value after it, which, in this case, is the data used to filter by last name.

Recall that the `.handle()` method takes `*args` and `**options` in its signature. When you implement `.add_arguments()`, the `options` parameter can be treated like an `argparse` namespace. That's the dictionary-like object that contains the positional arguments and flags passed to your management command.

To implement a filter based on a musician's last name, you first check the contents of `options["last_name"]`. If the `--last_name` (or `-l`) flags got used, the value passed to the flag gets included in `options`. If the flag wasn't present, then `options["last_name"]` contains `None`.

Back in chapter 4, you learned how to write database queries using the `.filter()` method. In particular, you can modify a query using double-underscore field-lookup modifiers. Passing `last_name__gte=value` to the `Musician` query returns all the `Musician` objectss with last names greater than or equal to the provided value. If `options["last_name"]` isn't empty, then you filter based on its content.

> **NOTE** To keep things simple, the name queries are case sensitive; otherwise, you have to deal with the fact that ASCII *a* > *A*. Querying a last name beginning with *Z* includes any last names that start with a lowercase letter.

Writing a filter based on first names is the same as last names, except using a `--first_name` flag and a `first_name__gte` field-lookup modifier. Filtering by birth date is a little trickier. To filter a database column that contains a date, you need to pass the query a `datetime` object. All command-line arguments are strings, so before you create your query, you need to convert the command-line flag into a date. Dates are problematic, as their format differs between regions. As a programmer, my default for handling this problem is to make everyone uncomfortable and require the year-month-day format (it's the only sane value numerically, and it's a standard: ISO 8601).

It is all well and good to write "just use my format," but of course, users don't always pay attention. There is a chance your user won't read the instructions and may pass you a date that `datetime` can't parse. You could just let `datetime` throw an error and get the resulting ugly stack trace, or you could catch the `datetime` error and throw your own. Django's management commands have their own exception: `django.core.management.base.CommandError`. If you throw one of these, Django formats a pretty error message and even color codes it if the user's terminal supports it.

Listing 9.3 has the updated code for the `musicians` management command, which now supports filtering based on the musician's first name, last name, and date of birth. For each of the three filters, a command line flag is available, so the user can specify the filter. To register a flag, you call `.add_argument()` on the parse object in the command's `.add_arguments()` method. Inside the `.handle()` method, you query the musicians and modify the query based on which flags got included. The `.filter()` query method supports field-lookup modifiers, allowing you to filter the contents based on the `Musician` `Model` fields. The `options` object contains the values of any flags used when a management command gets invoked.

Listing 9.3   Add filtering to your `musicians` management command

```
# RiffMates/bands/management/commands/musicians.py
from datetime import datetime
from django.core.management.base import BaseCommand
from django.core.management.base import CommandError
from bands.models import Musician


class Command(BaseCommand):
    help = "Lists registered musicians"

    def add_arguments(self, parser):
        parser.add_argument("--last_name", "-l",
            help=(
                "Query musicians whose last name is greater than or equal"
                " to this value. Note this is case sensitive."
            )
        )
        parser.add_argument("--first_name", "-f", help=("Query musicians "
            "whose first name is greater than or equal to this value. "
            "Note this is case sensitive."))
        parser.add_argument("--birth", "-b", help=("Query musicians "
            "whose birth date is greater than or equal to this value. "
            "Date must be given in YYYY-MM-DD format."))

    def handle(self, *args, **options):
```

Implement .add_arguments() to register command-line positional arguments and flags.

The parser object passed into .add_arguments() is an argparse parser. Use its .add_argument() method to register a flag. Flags are indicated by leading dashes.

The help parameter gets used by .add_argument() to add flag-specific information to the help screen.

```
                  musicians = Musician.objects.all()    ◁─┐  Start by querying all
                  if options['last_name']:                │  Musician objects.
                      musicians = musicians.filter(
                          last_name__gte=options["last_name"]    ◁──┐  Filter the query set,
                      )                                              │  using all names greater
                                                          ┌─── Filter based on the    than or equal to the --
                  if options['first_name']:    ◁─────────┘     --first_name flag.     last_name flag's value.
                      musicians = musicians.filter(
                          first_name__gte=options["first_name"]
                      )
                                                          ┌─── Parse the --birth value as year-
                  if options['birth']:                    │    month-day into a datetime
                      try:                                 │    object to be used in the filter.
                          birth = datetime.strptime(
                              options["birth"], "%Y-%m-%d"    ◁─┘       If parsing the date results in an
                          )                                             error, catch the error and raise a
                      except ValueError:                                CommandError instead; the output
                          raise CommandError(    ◁─────────────         is friendlier than a stack trace.
                              "Birth date must be provided in YYYY-MM-DD format")

                      musicians = musicians.filter(birth__gte=birth)

                  for musician in musicians:    ◁──────────────────┐
                      self.stdout.write(
                          f"{musician.last_name}, {musician.first_name} "
                          f"({musician.birth})"
                      )                          Loop through the query set result after all
                                                 filters have been applied, and then write each
                                                 musician value using self.stdout.write().
```

If the --last_name flag gets used, options["last_name"] contains the flag's value; otherwise, it is None.

With the code in place, it is time to test out your command. Here are some possible tests you can run:

```
(venv) RiffMates$ python manage.py musicians    ◁──┐  Command-line flags are optional;
Bonham, John (1948-07-31)                            │  without any, the management
Cousin, Nicky (2000-01-13)                           │  command runs no further filters
Hendrix, Jimi (1942-11-27)                           │  and outputs all musicians.
Lennon, John (1940-10-09)
Star, Ringo (1942-11-27)
Vai, Steve (1960-06-06)
(venv) RiffMates$ python manage.py musicians
➥ --last_name Loblaw    ◁──┐  A greater-than-or-equal filter can
Star, Ringo (1942-11-27)    │  be a full string or a single letter.
Vai, Steve (1960-06-06)
(venv) RiffMates$ python manage.py musicians --first_name J
Bonham, John (1948-07-31)
Cousin, Nicky (2000-01-13)          Flags can be combined. Although all musicians have
Hendrix, Jimi (1942-11-27)          a last name of B or greater, the first name restriction
Lennon, John (1940-10-09)           of O whittles the results down to just two. The filters
Star, Ringo (1942-11-27)            are implemented as an AND condition.
Vai, Steve (1960-06-06)
(venv) RiffMates$ python manage.py musicians --first_name O
➥ --last_name B              ◁──────────────────┘
Star, Ringo (1942-11-27)
Vai, Steve (1960-06-06)
```

```
(venv) RiffMates$ python manage.py musicians
➥ --birth 1950-01-30          ◄─── | Filtering based on a date
Cousin, Nicky (2000-01-13)          | in year-month-day format
Vai, Steve (1960-06-06)
(venv) RiffMates$ python manage.py musicians
➥ --birth tomorrow
CommandError: Birth date must be provided in YYYY-MM-DD format
```

Filtering based on a date in year-month-day format

datetime can't parse tomorrow, so a Command-Error is raised; this is more user friendly than a stack trace.

9.3.1 Built-in arguments

Now that you've added flags to the `musician` management command, the help screen has more stuff in it:

```
(venv) RiffMates$ python manage.py musicians --help
usage: manage.py musicians [-h] [--last_name LAST_NAME]
                           [--first_name FIRST_NAME] [--birth BIRTH]
                           [--version] [-v {0,1,2,3}]
                           [--settings SETTINGS] [--pythonpath PYTHONPATH]
                           [--traceback] [--no-color] [--force-color]
                           [--skip-checks]

       Lists registered musicians

options:
  -h, --help            show this help message and exit
  --last_name LAST_NAME, -l LAST_NAME
                        Query musicians whose last name is greater than or
                        equal to this value. Note this is case-sensitive.
  --first_name FIRST_NAME, -f FIRST_NAME
                        Query musicians whose first name is greater than
                        or equal to this value. Note this is case-sensitive.
  --birth BIRTH, -b BIRTH
                        Query musicians whose birth date is greater than
                        or equal to this value. Date must be given in
                        YYYY-MM-DD format.
  --version             Show program's version number and exit.
  -v {0,1,2,3}, --verbosity {0,1,2,3}
                        Verbosity level; 0=minimal output, 1=normal
                        output, 2=verbose output, 3=very verbose output
  --settings SETTINGS   The Python path to a settings module, e.g.
                        "myproject.settings.main". If this isn't provided,
                        the DJANGO_SETTINGS_MODULE environment variable
                        will be used.
  --pythonpath PYTHONPATH
                        A directory to add to the Python path, e.g.
                        "/home/djangoprojects/myproject".
  --traceback           Raise on CommandError exceptions.
  --no-color            Don't colorize the command output.
  --force-color         Force colorization of the command output.
  --skip-checks         Skip system checks.
```

The main help string gets set by the help attribute of your command class.

The --help flag gets created for you.

The help content for the --last_name flag based on the help parameter to .add_argument() and the flags for first name and birth date following it.

As before, your command class's `help` attribute is the main help message, but now, each flag you defined shows in the message as well. Django also provides a few more flags by default.

The `--version` flag prints out the Django version and exits. It isn't clear to me why they bother, as there is a `version` management command that does the same thing.

The `--verbosity` flag gets used by the built-in Django management commands to display more or less debug information as part of their output. Currently, using it with the `musicians` command does nothing, but `options["verbosity"]` is populated by the flag, so you could change your output based on its value.

The `-settings` flag changes which configuration Django uses, with the default being your settings.py file. Similarly, you can change your Python path if you need to add additional modules, using `--pythonpath`.

By default, raising a `CommandError` does not display a stack trace; instead, it prints a colorized error message. If you want to see the stack trace, the `--traceback` flag outputs it if an exception occurs.

Django automatically applies terminal colors to your management command if your terminal supports them. You can turn this off using `--no-color`, or if you're using the command in a situation where color is normally off (e.g., piping your command to another command), `--force-color` forces coloring to be turned on.

> ### Pretty pretty colors
> In addition to controlling your command's colors through the `--no-color` and `--force-color` flags, you can also change the colors themselves. This isn't done through the code but through an environment variable: `DJANGO_COLORS`. Django ships with three different palettes: dark, light, and nocolor. On a Unix-based machine using a bash-compatible shell, you change to the light palette with the following command:
>
> ```
> (venv) RiffMates$ export DJANGO_COLORS="light"
> ```
>
> This shell variable even allows you to control exactly which colors to use. For more information on controlling management command colors, see http://mng.bz/eEqw.

The same system checks that get run when the development server gets started are also available through the `check` management command. These checks also get run by default when you invoke your own commands. To skip them, use the `--skip-checks` flag. Alternatively, you can set your command class's `requires_system_checks` attribute to an empty `tuple` to disable checking programmatically.

9.4 *Testing, and using STDOUT and STDERR*

Chapter 8 was all about testing Django views; your custom management commands are code, so they deserve to be tested as well. To help with this, Django provides the `django.core.management.call_command` function, allowing you to invoke a management command from code.

A management command is often all about its output. For example, the `musicians` command displays musician information to the screen. Recall that I insisted you use `self.stdout.write()` instead of calling `print()`; testing is why. The `BaseCommand` class provides proxies to both STDOUT and STDERR, which the `call_command()`

function interfaces with. By using `self.stdout` and `self.stderr`, your tests can capture all of your command's output to a stream and then validate the stream's contents.

Consider testing the `musicians` command: first, you you need to create at least one `Musician` object during setup. Then, you'll need a test method that runs `call_command()`, a stream to capture the output, and assertion code that validates the contents of the stream. The following listing shows exactly that.

Listing 9.4 Test code for the `musicians` management command

```
# bands/tests.py
import io
from django.core.management import call_command
...
class TestMusiciansCommand(TestCase):
    def setUp(self):
        self.musician = Musician.objects.create(          ◄─┐  Create a Musician object
            first_name="First",                               in the test database.
            last_name="Last",
            birth=date(1900, 1, 1)
        )

    def test_command(self):                     Use a string
        output = io.StringIO()            ◄─┘   stream to        The call_command() function
                                                capture STDOUT.  takes the name of a command
                                                                 and optionally redirects
        call_command("musicians", stdout=output)       ◄─       STDOUT to a stream.
        self.assertIn("First", output.getvalue())       ◄─┐  Assert that the musician's
                                                             name ("First") is in the stream.
```

With the new test case created, you now run the `test` management command, which you learned about in chapter 8.

This example only invokes the simplest version of `musicians`, without any extra arguments. The `call_command()` function takes optional parameters, specifying the same kinds of positional arguments and flags that are used on the command-line. You can add `--last_name B` as parameter to `call_command()`, or if you prefer, you can also specify it as `last_name="B"`. To write a test case that checks all the functionality in `musicians`, you need a few more `Musician` objects and more invocations checking all flag combinations. I'll leave that to you to play with.

> **WARNING** If your test invokes `call_command()` multiple times, don't forget to create a new `StringIO` buffer each time; otherwise, you'll be including old results in your output

9.5   Exercises

1   Create a `venues` management command that lists all the `Venue` objects in your database. Include a `--rooms` flag to optionally display the names of the rooms associated with a venue. Hint: the `action="store_true"` parameter to `add_arguments()` changes your flag, so it acts as a Boolean flag and doesn't expect any additional arguments.

2 When you delete an object with a `FileField` or `ImageField`, Django does not remove the associated file. Write a `cleanup` command that searches through all the `Musician` and `Venue` objects for their associated pictures and compares this to the uploaded files, removing any orphans. Hint 1: use a Python `set` to contain all picture references and another to contain all file references, and then use the `set.difference()` method to determine the orphan list. Hint 2: convert the picture values into `pathlib.Path` objects before comparing them. Hint 3: test your code a lot, printing out results instead of deleting files until you're absolutely sure it works.

Summary

- A management command is a Python script that allows you to interact with your Django project from the command-line.
- You've used Django management commands throughout the book already, to create a superuser, create and migrate ORM tables, launch a Django-aware REPL, launch your database's command-line tool, save and load fixtures, and run your unit tests.
- Django comes with many management commands that give you the ability to create superusers, change passwords, import and export data, manage database interactions, run tests, and more.
- The `changepassword` management command allows you to change a user's password. It does not require authentication to do so, as Django expects people with access to the command-line to be administrators.
- The `diffsettings` management command displays the difference between the default configuration of a project and your own.
- The `flush` management command wipes all data from your database but keeps the table structure and current migration state. It is useful when developing a new project to clear out test data.
- The `sqlflush` and `sqlmigrate` management commands print out the SQL that would be run for the corresponding `flush` and `migrate` commands.
- Each management command is its own file associated with a Django app, living inside the app's management/commands directory. The name of the file is the name of the command. The directories are Python modules and require a __init__.py file.
- Django expects each management command file to contain a class that extends from `BaseCommand`.
- The `.handle()` method in your management command class is the entry point for performing an action. It is invoked by Django when the management command gets run.
- Instead of using `print()` in a management command, it is recommended to use `self.stdout.write()` and `self.stderr.write()`. Using these proxies to the output streams makes it easier to write tests for your management command.

- Command-line arguments are divided into two types: positional arguments and flags. Flags are typically optional and are denoted by a leading dash or double-dash.

- Django automatically creates a `--help` argument for your command and displays the message found within your command class's `help` attribute.

- The `BaseCommand` class wraps Python's `argparse` library for you, creating a command-line argument parser and parsing any additional arguments to your command.

- You can register command-line positional arguments and flags with the `argparse` parser by overriding the command class's `.add_arguments()` method. The method gets called with a reference to the parser, which you use to register arguments through its `.add_argument()` method.

- The `.handle()` method gets passed `options`, which contains the positional arguments and flags passed on the command-line to your management command.

- If you raise a `CommandError` in your management command, Django suppresses its stack trace, printing a colorized message instead. This behavior can be overridden using the `--traceback` flag.

- The `call_command()` function allows you to invoke a management command programmatically. This is particularly helpful for writing unit tests for your command.

- You can capture the output from a management command by passing an `io.String` stream to the `stdout` and `stderr` parameters of the `call_command()` function.

Migration

10

This chapter covers

- The internals of migration scripts
- Writing custom migrations, including manipulating existing data
- Combining and optimizing migration files
- Dealing with merge conflicts caused by changing a model

Django `Model` objects are proxies to tables in a database, and the migration system helps you maintain the relationship between the two. The migration system is a powerful tool that allows you to move forward and backward through state changes and manipulate data while doing so.

10.1 *Migration scripts in detail*

In chapter 4, you learned about Django's ORM and how `Model` classes act as a proxy to tables in the database. You used the `makemigrations` and `migrate` commands to push changes down to the database that correspond to the code in your model files. Managing changes to your models can be a bit complicated, and this chapter dives deeper into the migration system.

To better understand what happens during the migration process, it is time to create a new Django app. This app won't have much functionality in it, and for now, it won't even have any views, but by working with a fresh model file in a new app, you'll be able to see exactly what happens at each step in the migration process.

A lot goes on in the music industry besides music. There are some very big names that you've likely never heard of, without whom you might never have known your favorite bands. Promoters and managers are the people behind the scenes that make concerts happen and help bands fulfill their musical dreams. Our new Django app tracks promoters. To create the new app, you'll need to run the `startapp` management command, passing it `promoters` as an argument. You'll then also need to update `INSTALLED_APPS` in settings.py to register the app with your project. For a refresher on creating new apps, see chapter 2.

Throughout this chapter, you'll be modifying the `Promoter` model and examining the resulting migration files. You need to start this journey somewhere, so create a `Promoter Model` with a first and last name field to store the promoter's info. Add the code in the following listing to models.py in your new promoter app.

Listing 10.1   A short `Model` to use as a starting point for investigating migrations

```
# RiffMates/promoters/models.py
from django.db import models

class Promoter(models.Model):
    first_name = models.CharField(max_length=25)
    last_name = models.CharField(max_length=25)
```

You'll want some data in your database. The easiest way to do this is to build a `ModelAdmin` object for `Promoter`, and then use the Django Admin to enter some data. The following listing shows a simple `PromoterAdmin` object you can use to do data entry. For a refresher on the Django Admin and its classes, see chapter 5.

Listing 10.2   An Admin Model for the new Promoter object

```
# RiffMates/promoters/admin.py
from django.contrib import admin

from promoters.models import Promoter

@admin.register(Promoter)
class PromoterAdmin(admin.ModelAdmin):
    list_display = ("id", "first_name", "last_name", )
```

To save you the effort of digging through Wikipedia, table 10.1 has the data for four famous promoters you can use in this chapter.

Table 10.1   **Music industry promoters you can use to populate your database**

Name	Famous For	Lifetime
Allan Williams	The Beatles	1930/02/21–2016/12/30
Harvey Goldsmith	Live Aid	1946/03/04–
Phoebe Jacobs	Duke Ellington, Ella Fitzgerald	1919/06/21–2012/04/09
Michael Lang	Woodstock	1944/12/11–2022/01/08

Of course, to be able to enter the data, you need the corresponding tables in the database to exist. You'll recall from chapter 4 that you accomplish this by creating migration files and migrating them. To create a migration script, you use the `makemigrations` management command:

```
(venv) RiffMates$ python manage.py makemigrations promoters
Migrations for 'promoters':
  promoters/migrations/0001_initial.py
    - Create model Promoter
```

> The makemigrations management command takes the name of a Django app as an argument.

When run, the command reports that a new file has been created: promoters/migrations/0001_initial.py. Django uses this file to know which actions to perform on the database corresponding to changes in the `Promoter` class. The action required for a new model is table creation. Running the `migrate` management command causes this to happen:

```
(venv) RiffMates$ python manage.py migrate
Operations to perform:
  Apply all migrations: admin, auth, bands, content, contenttypes,
      promoters, sessions
Running migrations:
  Applying promoters.0001_initial... OK
```

Once you've performed the migration, the table for `Promoter` gets created. You can now use the Django Admin to enter some data. Go do that now, and I'll wait for you here. (See, that's funny because this is a book, and I'm not really here waiting at all. A joke isn't a good one unless you explain it.)

10.1.1 An initial migration

Nothing covered so far is new. You already knew how to create an app, create a new `Model` class with corresponding migration files, and migrate it to the database. In fact, you're probably also accustomed to my odd sense of humor by this point as well.

Although you've done migrations before, they've kind of been magic. It's time to look behind the curtain. It might seem an obvious point to make, but migration files are Python files. They aren't the most obvious scripts, though. They mostly consist of just data structures. The actual code that performs a migration is deep within the Django framework; the migration file provides data to inform the process.

Consider your newly created migration file for the promoters app: promoters/migrations/0001_initial.py. It contains a Migration class that encapsulates the actions needed in the database for the Promoter Model. There are three members of the Migration class: .initial, .dependencies, and .operations. The .initial value is a Boolean, which is True if this is the first migration to be performed for the app. The .dependencies list contains the names of other migrations that need to be run before this one, which, for 0001_initial.py, is empty.

The core of the Migration class is the .operations list. This consists of a series of objects that describe what actions need to be performed on the database. For 0001_initial.py, this list contains a single object: CreateModel. When the Django migration system sees a CreateModel object, it knows to create the tables in the database for the named model. For the Promoter model, there are three fields: the two you specified for first and last names and a third for the object's ID, which is automatically created by Django. Each field gets specified in the migration using the same classes you use when writing the Model class itself. For the first and last name, that is a CharField, and for the ID, it is a BigAutoField. The following listing shows the entire migration file.

Listing 10.3 The initial migration script for the Promoters app

```
# RiffMates/promoters/migrations/0001_initial.py
from django.db import migrations, models

class Migration(migrations.Migration):
    initial = True

    dependencies = []

    operations = [
        migrations.CreateModel(
            name="Promoter",
            fields=[
                (
                    "id",
                    models.BigAutoField(
                        auto_created=True,
                        primary_key=True,
                        serialize=False,
                        verbose_name="ID",
                    ),
                ),
                (
                    "first_name",
                    models.CharField(max_length=25)
                ),
```

Each migration file contains a Migration class definition that describes the migration's corresponding database actions.

.initial indicates whether this is the first migration for the app.

.dependencies is a list of migration filenames that need to be run before this one; for the initial script, this is empty.

The .operations list contains all the actions run by this migration

The initial migration for the Promoter object has a single operation: creating the model.

CreateModel contains a list of fields in the model that correspond to columns in the underlying database table(s).

By default, Django creates an ID field as a primary key, using the BigAutoField type.

The first and last name fields get specified using the same CharField as is used in your model specification.

```
        ("last_name", models.CharField(max_length=25)),
    ],
  ),
]
```

> **Why plural?**
> You may have noticed I keep writing *tables* rather than *table*. Remember that a single
> `Model` class may result in multiple database tables. The `Promoter` class is a single
> table with three columns, but any class with a `ManyToManyField` results in both a
> main table for the model and a relationship table containing the IDs of the related
> objects. And of course, a model can have more than one many-to-many relationship.
> Each `Model` class results in a main table plus another table for each many-to-many
> relationship defined.

The name of the migration file gets automatically generated when you run `make-migrations`. It is both important and unimportant at the same time. The run order of the files gets determined by the contents of `.initial` and `.dependencies`. Although 0001_initial.py implies it is first, it doesn't have to be. You could do something creative and muck with the names of the files, and things would still work if the member values got constructed properly. I've never tried this; I wouldn't recommend it, and although the name isn't important to Django, it really helps a programmer understand what order things happen in. Don't muck with the filenames.

10.1.2 *Changing a model*

The migration system hasn't been around for the entire lifetime of Django. In the olden days, coders had to manage changes to their models manually. This was painful. Several add-ons got created by a variety of coders to help manage this problem, with the most popular being called South. South became so popular that the Django core team decided to integrate it into the framework.

Consider what you would need to do if the migration framework did not exist. Having just the promoter's name in the database isn't enough information. To track why they're famous, you add another field. The corresponding database table now needs a new column to go with this field. Before the existence of the migration framework, you'd have to write a SQL script to take care of this change. If you forget during development that a `Model` class changed, and don't have a corresponding SQL script, your code would crash. Not only does Django detect changes in your models, but you can also run commands to check whether the state of the database matches the state of the models, helping ensure you haven't forgotten anything when you push your code live.

To see how Django handles the addition of a field, let's add a field. Before doing that, make sure you've put some promoter data in the database using the Django Admin. This data complicates things, and you want to see that complication. Once you've got the data in place, add a `CharField` called `famous_for`. The following listing shows the new version of the `Promoter` class.

Listing 10.4 Add `famous_for` **to the Promoter class**

```
# RiffMates/promoters/models.py
from django.db import models

class Promoter(models.Model):
    first_name = models.CharField(max_length=25)
    last_name = models.CharField(max_length=25)
    famous_for = models.CharField(max_length=50)
```

A new field to store what a promoter is known for

The purpose of migrations is to manage your database over time as your project changes. Once you've released code and your project is live, you'll have data in your database, which makes changing it messier than creating it. In `Promoter`, the first and last name are required fields, since you haven't specified `null=True`. The database expects all rows in the table to contain a value. First and last name are both text, which means the value can be an empty string. From the database's perspective, an empty string isn't empty, `NULL` is empty.

> **NOTE** Recall `null=True` specifies a value can be `NULL` in the database, while `blank=True` specifies whether the Django Admin and other forms allow you to enter an empty string.

The new `famous_for` field is also required. When the new column gets added to the table, the database won't allow the `famous_for` field on the existing rows to be `NULL`. You have to put something in each field, for the sake of database integrity. Your choices are to change `famous_for`, so it isn't a required field; provide a default value on the field; or provide a default value in the migration file.

When you run `makemigrations` on the changed `Promoter` model, Django detects that `famous_for` is a required field without a default value and prompts for content to insert during the migration. This wasn't needed when you created the table, as there was no content in the database, but there is now. Run the `makemigrations` command as follows, choosing Provide a One-Off Default when prompted:

```
(venv) RiffMates$ python manage.py makemigrations promoters
It is impossible to add a non-nullable field 'famous_for' to promoters
without specifying a default. This is because the database needs
something to populate existing rows.
Please select a fix:
 1) Provide a one-off default now (will be set on all existing rows
 with a null value for this column)
 2) Quit and manually define a default value in models.py.
Select an option:
```

When you select Provide a One-Off Default, Django opens a Python REPL for you where you enter the default value. The use of the shell here is rather clever; it means you can call functions that return a value. Note that if you do this, it is called immediately, and the value gets inserted in the script. The calculation isn't performed at migration time or per row in the database.

For the `Promoter` migration, an empty string for the `famous_for` field is sufficient:

```
Please enter the default value as valid Python.
The datetime and django.utils.timezone modules are available, so it is
possible to provide e.g. timezone.now as a value.
Type 'exit' to exit this prompt
>>> ""
Migrations for 'promoters':                              ◁─┐ A default value used by the
  promoters/migrations/0002_promoter_famous_for.py          migration script to populate
    - Add field famous_for to promoter                       famous_for in existing rows
```

The new migration file gets called 0002_promoter_famous_for.py. The name is rather helpful. It indicates that this is the second migration file to run (there are exceptions to this—more on that later), it touches the `Promoter` class, and the change is the `famous_for` field. Like with 0001_initial.py, the new migration script contains a `Migration` class declaration. This time, the `.dependencies` attribute got populated, indicating that the 0001_initial.py migration must be run before this one. This time around, the operation is `AddField`, which adds the new `famous_for` field. The complete contents of the second migration file are in the following listing.

Listing 10.5   The migration file for adding the `famous_for` field

```
# RiffMates/promoters/migrations/0002_promoter_famous_for.py
from django.db import migrations, models

class Migration(migrations.Migration):
    dependencies = [
        ("promoters", "0001_initial"),        ◁─┐ This migration depends on
    ]                                             0001_intitial.py in the promoters app.

    operations = [
        migrations.AddField(        ◁─┐ AddField describes the addition of the
            model_name="promoter",       famous_for field to the database.
            name="famous_for",
            field=models.CharField(default="", max_length=50),
            preserve_default=False,
        ),
    ]
```

Now that you've seen a second migration file, hopefully, you're getting the idea of how these pieces fit together. Don't forget to run the `migration` command to invoke this latest change. If you wish, you can also populate your `famous_for` fields using the Django Admin. The migrations you've seen so far have been purely structural, but once you're using your database, any changes could also impact existing data. The next section outlines the extra work you need to do in this case.

10.2   *Migration with existing data*

When you added `famous_for` to the `Promoter` model, you gave Django a value for existing rows in the database. Adding content requires a little thought. *Deleting*, or moving content between columns, is a whole other challenge. Removing a field isn't hard, but the consequences should be considered fully first. The migration system is about the state of the table structures, not the contents of the tables. Removing a field in your model results in a column getting removed from the database. All data in that column goes away. There is no "undo." Unless you've made a backup of the database, the data is gone. Moving content is equivalent to adding a new column and deleting the old one, so it has all the challenges of deletion with added steps.

Changing your mind about the structure of your models can be problematic. In the `Promoter` model (and in others) you used a very Western-centric view of people's names. The assumption that everyone has a first and last name is wrong. Patrick McKenzie has written a great article on this topic, called "Falsehoods Programmers Believe About Names" (http://mng.bz/5o28). Add it to your reading list, as it is valuable information.

Falsehood programmers believe

Articles similar to Patrick's have become a genre unto themselves. There seems to be a lot of falsehoods we programmers believe. The following are a couple more that are seminal for your reading list:

- "Falsehoods Programmers Believe About Time" (http://mng.bz/6n2p)
- "Falsehoods Programmers Believe About Email" (http://mng.bz/orEy)
- "Falsehoods Programmers Believe About Geography" (http://mng.bz/n18V)

There are curated lists of these kinds of articles as well, Kevin Deldycke's "awesome falsehood" (http://mng.bz/vP5m) has a decent round-up.

A better way to store names than using a first and last name field is to store a full name and the name the person wishes to be called (the common name). This doesn't solve all the problems that Patrick enumerates, but it is a step in the right direction. To change the `Promoter` model to use this style, you have a problem: you already have data. Adding two new fields isn't a big deal, but what do you do about the existing first and last names?

Since the existing structure uses Western-centric assumptions, let's continue with the assumption that composing the first and last name together can constitute our full name, and the first name can be the common name. This doesn't fix any problems with the existing data's assumptions, but it does create a space from which you can move forwards. By transferring the first and last name data into full name and common name fields, you can then remove the first and last name fields, leaving your model in a better state.

This transformation is done in three steps:

1   Add the new full name and common name fields.

2   Construct the data for the full and common name fields based on the existing first and last names.

3   Remove the existing first and last names.

The first and third steps are things you already know how to do; you modify the fields in the model and migrate them. Django's migration framework provides programmatic hooks that allow you to perform the second step as part of a migration. The `migrations` module has an operation class called `RunPython`. This class takes two references to functions: one function to be called when moving forward in a migration and another to be called when moving backward (yep, you can move backward—more on how to do that later).

Let's de-Westernize `Promoter`. First, add the two new fields, and create the corresponding migration file. The following listing shows the state of `Promoter` after step 1.

Listing 10.6   Adding full and common name fields to the Promoter Model

```
# RiffMates/promoters/models.py
from django.db import models

class Promoter(models.Model):
    first_name = models.CharField(max_length=25)
    last_name = models.CharField(max_length=25)
    common_name = models.CharField(max_length=25)    ⟵  Add new common
    full_name = models.CharField(max_length=50)            and full name
    famous_for = models.CharField(max_length=50)    ⟵     fields to Promoter.
```

Note that the order you declare your fields in effects
the underlying table structure but doesn't have to
correspond to when you added things to your model;
`famous_for` can show up after the new fields.

With the change in place, create a new migration file by running the `makemigrations` management command. The resulting file has a rather unwieldy name: 0003_promoter_common_name_promoter_full_name.py.

The second step in the de-Westernization process is the new one. Inside of a migration file, you use a `RunPython` class as an operation by providing code that copies data from the first and last name fields into the full and common name fields. This new code goes in a custom migration file. To create one, call `makemigrations` with the `--empty` flag. This creates a migration file stub with an automatically generated filename. My obsessive need for control over details means I can't leave that alone, so I rename the file to be a little more clear. The process for creating and renaming the file is as follows:

```
(venv) RiffMates$ python manage.py makemigrations --empty promoters    ⟵
Migrations for 'promoters':                                    Create a stub migration file
    promoters/migrations/0004_auto_20230904_1552.py              in the promoters app.
(venv) RiffMates$ cd promoters/migrations/
(venv) migrations$ mv 0004_auto_20230904_1552.py 0004_data_fullname.py    ⟵
(venv) RiffMates$ cd -
                                                             Rename the file something
                                                                   more descriptive.
```

The resulting stub migration file looks like this:

```
from django.db import migrations

class Migration(migrations.Migration):
    dependencies = [
        ("promoters", "0003_promoter_common_name_promoter_full_name"),
    ]

    operations = []
```

The migration framework automatically makes the new script dependent on the previous one.

A stub migration script starts with no operations.

With 0004_data_fullname.py in place, you now have somewhere to write the data translation code. This script gets run after the 0003 migration, so the full and common name fields will exist. To populate those fields, enumerate all the existing rows, copying the first and last name contents into the full and common name fields. This work goes in a function that can live in the migration file. The migration system supports moving forward and backward in table state, so it is best practice to write code that undoes the translation work as well.

> **NOTE** In some situations, you simply can't move backward through a migration. The transformation on your data may be one-way. If you do not provide a function for moving backward to RunPython, Django raises an exception if someone attempts to undo this migration step.

To write a Django view that enumerates all Promoter objects, import Promoter and run Promoter.objects.all(). Unfortunately, life in a migration script isn't that simple. Importing Promoter gives you the current state of the model. The state of Promoter in a migration script may be different from the current state of the model—that's the purpose of migration scripts. Consider the case where you are on your 10th change to Promoter, the 4th migration script needs the state of Promoter six changes ago.

Django can build any version of your model from the information inside the migration scripts. You get at the version corresponding to the migration script by calling apps.get_model(), where apps is one of the two arguments sent in to the function called by RunPython. The second argument is schema_editor, and although it isn't something normal humans use, it has to be in the function signature. The migration system in Django is pluggable, and you can replace it with your own code. Doing so requires building SchemaEditor objects, which are what the migration system is passing to your function call. I've never met anyone, outside the Django core team, who has ever needed to do this though.

Listing 10.7 contains the code that translates the first and last name fields into their corresponding full and common name versions. It contains two functions, de_westernize_names() and re_westernize_names(), for migrating forward and backward, respectively. References to these functions are passed to a RunPython object, which is included in the Migration class's operations list.

Listing 10.7 A migration script that calls Python to transform data during migration

```
# RiffMates/promoters/migrations/0004_data_fullname.py
from django.db import migrations
```

This function gets called by RunPython when migrating forward.

The apps.get_model() method returns a Model class, whose state is the same as the current migration.

```
def de_westernize_names(apps, schema_editor):
    # Can't import Promoter Model, the current version may be newer than
    # the one in this migration. Use historical version instead.
    Promoter = apps.get_model("promoters", "Promoter")    ◄─────────┐
    for promoter in Promoter.objects.all():        ◄─────
        promoter.full_name = f"{promoter.first_name} {promoter.last_name}"
        promoter.common_name = promoter.first_name
        promoter.save()
```

Data translation for Promoter requires enumerating all objects, and for each one, constructing the .full_name field based on the .first_name and .last_name fields and then copying the .first_name field into the .common_name field.

This function gets called by RunPython when migrating backward. It is similar to de_westernize(), except it undoes the data translation.

```
def re_westernize_names(apps, schema_editor):    ◄──────
    Promoter = apps.get_model("promoters", "Promoter")
    for promoter in Promoter.objects.all():
        promoter.first_name = promoter.common_name
        length = len(promoter.first_name)
        promoter.last_name = promoter.full_name[length + 1:]

    promoter.save()

class Migration(migrations.Migration):
    dependencies = [
        ("promoters", "0003_promoter_common_name_promoter_full_name"),
    ]

    operations = [
        migrations.RunPython(    ◄──────
            de_westernize_names,
            re_westernize_names
        ),
    ]
```

RunPython is an operation that takes two function references: the first gets called when migrating forward, and the second when migrating backward.

Your data translation migration script is ready. The full process, including removal of the first and last name fields, is three steps, but that doesn't mean you should run them all together. Now is a good time to test. If you've made an error in your script, you might lose data. Your data is four sample lines of Promoters and can easily be re-entered. The real world is seldom that forgiving. You should take a backup of your database and test your scripts by running the `migrate` management command. Once you've done that, validate that the script did what you wanted. If it didn't, restore your backup, fix your bugs, and try again. Once you're satisfied that 0004 is working, you can move to the third, and final, step in the process.

The last step is to remove the first and last name fields. This step shouldn't contain any surprises. Open the model file, delete the appropriate lines, run `makemigrations`, and then migrate. The final state of `Promoter` is shown in the following listing.

> ### Listing 10.8   Promoter without a first and last name field

```
# RiffMates/promoters/models.py
from django.db import models

class Promoter(models.Model):
    common_name = models.CharField(max_length=25)
    full_name = models.CharField(max_length=50)
    famous_for = models.CharField(max_length=50)
```

The migration file for this change has the lengthy name: 0005_remove_promoter_first_name_remove_promoter_last_name.py. You need to run the `migrate` command to have it take effect. Don't forget, the changes you're making need to be reflected in the Django Admin, so you'll need to update your `PromoterAdmin` class if you wrote one.

> ### Database changes in the real world
>
> Depending on the size of your project, how many people are using it, and how many coders are involved, you may need to keep intermediate migration stages alive for long periods of time. Consider the de-Westernization of our `Promoter` model. If our project had an API that accessed `Promoter` or other developers had code that was dependent on `Promoter` containing a first and last name, you may not want to remove those fields immediately. Your production system could stay in stage 0004 for weeks or months, as others catch up to your changes. When you make the intermediary changes, you announce the deprecation of the first and last name fields and a target date for their removal. You only perform the removal after the date has passed and, depending on how much you like your colleagues, after you've verified they're ready for the change. A similar process can be used to rename columns: create a column with the new name, copy the data, keep both columns until the deprecation comes into effect, and then remove the original column.
>
> The `Promoter` case is relatively simple. If the data is only ever accessed through the `Promoter` object, you can write properties that mimic the first and last names without breaking anything. In large, complex systems, there is a chance someone else is integrated directly with your database though, and that requires the columns to continue to exist. This adds the complication of having to maintain consistency across the four name fields. Who said software was easy?

10.3   Squashing a migration

Each change you make to your models means another migration file. If you are frequently standing up new instances of your project from scratch, running all these migrations takes time. You may not need the whole state history of your project, only what things look like now. Django's migration system provides a mechanism for squashing migrations together. It takes two or more migration stages and produces a single file to replace them all.

To better understand the process of squashing migrations, let's add two new changes to `Promoter`, with a migration file for each. The first change is to add a date of birth field and the second is to add a date of death field. Apply each change separately, creating a migration after each. The end result of `Promoter` is shown in the following listing.

Listing 10.9   Two changes to Promoter to be squashed together

```
# RiffMates/promoters/models.py
from django.db import models

class Promoter(models.Model):
    common_name = models.CharField(max_length=25)
    full_name = models.CharField(max_length=50)
    famous_for = models.CharField(max_length=50)
    birth = models.DateField(blank=True, null=True)
    death = models.DateField(blank=True, null=True)
```

First, add the new .birth field, creating a migration immediately afterward. By using blank=True and null=True, this field is allowed to be empty in the database and the Django Admin.

After migrating the .birth field change, follow a similar process to add the .death field.

The migration files for these two changes get named: 0006_promoter_birth.py and 0007_promoter_death.py. If you've been coding along, your Promoters app's migration directory looks like this:

```
RiffMates/promoters/migrations/
├── 0001_initial.py
├── 0002_promoter_famous_for.py
├── 0003_promoter_common_name_promoter_full_name.py
├── 0004_data_fullname.py
├── 0005_remove_promoter_first_name_remove_promoter_last_name.py
├── 0006_promoter_birth.py
├── 0007_promoter_death.py
└── __init__.py
```

Once you have the two migrations, you can squash them together. Squashing is done using the `squashmigrations` management command. This command takes three arguments: the name of the app to be squashed as well as the start and end points of the squashing. The start and end points can either be the full names of the migration files or just enough of their name to uniquely identify them. You can type less by using the number portion of the filename. To squash the birth and death field migrations into a single file, you specify `0006` and `0007` as the squashing targets. The command is as follows:

```
(venv) RiffMates$ python manage.py squashmigrations promoters 0006 0007
Will squash the following migrations:
 - 0006_promoter_birth
 - 0007_promoter_death
Do you wish to proceed? [yN] y
Optimizing...
  No optimizations possible.
```

```
Created new squashed migration
  0006_promoter_birth_squashed_0007_promoter_death.py

  You should commit this migration but leave the old ones in place;
  the new migration will be used for new installs. Once you are sure
  all instances of the codebase have applied the migrations you squashed,
  you can delete them.
```

The command asks if you are sure and results in a new file that starts with the same number as the source of your squashing. The new state of your migration directory is as follows:

```
RiffMates/promoters/migrations/
├── 0001_initial.py
├── 0002_promoter_famous_for.py
├── 0003_promoter_common_name_promoter_full_name.py
├── 0004_data_fullname.py
├── 0005_remove_promoter_first_name_remove_promoter_last_name.py
├── 0006_promoter_birth.py                                        ◄
├── 0006_promoter_birth_squashed_0007_promoter_death.py           ◄
├── 0007_promoter_death.py             ◄
└── __init__.py
```

Original script for adding the .birth field

Squashed script containing the addition of both the .birth and .death fields

Original script for adding the .death field

As the note from the command tells you, you can leave the old files around. The Django migration framework ignores them. Of course, if you were willing to keep them around, there really wasn't a need to squash them in the first place, but if you want to keep them there until you're sure everything works, they do no damage. The more complicated your migration files are, the more work Django has to do to squash your migrations. There is a chance the tool can get it wrong, and the documentation recommends holding onto your old files until you've tested the squashed ones. See https://mng.bz/7ddx for more information and to better understand possible pitfalls.

10.4   *More migration choices*

So far, you've mostly been running the migrate management command without any options. When you call migrate without any arguments, it migrates the database forward to the current state of your model files. You can be more explicit, though, and specify the target state. Doing this, you can migrate forward or backward to any allowed position on the migration timeline.

For example, the current state of Promoter is the squashed migration script with the birth and death field additions. To back this migration out, you can migrate to stage 0005:

Specify both the Django app name and (partial) migration filename to target a specific state.

```
(venv) RiffMates$ python manage.py migrate promoters 0005     ◄
Operations to perform:
  Target specific migration:
    0005_remove_promoter_first_name_remove_promoter_last_name, from promoters
```

```
Running migrations:
 Rendering model states... DONE
 Unapplying promoters.0006_promoter_birth_squashed_0007_promoter_death... OK
```

The `--plan` option to `migrate` shows what would happen if you run `migrate` without any arguments. As you've just undone the squashed 0006 script, using `--plan` tells you that a migration is due:

```
(venv) RiffMates$ python manage.py migrate --plan
Planned operations:
promoters.0006_promoter_birth_squashed_0007_promoter_death
    Add field birth to promoter
    Add field death to promoter
```

Not only does `--plan` tell you which scripts will be executed, but it even includes the details about their effects. In this case, that is the addition of the birth and death fields.

Scary options to migrate

There are a few more arguments to `migrate` that allow you to muck around with the database. Recall from chapter 4 that Django keeps the current state of migration in a table called `django_migrations`. The `--fake` and `--fake-initial` options update this table as if a migration had run, without actually running it. The `--fake-initial` option restricts the change to only the initial migration. The `--run-syncdb` option creates tables for the apps but without running migrations. You use these three options if you have existing database structures you're trying to Django-ify or you're trying to bypass the migration system for performance reasons.

Using any of these options can result in the contents of the `django_migrations` table being out of sync with the migration files in your project. Be careful, as a mismatch may result in Django not detecting future changes or rerunning a migration that has already been done.

The `--prune` option removes any migrations from the `django_migrations` table that no longer exist. A few extra rows in the database are not going to hurt anything, so this really is a neat-freak kind of choice.

The `makemigrations` command also has some useful optional arguments. You can use `--dry-run` to see what the result of calling `makemigrations` would be, without it actually creating the migration script.

One challenge you may encounter when working with multiple developers is two people making a change to a model on different branches in the code repo at the same time. Whoever merges last gets a merge conflict. The `Model` state needs to be fixed by addressing the two overlapping changes. Additionally, you'll have two migration files with the same starting number, one from your change and one from your colleague's.

The `--merge` option to `makemigrations` operates on files with the same numbers, producing a new migration script named with the next number. The new script has no operations but depends on the two conflicting ones. This ensures future migration scripts are dependent on both files. Figure 10.1 illustrates this resolution.

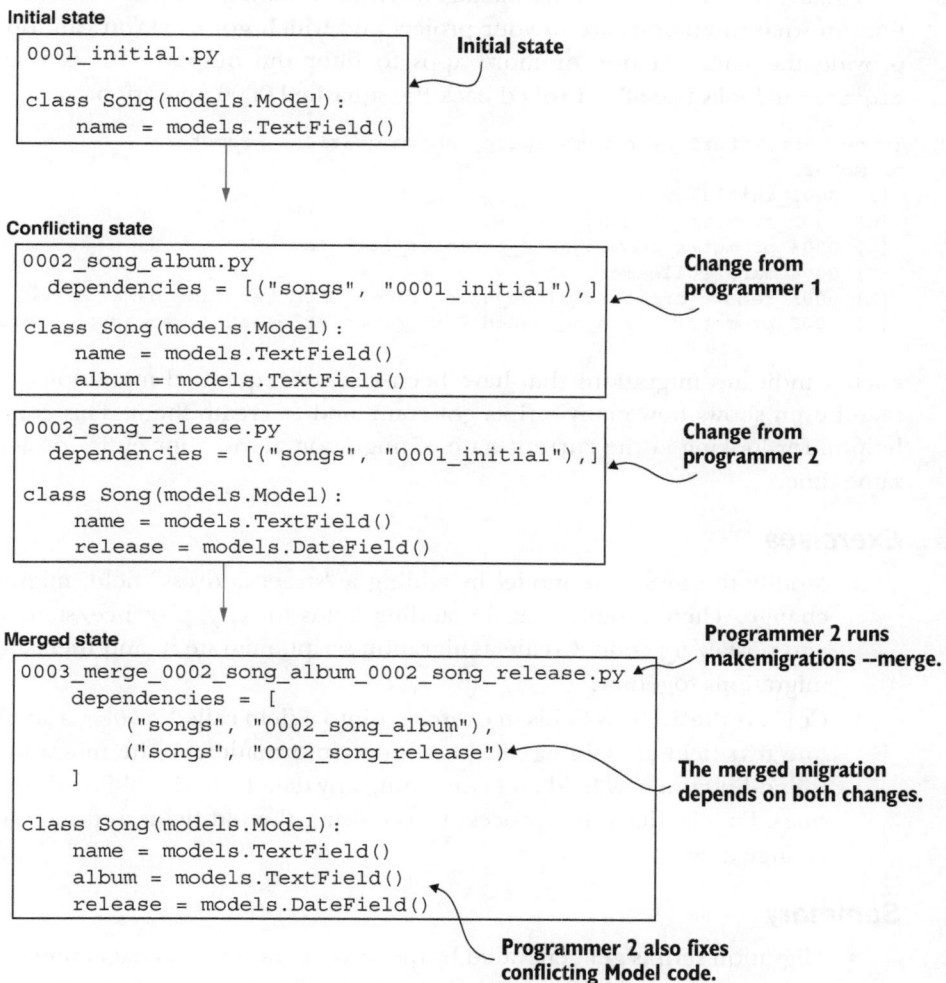

Figure 10.1   Dealing with a merge conflict containing migration scripts

If you go back and look at the output of `squashmigrations`, you'll notice it contains `Optimizing...`. During the squashing process, Django examines the operations and attempts to reduce the number of them, if possible. For example, if you are squashing together migrations that both create a new table and later add fields to that table,

Django replaces that with a single creation step that includes the added field. You can invoke this same optimization process on a single file that hasn't been squashed by using the `optimizemigration` management command. Personally, I've never used this; I do my best to keep my model changes as small as possible, leaving little need for optimization.

Finally, the `showmigrations` management command gives you detailed information on what migrations are in your project and which got run. You can, optionally, provide the name of one or more apps to filter the output. This is what `showmigrations` looks like after I rolled back the squashed 0006 migration:

```
(venv) RiffMates$ python manage.py showmigrations promoters
promoters
 [X] 0001_initial
 [X] 0002_promoter_famous_for
 [X] 0003_promoter_common_name_promoter_full_name
 [X] 0004_data_fullname
 [X] 0005_remove_promoter_first_name_remove_promoter_last_name
 [ ] 0006_promoter_birth_squashed_0007_promoter_death (2 squashed migrations)
```

Each x indicates migrations that have been run. For squashed migrations, the command even shows how many scripts got combined to create them. This command is helpful for looking at the current state of migration across your entire project at the same time.

10.5 *Exercises*

1   Modify the `Promoter` model by adding a "street address" field, migrating the change. Then, modify it again, adding fields for city, province/state, country, and postal/zip code. Create a migration script, migrate it, and then squash the migrations together.

2   Convert the address fields in exercise 1 into a field called *address*, a single multiline text field containing all the address information. Write migration scripts for adding the new field and converting any data from the old fields to the new ones. Finally, finish the process by removing the old fields and migrating that change as well.

Summary

- Migration scripts get generated by the `makemigrations` management command and are responsible for syncing the state of your `Model` files with the corresponding database tables.

- You use the `migrate` management command to invoke the migration scripts on the database.

- Migration scripts are Python programs that declare the `Migration` class, used to tell Django what changes need to be performed.

- The first migration script generated for a new Django app is named 0001 _initial.py, with subsequent files starting with an incremented number and the name of the class and field getting changed.

- The `Migration` class has three fields: a Boolean indicating whether this is an initial script, a list of other scripts that must be run before this one, and a list of operations to perform.

- The name of the migration script is a hint for developers regarding what the script does, but the number is irrelevant to the framework. Django determines the order of script execution based on the `depenencies` member of the `Migration` classes.

- The `operations` list in a `Migration` class contains one or more classes that indicate what changes need to happen. For example, the `CreateModel` operation indicates a new `Model` has been created and one or more tables need to be created in the database.

- The `CreateModel` operation has a `fields` member that contains descriptors of the fields in the `Model`. It uses the same classes to specify fields as a `Model` class.

- Changing an existing `Model` impacts the data in the table that is already there. You may need to provide default entries for existing rows in the database. The `makemigrations` script prompts you if this is the case and gives you access to a REPL to enter the default data to be used by the script.

- Migrations can be run both forward and backward.

- The `RunPython` operation allows you to call a function to perform side-effects on the database as part of the migration. `RunPython` takes two function references as arguments, the first to be called when migrating forward and the second for migrating backward.

- You can generate a migration script with no operations using the `make-migrations` command and passing it the `--empty` flag. This can be used to create a stub file for custom `RunPython` operations.

- Renaming or combining fields requires a three-step process: (1) add the new field and migrate the change; (2) add a custom migration script that uses the `RunPython` operation to migrate the data and migrate the change; and (3) remove the original fields and migrate the change.

- Not all custom migrations can be undone. If a migration can't be undone, the second argument to `RunPython` can be left empty. Django raises an exception if such a backward migration gets attempted.

- For efficiency, multiple migration files can be combined using the `squash-migrations` management command. This command does not remove the old files, which can be left in place, as they are no longer part of the dependency chain.

- The `--plan` flag of the `migrate` management command prints out what migrations need to be run.
- The `showmigrations` management command prints out the current state of all migrations in the system, indicating both those migrations that have been run and those that need to be run.

Part 3

Django projects

Parts 1 and 2 of the book gave you the basis for writing complex, multiuser websites. The chapters in part 3 explore some third-party libraries you can use to add even more capabilities to your project. The chapters in this part aren't interdependent, so feel free to read them in whatever order you please.

Chapter 11 is all about APIs. It will show you how to use the Django Ninja library to build the backend of a single-page application and add features to your site, so users can programmatically access your data.

Unmodified, Django's view mechanism favors multi-page applications, but newer tools, like HTMX, can provide dynamic interactions without the need to convert to full single-page application (SPA) frameworks, like React or Angular. Chapter 12 shows you how to use HTMX and partial-page snippets to increase the interactivity of your web pages.

Chapter 13 provides an overview of several popular third-party libraries. It discusses power tools, such as the Django Debug Toolbar, using Django Distill to create static sites, beautifying the Django Admin using Grappelli, and much more.

Finally, Chapter 14 points you to what's next. It briefly covers parts of the Django framework that didn't fit in the book, several third-party libraries that will help you write less code, as well as some helpful links to resources where you can learn more about Django and its ecosystem.

Adding an API to your project creates a way for other systems to access your data, including alternate frontend interfaces, such as mobile devices and single-page applications (SPAs). The most common API protocol on the web is REST, a mechanism built on top of URLs and HTTP calls. The third-party library Django Ninja allows you to build REST-based APIs using the same view functions you've used for your pages.

11.1 Why use an API?

When you think about a web-based software system, your first inclination is that your users are people. You shouldn't forget the people; they're definitely your primary audience, but sometimes, they aren't your only users. All that interesting information stored away in your database might also be useful to another piece of software. Like with people, you want to be able to control what other systems have access to, so you can't just let them attach to your database. By providing an *application programming interface* (API), your project can be accessed by other systems.

There are two common categories of systems that might use your API: the first is another computer accessing your data, while the second is a user interface. Mobile phone applications on iPhone or Android typically get built with custom software specific to those devices. These applications still need a backend, though, just like your web application does. An API provides a way for mobile apps to talk to your system. Larger projects might have both web and mobile interfaces, and using an API means the user can interact with their data, no matter which frontend they are using.

Another kind of frontend has become popular as well: SPAs. These are still web applications, but instead of the backend producing individual web pages, a single user interface that operates in JavaScript gets downloaded to the browser, and all further UI interaction gets done in place. The *single* in *single-page* means only one web page gets used: a single, bundled JavaScript application. Frameworks like React and Angular are built using this mechanism. Django can still get used as the backend for an SPA, through the use of an API. Of course, the world isn't quite that simple. There are mobile applications built using web technologies and multipage web applications that have interactive JavaScript on a page that also might use an API. Figure 11.1 shows this variety.

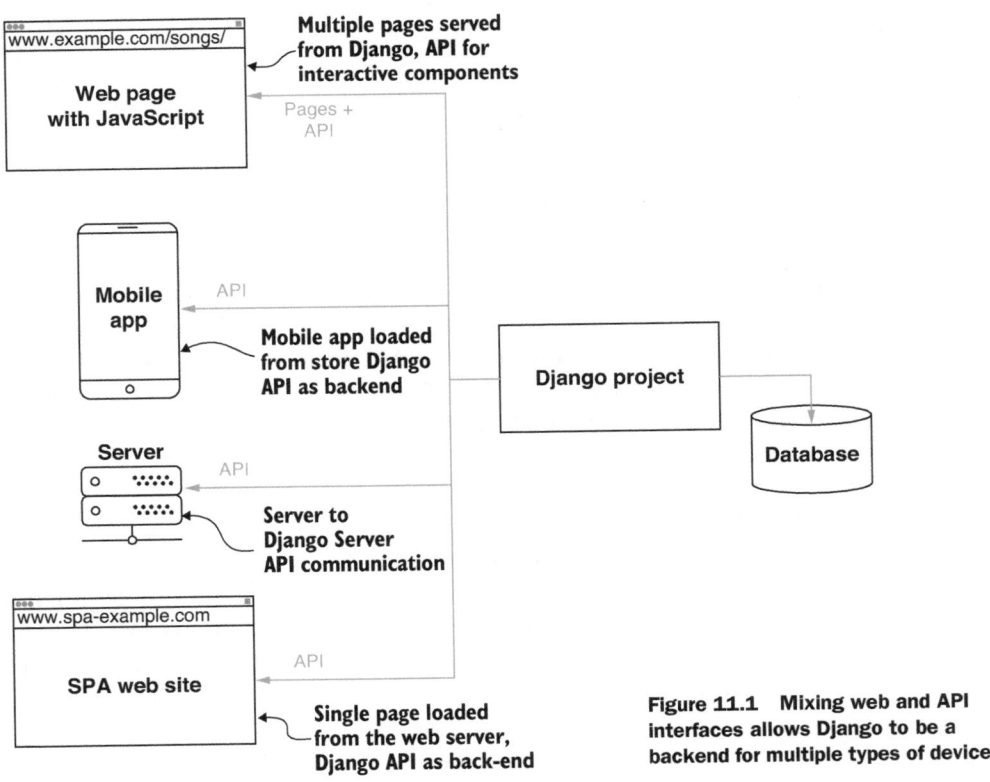

Figure 11.1 **Mixing web and API interfaces allows Django to be a backend for multiple types of devices**

Before discovering HTMX (see chapter 12), my go-to stack was Vue.js and Django. This allowed me to use regular web pages, where it was easiest, and sprinkle in Vue.js for interactivity. For me, at least, this was a faster method of creating applications than a pure SPA. It still needs an API, though. When Vue.js interacts with a page, it sometimes needs information from the backend.

11.1.1 CRUD and REST

Back in chapter 5, you learned about *CRUD*—that's *create, read, update,* and *delete.* It is still a fun acronym, and it is applicable in more ways than just the context of the Django Admin. Any time you're dealing with data, those four operations drive the interaction. This applies to APIs as well. All APIs implement at least one of these operations, and many provide an interface for all four. You can think of an API as comprising "nouns" and "verbs," where the nouns are the objects getting acted upon and the verbs are one or more of the CRUD operations.

A noun/object in an API call may not be the same as the object in your backend—in fact, it is almost always different. Usually, a data transformation has to happen between the actual object and its representation in the API. This might seem messy at first, but it is no different from what the ORM does for you: it abstracts away a row in the database. As the consumer of your API may not be using Django, and in fact, they may not even be using Python, an intermediary data representation is necessary. The process of changing your actual object into this representation is known as *serialization.*

The rules that bind the interaction of two machines is called a *protocol,* and you're already using one. Your browser on one machine and the web server on another talk using HTTP. The GET and POST HTTP methods you learned about in chapter 7 are part of this protocol. A natural way of building an API is to use the existing HTTP protocol, rather than re-invent the wheel. This isn't required, as there are APIs out there that have their own protocols, but for a web-based scenario, HTTP makes the most sense.

By far, the most common API protocol in the web world is *representational state transfer* (REST). Calling REST a protocol is actually an overstatement; it is a loosely defined set of conventions that has become a de facto standard. It is built on top of HTTP, though, and its lack of strictness is probably one of the influencing factors of its wide adoption.

REST uses the HTTP methods to enact the verbs in CRUD. You've already seen GET for read and POST for create or update within the context of forms. There are other HTTP methods as well, though, and the three that typically get used with REST are PUT, PATCH, and DELETE. When implementing REST, POST typically gets reserved for creation only, with PUT and PATCH being for updates. The difference between the two is based on what information gets provided. PUT expects all an object's fields, while PATCH expects only those that have changed. HTTP DELETE, quite sensibly, gets used for deleting.

Remember when I wrote *loosely defined* and *lack of strictness*? Well, POST, PUT, and PATCH are some of the sources of this slipperiness. REST doesn't enforce anything, and if you decide to use POST for both creating and updating, nothing is going to stop you. You have to read an API's documentation to know which methods it uses for what operations, but you'd have had to read the docs to implement it anyway, so that's not that big a deal.

That covers the verbs, but how about the nouns? Like with HTTP, REST uses URLs to determine what object is getting acted upon. Again, this isn't strictly enforced, but there are some best practices that should be followed. Typically, the URL starts with a namespace (e.g. *api*); optionally, includes a grouping (in Django, this might be the app); and then the noun of the object to interact with. REST URLs should not include verbs, as the HTTP protocol specifies the action. This means the same URL can be used for multiple operations. For example, http://example.com/api/song/42/ indicates the song with ID 42. Running GET fetches the song, running PUT expects data in the call to update the song's fields, and running DELETE would remove the song. That's one URL with three different actions.

A common practice is to use plural nouns to retrieve listings and singular nouns and an object ID to fetch specifics. For example, http://example.com/api/songs/ fetches a list of songs in the database, while the aforementioned http://example.com/api/song/42/ fetches a single song. The singular form, without an ID, typically gets used for creation. Following our example, http://example.com/api/song/ called using POST creates a new song.

The POST, PUT, and PATCH methods all expect data in the body of the request that specifies information about the change. This is typically the fields of the object being created or modified. All five HTTP methods usually include data in the body of the response, with everything except DELETE containing the serialized version of the object getting interacted with. DELETE is a special case; some APIs do return the content of the newly deleted object, while others simply return a flag indicating success or failure of the deletion. I tend to do the latter, but you may want the content of the deleted object if you want the user to be able to undo their operation by re-creating it.

REST does not specify the form of all this data getting sent back and forth. The most common format is JSON, while older interfaces still use XML. This is where REST can get a little messy, as there is no mechanism for determining what the body might contain, except making a request. This isn't as troublesome as it might sound. Nobody randomly queries a server with REST. If you're writing code that consumes a REST API, there is probably some documentation somewhere telling you what the API expects. Yep, that's the second reference to reading the docs. Maybe I'm suggesting you'll need to read the docs? Figure 11.2 summarizes the use of HTTP methods with JSON data to perform CRUD operations through a REST API.

This figure has all the operations needed to build a song API. Consider a mobile application where a user can input and modify a database of their favorite songs. The application's home screen lists all the songs in their database, by calling GET on /api/songs/. When the user clicks on the song "Fire" by Ohio Players, they see the details,

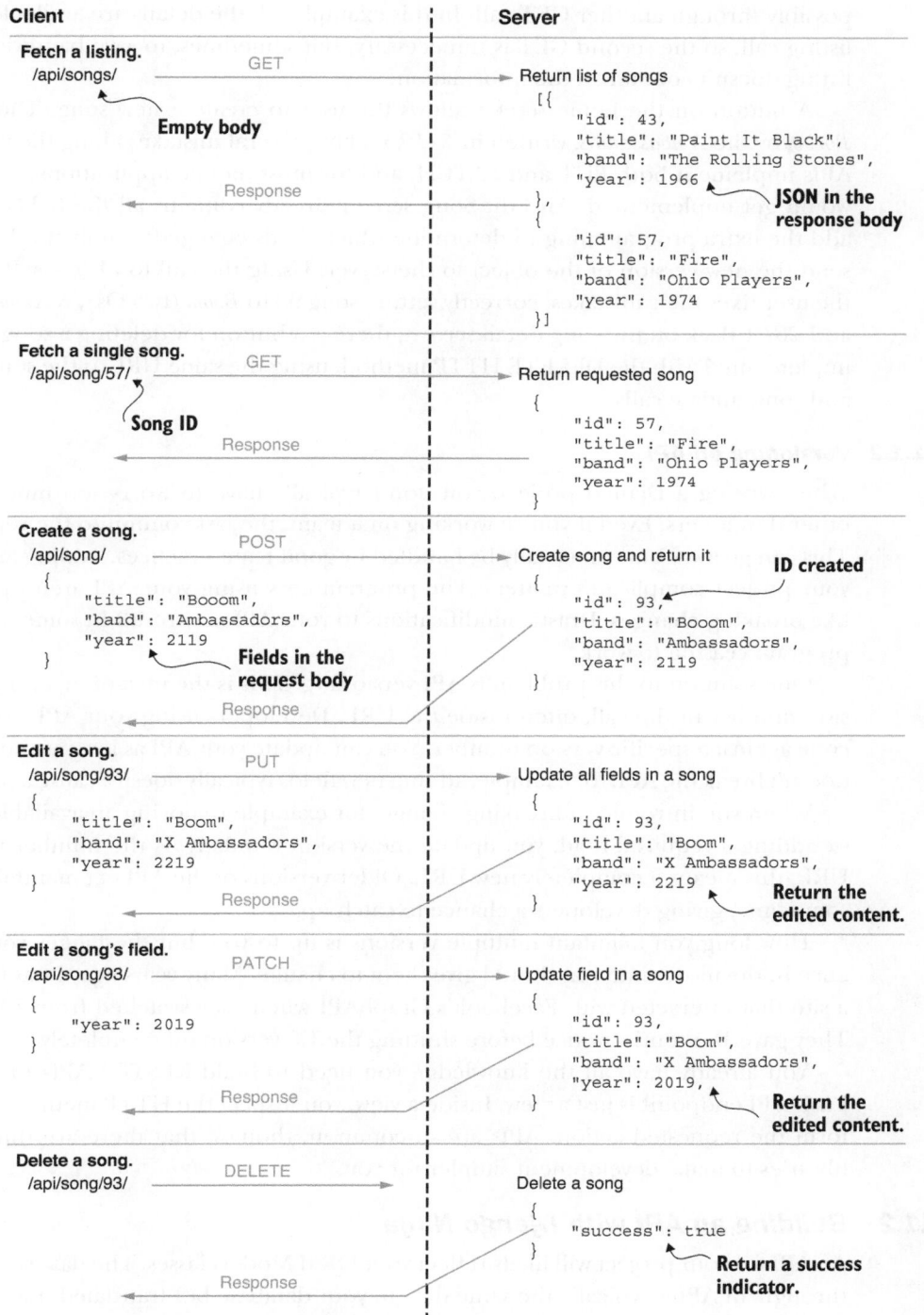

Figure 11.2 GET, POST, PUT, PATCH, and DELETE: HTTP methods for CRUD actions

possibly through another GET call. In this example, all the details are available in the listing call, so the second GET is unnecessary, but sometimes, to save bandwidth, the listing doesn't contain all the information.

A button on the home screen allows the user to create a new song. They enter *Booom* by the *Ambassadors*, written in *2119*, making several mistakes along the way. Few APIs implement both PUT and PATCH, and for most mobile applications, only PUT would get implemented. An Edit Song screen already contains all the fields, so why add the extra programming to determine which fields changed; simply use PUT and send the new version of the object to the server. Using the call to PUT (or PATCH), the user fixes their mistakes, correctly setting song 93 to *Boom* (two Os), *X Ambassadors*, and *2019*. Back on the song detail screen, there is a button for deleting a song. This is implemented with the DELETE HTTP method, using the same URL as the song detail and song update calls.

11.1.2   *Versioning an API*

When writing a Django project, you don't typically have to worry too much about other developers. Even if you're working on a team, the last commit to the repo wins. This can go awry but can usually be handled by good team practices. Adding an API to your project complicates matters. The programmers using your API aren't going to like breaking changes. Drastic modifications to your API may result in someone else's program ceasing to work.

One solution to this problem is API versioning. This is the idea of including a version number in the call, often inside the URL. Developers using your API write their code against a specific version number. You can update your API as long as the change doesn't break the API; for example, adding new fields typically doesn't cause a problem.

When you introduce a breaking change, for example removing an available object or adding a required field, you update the version number. As the number is in the URL, this means a completely new URL. Older versions of the API get maintained for some time, giving developers a chance to catch up.

How long you maintain multiple versions is up to you, but the bigger your audience is, the more time you should give them to change. Many years ago, I was building a site that interacted with Facebook's GraphAPI when they switched from 1.8 to 2.0. They gave 18 months notice before shutting the 1.8 version off completely.

You already have all the knowledge you need to build RESTful APIs in Django. Each API endpoint is just a view. Inside a view, you inspect the HTTP method and perform the requested action. APIs are so common, though, that there are third party libraries to make development simpler for you.

11.2   *Building an API with Django Ninja*

An API for your project will likely reflect your ORM Model classes. The data you expose through an API is typically the same data in your database but translated into another format. Most API endpoint views query an object out of the database, optionally perform actions on the object, and serialize the object, sending it in response. Consider the main objects in RiffMates: to build a full API, you need endpoints for musicians, bands, venues, and promoters. That's a lot of boilerplate code.

Enter Django Ninja (sneakily, of course—it is a ninja). Ninja (https://django-ninja .dev/) is a third-party library that reduces the amount of boilerplate code you need for your API endpoints. You turn a view into an endpoint using a decorator, and the serialization of objects into JSON is mostly done for you. Ninja knows how to serialize your Model classes and can use Python type hints to interact with non-Model fields as well. If you've ever used the FastAPI (https://fastapi.tiangolo.com/) web framework, you'll find Ninja familiar; it had heavy influence on the library's design.

To get started with Ninja, you'll need to install it. For full details on installing third party apps, see appendix A. Ninja is one of the simpler libraries to install; all you need to do is run `pip install django-ninja` and you're good to go. It is a rare Django library that technically isn't an app and so does not need to be registered in `INSTALLED_APPS`.

To build an API, you instantiate a `NinjaAPI` object. This should only be done once (or once per API, more on that later). Groups of API endpoints get collected in a `Router` object, and each router gets registered with the `NinjaAPI` object. It is called a *router*, as it is collecting view routes, just like your other views registered in urls.py.

The main Ninja object has a `.urls` property, which you use inside a `path` object in your urls.py file. `Router` object instances have methods that correspond to the HTTP methods and get used as decorators. The decorators turn view functions into API endpoints.

Let's start building an API by adding a `"Hello, world"`-inspired endpoint. Inside your RiffMates/home directory, create a new file called api.py. Inside this file, create a Ninja `Router` object, a view function that returns a string, and wrap the function with the `.get()` method of the router. The `.get()` method takes an argument: the last part of the URL for this API endpoint. The following listing contains this code.

Listing 11.1   An API endpoint that returns a string

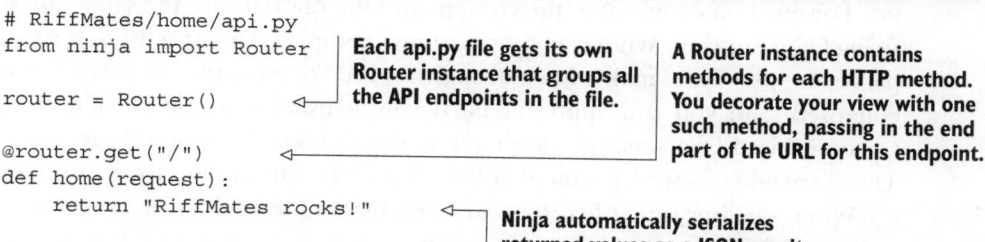

```
# RiffMates/home/api.py
from ninja import Router          Each api.py file gets its own       A Router instance contains
                                  Router instance that groups all      methods for each HTTP method.
router = Router()         ◄───┘   the API endpoints in the file.       You decorate your view with one
                                                                       such method, passing in the end
@router.get("/")         ◄────────────────────────────────────        part of the URL for this endpoint.
def home(request):
    return "RiffMates rocks!"     ◄──┐  Ninja automatically serializes
                                      │  returned values as a JSON result.
```

Now that you have declared an endpoint, you need to register it. Open RiffMates/ urls.py, and then add the code in the following listing.

Listing 11.2   Register routers with a `NinjaAPI` object and use it to create URLs

```
# RiffMates/RiffMates/urls.py
...
from ninja import NinjaAPI

from home.api import router as home_router          ←┐  Import the Router from the
                                                        RiffMates/home/api.py.
api = NinjaAPI(version="1.0")          ←┤  Create a single NinjaAPI object.
api.add_router("/home/", home_router)     ←┐  Register the home app's
                                               router with NinjaAPI.
urlpatterns = [
    # ...                                      Add the API endpoints as
    path("api/v1/", api.urls),         ←┘  URLs in your Django project.
]
```

I've made a couple of choices here that aren't necessary yet but help future-proof the API. First, when importing `router` from `home.api`, I alias it as `home_router`. If you guessed that I plan on adding api.py files to several apps, you'd be right. Second, I used the `version` argument when constructing the `NinjaAPI` object. This isn't required if you only have one API. If you wish to have multiple `NinjaAPI` objects, they must have unique version names. As I like to version my APIs anyway, I've done this from the start.

The `api.urls` property works similarly to `include()` in the `django.urls` module. All the API endpoints that are registered with the `NinjaAPI` object get included underneath the declared path. I've chosen `api/v1/` as my base path, first to name-space all the URLs as part of the API and second to include versioning information to future-proof any breaking changes.

That's it. You've got an API. Granted, it only has one endpoint, but it is an API. Fire up your development server and visit http://localhost:8000/api/v1/home/ to see it in action. Remember that Ninja's output is JSON, so it has a MIME type of `application/json`. Depending on what browser or tool you are using to hit the API, you may see different things. Firefox has a great JSON analysis tool built in. If you're using Firefox, you will see three tabs: the Content tab (RiffMates Rocks!), a Raw Data tab, and a Headers tab. For our home endpoint, the content and the raw data are the same: the serialized string from our view. When you move to more complex data structures, the content tab parses the JSON and makes it easier to deal with. For example, objects and lists can be collapsed, and you can apply filters. If you're using Chrome or one of the many Chrome-based browsers, you don't get all this fancy stuff—you only get the raw data. There are add-ons for Chrome that have similar features to Firefox's interface.

When dealing with APIs, the `curl` command-line tool (https://curl.se/) can be quite useful. This tool speaks numerous protocols, including HTTP, and can fetch any URL you give it. If you're interacting with a REST API that uses JSON or XML, doing so on the command line is sometimes easier. There are also dedicated tools, like `postman` (https://www.postman.com/product/rest-client/), if you prefer a GUI approach.

11.2.1 *Serializing objects*

Returning simple strings isn't much fun and is of limited value. Thankfully, Ninja serializes more interesting objects. Most native Python data types can be returned from a view, and Ninja will turn them into JSON. There are some restrictions, but they're the same restrictions imposed by Python's `json` library. This means lists of strings, or a good old dictionary, can be returned from an API view.

One of the exercises in chapter 2 had you add a view that showed your project's version information. In it, you returned a `JsonReponse` object that serialized a dictionary. The following listing shows the Ninja equivalent. Add it to RiffMates/home/api.py.

Listing 11.3 You can serialize a `dict` from a Ninja API endpoint

```
# RiffMates/home/api.py
...
@router.get("/version/")        ←  Declare a function that handles a GET
def version(request):              call for the URL ending in /version/.
    data = {
        "version": "0.0.1",
    }                           Anything the json module can serialize
    return data             ←  can be returned through Ninja.
```

Note the URL argument to `@router.get()` ends with a slash (/). You'll recall from chapter 8 that Django redirects any URLs not ending in a slash to their equivalent with a slash on the end. This is actually my only real complaint about Ninja—it doesn't handle this well. You can create API endpoints without the slash, but I've run into problems with them: there are cases where the redirect will trigger and others where it won't. Rather than trying to figure out which is which, always declare the URL ending in a slash and avoid the problem altogether.

Since the `version` API endpoint uses the existing `router` object in the file, and that router already got registered with Ninja, you have nothing else to do. Your API now supports two endpoints. Make sure your development server is running, and visit http://localhost:8000/api/v1/home/version/ to try it out.

As mentioned earlier in the chapter, the most likely thing you'll do with your API is expose your ORM Model classes. Django Model classes aren't compatible with Python's JSON serializer, but Ninja provides tools for converting your Model data to JSON with very little work.

Ninja is built on top of another third-party library, called Pydantic. This library is similar to the Django ORM, in that it provides tools for declaring fields in classes, but unlike the ORM, it uses Python type hints to do so. Ninja extends Pydantic's object model with a class called `schema`. You can declare your own serializable objects by inheriting from `schema` and declaring fields. If you've ever used Python's dataclasses module, it is similar. Pydantic has been around longer than dataclasses, which is why there are multiple ways of doing things now.

Ninja also provides a class that translates a Django ORM object into a `Schema` for serialization. You do this by subclassing a `ModelSchema` and configuring it based on your ORM Model class. This is similar to the `ModelForm` class discussed in chapter 7.

Consider, once again, a mobile application, this time with a screen that displays the promoters in your database. To do this, you'll need to add some API endpoints to the RiffMates `promoters` Django app. First off, create RiffMates/promoters/api.py. Inside this file, you declare `PromoterSchema`, which extends a Ninja `ModelSchema`. This class uses an inner class, called `Meta`, whose properties declare how the serialization works. At minimum, you need two properties: `model` points to the `Model` class to be serialized, and `fields` is a list of the fields to participate in the serialization. As its name implies, the `PromoterSchema` class gets used to serialize a `Promoter` Model. Note that the `Promoter` class got modified in the chapter 10 exercises; the example presented here is based on that version. If you didn't do the exercises, you'll need different values in the `fields` property.

> **NOTE** In early versions of Ninja, `Meta` was called `Config`, and `fields` was called `model_fields`. With the 1.0 release, the names were made consistent with Django's own ORM models

Once you've declared `PromoterSchema`, you use it with a `response` argument in a Ninja decorator. This informs Ninja that the schema gets used for serialization of the endpoint's return value.

The promoters screen in your mobile application would contain a list of promoters, similar to the list of songs mentioned before. The `promoters()` endpoint, shown in the following listing, returns a list of all the promoters used to populate that screen. You tell Ninja that a function endpoint returns a list by using Python type hints. With the correct type hint in place, all the function needs to do is return a `QuerySet` of `Promoter` objects, and Ninja takes care of the rest.

Listing 11.4 Serialize an ORM Model class with Ninja `ModelSchema`

```
# RiffMates/promoters/api.py
from ninja import Router, ModelSchema

from promoters.models import Promoter

router = Router()                          ◁── Each api.py file declares
                                               its own Router object.

class PromoterSchema(ModelSchema):    ◁──  Subclassing ModelSchema creates a
    class Meta:                             serializer for your Django ORM Model.
        model = Promoter                    This class serializes      List the fields to
        fields = ["id", "full_name", "birth", "death"]    a Promoter object.    participate in the
                                                                                serialization.

@router.get("/promoters/",
        response=list[PromoterSchema])     ◁── Tell Ninja that this endpoint returns
def promoters(request):                        a list of PromoterSchema objects.
    return Promoter.objects.all()      ◁──  Return all the Promoter objects.
```

---

list vs. List

The code in this book was written and tested with Python 3.12. Type hinting with built-in types got introduced in Python 3.9. If you're using Python 3.8 or earlier, the endpoint function declaration needs the `List` class from the `typing` module instead. It looks like this:

```python
from typing import List

@router.get("/promoters/",
        response=List[PromoterSchema])   ◁──┐ Note the use of List
def promoters(request):                       │ instead of list.
    return Promoter.objects.all()
```

As this is a new file with a new `Router` object in it, you need to register it with the `NinjaAPI` object in urls.py. The following listing highlights the changes needed there.

Listing 11.5 Register the `Router` for the `promoters` app

```python
# RiffMates/RiffMates/urls.py
...
from promoters.api import router as promoters_router      ◁──┐ Import the
...                                                              │ promoters Router
api = NinjaAPI(version="1.0")                                    │ object with an alias.
api.add_router("/home/", home_router)
api.add_router("/promoters/", promoters_router)          ◁──┐ Register the new router
...                                                            │ with the NinjaAPI object.
```

Note that you don't need to make changes to the `path` object; using the `add_router()` call is sufficient. Depending on how much playing around you did in chapter 10, you may or may not have promoter data in your database. Make sure you do, or your API won't have anything to return. You can either use the Django Admin to add some information, or for your convenience, the sample code has a fixture starting in the ch10g_exercises directory. Note that this fixture pairs with the changes in the chapter 10 exercises and will only work if you model matches that work.

Your new endpoint is http://localhost:8000/api/v1/promoters/promoters; visit it to see the results. The double noun of `promoters/promoters` is a little annoying but common practice. The first noun is the namespace, and the second indicates this is listing a series of objects. For the `promoters` app, this is overkill: there is only one model inside it. When you start building the APIs for bands, musicians, and venues, this kind of namespacing becomes important. Your results should look something like this:

```json
[{
    "id": 1,
    "full_name": "Michael Lang",
    "birth": "1944-12-11",
    "death": "2022-01-08"
},
```

```
{
    "id": 2,
    "full_name": "Phoebe Jacobs",
    "birth": "1919-06-21",
    "death": "2012-04-09"
},
{
    "id": 3,
    "full_name": "Harvey Goldsmith",
    "birth": "1946-03-04",
    "death": null
},
{
    "id": 4,
    "full_name": "Allan Williams",
    "birth": "1930-02-21",
    "death": "2106-12-30"
}]
```

As I write this sentence, Harvey Goldsmith is still alive and, therefore, doesn't have a death date (date of passing? expiration date? period-of-pushing-up-petunias?). Where Django uses Python's `None` value, JavaScript, and therefore JSON, uses `null`.

A shortcut you shouldn't use

Similar to the `ModelForm` class, `ModelSchema` supports two values that can save you typing in a long list of fields. You can set the `fields` property to `"__all__"` to include all the fields from a Model, or instead of using the `fields` property, you can use an `exclude` property.

Like with `ModelForm`, this isn't recommended. Explicitly listing your fields is safer. If you add a new field to your Model that shouldn't be serialized, it is better for the default to be exclusion. Inclusion, by default, means having to remember to edit the `ModelSchema` subclass to explicitly remove the new field.

Not all fields get used in all situations. For example, if you have a creation timestamp on your object that automatically gets set by Django, you might want it serialized when reading an object but not when updating it. You shouldn't be able to change the creation timestamp through the API. This can mean needing different serializers for reading and updating—more on this later.

11.2.2 Handling arguments

Ninja supports both URL query parameters and URL-based arguments. Typically, query parameters get used to modify a result, while URL-based arguments get used to identify a target object. It is quite common for an API to provide two GET methods for each target object, one that lists objects and the other to fetch a specific object. This is akin to the `musician()` and `musicians()` views you wrote in chapter 4.

You've already seen the `promoters()` endpoint, so let's add a new one to fetch a single `Promoter` object. The difference, in this case, is the URL must support an argument, which you dictate to Ninja through the use of brace brackets, similar to an f-string. The following listing shows how to tie a named value in the URL with the view function's arguments.

Listing 11.6 An endpoint to fetch a single `Promoter` object by its ID

```
# RiffMates/promoters/api.py
from django.shortcuts import get_object_or_404
...
@router.get("/promoter/{promoter_id}/",
    response=PromoterSchema)
def promoter(request, promoter_id):
    promoter = get_object_or_404(Promoter, id=promoter_id)
    return promoter
```

Denote URL arguments, using brace brackets.

This endpoint returns a single object and uses the PromoterSchema to serialize it.

Match the named URL argument with an argument to the endpoint view function.

Like in a page view function, use get_object_or_404() to find the requested object, and then return it.

To dive deeper into arguments and serialization, let's move on from promoters and start building a more complex set of API endpoints. The goal is to provide a full set of CRUD operations on the `Venue` model, including the ability to show a subset of venues at once through the application of a filter. Again, if this was for a mobile application, you'd start with the venue listing screen, but this time, you'd also have an input field that allowed you to only show those venues that match the name in the field.

Like with the other RiffMates apps, you need a new api.py file, this time in the `bands` app directory. To output a `Venue` object, you need a serializer, which is also based on a `ModelSchema` class. Earlier, I hinted that you can declare your own fields on a `Schema`. You can do this by building a serializer that is independent of a model, or you can augment a `ModelSchema` by adding fields. I'll show you the latter by defining the `VenueSchema` serializer.

I want to add two fields that aren't in the `Venue` model to the `VenueSchema`, both of which can be helpful for developers consuming your API. A *slug* is a term from the newspaper industry, meaning a short name for an article. Slugs sometimes get used on the web inside of URLs. Consider the readability difference between /song/43/ and /song/paint-it-black/; the latter is human readable and gives search engines a clue regarding what the URL points to. A common technique is to combine the two ideas: /song/paint-it-black-43/ keeps the human-readable content, while making it easy to parse the song's ID off the end of the URL. An integer-based primary key is typically significantly faster to find in a database than searching on a string. With the mixed technique, you don't even need to store the slug, as the 43 part is enough to do your look-up.

The second field to add to the serializer is a URL for the object's GET method. This provides a shortcut for developers using the listing GET and wanting to fetch more information on a specific object. If you've designed your API well, the URL will be the same for PATCH and DELETE, meaning the programmer doesn't have to know how to construct your API endpoint—they can just use the information in the serialized object.

Adding fields to a Ninja serializer only requires you to declare them in the class with a corresponding Python type hint. When an object gets serialized, the field gets populated by looking up properties with the same name on the object. To implement the slug and URL fields, you could add @property values to Venue. Ninja also provides a way of populating fields within the serializer class itself, using a static method named after the field with a resolve_ prefix. To implement our two fields, you create .resolve_slug() and .resolve_url(). Figure 11.3 shows how the .resolve methods get used by the serializer to produce the resulting JSON.

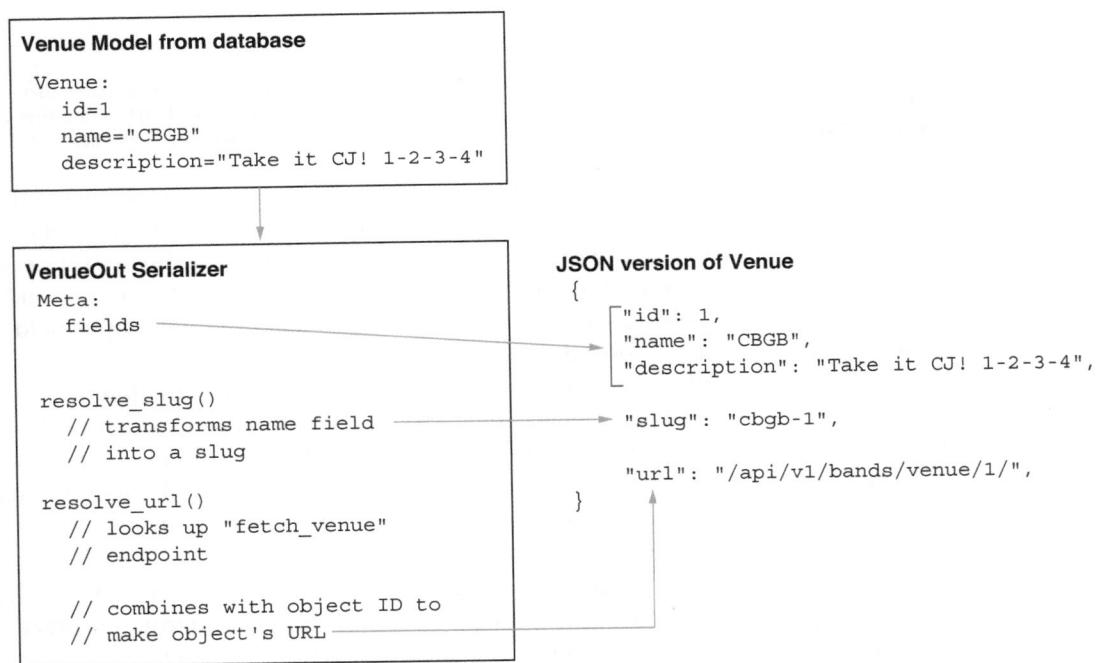

Figure 11.3   Using methods in a Ninja serializer to add content to an object's representation

Django has its roots in the newspaper industry and so comes with a slug method built-in. The django.utils.text module has a function called slugify(), which takes a string and returns a slug that is URL compatible. The slugify() function converts a string to ASCII (in case it contains Unicode); changes it to lowercase; removes leading and trailing spaces; replaces remaining whitespace with a single dash; and removes any characters that aren't alphanumeric, underscores, or hyphens. The .resolve _slug() method on the serializer calls slugify() on the Venue object's name and appends a hyphen and the object ID.

In chapter 5, you learned about the reverse() function, which gets used to look up a named URL. The .resolve_url() method uses reverse() to find the GET endpoint for a `Venue` object. Ninja's decorators support naming in a fashion similar to a `path` object in the urls.py file. The only complication is they are namespaced. If your `Ninja-API` object has no `version` argument, the namespace is `api-1.0.0:`. If your `NinjaAPI` object does have a `version` argument (like in our code), the namespace starts with `api-`, then appends the value of `version`, and finishes with a colon (`:`). In either case, the name you give the API endpoint comes after the `:`. The following listing contains the code for serializing a `Venue` object and the API endpoint for fetching a single instance.

Listing 11.7   API endpoint for fetching a `Venue` object

```
# RiffMates/bands/api.py
from django.shortcuts import get_object_or_404
from django.urls import reverse
from django.utils.text import slugify

from ninja import Router, ModelSchema

from bands.models import Venue

router = Router()                    ◄──┐ As this is a new api.py file,
                                        │ it needs its own Router.

class VenueOut(ModelSchema):            │ Additional fields get declared in a Schema or
    slug: str            ◄──────────────│ ModelSchema class, using Python type hinting.
    url: str

    class Meta:                                            │ Serialize the id, name,
        model = Venue                                      │ and description fields
        fields = ["id", "name", "description"]   ◄─────────│ from the Venue object.

                                        │ Ninja uses .resolve_X() static methods to populate
                                        │ the corresponding field. The .resolve_slug()
    @staticmethod                       │ method uses Django's slugify() function to create a
    def resolve_slug(obj):   ◄──────────│ slug based on the Venue object's name and ID.
        slug = slugify(obj.name) + "-" + str(obj.id)
        return slug
                                        │ The .resolve_url() method looks up
    @staticmethod                       │ the API endpoint named fetch_venue
    def resolve_url(obj):    ◄──────────│ and returns the corresponding URL.
        url = reverse("api-1.0:fetch_venue", args=[obj.id, ])
        return url

@router.get("/venue/{venue_id}/",       │ The url_name argument to a Ninja decorator
    response=VenueOut,                  │ declares a name for the endpoint that can
    url_name="fetch_venue")   ◄─────────│ be looked up with a call to reverse().
def fetch_venue(request, venue_id):
    venue = get_object_or_404(Venue, id=venue_id)
    return venue
```

In addition to adding the code in listing 11.7, don't forget to register the new `router` with the `NinjaAPI` object in urls.py, using `bands` as the router's base name. Once done, you can run the development server and visit http://localhost:8000/api/v1/bands/venue/1/. If you followed along way back in chapter 4, you will get the following result:

```
{
    "id": 1,
    "name": "CBGB",
    "description": "Take it CJ! 1-2-3-4",
    "slug": "cbgb-1",
    "url": "/api/v1/bands/venue/1/",
}
```

Including the `url` field here may seem a little strange: you had to hit that URL to get this result, but the same serializer gets used in the listing code, which is where that value becomes useful. Are you ahead of me? Are you mumbling, *well, then let's add the listing code?* Who am I to argue? To add a bit of flair, the `Venue` listing endpoint also supports a filter. It takes an optional query parameter *name*, which, if given, filters the venues that begin with that value. The following listing shows the first attempt at this endpoint.

Listing 11.8 Venue object listing API end-point

```
# RiffMates/bands/api.py
...
@router.get("/venues/", response=list[VenueOut])    ┐  Support a query
def venues(request, name=None):                   ◄──┘  parameter called name.
    venues = Venue.objects.all()
    if name is not None:
        venues = venues.filter(name__istartswith=name)   ◄──┐ If a name got provided,
                                                             │ include only venues
    return venues                                            │ that start with it.
```

Endpoint view arguments get used by Ninja to support either URL arguments or query parameters. If a view argument has a corresponding brace-bracket surrounded value in the URL, it is a URL argument. Otherwise, it is treated as a query parameter. To make the query parameter optional, simply provide a default value to the function argument.

To filter listed results based on a name query parameter, you use the `QuerySet` object's `.filter()` method. Like with the `promoters()` endpoint, this endpoint function returns a list, indicated to Ninja through a Python type hint in the decorator. Make sure your development server is running, and visit http://localhost:8000/api/v1/bands/venues/ to see the results of your work.

11.2.3 *Filtering your listings*

A few paragraphs back, I wrote *first attempt*, did you catch it? Filtering lists is such a common activity that Ninja provides tools for it. For our `Venue` example, the tool is overkill: it takes more code with the tool than without. But if you want to support filters on multiple fields of an object, it can save you some work. To define a filter you build a `FilterSchema`, it is very similar to the other kinds of schemas you've seen so far, using Python type hints to declare the fields that can be filtered.

To filter the `venue` listing, there are a couple of wrinkles. First, you need to use the `Optional` type hint to specify that this query parameter isn't required. Second, by default, the filter is an exact match. To perform starts-with, you need some extra stuff. Ninja uses Pydantic's `Field` class to give you more control over how a field behaves. Without the `Field` class, this would simply match the name of the field. With it, you can specify the `q` argument to a `QuerySet.filter()` call, using the `__istartswith` field look-up you learned about in chapter 4. The following listing contains the `VenueFilter` code.

Listing 11.9 Declare the fields that participate in a Ninja filter

```
# RiffMates/bands/api.py
...
from typing import Optional
...
from ninja import Field, Router, ModelSchema,        Add Field and FilterSchema to
➡ FilterSchema                                        the list of imports from ninja.

                      Inherit from FilterSchema
                        to create a filter class.
...

class VenueFilter(FilterSchema):                      Declare the name field, using Python type
    name: Optional[str] = Field(None,                 hinting to define it as an optional string
        q=['name__istartswith'])                      and the Field class to change how it filters.
```

With the filter class ready, you need to make changes to the `venue` listing endpoint. Replace the `name` argument of the function with the more generic `filters`. The key to Ninja understanding this is the Python type hint you provide. Ninja includes a `Query` type hint, which you combine with your `VenueFilter` class to specify that `filters` is a query filter.

Type hinting, a little deeper

The next chunk of code includes a bit of magic: Python's ellipsis (...). If you're not very familiar with type hinting, or don't really care, you can simply type it in as it is, and you'll be fine.

Type hinting is all about telling your tools what kinds of values to expect. For a complex filter, you could have a variable number of arguments. For `VendorFilter`, there is only name, but for a heavier object, you could filter on many fields.

The ellipsis literal in Python acts as a placeholder. You've seen it in the sample code, indicating I've skipped over stuff. The wonder of the ellipsis is that it is valid Python. If you copy and paste some sample code containing ..., Python won't complain. The ellipsis commonly gets used to create stub functions as well: define the function header, and make the body just ....

In type hinting, the ellipsis literal indicates a variable number of arguments. As the filter can have zero or more arguments, the syntax for the type hint is `filters: VendorFilter = Query(...)`.

The `FilterSchema` base class contains a method called `.filter()`, which takes a `QuerySet` and filters it based on the instantiated values of the `FilterSchema` object. I tried to write the word *filter* twice more in that last sentence to make it clearer but couldn't sneak them in. Remember, as complicated as this sounds, it is just a set of query parameters. Ninja uses the query parameters to build a set of fields to perform a filter and provides a class that encapsulates this operation for you. The following listing has replacement code for the `venues()` endpoint.

Listing 11.10   Declare the fields that participate in a Ninja filter

```
# RiffMates/bands/api.py
...
from ninja import (Field, Router, ModelSchema,      Add the Query type hint class
    FilterSchema, Query)                         ◁─┘ to your list of imports.

...                                      Declare a query parameter, using
                                         the VenueFilter type, which takes a
                                         variable number of arguments.
@router.get("/venues/", response=list[VenueOut])
def venues(request, filters: VenueFilter = Query(...)):   ◁─────────────
    venues = Venue.objects.all()
    venues = filters.filter(venues)   ◁──┐ The filters object is an instance of VenueFilter
    return venues                        │ with a method that filters the venue's
                                         │ QuerySet based on the query parameters.
```

To see the new endpoint in action, you'll want some additional `venue` objects: filtering when you only have one in the database isn't much fun. Use the Django Admin to add a couple more venues, and then visit http://localhost:8000/api/v1/bands/venues/ ?name=c. Your results will be dependent on what data you created, but it will be something like this:

```
[{
    "id": 1,
    "name": "CBGB",
    "description": "Take it CJ! 1-2-3-4",
    "slug": "cbgb-1",
    "url": "/api/v1/bands/venue/1/",
},
{
    "id": 8,
    "name": "Cherry Bar",
    "description": "Australia's best after party",
    "slug": "cherry-bar-8",
    "url": "/api/v1/bands/venue/8/",
}]
```

Don't forget to test it without a query parameter filter as well, to make sure you didn't break anything.

Filtering with django-filter

This filter concept is a cool idea, and it can be applied to your regular views as well. You could go through the effort of handling all the query arguments to provide filters on your views, or you could use django-filter (https://pypi.org/project/django-filter/). This third-party library works similarly to Ninja's `FilterSchema`: you build a `django_filters.FilterSet` class and then use it to fetch operate on your `QuerySet` in a view, passing in the request and all the possible query parameters. With just a few lines of code, any of your Django views can support filtering.

11.2.4 Nesting data

Sometimes, even your data has data. Consider the rooms that belong to venues. You could write an API endpoint that lists rooms that took a venue ID as an argument, but then, determining the rooms that belong to a venue would take two calls. A list of all venues and their corresponding rooms would take $N + 1$ calls, one to list the venues and N more for each of the corresponding rooms. This is expensive on the network and, for a long listing, hard on the database in the backend. A better solution is to nest the room information inside the venue data.

Ninja makes data nesting straightforward: add a serializer for the nested object, and set an appropriate Python hint in the enclosing one. Recall that each `Room` model gets connected to a `Venue` through a many-to-many relationship. Each `Venue` object has a `.room_set` query manager that you can use to find associated rooms. Ninja knows how to do this. By defining a schema for a room and adding a `room_set` field to `VenueOut`, Ninja automatically performs the subquery and nests the data.

The name `room_set` is very Django-esque. Developers using your API might not understand what that means, and *rooms* would be easier to understand. Ninja allows you to rename fields using the `Field` class—in fact, that's what was going on when you aliased the `name__istartswith` query parameter. The following listing contains the code for a room serializer and the change to `VenueOut` to include the nested data.

Listing 11.11 Nesting `Room` data inside serialized `Venue` objects

```
# RiffMates/bands/api.py
...
from bands.models import Venue, Room        ← Add the Room model
                                               to your imports.
...

class RoomSchema(ModelSchema):              ← Create a serialization
    class Meta:                                schema for rooms.
        model = Room
        fields = ["id", "name"]

class VenueOut(ModelSchema):
    slug: str
    url: str
```

```
rooms: list[RoomSchema] = Field(...,
    alias="room_set")
...
```

To nest the room data, use a list of RoomSchema type hint, which, when combined with the Field class, allows you to rename it from room_set.

Ninja's pretty cool; with very little code, you've got nested data. Rerun your query on the CBGB venue, and you'll now get the following:

```
{
    "id": 1,
    "name": "CBGB",
    "description": "Take it CJ! 1-2-3-4",
    "slug": "cbgb-1",
    "url": "/api/v1/bands/venue/1/",
    "rooms": [
        {
            "id": 2,
            "name": "Blue"
        },
        {
            "id": 1,
            "name": "Red"
        }
    ]
}
```

Nested room data associated with CBGBs

11.2.5 *Authenticating your API*

So far, you've only been doing the *R* from *CRUD*. What about the other three choices? You've used Ninja's .get() decorator to read values. It also has .post(), .put(), .patch(), and .delete() decorators to take care of the other parts of CRUD (still a fun acronym). But you might not want just anybody adding stuff to your database. Before considering create or delete, it is time for a tangent about authentication.

Ninja supports a variety of authentication mechanisms. You can specify authentication globally through the NinjaAPI object, at the Router level, or endpoint by endpoint. In each case, you provide an auth argument, the value of which determines the kind of authentication to perform. In this section, I'll be discussing two mechanisms: Django's auth and an API key. For a full list of the other supported types, see https://django-ninja.dev/guides/authentication/.

Authentication for an API doesn't have to be restricted to modification. Everything discussed here can also be used for your GET methods if you want to limit who can access your data.

What kind of authentication to use depends on your use case. As Django has authentication built-in, at first glance, that might seem like the right answer. If you've already got user accounts and all that fun password management stuff covered in chapter 6, why not use it for your API as well? The problem is the authentication step: if you're not authenticated, Django redirects you to the login page. If another system is talking to your project, that means it has to fill in a web form.

There really is only one case where Django-based authentication should be used: when the API is for a web-based interface. If your API is there to support an SPA or provide data to libraries like Vue.js, then the redirect isn't a problem. You can capture the redirect in your code and send the user to the login page. To implement this kind of authentication, simply import `django_auth` from `ninja.security` and pass it as the value to the `auth` argument in an endpoint function or the `NinjaAPI` class.

If Django-based authentication isn't the answer, then what is? A common mechanism out there is to provide a key. Keys can be simple, a global string which all API consumers know, or more complex, a value stored in the database and validated. For public-facing APIs, you're going to want a key management system, so you can revoke keys from problematic users. If you're just using the API for your own tools, you can take a simpler approach. Be careful with keys; they are essentially passwords. If you're passing them around in the clear, someone might see them and then gain access to your API. For simplicity, I'm going to ignore this advice here and just use a hardcoded global value.

Getting key management right

Like password management, key management can be tricky. If you're building a public API, you should do some research on key management first. A good place to start is freeCodeCamp's website: https://mng.bz/maan.

The major cloud providers, like AWS (https://aws.amazon.com/what-is/api-key/) and Google Cloud (https://mng.bz/5IO4), both have in-depth documentation on how they handle API keys at scale, to give you some ideas as well.

When you authenticate with Django, it sets a cookie in your browser and uses that to validate who you are in future calls. This requires managing a user's session. For an API, it is far simpler to require the key to be included in every single call. HTTP supports metadata getting attached to a method through the use of a header. HTTP has its own headers but reserves anything that begins with *X-* as a namespace to be used by developers. Ninja provides the `APIKeyHeader` class, which you extend to create a key-based authentication mechanism.

Your subclass of `APIKeyHeader` needs two things: the name of the HTTP header to use for the key and an `.authenticate()` method. The authentication method returns the key to indicate success or `None` for failure. You provide an instance of your subclass as the `auth` argument in the places you wish authentication to happen. In the following examples, I'm going to put it on the endpoints. There should only be one instance of the `APIKeyHeader` subclass, so it is useful to put it in a file separate from api.py files in your apps. It doesn't really matter where it goes; it just needs to be importable. Create RiffMates/api_auth.py, and add the code in the following listing.

Listing 11.12   Creating an authentication handler based on a key

```
# RiffMates/api_auth.py
from django.conf import settings

from ninja.security import APIKeyHeader

class APIKey(APIKeyHeader):          The name of the HTTP header
    param_name = "X-API-KEY"         where the key gets found

    def authenticate(self, request, key):      Compare the key sent in to a
        if key == settings.NINJA_API_KEY:      hardcoded value in settings.py.
            return key                          Return the key if the values match;
                                                otherwise, use the default return
                                                value of a function: None.

api_key = APIKey()        Create a single instance of
                          APIKey to be used by the apps.
```

Don't forget to add a new configuration value, called NINJA_API_KEY, in your set-tings.py file. I've set mine to the very cryptic *notsecure*. As mentioned earlier, this is a bad idea. Do proper key management, or at least use an appropriately cryptic long value, for your key.

11.2.6 *Creating objects with the API*

With your key-handling class in place, you can now write an endpoint for creating a venue that is behind the authentication wall. You may have noticed that I named the serializer for venues VenueOut. That's because there needs to be a VenueIn. The fields involved in displaying a venue are different from those for creating one. Venues being output should include their ID, whereas venues getting created don't have an ID yet. In this case, the only difference between the *in* and *out* versions is the ID, so you could choose an ID value of 0 for creating, but in more complex cases, there may be bigger differences.

When using the .post() decorator for the creation method, you declare an argu-ment to the function for the field values. This is similar to the contents of POST when handling a form, but in this case, the payload is a JSON dictionary. You tell Ninja what kind of data to expect by using a Python type hint for the payload argument. The Schema class has a .dict() method that returns the contents as a dictionary. This can be combined with Python's double-star (**) feature, like you do with **kwargs, to use the contents of the dictionary as key–value pairs for the Venue object constructor. The following listing contains the new VenueIn serializer along with the POST endpoint for creating a venue.

Listing 11.13   A create endpoint for venues

```
# RiffMates/bands/api.py
...                                  Import the instance of APIKey to
from api_auth import api_key         specify the authentication method.
```

```
...
class VenueIn(ModelSchema):          ◁——  A new serializer specific to creating
    class Meta:                            venues, which doesn't require an ID
        model = Venue
        fields = ["name", "description"]
...
```

The response from a creation action is the resulting Venue. By specifying the auth argument, you restrict access to this endpoint.

```
@router.post("/venue/", response=VenueOut, auth=api_key)   ◁——
def create_venue(request, payload:VenueIn):
    venue = Venue.objects.create(**payload.dict())   ◁——
    return venue
```

Using VenueIn as a Python type hint tells Ninja how to handle the payload body.

Venue.objects.create() expects key–value pairs for the fields in a Venue object; using the ** notation turns a dictionary into this format.

If you're concerned about how to test this, thinking you'll need to manually create an HTTP call with the appropriate header, don't worry—Ninja has your back. Similar to how Django provides the Admin, Ninja provides a tool for interacting with your API. It is called *docs*, and you invoke it by adding *docs* to the end of your API's URL. You'll recall me complaining about Ninja's lack of consistency with trailing slashes; this is one of those cases: putting a slash on the end of the URL won't work. To see the interface for your own API, visit http://localhost:8000/api/v1/docs.

Unit testing Ninja calls

Although it is great to have the Ninja docs interface to play with your API, in a real project, you're still going to want to write unit tests. In chapter 8, you saw how to use the `.client.get()` and `.client.post()` member methods of the `TestCase` class. These work equally well with Ninja. There are also methods for `.put()`, `.patch()`, and `.delete()`.

The `.post()`, `.put()`, and `.patch()` methods that are used for creating and updating content all support an optional argument: `content_type`. By setting this value to `application/json`, Django automatically converts your data argument into JSON. In your unit tests, create a Python dictionary containing the key–value pairs for your content, and then pass it into the call using the JSON content type, and Django's test framework takes care of the rest.

Another useful optional argument that is supported by all the HTTP method calls is `headers`. This value takes a dictionary with key–value pairs specifying additional headers to include in the call. This is how you test against calls guarded by key-based authentication. The following example combines both these ideas:

```
from django.conf import settings
from django.test import TestCase


class APITests(TestCase):
    def test_venue_api(self):          A dictionary containing the
        headers = {              ◁——  API key's HTTP header
            "X-API-KEY": settings.NINJA_API_KEY,
```

```
(continued)
        }
                            ┌─  The payload data for
        data = {         ◁──┘   the POST call              Using a JSON content
            "name": "some venue name",                     type and the headers
            "description": "some venue description",        dictionary to post to
        }                                                   the API endpoint
        response = self.client.post("/api/v1/bands/venue/", data,
            content_type="application/json", headers=headers)   ◁──────────
        # Asserts about the response go here
        ...
```

In the Ninja docs interface, every endpoint in your API gets displayed as a collapsible line. You can expand any endpoint to see more details about each call. In the expanded view, there is also a Try it Out button. This button is a little misleading; it should read Get Ready to Try it Out. Pressing it creates another button labeled Execute, which you press to actually do something. It is a two-step process for the scenarios where you need to provide data. For a GET with no arguments, it is an extra step. Try executing one of your GET endpoints to see the results. Ninja gives you a bunch of info: the `curl` call equivalent of what you just ran, which you can copy/paste into a terminal, the URL you just executed against, the response body, and the headers that came back with it.

If you attempt to run the POST for creating a `venue`, you will get a Permission Denied response. This is because you didn't provide an authentication key. To do so, scroll to the top of the screen, and click the Authorize button. This pops open a new window, which in our case, shows the name of the HTTP header and an input box for the key. Fill it in, press Authorize, and all subsequent calls will include the authentication header. Note that this information isn't long-lived. If you exit your development server and come back, you may need to re-enter the key.

Once you've authenticated, expand the POST call for creating a venue, and then press the Try it Out button. A text field gets added, containing a template of the JSON payload needed for the call. Replace the placeholder values with actual content, and then press Execute. Like with the GET calls, you'll see the `curl` command, the URL used, and the response header and content.

If you scroll to the bottom of the docs interface, you'll see a listing of all your serialization schemas. Expand any of these to see the required format for the fields. The docs tool is very handy for testing and can be left on for developers working with your API. If you've secured everything with keys, this interface really is no different from the API itself. If you want to be a little more subtle about things, you can ask Ninja to use Django authentication before giving access to the interface or turn it off altogether. Details on how to do that can be found here: https://django-ninja.dev/guides/api-docs/.

Object relationships

Each room belongs to a venue, so to create a `Room` object using the API (or in the docs interface), you need to associate it with a `Venue`. To do this, use the numeric ID of the related object. A `RoomIn` schema would include a field named `venue`, which you populate with the integer ID of the room's related `Venue` object.

11.2.7 Updating and deleting with the API

Two letters down, two to go; it's time to address *U* and *D*. Updating an object is rather similar to creating a new one—in fact, if you're using the PUT method, the same serializer can be used. As you're editing an existing object, include the ID of the object to be changed in the URL. Ninja doesn't provide any shortcuts for updating the fields on an object, so you need to loop through the payload and apply each field using a call to `setattr()`. The following listing contains a new API endpoint that updates all the field values on an existing `Venue` instance.

> **NOTE** `setattr()` is a Python built-in method that allows you to set a property on an object by giving its name as a string and the new value.

The following listing contains a new API endpoint that updates all the field values on an existing `Venue` instance.

Listing 11.14 A update endpoint for venues

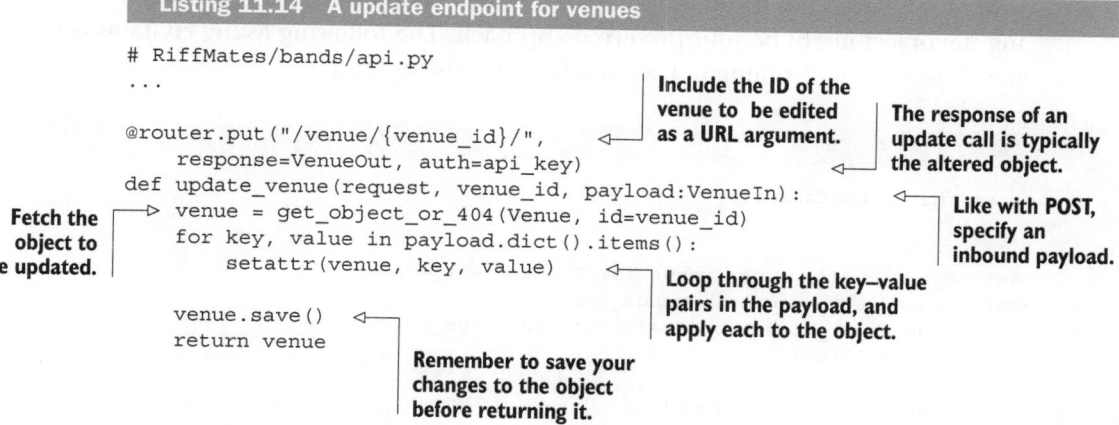

```
# RiffMates/bands/api.py
...

@router.put("/venue/{venue_id}/",
    response=VenueOut, auth=api_key)
def update_venue(request, venue_id, payload:VenueIn):
    venue = get_object_or_404(Venue, id=venue_id)
    for key, value in payload.dict().items():
        setattr(venue, key, value)

    venue.save()
    return venue
```

Include the ID of the venue to be edited as a URL argument.

The response of an update call is typically the altered object.

Fetch the object to be updated.

Like with POST, specify an inbound payload.

Loop through the key–value pairs in the payload, and apply each to the object.

Remember to save your changes to the object before returning it.

Ninja supports both the PUT and PATCH methods as decorators. You seldom need to implement both. PUT gets used when the client provides all fields, whereas PATCH only sends fields that changed. PATCH takes up less bandwidth but typically requires its own schema. A `ModelSchema` subclass decides which fields are required based on its ORM Model. For example, if *first_name* is a required field, it will be required in the schema. To implement a PATCH, required fields need to be optional instead, as you are only sending the changed values. There is no easy way to do this, so you have to construct the schema by hand and use the `Optional` Python type hint. Implementing PATCH means you have to write more serializer code, so it needs to be worth it. The custom schema notwithstanding, PATCH code is otherwise identical to a PUT: loop through the fields sent and update the object, saving it when you're done.

Choosing between PUT and PATCH is based on how you're passing objects around. For an SPA or a mobile app, there is a good chance the entire object gets sent to the browser or device, and the browser or device doesn't track changes at the field level. In this case, it is simplest to send all the information on the client side to the server through a PUT. Alternatively, for models with many fields or for data-intensive fields, like attachments, you might use PATCH. It is up to the client device to know what fields got edited in this case.

Last, but not least, is DELETE. OK, technically it is least, as in the least likely thing you'll need to implement. I've never counted, but I suspect less than a quarter of the APIs I've built have implemented delete capabilities, but that will depend on what you're using the API for. If your API is to make data available programtically (like an RSS feed), it will likely be read only and not need DELETE. If your API is the interface to a mobile front end, you'll likely need the whole range of CRUD.

To delete an object, you need to find it. Like with PUT and PATCH, the URL for DELETE contains an object ID. What the body of a delete call's response should contain is somewhat debated. The two schools of thought are (a) return the deleted object or (b) return some meta-information expressing success or failure. I lean toward the latter, but if you want to give the user undo or re-save capabilities, returning the object might be your preferred approach. The following listing contains code to delete a venue. Nothing in it should be a surprise at this point.

Listing 11.15   A delete endpoint for venues

```
# RiffMates/bands/api.py
...

@router.delete("/venue/{venue_id}/", auth=api_key)
def delete_venue(request, venue_id):
    venue = get_object_or_404(Venue, id=venue_id)
    venue.delete()

    return {"success": True}
```

Use the Ninja docs interface to try out your new delete endpoint. Once you're done, run a GET on the newly deleted ID. On the server side, this causes a 404, as the lookup in `get_object_or_404()` throws an error. It is worth trying out to see how Ninja handles a 404. The HTTP status code gets set, of course, but it also automatically sends a JSON dictionary containing a key named *details*, whose value is the error string from the exception. This can be useful in a user interface: you can show the error in a pop-up dialog.

> ### Alternate Ninja architecture structures
>
> Putting the `NinjaAPI` object in urls.py and using `Router` instances to group API endpoints is just one approach. This tends to be how I organize my code, as it keeps the endpoint definitions in the same app as their model and view code. On occasion, I also separate out the schemas into their own file, creating a schemas.py to go along with the api.py file.
>
> An alternate structure I've used in the past is to make the API its own Django app. In this case, you don't need the `Router` instance. Instead of calling `.add_router()` on the `NinjaAPI` object, you can use the instance of the `NinjaAPI` object directly: the HTTP method decorators are available on it as well. If you want to put all of your API code together in an app, you can create the `NinjaAPI` object in that app and import the instance into whatever files contain your endpoints.
>
> This style of structure is common when using an alternate to Ninja called the Django REST Framework (as discussed later in the chapter). It is done this way, as the DRF requires a few more files to configure, and keeping it all in the same directory makes more sense.

11.3 Other API libraries

Ninja is definitely my preferred library for building APIs with Django. There are other choices out there, though. Predating Ninja is the *Django REST Framework* (DRF). The DRF (https://www.django-rest-framework.org/) is the granddaddy of Django REST API tools, and its first version was built before Python type hints existed. As such, there is a lot more code that needs to be written to build an API, code that Ninja does for you by understanding Python type hints.

The same basic ideas apply, though. Instead of functions, you typically use class methods, implementing a class for each object with methods corresponding to the GET, POST, and other HTTP actions. Classes also get used to declare serialization, and tools that map Django ORM objects are available. Like with Ninja, a multitude of authentication mechanisms are provided.

Like Ninja, the DRF comes with a web-based interface to interact with the API, which is very useful for testing. Unlike Ninja, the DRF supports several response-body formats. By using its serialization classes, changing from JSON to XML is a matter of a configuration parameter. DRF does this through the use of `Renderer` classes, and in fact, its web interface is built using this same technology. The DRF ships with renderers for JSON, HTML forms, Django templates, and more. There are also third-party add-ons for XML, YAML, three variations on JSON, MessagePack, Excel, CSV, Pandas, and Latex.

If your project needs payloads that are something other than JSON, then DRF is the way to go. This can also be used as a data export tool. For example, you could build an API with a single call whose output is YAML based on a group of nested serializers.

The DRF is definitely richer than Ninja, having more features and giving more control over how things work. The downside is it requires a lot more code, and for most REST APIs, Ninja is sufficient. Ninja is also a younger library, and features are getting added frequently; it may handle your need soon.

I've mentioned several times in this chapter the importance of a REST API's documentation, especially considering how loosely defined the protocol is. While both Ninja and the DRF come with web-based interfaces that can be used as docs, the developers consuming your API would appreciate actual documentation. Since API endpoints get exposed through views and classes in Ninja and DRF, the usual Python tools are sufficient. My personal preference is Sphinx (https://www.sphinx-doc.org/), but any Python documentation tool will work.

There are non-REST alternatives to providing an API as well. A popular mechanism is GraphQL. A GraphQL interface has a single endpoint that takes a JSON-like document that specifies a query. There are no HTTP methods to "verb" an object, and you don't need to specify multiple URL endpoints.

To build a GraphQL API interface with Django, you use a third-party library called Graphene (https://docs.graphene-python.org). Like with Ninja or the DRF, you specify a series of schemas that indicate what data can be returned from your interface and how it maps to the ORM. Since GraphQL doesn't use HTTP methods, you also need to define query classes that specify those actions that can be performed. Different types of query classes map to CRUD operations. This is essentially similar to REST endpoints, but it is built into the query language instead.

Graphene schemas and query classes get registered against a single `GraphQLView` object, which, itself, is registered as a view. This view is your API's endpoint. I have written systems that interact with upstream servers using GraphQL, but I've never built an API based upon it. The argument for GraphQL is flexibility on the client side. By specifying a schema, you get filtering and more complex queries for free. For example, you can ask for an object and limit what data comes back, minimizing your bandwidth usage. It is akin to an SQL call, where you can limit the response to only the columns you're interested in. There are two main arguments against GraphQL. First, the flexibility comes with the cost of the developer using the API having to write the queries to consume the data. Contrast this with REST, where they simply hit a URL. The second argument against is a provisioning one: due to the flexibility, the load on your server gets determined by the complexity of the query the downstream developer has written. This makes it much harder to predict load cost.

If you're writing your first API, I'd suggest sticking with Ninja. If you're already comfortable with GraphQL from other projects or frameworks, then Graphene could be the answer you're looking for.

When weighing which API framework to use, consider that Ninja has a few other features not covered in this chapter. For example, it supports the following:

- Endpoints implementing multiple HTTP methods
- HTTP methods not covered by the decorators
- Pagination
- Dynamically creating schemas

- Exception handling
- Injecting additional headers into a response
- Custom content renderers
- Support for `async` calls

All else being equal, I'd recommend you start by using Ninja, only moving to other libraries if you have deeper needs that aren't covered. Finally, I'd really like to point out the self-control involved in getting all the way through chapter 11 without making a bad bankruptcy joke.

11.4 Exercises

1 Write an API to list all the `Band` objects in the system with the corresponding `Musician` data nested within each `Band` object.

2 Write an API to update the fields of a `Musician` object, requiring authentication to do so.

Summary

- An API interface can provide access to the data in your project to outside systems.
- Web pages based on the Django Template Engine aren't the only kind of frontend you might build, and by building an API, these other interfaces can use the same logic from your views and the same data in your project.
- *CRUD* is short for *create, read, update,* and *delete*, the actions you perform on data in your system. This is true whether you're dealing with the objects directly, through the ORM, or indirectly, through the Django Admin or an API.
- REST is a loosely defined protocol built around URLs to define "nouns" in your system and HTTP methods to act as "verbs" to access them.
- REST uses HTTP GET to fetch content, POST to create or modify content, PUT and PATCH to update content, and DELETE to remove content.
- REST does not specify what data is in a call, but two common formats are JSON and XML.
- To use a REST API, you need to know which HTTP methods are used and the format of the payload.
- Versioning an API means including a version number in the base of the API's URL. This can allow you to future-proof breaking changes, giving your users time to continue to use a deprecated version of the API.
- Django Ninja is a third-party library that uses decorators to turn Django view functions into API endpoints.
- In Ninja, you define a single `NinjaAPI` object as a central collector for API endpoints and use its `api.urls` property to register the API's URLs as Django routes.
- API endpoints can be grouped together, using a Ninja `Router` object, with each router registered with the central `NinjaAPI` object. It is common practice to use

a separate api.py file for each of your project's apps that participates in the API, with a `Router` in each of those files.

- You create API versioning with Ninja in two steps: (1) use the `version` argument to the `NinjaAPI` object, and then (2) include the version number in your route declaration.
- Ninja provides `Schema` objects to specify how data gets translated into and out of JSON payloads.
- Ninja's `ModelSchema` class is a shortcut for basing a schema on an existing Django Model class.
- Each HTTP method has its own decorator in Ninja. Arguments passed to the decorator can register the ending part of the URL, determine the schema of the view's response, provide a look-up name for the endpoint view, and define the use of an authentication mechanism.
- Ninja endpoints can handle URL-based arguments and query parameters. Both cases get specified using an argument to the endpoint view function, with the URL-based arguments requiring an additional brace-bracket-wrapped token in the URL.
- Python type hints are used within schema definitions to indicate how fields get serialized. The declaration of a schema is similar to Python's `dataclasses` library.
- Ninja schemas look for static class methods with a prefix of `.resolve_` to populate fields. For example, `.resolve_slug()` is called to populate a field named `slug` on the class. The methods get called with an instance of the object getting serialized and should return the field's value.
- Schemas in Ninja can contain fields that reference other schemas, allowing you to nest data. For `Model` classes, a field name corresponding to related objects automatically gets populated. A Python type hint of `list[]` gets used to support the nesting of multiple related objects.
- The `Field` class is a Python type hint that gets used to give fine-grained control over field definitions, including providing default values and field name aliasing.
- Ninja supports a variety of authentication mechanisms, including Django's own authentication system and one based on API keys.
- Authentication can be linked to the `NinjaAPI` object, a `Router` object, or specific endpoint view functions.
- Using an API key that is included in an HTTP header is good practice, as it doesn't require an authentication session on the server, like a Django login does.
- The Django REST Framework is a popular alternative to Django Ninja. It requires more code to implement but also provides more flexibility.
- A GraphQL API can be built into your Django project, using the third-party library Graphene.

Making your pages more dynamic with HTMX

On its own, Django is structured for older-style web interactions, with each action causing a new page to be loaded. Modern web frameworks, like React and Angular, can be used on top of an API, but the HTMX library allows for a high degree of interactivity without a lot of additional JavaScript code.

12.1 Dynamic web pages

Django was created in a time when there was a one-to-one relationship between a URL and a web page. Web pages were relatively static, with JavaScript mostly used to snazz the page up a little, by highlighting the current page in the nav or doing a bit of calculation in a form. This time period now gets referred to as Web 1.0. As computers got faster and browsers added features, new degrees of interactivity got added to web pages. Many tools grew out of this time period, and web pages evolved into fully contained applications. Meanwhile, Django kept chugging along in its rather old-school way.

Web 2.0 can require a lot of JavaScript tooling. Frameworks like React and Angular mean potentially writing in TypeScript and adding a compilation stage to your web development. Libraries like Vue.js straddle the line, allowing you to mix and match 1.0-style pages with 2.0-style dynamics. If you want to build a web-based spreadsheet, these heavy-duty frameworks are a must. You wouldn't want the page to reload every time the user edited a cell; a high degree of interactivity is required. Single-page applications are really full programs running in your browser, rather than being paged based. The vast majority of business applications don't need this degree of interactivity. Most business applications really are just CRUD interfaces to a database. A sprinkling of interactivity is often enough.

HTMX is a JavaScript library that can meet a significant percentage of your dynamic web page needs. It works by adding the capability of replacing a portion of a web page through a URL call. Essentially, it brings the web 1.0 principle of visiting a URL and getting a page back to parts of the page. This works quite well with Django. HTMX modifies a loaded page on the fly by fetching part of a page from a Django view.

HTMX isn't meant to replace the heavier frameworks for situations like building a web-based spreadsheet, but it does provide a degree of interaction with very little JavaScript. The structure of your project can be very similar to Web 1.0, while the dynamic interactions on your pages get brought into the 2.0 era.

12.2 *HTMX attributes*

The HTMX library adds a set of attributes to HTML that you can place on almost any tag. These new attributes center around HTTP methods, and so are very similar to the REST concepts covered in chapter 11. When a user interacts with an HTML tag containing an HTMX attribute, the corresponding HTTP method gets invoked. Other HTMX attributes specify what to do with the response from the REST-like call. A typical example is to replace the activated tag with the response from the server. When using HTMX with Django, the only difference is that some Django views now return part of a web page, rather than a complete one. These component pieces are known as *partials*.

Consider a web page that shows the user the details of a random song and a link that swaps the song for another one when clicked. In the Web 1.0 world, clicking a link loads the whole page again to fetch a single new song. With HTMX, the link executes a GET to fetch an HTML partial containing the new content, which HTMX then replaces in the page for you. Dynamic!

All HTMX attributes begin with an `hx-` prefix. The `hx-get` performs an HTTP GET operation when the attached tag gets interacted with. The `hx-target` and hx-swap tags indicate what to do with the resulting content, with the target identifying what tag to replace and the swap attribute indicating how to replace it. A value of hx-swap="innerHTML" means to replace the contents inside the tag identified as the target. Figure 12.1 shows you this interaction.

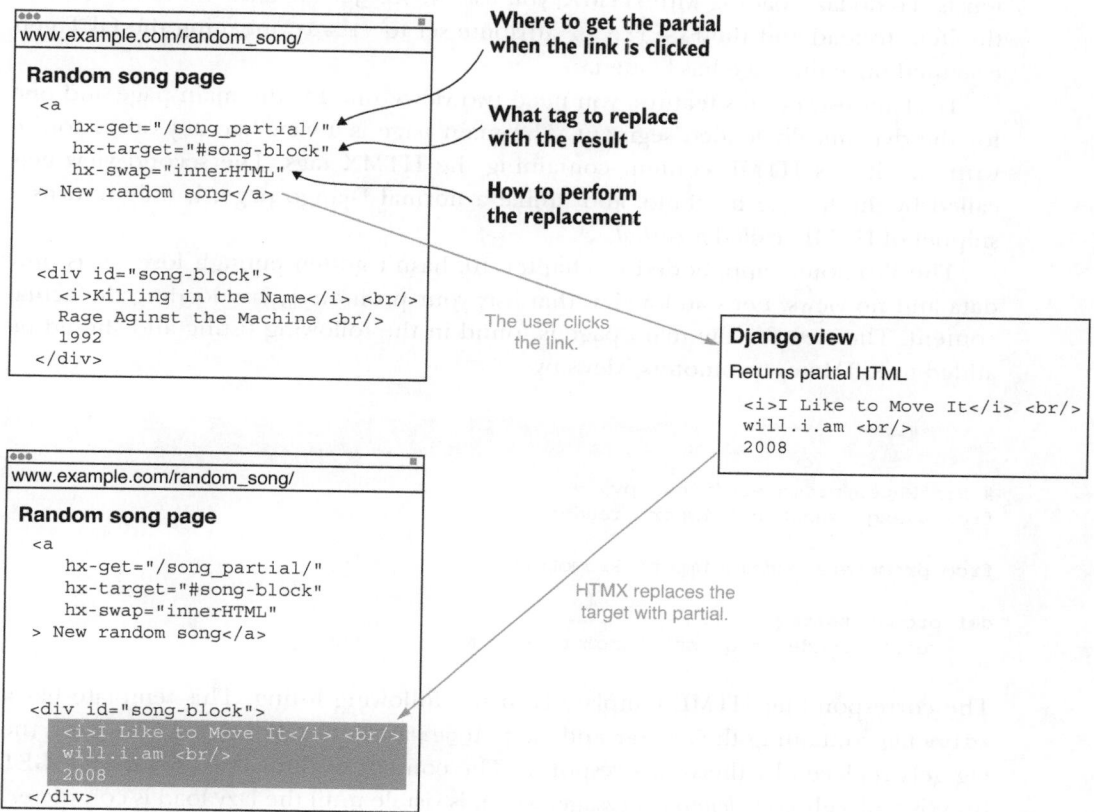

Figure 12.1   Using HTMX attributes to change a link into an action that replaces a portion of the page

HTMX operation attributes, like hx-get, are aware of their context. For example, when paired with an <input> tag, the hx-get is capable of including the value inside the input box as a query parameter in the URL it calls. Likewise, hx-post is aware of any forms it is attached to. The hx-trigger attribute allows you to specify when an action occurs. In conjunction with an input box, the trigger can be related to a keypress event. You can also trigger actions based on a tag becoming visible or the page getting loaded. With just a handful of attributes and the same view-based mechanisms you're already using in Django, HTMX provides a lot of possibilities.

12.3 Lazy loading

Let's dip our toes into the HTMX waters by doing lazy loading. Sometimes, elements on a web page take a while to calculate or can be slow to load. In some cases, this means the whole page stalls out waiting for a single item. Lazy loading is the idea of showing a page while dynamically inserting the slower content into the page afterwards. To do lazy loading with HTMX, you use the `hx-get` attribute set to the URL of the item to load and the `hx-trigger` attribute set to `"load"`, meaning the GET gets executed once the page has loaded.

To demonstrate this feature, you need two views: one for the main page and one for the dynamically loaded segment. The main page is a view like any other you've written, with its HTML content containing the HTMX tags. The second view gets called by the `hx-get` attribute, and unlike a normal Django page, it only returns a snippet of HTML, called a *partial*.

The Promoters app, added in chapter 10, hasn't gotten enough love—it is only data and no views. Let's add a view that lists your promoters, lazy loading the actual content. The view for the main page is found in the following listing and should be added to RiffMates/promoters/views.py.

Listing 12.1   A promoters listing view

```
# RiffMates/promoters/views.py
from django.shortcuts import render

from promoters.models import Promoter

def promoters(request):
    return render(request, "promoters.html")
```

The corresponding HTML template is in the following listing. This template has a `<div>` tag containing the `hx-get` and `hx-trigger` attributes. When the GET fires, the tag gets replaced by the view's response. The content of the `<div>`, before the GET fires, is a placeholder *loading* message, which is visible until the lazy load is complete.

Listing 12.2   A promoters listing template

```
<!-- RiffMates/templates/promoters.html -->
{% extends "base.html" %}

{% block title %}
  {{block.super}}: Promoter Listing
{% endblock %}

{% block content %}
  <h1>Promoters</h1>

  <div
        hx-get="/promoters/partial_promoters/"    ◁──  hx-get replaces this tag
                                                       with the contents
                                                       returned from the URL.
```

```
      hx-trigger="load">
   <i> Loading promoters... </i>
</div>
```

hx-trigger specifies when
the GET occurs—in this
case, on page load.

Placeholder text visible until
the lazy load completes

```
{% endblock content %}
```

The `hx-get` tag fires when the page loads and calls the associated URL. The following
listing contains the view this GET invokes.

Listing 12.3   An HTMX-invoked promoters listing view

```
# RiffMates/promoters/views.py
from time import sleep
...
def partial_promoters(request):      │ A two-second delay to simulate
    sleep(2)                         ◁─┘ lazy loading taking a while
    data = {
        "promoters": Promoter.objects.all(),
    }
    return render(request, "partials/promoters.html",
        data)
```

HTMX results get rendered
the same as any other
template, but the contents
are only a partial page.

The following listing contains the partial HTML segment, rendered by the
`partial_promoters()` view. I keep all my partials together in a subdirectory, created
under templates. This first partial is named RiffMates/templates/partials/
promoters.html.

Listing 12.4   A snippet of HTML that gets rendered in response to an HTMX GET call

```
<!-- RiffMates/templates/partials/promoters.html -->
<ul>
   {% for promoter in promoters %}
      <li>
         {{promoter.full_name}}
         {% if promoter.birth %}
         (
            {{promoter.birth}} -
            {% if promoter.death %}
              {{promoter.death}}
            {% endif %}
         )
         {% endif %}
      </li>
   {% empty %}
      <li> <i>No promoters in the database</i> </li>
   {% endfor %}
</ul>
```

Loop through
all promoters.

Render each promoter
as a list item.

An alternate message if
there are no promoters

To test all this out, you need to add a urls.py file to the `promoters` app, register the two
new views, and include the URL routes in the main RiffMates/urls.py file. You'll also
need some promoters if you haven't created them already. You can do this with the

Django Admin or the `ch10h_exercises` sample code directory, which includes a fixture with some data.

One last thing needs to be done before it will work: you need the HTMX JavaScript file. You reference this file in base.html, so it can be loaded into all of your pages. The `<script>` tag that includes the library can reference a CDN, as follows:

```
<script src="https://unpkg.com/htmx.org@1.9.8"></script>
```

> **NOTE** A *content delivery network* (CDN) is a giant cache on the internet, which many popular tools use to centrally locate their content, meaning your browser can cache files common between different sites.

Or if you prefer not to use a CDN, you can download the file for yourself and serve it as static content, like you learned about in chapter 7. This is the approach I've taken, as I don't always trust CDNs to keep their files around for a long time. This comes at the cost of page load time; the user's browser can't use a cached copy from a different site because it doesn't know it is the same content as HTMX elsewhere. The change I made to base.html to load the HTMX library from the project directly is shown in the following listing.

Listing 12.5   Add the HTMX library to the base template

```
<!-- RiffMates/templates/base.html -->
{% load static %}          ◄─┐ Load the
<head>                       │ {% static %} tag.
  <!-- ... -->
  <script src="{% static 'js/htmx-1.9.8.min.js' %}"    ◄─
    ></script>

</head>
```

Use the downloaded copy of the library found in RiffMates/static/js/htmx-1.9.8.min.js.

Restart your development server, and visit the `promoters()` view. I put mine at http://localhost:8000/promoters/promoters/. As there is a 2-second delay in the view called by the lazy load, you should see the Loading… message, followed by your list of promoters filled in dynamically.

12.4 *Search-as-you-type with infinite scroll*

A common dynamic interaction on a web page is search-as-you-type, where a search page has an input box and as you enter search terms, the results are populated below. Another dynamic concept is infinite scroll. Consider your favorite social media feed: as you scroll, new content gets added to the bottom. Both of these concepts can be built with HTMX, requiring little more code than a regular view.

Before considering the HTMX version, let's start with a musicians search view, making sure it works before adding the interactive part. The view uses a query parameter to get the search text—it'll be clear why, when the HTMX part gets wired in.

To search a model, you need to construct a query based on the search text. For a `Musician`, you want to search by first and last names. Instead of looking for exact matches, it is better to look for names that start with the search terms. All the queries you've performed so far with the `.filter()` method have had their clauses AND-ed together. To search for a first or last name beginning with a search term, you need clauses OR-ed together.

In Django, you can create more complex queries by using the `Q` object, found in the `django.db.models` module. `Q` is short for *query*, and you build the objects using the same arguments as you pass to `.filter()`. You can combine `Q` objects together to compound them, using Python's binary operators, like AND (`&`) and OR (`|`). This allows you to form arbitrarily complex queries, and then submit the resulting `Q` object as a single argument to a `.filter()` call. In chapter 11, when you passed `q=name__icontains` into a `Field` class to modify a related-object query, it was using this same technique under the covers.

In addition to searching using both first and last name, it would be nice to allow the user to enter multiple search terms. To support this, the code needs to parse the text based on whitespace, use each term in two `Q` objects for the first and last names, and then combine all the `Q` objects with an OR (`|`). The finished query searches for instances of any of the search terms in either name. The following listing contains the first attempt at a search view.

Listing 12.6   A search view for musicians by their names

```python
# RiffMates/bands/views.py
...
from django.db.models import Q
...

def search_musicians(request):
    search_text = request.GET.get("search_text", "")       # Retrieve the search terms
                                                            # from the query parameter.
    search_text = urllib.parse.unquote(search_text)        # A URL parameter gets
    search_text = search_text.strip()                      # encoded. Turn it back
                                                            # into a regular string.
    musicians = []

    if search_text:                                         # Split the search
        parts = search_text.split()                         # terms into a list.

        q = Q(first_name__istartswith=parts[0]) | \         # Build Q objects OR-ed together
            Q(last_name__istartswith=parts[0])              # to search for this term in both
                                                            # the first and last name fields of
        for part in parts[1:]:                              # the Musician object.
            q |= Q(first_name__istartswith=part) | \        # OR another set of Q objects
                Q(last_name__istartswith=part)              # to the combined query.

        musicians = Musician.objects.filter(q)              # Perform the database search
                                                            # by calling .filter() with the
    data = {                                                # combined Q objects.
        "search_text": search_text,
        "musicians": musicians,
    }

    return render(request, "search_musicians.html", data)
```

Loop through subsequent search terms.

For the sake of brevity, I'll leave it to you to create the first version of RiffMates/ templates/search_musicians.html. It only needs a {% for %} tag to loop over the resulting musicians.

Once you've written the proof-of-concept template, add a route for the new search view in RiffMates/bands/urls.py, and then test your view by calling http:// localhost:8000/bands/search_musicians/?search_text=J V. (Yes, that space in the URL will work in your browser.) If your data is the same as mine, you'll get back John Bonham, Jimi Hendrix, John Lennon, and Steve Vai. The first three match the *J* with the first name field, while Steve Vai is a match for the *V* on the last name field.

With the initial view in place, let's add some HTMX. The real version of the page has an <input> tag for entering the search terms and an area where results get appended. The results area gets populated using an infinite scroll mechanism, meaning smaller sets of results are returned by the server, and as the user scrolls down on the page, more results are added. This is an efficient way of doing things, especially if there are a lot of results. It is essentially pagination without the user having to click Next Page. In case that's not fancy enough, we're also going to update the browser's URL as the user types in their search terms. Doing this means the search can be bookmarked or shared between users as a deep link. One complication of this feature is that the initial view of a deep-linked page must render search results. So either the initial render or an infinite scroll event can add results to the page. Figure 12.2 outlines the end goal of our search page.

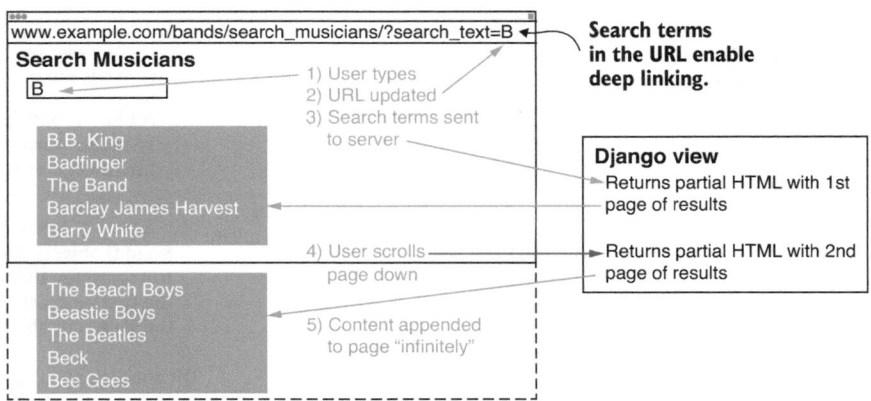

Figure 12.2   A search-as-you-type page with infinite scroll and deep linking

Let's start building the page by adding the <input> tag, which uses an hx-get attribute, sending the search terms to the server when the user types. You connect typing with a GET call through the hx-trigger attribute. A value of hx-trigger="keyup" causes GET to be performed when a key gets pressed and released.

The trigger also supports additional parameters. Using `"keyup changed delay:500ms"` adds a filter to the trigger. Now, only key releases that change the value of the field invoke the GET. Pressing an arrow key won't cause the trigger. The `delay` tells HTMX to wait until typing has stopped, or at least paused. The trigger doesn't activate until 500 milliseconds after the last keypress. If the user is typing quickly, the page waits a bit before invoking the trigger, so as not to overwhelm the server.

Search results get inserted in a `<div>` tag on the page. The `<div>` has an ID, which the `<input>` tag targets with an `hx-target` attribute. The GET call's results get inserted into the target tag.

HTMX allows you to tie the content of the input box to the browser's URL by using the `hx-push-url` attribute. With this attribute set to `"true"`, anything the user types in gets appended to a query parameter in the URL. This allows for deep linking. You can copy and paste the URL into another window to perform the same search results. This also means your search can be bookmarked. Because of this, the initial rendering of the page may need to include search results, but you don't need to use HTMX for this—you can instead include it as part of the page rendering like with non-HTMX views. The `<div>` tag where results go starts with rendering any initial results and is the target for any appended results. As this chunk of HTML is needed in two places (the initial and update calls), I've encapsulated it into its own file, so it can be included by the template engine. The following listing contains the main search page.

Listing 12.7   The template for the search page

```
<!-- RiffMates/templates/search_musicians.html -->
{% extends "base.html" %}

{% block content %}
  <h1>Search Musicians</h1>

    <input name="search_text"
      placeholder="Search for musicians..."
      type="text"
      value="{{search_text}}"
      hx-get="{% url 'search_musicians' %}"
      hx-trigger="keyup changed delay:500ms"
      hx-target="#results"
      hx-push-url="true">

    <div class="results" id="results">
      {% include "partials/musician_results.html" %}
    </div>
{% endblock content %}
```

The URL to call when the search terms change

The input box for search terms

When the page is deep-linked, render the search terms in the input box.

Trigger a GET when a keyup event changes the content of the input box.

Returned results get rendered in the tag matching this CSS query selector.

The parent tag for any results

The partial HTML segment that renders the resulting list of musicians

Turning on hx-push-url causes the URL's search_text query parameter to be updated with the contents of the input box.

The subtemplate that both gets included by the search page and used as a partial HTML result is shown in the following listing.

Listing 12.8   The inner template for the search results

```
<!-- RiffMates/templates/partials/musician_results.html -->
<ul>
  {% for musician in musicians %}                    ◄──────────┐  Loop through and display
    <li> <a href="{% url 'musician' musician.id %}">            │  all the musicians.
      {{musician.last_name}}, {{musician.first_name}}
    </a> </li>
  {% empty %}
    <li> <i>No matching musicians</i> </li>
  {% endfor %}
</ul>
```

An HTMX-enabled search page isn't very different from a regular one; with a few extra attributes, you have search-as-you-type. The only thing missing now is a view that returns the results as partial HTML. In the `promoters()` view early in this chapter, you used separate views for the main page and the partial, but like with GET and POST sections in a form view, it is cleaner to put it all in the same place.

For a view to be able to render both the page and the partial segment, it needs to know its invocation mode. Any call that HTMX makes includes a header called `HX-Request`. In your view, you check for this header and behave accordingly. You could do this manually, but there is a very handy library that makes it simpler: django-htmx. To install this library, call `python -m pip install django-htmx`, add `"django_htmx"` to your `INSTALLED_APPS`, and add `"django_htmx.middleware.HtmxMiddleware"` to the `MIDDLEWARE` list in your settings.py file. For more details on installing third-party libraries, see appendix A.

The `HtmxMiddleware` component of `django-htmx` adds an `htmx` object to the `request` in your view. This object contains details about the HTMX call and, usefully, can be used in a Boolean context to determine whether the HTMX invoked the call. The following listing contains the new version of the search musicians view.

Listing 12.9   An HTMX-capable search view

```
# RiffMates/bands/views.py
...
def search_musicians(request):
    search_text = request.GET.get("search_text", "")
    search_text = urllib.parse.unquote(search_text)
    search_text = search_text.strip()

    musicians = []

    if search_text:
        parts = search_text.split()

        q = Q(first_name__istartswith=parts[0]) | \
            Q(last_name__istartswith=parts[0])
        for part in parts[1:]:
            q |= Q(first_name__istartswith=part) | \
                Q(last_name__istartswith=part)
```

```
    musicians = Musician.objects.filter(q)

data = {
    "search_text": search_text,
    "musicians": musicians,
}
if request.htmx:          ◁──┐  If this is an HTMX call, render
    return render(request, "partials/musician_results.html", data)   only the partial page.

return render(request, "search_musicians.html", data)
```

That's it! Now, you have search-as-you-type. The equivalent in Vue.js requires a couple dozen lines of JavaScript. With HTMX, you add a few attributes, write a search view, and you're there. Go back to the development server, and this time, type your search terms in the input box to test it out. Note how the URL updates as you enter your terms.

Other django-htmx features

In this chapter, I'll only be using the `request.htmx` object as a Boolean to determine if the call is HTMX or not, but the library also has the following:

- Full access to all the headers HTMX sends, including which URL got called and why it got triggered
- An extension JavaScript library that enhances HTMX's error reporting and interaction with the template engine
- Response classes allowing you to perform redirects, refreshes, and other actions as part of HTMX-triggered views

---

Let's add another feature to your search page: infinite scroll. If your site has a lot of data, you might paginate the results. With infinite scroll, instead of forcing the user to click to get the next page of data, they simply scroll down, and the new data gets added to the bottom. Two things need to be done to add infinite scroll to your existing search feature: first, you need to paginate the data in your view, and second, you need an HTMX trigger that renders the next "page" of data.

You've seen pagination before. It was used in the `musicians()` view way back in chapter 4. As a quick recap, Django provides the `Paginator` object that divides query results into pages of data, and then you use a query parameter to specify which page is displayed. The following listing contains the modifications to the search musicians view to add pagination. It takes advantage of the existing `_get_items_per_page()` and `_get_page_num()` utilities, written in chapter 4's exercises.

Listing 12.10 An HTMX-capable search view

```
# RiffMates/bands/views.py
...
from time import sleep
...
```

```
def search_musicians(request):
    ...

    # Query results are in the "musicians" object by this point in the code

    items_per_page = _get_items_per_page(request)
    paginator = Paginator(musicians, items_per_page)          Paginate the results
    page_num = _get_page_num(request, paginator)              of the search.
    page = paginator.page(page_num)

    data = {
        "search_text": search_text,                      "musicians" now contains
        "musicians": page.object_list,                   only this page of results.
        "has_more": page.has_next(),
        "next_page": page_num + 1,                        The value of the
    }                                                     next page of data

    if request.htmx:
        if page_num > 1:                    If you are rendering after the
            sleep(2)                        first page, wait 2 seconds.

        return render(request, "partials/musician_results.html", data)

    return render(request, "search_musicians.html", data)
```

True if there is more data → `"has_more": page.has_next(),`

You'll note that like with the promoters partial view, I've included a time delay in this code. On your local machine, using a development server, it can be hard to see the call for the next data, as it happens so fast. To help check things are working properly, I've intentionally made the call take at least 2 seconds.

The search view now supports pages of data. To add infinite scrolling, you need an HTMX trigger for when a tag scrolls into view. This trigger value is `"revealed"`. At the bottom of the results page, insert a `<div>` that calls the next page of results when it gets revealed on the page. Of course, `<div>` tags are invisible, so the user doesn't see anything, but the browser doesn't care. The tag is either within the browser's view port, or it is not, and the first time it "shows" in the view port, the HTMX call gets triggered. Add the code in the following listing to the bottom of RiffMates/templates/partials/musician_results.html.

Listing 12.11   The inner template for the search results

```
<!-- RiffMates/templates/partials/musician_results.html -->
<!-- ... -->
                            The view sets has_more to True
                            if there are more pages of data.
{% if has_more %}
  <div
    hx-get="{% url 'search_musicians' %}?page={{next_page}}
      &search_text={{search_text}}"
    hx-trigger="revealed"              Trigger the HTMX call
                                       when this tag becomes
                                       visible on screen.
```

GET invokes the same search view with query parameters specifying the next page number and the search text.

```
hx-swap="outerHTML">
    <i> Loading... </i>
</div>
{% endif %}
```

Display a Loading...
message until the
results are available.

A value of "outerHTML" means to
replace the entire <div> with
the results from the GET call.

This new addition to the results partial implements infinite scrolling. It is common to indicate that something is loading if it takes a bit of time; I've used text here, but you could use an animated spinner GIF instead. Since the search view has a delay in it, you should see the Loading... text on the screen for 2 seconds before more results get shown.

You could test this out now, but as you don't have many musicians, there won't be enough data to trigger the infinite scroll feature. That is easily fixed. Invoke your Django shell with the `shell` management command, and enter the following code:

```
>>> from datetime import date
>>> from bands.models import Musician
>>> for n in range(1, 81):
...     Musician.objects.create(first_name=f"X{n:02}", last_name="Z",
...         birth=date(1900, 1, 20))
...
```

You now have an extra 80 musicians, all of whom conveniently have a first name starting with the same letter. Restart your development server, and try out your search results page with infinite scroll. Don't forget to keep scrolling until the data is consumed; you want to make sure the last page is working as well.

12.5   Click to edit

The Django Admin is very Web 1.0. It starts with a list of items, and to edit one, you click it and go to the next screen. With HTMX, you can perform inline editing, modifying the page to replace an item with the form to edit it. This is known as *click to edit*. The concepts are similar to what you've seen already: `hx-get` to replace a tag with a new partial, where the partial contains the edit form. HTMX supports all the HTTP methods you're familiar with, so as you might guess, the form gets submitted with `hx-post`.

To demonstrate click-to-edit, let's build an editor for the rooms associated with a venue. For this feature, you'll need three views: the main page displaying a venue's rooms, a view that handles the room-editing form, and a third view that can display a room partial on its own. The third view is necessary to give the user the ability to cancel out of the edit.

The main page view for editing rooms takes the ID of a `Venue` object and displays its associated rooms. The view is about as simple as is possible. The following listing shows the view I've added to RiffMates/bands/views.py.

Listing 12.12   A view to display the rooms in a venue

```
# RiffMates/bands/views.py
...
from django.contrib.auth.decorators import login_required
from django.shortcuts import render, get_object_or_404
```

```
...
@login_required          ◁——————————————————      Only logged-in users should
def room_editor(request, venue_id):                be able to edit a venue.
    venue = get_object_or_404(Venue, id=venue_id,
        userprofile=request.user.userprofile)  ◁—┐  Find the given venue and
                                                    ensure the logged-in user
    data = {                                        is associated with it.
        "venue": venue,
    }

    return render(request, "room_editor.html", data)
```

The HTML for the room editor is broken down into two parts: the main page and the partial that renders a room. You saw a similar pattern with the search musicians feature: the partial that needs to be rendered is often also included into the main page as well. The following listing contains the main page.

Listing 12.13   The main room editor page

```
<!-- RiffMates/templates/room_editor.html -->
{% extends "base.html" %}

{% block content %}
  <h1>Venue: {{venue.name}}</h1>

  <ul>
    {% for room in venue.room_set.all %}
      {% include "partials/show_room.html" %}   ◁——   The same subtemplate is used
    {% empty %}                                        as the partial for another view.
      <li><i>No rooms for this venue</i> </li>
    {% endfor %}
  </ul>

{% endblock content %}
```

The corresponding subtemplate for each room is shown in the following listing.

Listing 12.14   The main room editor page

```
<!-- RiffMates/templates/partials/show_room.html -->
<li id="room-row-{{room.id}}">
  {{room.name }}         ◁—|  Display the room's name.         The Edit link uses an
  <a                                                                    HTMX GET to retrieve
      hx-get="{% url 'edit_room_form' room.id %}"   ◁——————             the room-editing form.
      hx-target="#room-row-{{room.id}}"           ◁———
      style="cursor: pointer; text-decoration: underline"   ◁——         When GET
    > (Edit) </a>                                                        gets invoked,
</li>                                       As the <a> tag has no href, the   replace the
                                            browser doesn't style it; add the entire <li> tag.
                                            underline and pointer cursor back to it.
```

With the two templates in place, you can test the room editor view. Don't forget to register the room_editor() as a route in bands/urls.py, and make sure you include the name argument, as you'll want to reference this view in your HTML. As you haven't written the view for the form partial, clicking the Edit link won't work, but you can see the main page. Visit http://localhost:8000/bands/room_editor/1/ to see the rooms associated with the CGBG venue.

The next step is to add the view that handles the form to edit a room. Similarly to the form views covered in chapter 7, this view is responsible for both displaying the form and handling the submit. For this view, the HTML rendered is a partial segment in both cases, but otherwise, the idea is the same. The form, in this case, is simple enough that you could handle the `request.POST` manually, but I'll stick with best practices and create a `ModelForm`, shown in the following listing.

Listing 12.15   A form for editing Room objects

```
# RiffMates/bands/forms.py
from django import forms
...
from bands.models import Room
...

RoomForm = forms.modelform_factory(Room, fields=["name",])
```

The view that handles the room form has both a GET and POST case. The GET renders the form with the given room data. For the POST, the form gets validated, and the submitted data gets saved, replacing the values in the associated room. In both cases, the output is a partial, so HTMX can either replace the display information with the form or the form with the display information. The following listing shows the view.

Listing 12.16   An HTMX view for handling a room-editing form

```
# RiffMates/bands/views.py
...
from bands.forms import RoomForm
...
@login_required                          ◁─┘ Editing data requires
                                              the user to be logged in.      Edit the Room object
def edit_room_form(request, room_id):                             ◁─┘ for the ID passed in.
    room = get_object_or_404(Room, id=room_id,
        venue__userprofile=request.user.userprofile)        ◁──
                                                                      Fetch the Room, and
                                                                      ensure it is associated
    if request.method == "POST":                    ◁─               with a venue that is
        form = RoomForm(request.POST, instance=room)                 associated with the user.
        if form.is_valid():         ◁─┐ Validate, and then
            form.save()                 save the submitted      The view handles form
            data = {                    room data.              submission through a
                "room": room,                                   POST method.
            }
            return render(request, "partials/show_room.html",
                data)
    else:                                           For the GET scenario, build the
        form = RoomForm(instance=room)       ◁─┘ form based on the Room object.

    data = {
```

After saving the changes, show the partial displaying the room info. (annotation pointing to `return render(request, ...)`)

```
            "room": room,
            "form": form,                           Render the room
    }                                               editing form as a
                                                    partial.
    return render(request, "partials/edit_room_form.html", data)
```

The partial for the room-editing form is similar to the forms you built in chapter 7. The following listing shows the form, which uses an `hx-get` to cancel the editing action, and an `hx-post` to submit the form.

Listing 12.17 The HTML form for editing a room

```
<!-- RiffMates/templates/partials/edit_room_form.html -->
<li id="room-row-{{room.id}}">                 All forms require CSRF protection; see
    <form>                                     section 7.1.2, on CSRF, for more details.
        {% csrf_token %}
        {{form.as_p}}                                          Submit the form,
        <button                                                using hx-post.
            hx-post="{% url 'edit_room_form' room.id %}"
            hx-target="#room-row-{{room.id}}"        When triggering the POST, replace the
        >Save</button>                               parent <li> tag with the response.
        <button
            hx-get="{% url 'show_room_partial' room.id %}"
            hx-target="#room-row-{{room.id}}"
        >Cancel</button>                    Cancel editing the form by
    </form>                                 fetching the display
</li>                                       information with hx-get.
```

Render the RoomForm object as a `<p>` tag.

The beauty of HTMX is its similarity to regular Web 1.0 HTML coding. The form handling here uses the same patterns you used in chapter 7, but with the `hx-` attributes, the behavior becomes dynamic within the page.

The only thing you're missing now is the view called when cancelling the edit form. This view displays the existing room info partial template. The following listing shows this view.

Listing 12.18 An HTMX view for handling a room editing form

```
# RiffMates/bands/views.py
...
@login_required
def show_room_partial(request, room_id):
    room = get_object_or_404(Room, id=room_id,
        venue__userprofile=request.user.userprofile)

    data = {
        "room": room,
    }

    return render(request, "partials/show_room.html", data)
```

Completing the `@login_required` security check and validating the room is associated with the user aren't strictly necessary here, as the user can get the same information from the public venue listing page built in the exercises in chapter 4. I prefer the consistent approach, though; having a habit of "if it is for editing, it should be secure" is a good one.

Your code is now complete. Make sure to register the views as routes you haven't done so far, and revisit http://localhost:8000/bands/room_editor/1/ to play with the CBGB venue's rooms.

A true room editor would also allow you to create and delete rooms. These features can be added using the same techniques you've used so far. An Add link on the page could dynamically render the Edit form with empty data. Your room editing view would need to handle the ID = 0 case, or you could write a separate view for adding, if you prefer. Delete is just another link, like Edit. You can use `hx-delete` in the view if you like, but `hx-get` works equally well. The only trick with deletion is to remove the display tag afterwards, so the partial returned from the view needs to be empty. HTMX even has an `hx-confirm` tag, which presents an *Are You Sure?* dialog that you can use in the delete case. See https://htmx.org/docs/#confirming for more information.

HTMX may not be as powerful as full SPA frameworks, but it does allow you to inject a large degree of interactivity into your project with very little change in your code. For most CRUD-based websites, HTMX is more than enough, and the overhead is far smaller than a full SPA framework. The HTMX website includes a couple of case studies in which companies converted React-based projects to HTMX. The conversion significantly shrank the size of their code base; reduced the load time of their pages; and, due to the smaller memory footprint, actually enabled the application to handle more data on the screen at a time. See the Essays section of the HTMX website for more information: https://htmx.org/essays/.

12.6 Exercises

1 Add search functionality for your ad content, similar to the musicians search page. Implement both search-as-you-type and infinite scrolling.
2 Create a page that has two tabs: one for musicians and one for venues. You'll need a new view for the page, but the existing listing views for musicians and venues can be used to populate the tabs. An example covering how to write tabs is provided on the HTMX site: https://htmx.org/examples/tabs-hateoas/

Summary

- Django is constructed using a Web 1.0 architecture and requires integration with JavaScript libraries to make pages more interactive.
- HTMX enables replacing part of a page using similar techniques to clicking a link in the Web 1.0 world.
- HTMX adds a series of HTTP method attributes that can be assigned to tags in your HTML. Interacting with such a tag causes a GET, POST, or other method to be invoked on the server.
- All HTMX attributes begin with `hx-`.
- HTMX has attributes that control when the HTTP method gets invoked, such as when clicking a tag, when a page gets loaded, when a tag becomes visible, or when an event like a keypress occurs.

- The `hx-target` and `hx-swap` attributes control what parts of a page get modified when an action gets invoked. The target uses a CSS selector to determine what tag gets replaced, while the swap attribute determines which part of the tag changes.
- Lazy loading allows you to add content to the page after it has been displayed and is typically used for assets that take a long time to be generated or downloaded.
- To build lazy loading with HTMX, you use the `hx-trigger` attribute, set to a value of `"load"`, along with an `hx-get`, pointing to the URL of the asset to be fetched.
- Since HTMX uses HTTP methods, the Django portion of the code can be the same kinds of views you've written before.
- HTMX sets a header to indicate a call invoked by the library; this allows you to write views that serve both the full page and the replacement segment for an HTMX call.
- The segments of HTML returned in response to an HTMX call are known as *partials*.
- HTMX appends the contents of input boxes onto an `hx-get` URL as a query parameter.
- Search-as-you-type is a feature that populates search results dynamically as the user enters search terms in an input box.
- To build search-as-you-type in HTMX, you combine an input box with an `hx-get` call to the search view. An `hx-trigger` based on the `keyup` event invokes the GET when a key is pressed and released.
- When using an `hx-triggerkeyup` event, you can filter events with `changed`, so only keypresses that change an input box's value invoke the GET call.
- The `django.db.models.Q` object allows you to create arbitrarily complex ORM queries, using both AND and OR terms.
- Infinite scroll is a feature that adds additional data to the page when the user scrolls to the bottom.
- You can implement infinite scroll in HTMX by using the `hx-trigger` attribute with a value of `revealed`. When the tag scrolls onto screen, it triggers a GET call to fetch more content.
- Infinite scroll in Django is best handled using a `Paginator` class, with a page of data returned for each invocation of the associated view.
- The `django-htmx` library provides a middleware component, which can be used to test whether the view got called by HTMX or a regular page view.
- Click-to-edit is a feature displaying data as well as a button or link, which, when clicked, changes the display data into an edit form.
- You implement click-to-edit with HTMX by using `hx-get` to change viewable data into a form and `hx-post` to submit the form. This can be combined with an additional `hx-get` to cancel out of the edit.

Django power tools

This chapter covers

- Django Debug Toolbar
- General-utility libraries
- Django Admin beautification
- Prettier forms
- Favicons
- Feature flags
- Generating static sites

One of Python's mantras is *batteries included*, meaning the language should include everything you need to build your project. Ironically, Python has an incredibly rich ecosystem of add-ons. The batteries may be included, but there is a pretty big battery store with all sorts of variety. Django embraces this same attitude: the framework contains everything you need to build a website. Like with Python, Django has plenty of third-party tools to make your life easier. This chapter covers a few of the libraries I just can't live without. Before writing any kind of code, you should always check https://djangopackages.org/ to see if someone else has done it for you.

Most third-party packages for Django are installable Django apps. To install one, you use the `pip` tool and typically add the app's name to your INSTALLED_APPS configuration in settings.py. Some packages have other things you need to do to get them to work, like add additional configuration or run the `migrations` command. Appendix A contains general instructions for installing packages: in this chapter, I'll only be highlighting the key parts. If you're going to use a package, you should check its documentation. Some packages' instructions may have changed since this book was published, or there may be variations, depending on the versions of Python and Django you are using.

This chapter covers a variety of tools I've found useful over the years. The first section is on the Django Debug Toolbar, an add-on that shows an overlay on top of your view, giving you loads of information about the performance of the view and what resources were used to build it. The second section covers a couple of toolboxes. There are many libraries that are collections of small tools and `Models` you can take advantage of; I've covered Django Extensions and Django Awl here. After that, I delve into look-and-feel tools, things that make your Django prettier.

The fourth section is on feature flags: the ability to turn code on and off in production, depending on who is using it. This is a great way to beta test new code in a production environment. And finally, I go full circle by returning to static sites, which were introduced in chapter 1. Django Distill is a great tool that uses Django templating techniques to create a static site generator.

13.1 *Django Debug Toolbar*

What's in a name? Well, the Django Debug Toolbar (https://pypi.org/project/django-debug-toolbar/) doesn't require any debate about the smell of roses—it is what it claims. The Debug Toolbar is an overlay for your development server that tells you all sorts of interesting information about what is going on in a page.

The Debug Toolbar is a third-party library and can be installed using `python -m pip install django-debug-toolbar`. It requires a bit more configuration than your typical app. It needs the `django.contrib.staticfiles` app with its corresponding STATIC_URLS setting, and the APP_DIRS value of the TEMPLATES setting must be `True`. If your project is configured like RiffMates, you already have both of these settings.

The toolbar itself is an app, so you must register `"debug_toolbar"` in INSTALLED_APPS and add `"debug_toolbar.middleware.DebugToolbarMiddleware"` in MIDDLEWARE. The order of the middleware is important; it needs to be included as high as possible on the list but after any encoding middleware, like `GZipMiddleware`. The toolbar is a series of views, and the corresponding routes need to be added to your urls.py file. The typical prefix used for the toolbar's routes is *double-underscore debug*: `path("__debug__/", include("debug_toolbar.urls"))`. Finally, for security reasons, the toolbar only works on your local environment, and it needs `"127.0.0.1"` added to the INTERNAL_IPS setting. For complete details on installing the toolbar, see https://django-debug-toolbar.readthedocs.io/en/latest/installation.html.

That's a lot of configuration, but once you've got it going, you can run your development server and visit any page in your project. Try going to http:localhost:8000/bands/musicians/. If you got all that config right, you'll see a callout on the right side of the page showing all the tools that come with the Debug Toolbar. Figure 13.1 shows the result.

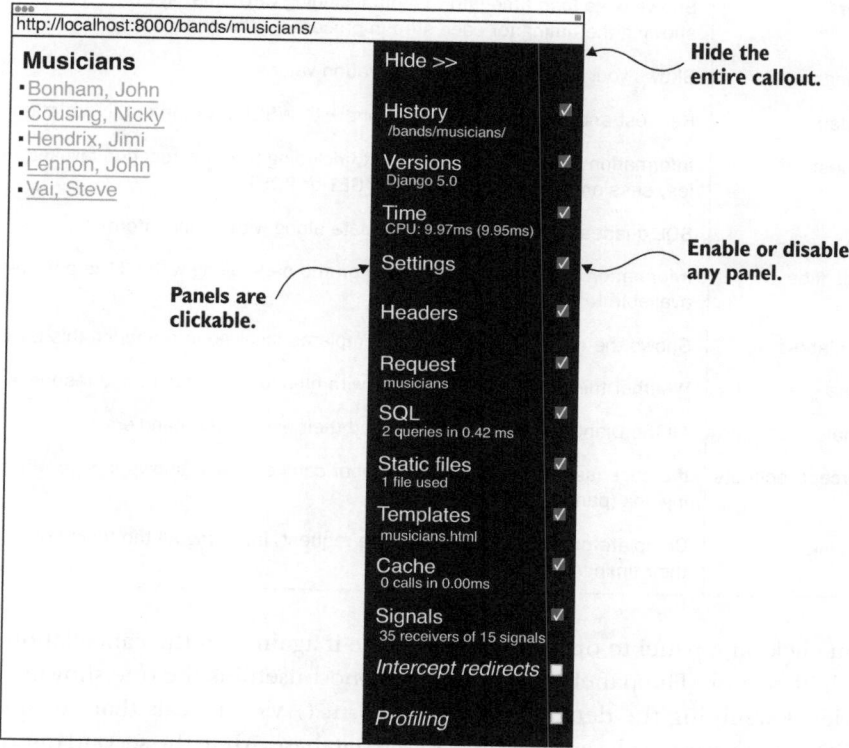

Figure 13.1   Django Debug Toolbar on the musician listing page

The toolbar is composed of a series of reports, with each showing information about the page. The Debug Toolbar calls these mini-reports *panels*, and in fact, you can customize what panels show in your toolbar and even install third-party additions. Gathering debug information can take a bit of time, so for performance reasons, you can turn off any panel using the corresponding check mark.

Some panels show quick information; for example, the Time panel indicates how long it took for the page to show, while the SQL panel tells you how many database queries got run. Clicking a panel opens it, covering your page and revealing detailed information. Table 13.1 describes each of the panels that come with the Debug Toolbar by default.

Table 13.1   Django Debug Toolbar panels

Panel	Description
History	History of requests made, which also includes the ability to view the debug info for past visits
Versions	Shows the versions of Django, Python, and installed apps (if possible)
Timer	Shows page load time information, including CPU time, system time, and a graph showing the timing for each step in processing the page
Settings	Shows your current project configuration values
Headers	Request and response headers along with WSGI environment information
Request	Information about the HTTP request, including the view function invoked, any cookies, session data, and data for the GET or POST
SQL	SQL queries run to get the page's data along with timing information
Static files	Information on the static files used on the page along with all the possible files available to the {% static %} tag
Templates	Shows the template path and all templates involved in rendering this page
Cache	Whether the cache got used along with hit-and-miss counts and response times
Signals	All the Django signals registered and their associated handlers
Intercept redirects	If a page issues a redirect, the toolbar catches it and shows a page with the resulting link (panel off, by default)
Profiling	Complete profile information on the request, including all the functions called and their timings (panel off by default)

If you click on a panel to open it, you can close it again with the cancellation *X* in the top right corner. The panel I personally find most useful is the one showing the SQL queries. Examining the details for the `musicians()` view reveals that two queries got run. The first counted all the musicians in the database, while the second queried using the musicians limiting the number of results. This two-step process occurs because the musicians view uses the `Paginator` object; the first call checks how many items there are in the entire database, while the second limits how many come back in a page.

The most likely performance bottleneck you'll have on a page is from the database. One of the downsides of an ORM is you're not always cognizant of your query's complexity. If you're finding your page load is slow, the Time and SQL panels can help you get to the bottom of it.

13.2   *Tool libraries*

Django is a large framework with lots of features, but there are always situations where there could be more. Often, these features are small and not worthy of their own library. As a result, there are several third-party libraries that are collections of miscellaneous tools. This section covers two of these tool kits: Django Extensions and Django Awl.

13.2.1 Django Extensions

The Django Extensions (https://pypi.org/project/django-extensions/) library is one of the most popular tool kits out there. Installation is simple: run `python -m pip install django-extensions`, then add `"django_extensions"` to `INSTALLED_APPS`. This library is quite large and is broken down by feature area, with extensions for the following:

- Commands
- Signals
- Debugging
- Fields
- Job scheduling
- Models
- Permissions
- Validators

Even with that extensive list, there is still another section called Utilities, the miscellaneous area of the ultimate miscellaneous tool kit. There is way too much in here to cover it all in detail, so I'll highlight a couple of key items.

Inside the Commands section, you'll find `shell_plus`: a management command that adds features to Django's `shell`. The key differentiator here is that it pre-imports many of the modules, classes, and functions you are likely to use when interacting with a Django shell, including `settings`, `reverse`, `Q`, and more. You can configure what gets imported, allowing you to include your own frequently used models. This can save a lot of typing.

Another useful command is `validate_templates`. This checks for syntax errors in any of your template files, allowing you to verify them first, rather than catching the error at run time. This command can be particularly useful as part of your continuous integration process, or as a commit hook, disallowing invalid templates in your repo.

The Fields section of the Extensions library has new Django Fields for your models. It includes fields for automatically generating a slug, creating random values, and using timestamps to track object creation and modification as well as a short UUID container. Along with the fields are some premade `Model` classes. When you inherit from one of them, you automatically get collections of fields that work together. For example, the `ActivatorModel` is an abstract model class that has a status field and two date fields. The status field indicates whether the object is "active," while the date fields track when an object was made active or inactive. Using this `Model`, you can quickly query only active items. This can be useful for things like blog posts, allowing you, for example, to hide a post that isn't ready for launch yet.

13.2.2 Django Awl

Similar to Django Extensions is Django Awl (https://pypi.org/project/django-awl/). Full disclosure, this is one of my own extensions. On one hand, you can mock the hubris of me including it here; on the other hand, I'm open to pull requests, so if you've got something you think should be there, drop me a line. When building Django projects for clients, I frequently found that there were certain kinds of code I was writing over and over, so eventually, I stuck it all in a library, with the result being Awl. Features found here include the following:

- Models
- Admin tools
- View decorators
- Context processors
- Commands
- Template tags and filters
- Testing utilities

You install Awl by running `python -m pip install django-awl` and adding `"awl"` to `INSTALLED_APPS`. As with Django Extensions, there is too much here to go through it all, but I'll describe a few things I use most often. There is an abstract `Model` you can inherit that adds create and update timestamp fields, `Model` classes for counters and locks, and a specialty `Model` for including a rank number for situations when your objects need an order. The ranked `Model` includes plugins for the Django Admin, providing you with up and down buttons to change an object's rank.

Often, when I'm playing around in Python, I create a quick script to test out an algorithm or double-check that weird syntax thing I just can't recall. The REPL is good for this, but it doesn't have the friendliest interface for typing a lot of code, so a quick script is often the answer. With Django, that's problematic. You can't just run a script within a Django context—you have to complete extra setup for the script to work. Enter the `run_script` command. It takes a Python file as an argument and loads and runs it, but within a Django context. This can be faster than writing a custom Django command and useful if you need a quick one-off.

Writing `ModelAdmin` classes can require a fair amount of boilerplate code, especially if you want to include cross-object links, like you were shown in chapter 5. The `awl.admintools.FancyModelAdmin` is a factory for `ModelAdmin` classes that supports additional features for the `list_display`. With a single line of code, you can add columns that have a default value when empty, links to related objects, and columns populated based on a template.

The feature I use most in Awl is a module called *Waelsteng*, an Anglo-Saxon word for *spear*. This module is a helper for testing; it includes tools for testing your Django Admin code and an object for faking requests if you want to call a view directly. It also has a custom test runner that supports managing dummy directories for uploads and, my personal favorite, a shortcut for running a specific test. The default Django test runner allows you to run a test with its full module name—for example, `python manage.py test bands.tests.TestBands.test_musician_view`. That's a lot of typing. Awl's replacement runner supports shortcutting with an equal sign (`=`). The same test could be run with `python manage.py test =musician_view`.

13.3 Look and feel

The web is an ever-changing place, and new tools pop up all the time, especially to make your site look more interesting. There are many third-party packages that integrate UI tool kits and other web goodness into Django. This section covers two tools and one technique. Django Grappelli is a drop-in replacement for the Django Admin, bringing pretty to your favorite administration tool. Crispy Forms is a series of libraries offering fine-grained control over form rendering with reusable components. Favicons are those funky little icons in your browser's tabs, and as they're a little messy; you'll need a couple of tricks to make it easier to serve them from Django.

13.3.1 Django Grappelli

One of the common complaints about the Django Admin is its lack of visual appeal. OK, let's be blunt: it's ugly. The Django Admin is only meant as a support tool. Its lack of aesthetic appeal isn't important, but you can do something about it. Django Grappelli (https://pypi.org/project/django-grappelli/) is a drop-in replacement for the Django Admin's templates.

You install Grappelli using `python -m pip install django-grappelli`. Note that if you're using an older version of Django (prior to to 4.0), you will need a different version of Grappelli. Check the docs for specific information. Once you've got it installed, add `"grappelli"` to `INSTALLED_APPS`, ensuring you put it before the line for `"django.contrib.admin"`. Grappelli has a few of its own views that need to be registered as routes: `path("grappelli/", include("grappelli.urls"))`, which also needs to be included before the admin routes. You also need to make sure the `context_processors` configuration in `TEMPLATES/OPTIONS` includes `django.template.context_processors.request`, which it does by default.

That's pretty much it; once configured, your Django Admin has a more modern look. It uses a grid based layout, changes the side panels into drop-down menus, and adds a cleaner header and footer. Figures 13.2 and 13.3 show you the difference between the default and Grappelli styling, so you can decide which appeals to you more.

13.3.2 Crispy forms

Let's face it, the look and feel of vanilla web forms is so yesterday—in fact, it's probably more like yesterday's yesterday. Most websites use frontend frameworks, such as Bootstrap and Tailwind to help with both layout and styling. Django's form tools are built around vanilla forms, and although you can add styling, it is a bunch of extra work. Django Crispy Forms (https://pypi.org/project/django-crispy-forms/) is a third-party library that helps you write reusable web forms.

Crispy Forms is broken into separate packages: the main package contains the form helper, while secondary template packs are for particular UI tool kit libraries. To install Crispy Forms, you need to run `python -m pip install django-crispy-forms` and register `"crispy_forms"` in `INSTALLED_APPS`. Then, depending on your choice of

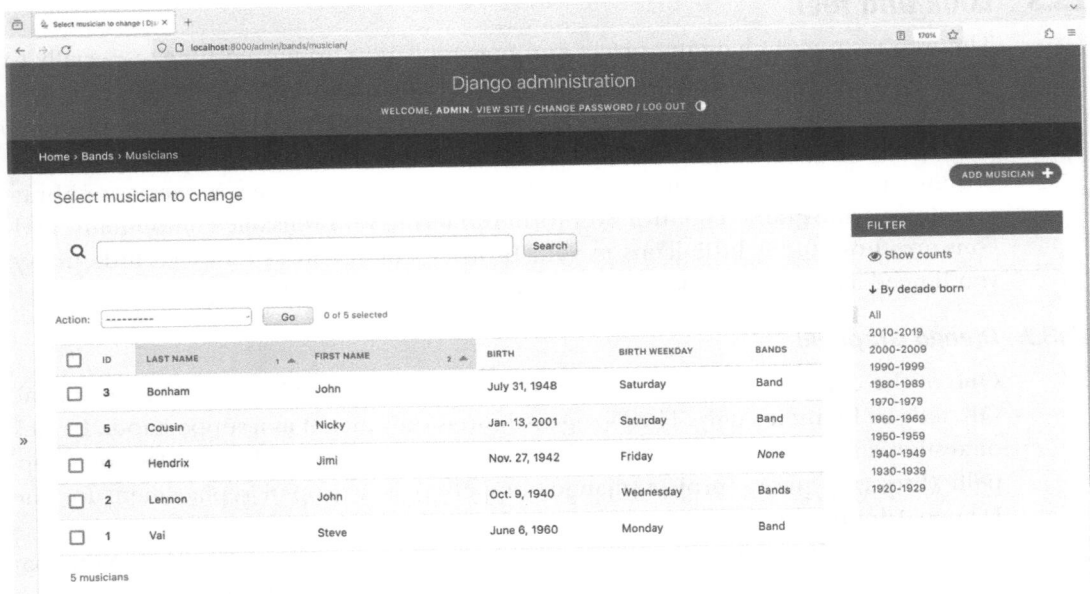

Figure 13.2   Default styling of the Django Admin

Figure 13.3   Grappelli styling of the Django Admin

UI tool kit, you install another package. For example, to use Bootstrap 5, run `python -m pip install crispy-bootstrap5`, add `"crispy_bootstrap5"` to `INSTALLED_APPS`, and add two new configuration values: `CRISPY_ALLOWED_TEMPLATE_PACKS = "bootstrap5"` and `CRISPY_TEMPLATE_PACK = "bootstrap5"`.

There are two ways to use Crispy Forms in your Django templates. The first is the `| crispy` filter. This filter gets applied to a form object inside your template, so instead of using `form.as_p` to output the form, you use `form | crispy`. This filter outputs a canned layout and style based on the installed template pack. There is no extra control over the look; you can't customize it at all. Consider it an opinionated layout, like `.as_p`, but with your template pack add-on.

The second way to use Crispy Forms is with the `{% crispy %}` tag. This is more complicated than the filter but more powerful as well. Within the template, you use the tag, giving the form object as an argument. To fully take advantage of the tag, you add Crispy Form's `FormHelper` class to your `ModelForm` class. Between the helper and an associated `Layout` object you get fine-grained control over the form's HTML, including tag IDs, CSS classes, the form action, and the HTTP method. Specific template packs also have their own tool-kit-specific attributes, which you can modify. For example, when using the Bootstrap pack, you can change whether error messages get rendered inline or as a block by setting `.error_text_inline=False`. As all this customization is done in your Python code, rather than in your templates, you can programmatically control the form inside a view. Crispy Forms provides as much or as little control as you want, with helpful defaults to make things prettier with little effort.

As mentioned in chapter 7, Django 5 has added a feature to make it easier to override and control the templates associated with a form field. This feature makes it easier to do the things Crispy Forms does for you, but it still means you have to write the underlying template widgets. Unless you're using a UI tool kit that isn't supported by a Crispy Forms template pack, you're better off using Crispy Forms, as someone else has done all the work of creating those templates for you.

13.3.3 Favicons

The little icon that appears on your browser's tab next to the page title is known as a *favicon*. This is another one of those nonstandard standards. It came about as a feature in Microsoft's Internet Explorer 5, which checked for the existence of a file named favicon.ico in the root directory of a website. Eventually, enough browsers adopted this practice that it became a World Wide Web Consortium (W3C) standard. As part of the standard, you can use a `<link>` tag in your HTML document's head to specify where to look for the image and which image format gets used. Unfortunately, adoption of the standard was a bit spotty, and different browsers support different image types, sizes, and variations of the attributes in that `<link>` tag.

Favicons are images, so from a Django perspective, they should be stored in your static folder. Django serves static files under the URL directory you configured with `STATIC_URL`, which is typically /static/ (see chapter 7 for more info). You can write your `<link>` tags to point at files in /static/, or you can define redirects that point to your own routes.

Django comes with a series of views as classes, which are handy utilities to quickly serve a file or perform redirects. The `RedirectView` class found in `django.views .generic.base` can be used directly inside your urls.py file, specifying the destination of a redirected URL. The following code redirects a request for /favicon.ico, sending it to /static/img/favicon.ico:

```
from django.urls import path
from django.views.generic.base import RedirectView

urlpatterns = [
    path('favicon.ico',
        RedirectView.as_view(url='/static/img/favicon.ico')),
    # ...
]
```

HTML 5 recommends you provide multiple sizes for your favicon, so it can be used in different resolutions in different contexts. This can lead to requiring half a dozen `<link>` tags in your HTML to get all the possible choices. The RealFaviconGenerator website is a free tool that handles all the cases and provides helpful instructions on what you'll need: https://realfavicongenerator.net/.

13.4 *Feature flags*

Over time, your Django project may become a product: a site your users are deeply invested in. With this fun comes feature requests. Every code change you make to your site comes with the risk of introducing problems. Of course, like you learned in chapter 8, you should have unit tests, which can help prevent this problem. Even with a good test suite in place, you can still make bad design decisions or misunderstand a requirement. One modern development practice that limits your risk is *feature flags*. The idea is to wrap new code in a conditional block and then allow only certain users to use that code. This technique means you can have users beta test a feature in your production code: only those with the feature flag turned on get to see it.

The cleverly named Django Waffle (https://pypi.org/project/django-waffle/) is a feature flag library. Waffle provides three controls: switches, samples, and flags. A switch is an on–off configuration value; a sample is a control for a percentage of visitors; and a flag goes the whole way, offering fine-grained control over who sees a feature.

You install Django Waffle with the usual `python -m pip install django-waffle`. It requires `"waffle"` in `INSTALLED_APPS` and needs `"waffle.middleware.WaffleMiddle-ware"` added to the `MIDDLEWARE` configuration. Waffle has its own database tables, which it uses to track state, so you need to run the `migrate` command after installation.

Waffle's simplest control is the switch, which it provides as a `Model`. You can use either the Django Admin or a command management tool to create switches and turn them on or off. Within your code, you query a switch with the `switch_is_active()` function, passing it the name of your `Switch` instance. The function returns a Boolean value, which you use to evaluate your conditional feature block.

The next step up in complexity is the `Sample Model`. Like with `Switch`, you can create instances of it in the Django Admin. Unlike the switch, it isn't on all the time. Each call to `sample_is_active()` returns a Boolean based on a random value. When you create a `Sample`, you specify the percentage of time it is active. Note that subsequent calls to `sample_is_active()` return a new value, so if you want the same result in a view, you should store the return value and reuse it.

Finally, Waffle's most powerful mechanism is the flag. This allows you to roll out a feature for specific users, groups of users, users that pass a test, or a percentage of visitors. A `Flag` gets associated with a request and gets accessed within a view. Calling `flag_is_active()` checks whether a global override is on, whether the flag is in testing mode, whether the current user meets the flag's criteria, whether the current user has a cookie (they've met the criteria in the past), and whether there is a random chance the feature should be enabled. The `Flag Model` contains the following attributes:

- Flag name
- On for everyone
- Testing mode
- Percentage allowed
- On for superusers
- On for staff
- On for authenticated
- On for a specific language
- A list of groups
- A list of users

By combining these criteria, you get a lot of control over who sees your conditional feature.

In addition to the `Model` classes, Waffle provides view decorators, mixins, and template tags. There are several other feature flag libraries out there, but Waffle is one of the longest-standing ones and is rock solid.

13.5 *Static sites*

Way back in chapter 1, I explained the idea of a static site: one where each URL maps directly to a file on the web server's hard drive. These sites are quite performant, as they require no additional database queries and are easily cacheable. Sometimes, a dynamic site is overkill. Of course, if you're building a static site, you still want a consistent look and feel, and it would be great to define the nav bar once and re-use it. Static site generators are tools that allow you to compose websites. You define pages that include reusable components, like your nav bar, and then the generator mushes everything together and outputs a set of files for your site.

There are quite a few static site generators out there, and they each have their own syntax and quirks. You've just spent a whole lot of time learning Django's syntax and quirks, so why go somewhere else? Django Distill (https://django-distill.com/) is a third-party library that turns your Django project into a static site. You install Distill using the familiar `python -m pip install django-distill` and add `"django _distill"` to `INSTALLED_APPS`.

Distill works by replacing the `path()` function in your urls.py files with its own: `distill_path()`. This function overrides `path()`, so your site continues to work as it did before. The new version of the function also allows you to run a management command that outputs a static version of all the URLs mapped by Distill. The `distill_path()` function takes at least one more argument than the regular kind: the name of the file to generate for the view.

As an example, I maintain an online cookbook for my family, containing some of our favorite recipes. Since the site is just for the family to use, and I'm the only one to ever edit it, using a content management system seemed like overkill. The original version of the site was built on a third-party Django project that required Django 2.1. As the library never got updated, maintaining the site became problematic. Instead of rewriting someone else's project for my own use, I decided to downshift to a static site. The recipes are in data files, and a simple view renders them as HTML. Instead of hosting a Django site, I use Distill to create a static site with all the recipes. As it's a static site, hosting it is as simple as zipping it up and sending it to a server.

There are a few restrictions to what Distill can do. First off, it only works with the GET mode of views. This makes sense, as doing a POST is part of a dynamic site; there won't be any Django on the backend to handle a POST with statically generated files. Second, if your view takes arguments, you need to specify which of those arguments to use when generating the static site. Distill allows you to pass in a function to generate the arguments, meaning you can dynamically build queries at generation time. In fact, I use this in my cookbook: in that case, the function examines the data directory for each recipe file and calls the view with the recipe name. The result is that Distill generates an HTML static page for each recipe.

Appendix B provides an overview of how to put your Django project into a production environment. Part of this process includes taking the static files in your project and deploying them to a web server, letting it serve them. It is inefficient to have Django serve static files, and you should only do it that way during local development. There is a management command called `collectstatic`, which is responsible for copying your static files to the web server's required destination. Distill expects this to be set up and working; it uses the same destination to source any static files for the generated site.

Once you have your URLs configured and your static files properly organized, you run the `distill-local` management command. This takes one argument: the output directory for your generated site. Once your site gets generated, you can zip up the output directory and deploy it wherever you plan on hosting your static site.

I really like Distill. Being familiar with Django already, it requires very little extra effort to build a static site. I already know Django's template language; I know how views work; I can test the site using the development server; and, most importantly, I don't have to learn some other static site generating tool.

Summary

- There are many third-party libraries available to help write less code when building your Django project. You can find many of them here: https://django packages.org/.
- The Django Debug Toolbar is an add-on that puts an overlay on top of your views to provide you with detailed information about the view's execution.
- The Debug Toolbar is divided into panels, each providing different information. Some key panels include execution time, SQL queries, HTTP request info, and profiling.
- The timing and SQL panels are key to solving slow page load times.
- Django Extensions is a collection of miscellaneous tools, including management commands, signals, fields, Models, and more.
- The `shell_plus` management command automatically loads key libraries into a Django-enabled REPL, saving you from having to do it yourself. You can even define what modules get loaded, including your own `Model` classes.
- Django Extensions comes with several Django fields and `Model` classes. For example, the `ActivatorModel` gets used to create objects that can be activated or deactivated, such as a blog page being published or not.
- Django Awl is another collection of useful tools. It also has additional `Model` classes, admin tools, view decorators, context processors, and commands as well as a custom test runner.
- Awl's `FancyModelAdmin` reduces the amount of boilerplate code you need when writing `ModelAdmin` classes and includes that ability to add columns in the Django Admin for related objects and those based on a rendered template.
- Django Awl comes with a replacement test runner, which has the handy feature of searching for a test using a shortcut to its name.
- Django Grappelli is a drop-in replacement for the Django Admin, providing a grid-based layout and a nicer look and feel.
- Crispy Forms is a collection of libraries that provide tools for writing better forms.
- Crispy Form template packs include HTML based on Bootstrap, Tailwind, and more, allowing you to build forms using the same styling as the rest of your site.
- A Crispy Form gets rendered with either the opinionated | `crispy` filter or the very flexible `{% crispy %}` template tag.
- Favicons are the small icons that your browser puts on the tab, showing the page's title.
- The favicon standard is messy, with lots of different files and sizes.
- Originally, favicons had to be served out of the root of the URL directory. You can accomplish this in Django using the built-in `RedirectView`.
- Feature flags allow you to conditionally expose a new feature to a subset of your site's visitors.

- Django Waffle has three kinds of conditional `Model` classes: switches, samples, and flags.
- A Waffle `Switch` is a global flag, while a `Sample` is on for a percentage of visitors.
- A Waffle `Flag` allows you to determine which visitors see a feature, depending on their role, account, language, group, and additional factors.
- A static website is one for which the URL maps directly to a file getting served.
- Static site generators are tools that use templates to build static sites.
- Django Distill overrides the `path()` function to allow you to output a subset of your project as a static site. This means you can use your existing knowledge of Django's templating instead of learning another tool's syntax.

Where to go next

14

This chapter covers

- Other Django features
- Configuration libraries
- Data libraries
- Web tools
- Asynchronous tools
- The Django ecosystem

This final chapter gives you a hint about what else exists in the Django ecosystem. While *Django in Action* intends to provide a comprehensive introduction, there are still parts of the framework we couldn't cover, not to mention the wide world of third-party libraries.

14.1 Within Django

Even if you've diligently worked through everything in this book, the Django framework itself has more to offer. Some features are corner cases that make your life easier when doing specific things, some are for more complex problems, and

315

some can be used as a matter of preference. What follows is a list of topics you might want to dig into:

- *Class-based views*—Throughout this book you've seen views as functions, Django also supports views based on classes. Django provides classes you can use directly or inherit from to define your own. Class-based views (CBVs) can mean less code is needed when dealing with multiple HTTP Methods, as you use one class method per action. You can learn more about CBVs here: https://mng.bz/ 67YG. The community is somewhat divided on the use of this feature, and personally, I prefer function-based views, as they are a little less abstract, but there are plenty of coders who prefer using CBVs. A great, in-depth article by one of the core Django developers explains why he still uses function based views most of the time: https://mng.bz/oe0N.

- *Middleware*—In the last few chapters, you've seen third-party libraries that have middleware components. Middleware is code that gets run before or after a view, allowing global actions on all requests or responses. You can write your own middleware using a factory function or a class. If you find you're writing the same snippet of code in many of your views, middleware might be a better approach. Writing middleware is covered in the Django documentation: https://mng .bz/ng0v.

- *Custom template tags and filters*—Django is structured around a few core concepts, with everything else being a pluggable component. Template tags and filters are no different. You can write your own tags and filters, and in fact there are shortcut mechanisms that make certain kinds of tags just a few lines of code. The Django Awl library, covered in chapter 13, has a few tags I've written to make my templating life easier—for example, {% qif %} is an inline if conditional, for those cases where a block takes up a lot of space. To learn how to write your own tags and filters visit the docs: https://mng.bz/v8Jx. Alternatively, if you aren't tired of my writing style yet, you can try this article: https://mng.bz/4JpB.

- *Validators*—A validator is code that checks a value and raises a ValidationError if it doesn't meet some criteria. Django ships with over twenty built-in validators, and some Model fields are simply a CharField with a specific validator attached. Of course, you can also write your own. To learn more, you can read about the topic here: https://mng.bz/QZVm.

- *Complex database operations*—In chapter 12, you got a quick introduction to Q objects, which get used to build complex ORM queries. Throughout this book you've been using .filter() and .all(), but the query language is far deeper than that. Full documentation on the API is available here: https://mng.bz/ X1VY. If that's not enough, Django also supports query expressions that perform calculations in the database without pulling the object into memory. This includes performing arbitrary math on a field and building aggregates like sums. Documentation on query expressions is available here: https://mng.bz/ y8oJ. A very useful cheat sheet on all things ORM is also available on the following web page: https://djangocentral.com/django-orm-cheatsheet/.

- *Generated fields and database-computed values*—Django 5 added the ability to perform even more computations in the database. In a field, the new db_default argument enables computation of a value when a row gets created. For example, the database can determine and store the current time. Examples for this field are found here: https://mng.bz/MZ12.

- The other new addition is the GeneratedField class, which is used to compute a field's value based on the combination of other fields. This is done in the database, meaning the object doesn't have to be brought into Django's memory to determine its value. The mechanism allows both stored values (computed and stuck in the table) and virtual values (computed on the fly). Details on the GeneratedField class can be found here: https://mng.bz/aEVJ. Both of these features are highly dependent on your database's capabilities.

- *Syndication feed framework*—RSS and Atom feeds are API-like summaries of the content on your site, meant to be consumed by users or tools. When looking for the lastest episode of my favorite podcasts, I read the site's RSS feed rather than dig through all the "fancy-shmancy" HTML. Django has a class to build these kinds of feeds, called Feed. To build a Feed class, you tie a query to the values you want in the feed and register it as a route. You can learn more about syndication here: https://mng.bz/gvAR.

- *System check framework*—When you start the development server, Django runs a check on your project. You can invoke the same process with the check management command. Django allows you to register your own classes to be run as part of the check process, giving you a hook on code validation or other activities. Instructions on how to write and register your own checks are provided here: https://docs.djangoproject.com/en/dev/topics/checks/.

- *Generic foreign keys*—In chapter 4, you learned about foreign key relations and many-to-many relations, but Django has one more relationship type. Django tracks the kinds of Model classes in your system using something called the *content types framework*. This framework enables you to build a foreign key that relates to more than one kind of Model. The GenericForeignKey field tracks the ID of a Model class's content type and the specific object ID. Consider a media database with Audio, Video, and Text Model classes. The cross-media top-10 list could be built using a ListItem Model. This Model would use a generic foreign key that could point to any of the three media types. An instance of ListItem points to a Song by using the content type ID of the Song class together with the ID of the Song object instance. Details on the content type framework can be found in the documentation: https://mng.bz/Ddp0.

14.2 Configuration

The use of settings.py is a bit limiting in modern engineering environments. Commercial-grade systems tend to be developed using multiple environments: development, testing, staging, and production. The need for different configurations in different environments becomes that much more complicated with containerization. When working in cloud computing, with its premade bundles of operating systems and libraries, you often need to inject configuration information from the outside. Appendix B touches on a few options for these situations, but there are also third-party libraries out there that can make managing multiple configurations easier:

- *Database URLs*—Different system environments need to connect to different databases and, sometimes, even different types of databases. The dj-database-url (https://pypi.org/project/dj-database-url/) library allows you to specify database configurations in a single URL, which can be injected into your project through an environment variable.
- *Django configurations*—The need to have different settings for each environment is one that has been solved several ways by third-party libraries. The django-configurations (https://pypi.org/project/django-configurations/) tool kit allows you to create classes inside of settings.py that group configurations together. You then use an environment variable to specify which class gets instantiated.
- *Django environ*—Another approach to the settings problem is django-environ (https://pypi.org/project/django-environ/). As the name implies, it provides tools for getting configuration values out of environment variables. This is a common approach when dealing with container systems, like Kubernetes.

14.3 *Dealing with data*

A core element of dynamic websites is the data they store, manipulate, and then present to the users. There are many kinds of data you might use, and there are libraries out there to better define, store, and interact with it in your projects:

- *Money*—Representing money in software is more problematic than you might first think. A naive approach is to use floating-point numbers for currency, but that creates inaccuracies. Floating-point numbers do not contain an exact decimal representation. Open a REPL and try `0.1 + 0.2` to see what I mean (`0.30000000000000004`). The Python standard library includes the `Decimal` class, which does have exact representation, and the third-party library django-money (https://pypi.org/project/django-money/) can be a big help. It comes with a `Model` field for storing monetary values and even includes a currency attribute to handle exchange.
- *Import and export*—If you have data in your system, you will likely find yourself needing to get data into and out of it on a regular basis. The django-import-export (https://pypi.org/project/django-import-export/) library provides a series of Django Admin tools for importing and exporting `Model` data. It supports CSV, JSON, Excel, and many other formats, and it even has a preview mode where you can see the proposed changes before enacting them.
- *Tagging*—One way of categorizing data is to tag it. This approach is quite common in publication systems, where each article has one or more tags that indicates what it is about, allowing users to easily find other articles on the same

topic. The django-taggit (https://pypi.org/project/django-taggit/) library comes with a `Model` that represents a tag that can be applied to any object in your database. You can then query other objects with similar tags.

- *Storage*—The content in your database isn't the only data in your system. In chapter 7, you learned about users uploading files to your project. Both the upload and static file mechanisms are built on top of Django's storage API (https://mng.bz/lMrz), with the default implementation using the filesystem. The django-storages (https://django-storages.readthedocs.io/en/latest/) library provides other storage API classes, allowing you to store content in places other than the filesystem. It currently supports Amazon S3, Apache Libcloud, Azure Storage, Backblaze B2, Digital Ocean, Dropbox, FTP, Google Cloud, Oracle Cloud, and SFTP.

14.4 Web tools

Django has everything you need to get a website up and going, but there are still things that could be easier. Plenty of libraries help you with other website complications, including getting new projects started, managing JavaScript files, and providing authentication through third parties, like Google and Facebook:

- *Cookiecutter site creator*—Although the `startproject` management command creates the minimum structure of a Django project, it is still the minimum structure. Most projects use template and static file directories, and all projects begin with at least one app. The django-cookiecutter (https://mng.bz/Bdgq) tool helps you start a new project, with a lot of the features you use already inserted for you. Cookiecutter supports Bootstrap 5, uses SSL by default, and allows integration with several email clients, among many other useful features. When you run the script, it asks a series of questions and outputs a new project structure for you based on the answers.

- *JavaScript and CSS compression*—As your projects get larger, they're likely to include more JavaScript and CSS. The average webpage today is significantly larger than the days of yore. Both JavaScript and CSS can be minified; you'd be surprised how much space can be gained by removing whitespace and renaming some variables. The django-compressor (https://pypi.org/project/django-compressor/) library provides template tags that surround the JavaScript in your HTML files and compresses and rewrites these and your static CSS files. Minification means smaller pages, which means faster page loads and, therefore, happier users.

- *Customizing the Django Admin*—The Django Admin is designed around the `Model` classes in your project, but sometimes, there is value in having other kinds of pages in the Django Admin. For example, you might want a report that only administrators get to see. Instead of writing a separate view outside the Django Admin, django-custom-admin-pages (https://mng.bz/d6Zz) allows you to write CBVs that appear in the Django Admin navigation.

- Another Django Admin customization alternative is django-admin-extra-buttons (https://mng.bz/rV1E), which provides tools for adding buttons and wizards to the Django Admin. These can be used to create specialized filters, generate links to outside pages, or wrap views that perform bulk operations.
- *Social auth and account management*—Authentication is a key part of a multi-user website, and even though all of chapter 6 was dedicated to it, there are still plenty of other options out there. Django allows you to build custom user models and modify the authentication backend. A common customization is to replace usernames with email addresses as the login token. Details are available in the documentation: https://mng.bz/Vx2r.
- Of course, why would you build it yourself when others have done it for you? The django-allauth (https://github.com/pennersr/django-allauth) library is a comprehensive approach to authentication. It provides logins based on usernames, email addresses, and social media accounts. It supports Open ID Connect and Oauth 1.0/2.0, meaning over 100 different account providers can be used. It also supports SAML, allowing integration with single sign-on systems as well as two-factor authentication. Even if all that is overkill, it provides a password-management workflow, as covered in chapter 6. Yep, You could have skipped the chapter and simply installed django-allauth instead.

14.5   *Asynchronous actions*

The basic workflow in Django is synchronous: the user enters a URL, control goes to Django and your views, and the user waits until a response gets returned. A synchronous process covers most of your needs on the web but not all of them. There are two varieties of asynchronous workflows. The first is out-of-band activities, like scheduled jobs. The simplest approach to this is to use a Django management command and your operating system's scheduling tools, like cron. For more complex systems, you might need something deeper. The other kind of asynchronous activity is that which interacts with the user. Consider a live-chat session on a web page: the server needs to send information down to the user without it being requested. Django has slowly been adding features to enable this, but even before it did, third-party libraries were capable of handling this scenario:

- *Celery*—A distributed task queue is a system that runs independent jobs across multiple machines. One of the most popular is Celery (https://docs.celeryq.dev/). A Django project that needs an asynchronous task uses a view to kick off a Celery job. Views then periodically query Celery to see if the job is complete. This integration is so common that Celery ships with hooks to work with Django. There is also an extension called django-celery-beat (https://django-celery-beat.readthedocs.io/) that allows you to manage your Celery jobs through the Django Admin. For a good overview on how to get started with Celery and Django, see the following article: https://mng.bz/x26q.

- *Asynchronous views*—The other kind of asynchronous activity is one that allows Django to transmit information down to the user without them requesting it. This is typically done through a browser feature called *websockets*. The Django Channels (https://channels.readthedocs.io/) library adds asynchronous features to Django. Special views communicate over an open websocket, sending information down to the user. This allows you to implement an event-based system, meaning you can build things like notifications, chat systems, and more.

14.6 A wide world

Django is huge. I've been using it since its 1.1 days, and I still discover new things frequently. The community is vibrant, and both the framework and the third-party library ecosystem are growing and changing all the time. Staying on top it all can be a challenge. The Django framework's home page has two areas that provide up-to-date information:

- *Django's News page*—https://www.djangoproject.com/weblog/
- *Django's Community page*—https://www.djangoproject.com/community/

There are also plenty of other sites that report on the Django ecosystem:

- *Django News*—(https://django-news.com/) A weekly email newsletter
- *Django Chat*—(https://djangochat.com/) A biweekly podcast from two of the core developers

For inspiration on what to build or to learn about the many packages out there, visit the following web pages:

- *Django Projects*—https://builtwithdjango.com/projects/
- *Django Packages*—https://djangopackages.org/

Django is so big that it is one of few libraries that has dedicated conferences. Yes, plural—*conferences*:

- *Django Con US*—https://djangocon.us/
- *Django Con EU*—https://djangocon.eu/
- *Django Con Africa*—https://djangocon.africa/

I sincerely hope this book has been valuable to you and that Django provides you many hours of productivity and joy. Happy web coding!

appendix A
Installation and setup

Python's growth in popularity means it has become more common for it to be installed on your system by default, but that isn't always the case. And sometimes its presence on your system is a problem: some versions of macOS ship with Python but use a much earlier release. This appendix briefly outlines some of the choices you have when setting up your system and where to find more information.

A.1 Installing Python

There are several ways of getting Python onto your computer, some of which are specific to an operating system. Personally, I use https://www.python.org/, the home of Python, and download the installable packages directly. Packages are available for Windows (in 32-bit, 64-bit, and ARM64 variations), on macOS as a universal installer (both Intel and Apple silicon), and directly as source code. There is also a reference page for where to locate ports to other platforms.

Most Linux distributions include a variety of versions of Python using their built-in package managers. Building from source is also always an option.

To determine whether you have Python installed on your system and what version it is, do the following at a terminal:

```
$ python --version
Python 3.12.2
```

On Windows, you can use the same command running from a PowerShell.

A.1.1 Windows installation options

There are two other common options for installing Python on Windows:

- Microsoft Store package
- Windows Subsystem for Linux (WSL)

Python is now available in the Microsoft Store. Use the store app, search for Python, and Windows will take care of the rest for you.

As of Windows 10, you can run Linux inside Windows using the Windows Subsystem for Linux. Running Python inside the WSL is slightly more complicated than running it directly from Windows, as you need to be inside the Linux environment, but it has the added benefit that most deployment scenarios are Unix based. By using the WSL, your development environment will likely be a closer match to your production environment, which tends to lessen the challenges experienced during deployment. Documentation on installing the WSL is available here: https://learn.microsoft.com/en-us/windows/wsl/install.

A.2 *Virtual environments*

When you install a third-party package in Python using `pip` or its equivalent, the tool downloads Python code from the *Python Package Index* (PyPI) and puts it in the site-packages directory. When you `import` a package in your code, Python looks in this directory as well as a few other places.

The Cheese Shop
Python isn't named after the snake but after the British comedy troupe Monty Python. When it came to building a site to manage Python packages, the coders called it the "Cheese Shop," after a famous Monty Python skit. Eventually, reason won out, and it was renamed the Python Package Index, but it is still affectionately referred to by its original moniker on occasion.

It is really handy to be able to choose from the over 500,000 freely available Python third-party libraries, but there is a complication. Packages change over time, and multiple versions are available. If you created a website using Django in 2021, you likely were using Django 3.2. In the following year Django 4.0 was released. You may not want to go back to your original project and upgrade it, as installing Django 4.0 overwrites Django 3.2, possibly breaking your original site.

If all that isn't messy enough, most packages have dependencies on other packages. In 2022, when you installed Django 4.0, you automatically got asgiref 3.4.1 and sqlparse 0.2.2. What if you also wanted to insall Apache Superset, the data visualization platform, which also uses sqlparse? How do you know that the version used by Django and the version used by Superset don't conflict?

The answer to all these questions is to use *virtual environments*. A Python virtual environment creates small copies of all the directories that Python requires in their own place and sets up a separate site-packages directory. The important stuff, like the interpreter itself, is linked to, so it doesn't take up too much disk space. Each virtual environment is self-contained, so you can install a package into an environment without affecting any other environment, including the default install location.

To use a virtual environment, you activate it. Activating an environment changes your shell so that the environment's link to the Python interpreter is first in your path, meaning it is the one your terminal finds when you run a script. It is best practice to have a separate virtual environment for each project you create. This avoids any library conflicts and means you can switch back and forth between projects without worrying about whether they'll still work.

There are several virtual environment management tools out there. In this book, all the examples use venv, which ships with Python. To create a virtual environment using venv, type the following:

```
$ python -m venv my_environment
```

NOTE If you have multiple versions of Python installed on your system, make sure to use the version that you want to use inside the virtual environment.

This example creates a directory named my_environment, containing the virtual environment. Common practice is to name the folder **venv** or **.venv**. With the directory created, you activate it. On Windows, run the following:

```
C:> my_environment/Scripts/activate.bat
```

On macOS and Linux, use

```
$ source my_environment/bin/activate
```

You can switch to a different environment by activating it instead. If you wish to stop using the environment, you use the deactivate command, which is the same on all operating systems:

```
$ deactivate
```

For more information on venv, see the documentation: https://docs.python.org/3/tutorial/venv.html.

Virtual environment directory location

The venv tool gets used to create the directory containing the virtual environment in the folder location where it is run. There are two schools of thought on the placement of this directory: (1) in your project or (2) in a central location.

Keeping your virtual environment with your project makes it clear what environment goes with the project and keeps things all together. There are even tools out there that can automatically switch your virtual environment based on what folder you are in. There are two downsides to this approach: you can't easily share virtual environments, and it complicates the use of some command line tools. Sharing virtual environments isn't too important, but it can be handy if you have multiple pieces of software that will all be using the same environment in production.

Depending on how often you use command-line tools, virtual environments inside a project folder can add extra complications. I often run a Unix find command to look for files or grep -r to look for content in files. By having the virtual environment directory in the project, you end up searching all those files as well. As most Python third-party libraries contain Python, searching for or in files ending in .py tends to return a lot of false positives.

> **(continued)**
> Alternatively, you can keep you virtual environments in a central location. The pros of
> this method are the cons of the other, and vice versa. Your project directory now only
> contains your project files, but now, you have to remember which project goes with
> which virtual environment.

There are also alternatives out there to using venv: two popular tools for managing virtual environments are virtualenv (https://virtualenv.pypa.io/en/latest/) and Conda (https://docs.conda.io/en/latest/). Personally, I use virtualenv on my own projects, but it requires an extra install step compared to venv. I'm not sure I can even argue in favor of my preference: it was the tool I discovered first, and inertia has kept me there.

A.3 *Editing tools*

The first line of original code I ever wrote was in the 1980s on an IBM PCjr. It had a whopping 4.77 MHz CPU (that second 7 seemed really important at the time). As I progressed to Unix, my coding world was still very much based on terminals, and to this day, I still prefer to use Vim (https://www.vim.org/) while running the Django development server in another terminal.

This isn't for everyone, especially if you're just getting started. The two most popular *integrated development environments* (IDEs) for developing Python are Visual Studio Code and PyCharm. As Python is text, any editor you're happy with will work. If you are using an IDE though, there is some extra configuration that makes your life easier.

IDEs have debugging tools built in. Because Django is a framework, and you're not really running a script, you need to perform extra steps to be able to use the debugger with code run through the Django development server. Once you've created a project in the IDE, you need to modify the run/debug profile to tell it to use the Django development server.

For Visual Studio Code, full instructions on creating a Django project and debugging can be found here: https://code.visualstudio.com/docs/python/tutorial-django. The equivalent document for PyCharm is here: https://www.jetbrains.com/help/pycharm/creating-and-running-your-first-django-project.html.

If you're using the IDE just to edit the files and running the development server in a terminal, the extra isn't required. If you're used to using the debugger and would miss coding without it, then you'll need to make those changes.

A.4 *Installing third-party libraries*

Django is more than a framework—it is an ecosystem as well. There are thousands of freely available libraries out there that can make a developer's life significantly better. Don't write something yourself if someone else has already done the work, especially if they've built tests to go with it. The Django Packages site (https://djangopackages.org/) is a directory of tools that can augment your Django project, and it has over 4,000 entries. You should check it out to see just what is out there.

In chapter 2, you learned about Django apps: the modules that Django uses to group code components together. The RiffMates project has multiple apps inside, organizing your code. These kinds of apps can also be packaged separately from a project and distributed on their own. Like other Python libraries, they are available on PyPI and installable through `pip`.

> **NOTE** Building installable apps is beyond the scope of this book. You can see my article "How to Write an Installable Django App" (https://realpython .com/installable-django-app/) for more details though.

Part 3 of this book covers a number of third-party libraries, each with its own installation requirements. This section covers the installation of the Django Debug Toolbar in detail as an example of how third-party libraries get installed.

First and foremost, when dealing with a third-party library, RTFM (read that funky manual)! I know, reading is hard, but each library has its own needs. The Django Debug Toolbar is a relatively complicated install, and it serves as a decent example. The toolbar's docs are available at: https://django-debug-toolbar.readthedocs.io/en/ latest/index.html.

As the name implies, the Django Debug Toolbar is a developer's tool to help you debug your application. It works as an overlay inside the browser, allowing you to inspect the details of any page you are viewing. How to use the toolbar gets covered in chapter 13.

Third-party Django apps get packaged like any other Python package, so installation starts through the use of the `pip` command. Don't forget to be inside your virtual environment:

```
(venv) RiffMates$ python -m pip install django-debug-toolbar
```

Most, but not all, Django third-party libraries name themselves with a *django-* prefix. Likewise, most, but not all, use dashes between the words of their names. Be careful when installing any Python package, as nefarious people sometimes upload bad things to PyPI with names similar to popular packages. The awesome folks at PyPI do a great job of finding and removing evil packages, but it is good to be mindful.

Once you have a package installed in your virtual environment, it is time to tell your Django project about it. Almost all Django third-party libraries are Django apps, so they need to be added to the `INSTALLED_APPS` configuration value in settings.py:

```
# RiffMates/RiffMates/settings.py
...
INSTALLED_APPS = [
    "django.contrib.admin",
    "django.contrib.auth",
    ...
    "home",
    "bands",
    ...
    "debug_toolbar",      ⟵┘ Add the Django Debug Toolbar's
]                              module name to register its app
```

This is another place to be careful; the name of the package you downloaded is typically different from the name of the module. Here, the package is django-debug-toolbar, while the Django app is named debug_toolbar. It is the app's name that goes in INSTALLED_APPS.

For simpler third-party apps, this is often all you need to do to get going. The Debug Toolbar isn't one of those simpler apps. For example, it is dependent on other apps and configuration, as explained in the documentation:

- The django.contrib.staticfiles app must be in INSTALLED_APPS (which it is by default).
- The STATIC_URL value must be configured (which is done to RiffMates in chapter 7).
- The TEMPLATES configuration must have the "APP_DIRS" key set to True (which it is by default).

Follow the installation guide, and you'll be fine. Some third-party libraries install views, and for the view to be useful, it needs to be registered as a route. For the Django Debug Toolbar, you do this by adding a *path* inside urls.py:

```
# RiffMates/RiffMates/urls.py
...
urlpatterns = [
    # ...
    path("__debug__/", include("debug_toolbar.urls")),
]
```

In chapter 2, you wrote your first Django view. When the web server handles a request from the browser, it passes this down to the Django framework. Django maps the URL to a view and calls your code. There is a step in-between though: if you wanted to change the behavior of every single view, rather than write the code over and over, Django has a way of hooking all view calls. This is called *middleware*, named as such because it sits in the middle of a request call. Some third-party libraries come with middleware, and the Debug Toolbar uses its middleware to add information about your views into the request, so it can be displayed by the debug overlay. To register middleware, you add its name to the MIDDLEWARE configuration value in settings.py. For the Debug Toolbar, it looks like this:

```
# RiffMates/RiffMates/settings.py
...
MIDDLEWARE = [
    # ...
    "debug_toolbar.middleware.DebugToolbarMiddleware",
    # ...
]
```

The order of declaration inside MIDDLEWARE defines the execution order of the middleware code. As each piece of code has an effect on the request, the order is important. Be careful to follow the library's installation instructions on the position of any middleware with respect to its siblings.

For almost all third-party libraries, that's everything you need to know. As you might have guessed from the *almost* in that sentence, the Debug Toolbar is an exception. As you don't want your debug information leaking into your production code, the Debug Toolbar is sensitive to the value of INTERNAL_IPS in settings.py. To ensure the Toolbar can only be used locally, the IP address of localhost must be in INTERNAL_IPS:

```
# RiffMates/RiffMates/settings.py
...
INTERNAL_IPS = [
    # ...
    "127.0.0.1",
    # ...
]
```

This kind of additional setting is why it is important to read the library's documentation: simply assuming you can get away with pip install and adding the module to INSTALLED_APPS is a recipe for problems if the library is more complex than that.

appendix B
Django in a production environment

If you've come from a world where most of your Python gets run locally or you send your script to a friend through email, moving to the world of the web can be rather daunting. Even if you're an old pro at packaging things and submitting them to PyPI, the web has its own set of challenges. When you write something using Django, or any other web framework, you're no longer just writing code. If you want to put your project on the web, you're now dealing with infrastructure. It isn't quite as scary as it sounds, but there are some things you need to be aware of.

> **NOTE** Throughout this appendix, I will be mentioning companies that provide a variety of hosting services. This is not an endorsement; searching the web for a provider name and "alternatives" or "competitors" is a good way to get a list of choices to choose from.

Ask five different developers on the best way to put Django into production, and you'll likely get at least six opinions. Part of that has to do with scale: Is your site for you and your friends, or is it going to handle a gajillion users? How you go into production depends on this question and, of course, the associated question of the costs therein. This appendix isn't meant as an authoritative guide but more as an overview of the choices that are out there.

B.1 Parts of a web deployment

Throughout this book, you've been using the Django development server, which, as is deftly found within its name, is only for development. It isn't hardened against attack, and it isn't optimized for performance. Even if it was, a lot of the content on your web page doesn't need Django. For many of the parts of a page, the framework is overkill. Think about all the steps involved in running a view: a mapped route gets looked up, the request gets passed through multiple middleware processors (authentication, session management, CSRF handling, and more), and then finally your code gets run. And of course, your code is Python, which is not the speediest language out there. Static content, like CSS files, site images, and Java-Script, shouldn't be served by Django; they don't need all that extra overhead. Likewise, any user-uploaded content also doesn't typically need all the mechanics your view requires.

Django is invoked through either a WSGI or ASGI interface, with a web server responsible for handling the actual call and passing it down to Django. Therefore, when you go to production, you need a web server. With such a beast in place, it makes a lot of sense to have the static and uploaded files served directly, skipping all that Django overhead. Figure B.1 shows the typical architecture with a web server fronting Django and directly hosting the static and uploaded files.

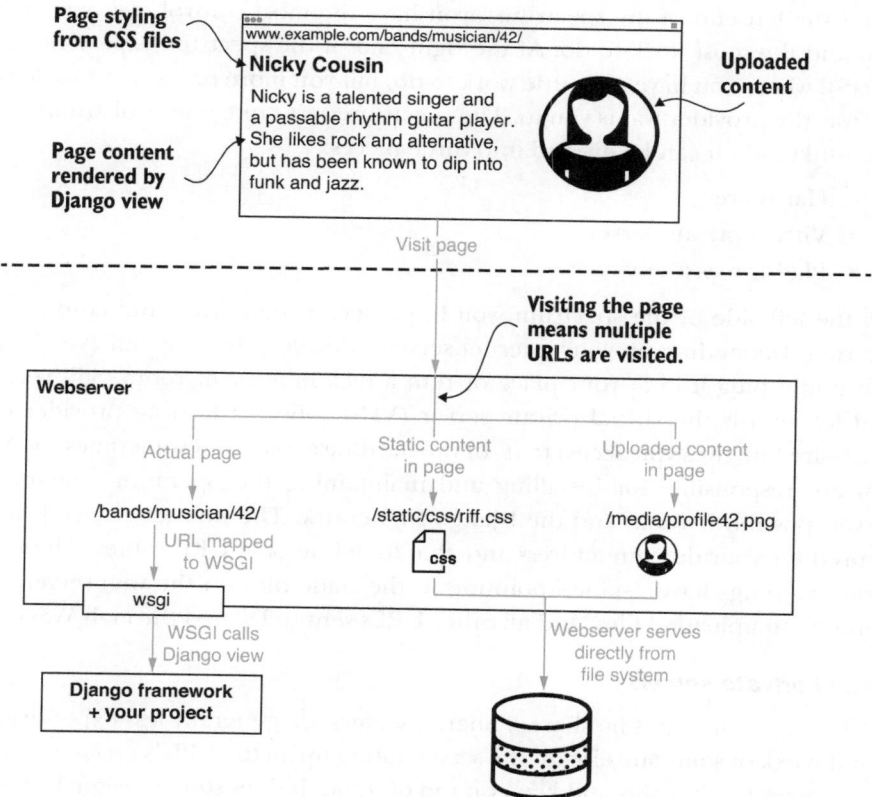

Figure B.1 Django through WSGI and other files served directly

When you go to production, you can implement everything in figure B.1 yourself, or there are providers that abstract this away for you, to varying degrees. However you deploy, the same concept is still happening underneath.

> **Serving static content from Django**
> When it comes to hosting architecture, there are plenty of choices, even the decision to serve static files from a web server isn't the only way. Django WhiteNoise is a third-party package that installs as middleware and serves static files directly from Django. It does this by bypassing all those extra steps I just mentioned. It isn't quite as fast as a web server, but it handles file changes and selective compression quite elegantly.

B.2   *Server hosting vs. platform as a service*

You can think of your hosting options as being on a spectrum. At one extreme (we'll call it the left end of the spectrum), you have the most control over your configuration and the most work to do. At the right end of the spectrum is *platform as a service* (PaaS), where you have very little work to do, but you more or less have to do it exactly the way the provider wants you to. The spectrum isn't quite evenly distributed; it's sort of chunky, and it can be divided into three pieces:

- Hardware
- Virtual private server
- Platform as a service

On the left side of the spectrum, you buy a server, plug it in, and connect it to the internet. Depending on your internet service provider, this may not even be allowed. You might plug it in at your place or rent a rack in a server room. Still very close to that left end is the virtual private server (VPS), where a hosting provider owns the hardware but gives you access to it. In the hardware case, and sometimes the VPS case, you are responsible for installing and maintaining the operating system, the web server, possibly Python, and the Django framework. The web server needs to be configured for your domain address and able to define base URL routes. The most common mappings have /static/ pointing to the static files on the web server, /media/ pointing to uploaded files, and all other URLs sent to Django through WSGI.

B.2.1   *Virtual private servers*

A VPS may or may not be shared. Shared servers are generally less expensive, but you run the risk of someone else on the server eating up all the CPU's cycles. Good hosting companies monitor this and keep on top of it, but it does still occasionally happen.

Even within the world of the VPS, there is a spectrum. Providers such as Linode and DigitalOcean (with their Droplets offering) start out with a Linux image, which you install on top of. They also offer pre-installed packages that include a web server, which means you have less to install yourself. A little further along the spectrum is a provider like OpalStack, whose dashboard includes installation modules that connect to their web server. On OpalStack, you would install three modules: Django and two file-serving modules (one for your static files and the other for uploads).

One downside of a VPS is it may be up to you to maintain your associated software. For example, if you've installed your own Apache web server, you are responsible for patching it. This comes back to the spectrum: a near-bare-metal Linode instance requires more work than an OpalStack account, where most of this is taken care of for you.

If your Django project uses a database, well, that's one more thing you have to worry about, isn't it? On the extreme left, you install and configure a database yourself. I generally recommend against this. Most VPS providers also offer cloud services, including databases. This is the better choice, as the database gets tuned by a professional and backups typically get handled for you.

If you have the good fortune of your site becoming very popular, you also have a new problem: scaling. With enough traffic, a single instance of a VPS is insufficient. Most VPS providers offer some load-balancing mechanism that splits traffic among different servers, but this requires more configuration.

B.2.2 Platform as a service

We find PaaS providers on the right side of the deployment spectrum. These hosting companies abstract away all the details of deployment. They tend to be a little more expensive than VPS, but there is a lot less work, in both getting them going and maintaining them. DigitalOcean has a separate offering from their Droplets VPS, called the App Platform; this and Heroku are common PaaS choices. The interface to Heroku, for example, is a GitHub repository. You point your Heroku account at your repo, and when you update the main branch, Heroku automatically deploys. Their system understands Django intimately and knows exactly where the different kinds of files go and how to host them. You can even include a configuration file in your repo to fine-tune your deployment options.

There is also the container approach, using Docker or Kubernetes. If you're new to Django and the web world, I wouldn't recommend going down this path, unless you are already very familiar with containers. Containers can help you scale massively, but most sites don't need them to get going. There is a fairly steep learning curve to using containers, and if you're already experimenting with your first Django deployment, adding containers on top of that makes for a difficult hill to climb. If you are keen on Docker, the PaaS host Fly.io might be the right choice for you.

The previous paragraph can more or less be repeated, replacing the word *container* with the word *serverless*. Serverless configurations, like AWS Lambda, can provide massive scaling options at the cost of warm-up time (how long it takes to start a new instance in the background), but a lot of moving parts are needed to get Django going on Lambda. You'll need an S3 instance for storing your files, an RDS database, Lambda itself, and several other services to wire all this together. As with containers, if you aren't already intimately familiar with AWS, this isn't the place to start.

Choosing a hosting provider

Except for the most basic recommendations, the answer to *What should I do?* is always going to be *It depends*. I have been using Linux since Slackware 3.2 (that's the late 90s), so a VPS is fairly comfortable for me. If you're familiar with the Unix world and have installed software like web servers and databases before, the VPS will likely be a good fit. For my smaller clients, I usually start with OpalStack; it gives full shell access and control, but they take care of the database and web server instance, so it is a nice middle ground.

At scale, you'll want more control over how many servers you're running, how they're load balanced, and where background tasks operate. Within the VPS world, this means more work, but you can tune it to your heart's content.

PaaS services tend to be a bit more expensive. Heroku used to be the go-to because it was free, but that ended in November 2022. That isn't a reason not to use their platform; all the other PaaS providers charge as well. And you get what you pay for: full-time professionals take care of the servers, infrastructure, and rollout scripts for you.

I personally don't use PaaS for my clients, but I have worked with folks who do, and they swear by it. At scale, PaaS can become expensive, but if you're serving a lot of users, automatically adding more instances to keep the site running smoothly is a big win.

B.3 *Synchronous vs. asynchronous*

WSGI is the Python standard interface for interacting with a web server, and ASGI is its asynchronous equivalent. When you interact with a server synchronously, it doesn't return a result to you until the result is ready. With a web page, that means getting the HTML all in one go. Synchronous systems tend to be pull based, meaning it is up to the client (the web browser) to ask the server for something.

Asynchronous systems tend to be bidirectional. You might ask for something and get a response, or the system might send you something on its own. Chat typically gets built using asynchronous technology: the server notifies you when you receive a message. To implement chat in a synchronous server, your client has to ask the server *Is anything new for me?* with some regularity. This is known as *polling* the server.

In the last few years, there has been a trend towards asynchronous based web frameworks. Django originally was a synchronous-only tool kit, but asynchronous features have been introduced over time. Daphne, Uvicorn, and Hypercorn are all asynchronous web servers that can interact with Django over ASGI.

For a "normal" Django project, switching to using Daphne and the like is as simple as pointing Daphne at asgi.py instead of wsgi.py in your project configuration folder. Typically, though, the reason for going asynchronous is to take advantage of the features it enables. If you want to build a chat server using Django, you're going to need extra tools. The django-channels third-party library integrates WebSockets with Django, allowing full bidirectional communication with your web server over JavaScript, and as it is Django based, it uses views to do this.

NOTE WebSockets are a protocol that sit on top of HTTP, allowing for asynchronous, bidirectional communication on the web. They require JavaScript to work in the browser.

B.4 Readying Django for production

Once your infrastructure is in place, you have to deploy your project for the first time. Your code needs to be put on the server, your server may need configuration, your production database needs to be synchronized with your ORM through the `migrate` management command, your static files need to be copied from your project folder to the web server's folder, and possibly more. This section walks you through each of these tasks.

B.4.1 Environment-specific configuration

At minimum, you have two environments for your code: development (usually your local machine) and production (available to the world). More complex setups are possible, and quite common, in industry. In large organizations, you might have a local machine, a development server, multiple levels of testing servers, and then production.

Some configuration in settings.py is common to all deployment environments, but some is environment specific. For example, `DEBUG` should be `True` in dev and `False` in production. There are two general approaches to dealing with these differences: using environment variables and importing values.

There is a reason settings.py ends in *.py*: it is a Python file. Throughout the book, you have added Python variables as configuration values in settings.py, but you can also run code. You don't want to do this very much, but a few lines can offer you conditional configuration based on your deployment target.

Your operating system allows for the setting of environment variables that are accessible within a program. If you are on a Unix-based system and running bash (and most other shells), the `env` command shows how many variables are currently set. In Python, the `environ` dictionary inside the `os` module contains all of these environment variables. Inside settings.py, you can set a value based on the contents of `os.environ`. This is particularly handy for things like passwords and keys that you don't want committed to your code repo. Here is an example that sets the `SECRET_KEY` value:

```
# RiffMates/RiffMates/settings.py
...
import os
...
SECRET_KEY = os.environ["RIFFMATES_SECRET"]
```

Instead of using environment variables, you can manage the settings.py file itself. A low-tech solution is to have settings_dev.py and settings_prod.py and, as part of your deployment, copying the appropriate file to settings.py. There are a couple of drawbacks to this approach: (1) many values will be common to both, and (2) you still have the problem of not storing secrets in your repo, which means you may not want to store either of these files in your code repository.

You can also import values into a settings.py file. The mechanism I use personally is a little convoluted, but I'm happy with it. I use settings.py for values common to all environments, and then import extra files based on the deployment environment. The module of the extra files is itself read out of a file. This level of indirection allows you to store all the files in your repo but configure for the deployment target by changing the contents of the indirection file.

I store all the environment files in a directory called *local_settings*, and the indirection file is named *import_redirect*. This file contains the name of the modules to import into the configuration. Code at the bottom of settings.py reads the module name from import_redirect and then dynamically imports that module.

Additionally, there is also a directory called *secrets*, containing the files with the same names as the local settings. These files contain configuration values that should not be stored in the code repo, like passwords and secret keys. The relationship between all these files is shown in figure B.2.

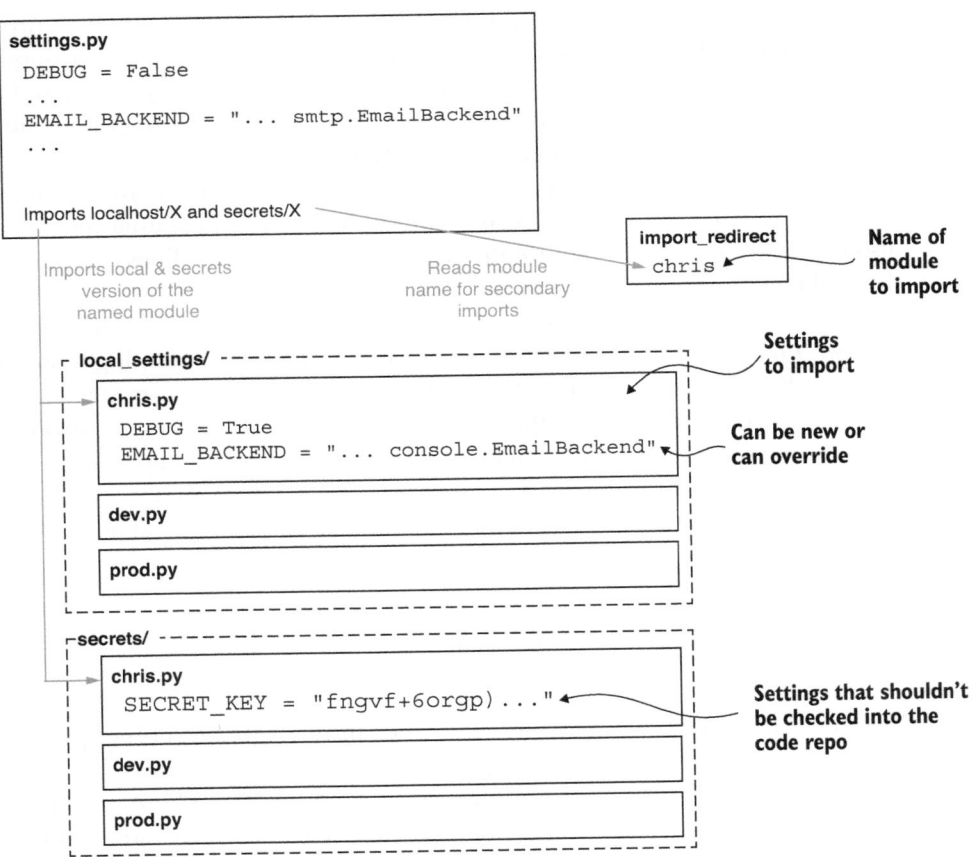

Figure B.2   Using separate subsettings files for environment-specific settings and secrets

This is probably overkill for a small project, but when you have multiple environments and a team of developers, it allows you to set configuration values specific to both a deployment target and, if necessary, a developer. For example, if we were working together and you wanted to use the Django Debug Toolbar but I didn't, this would be possible because we'd both have our own configuration file. An example file tree looks like this:

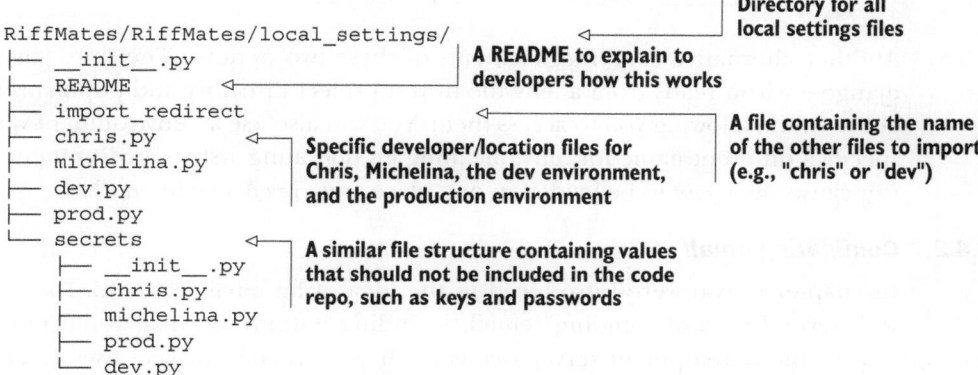

The import_redirect file and the secrets directory aren't included in your code repo. Adding the following to .gitignore ensures they won't be committed accidentally:

```
# .gitignore
...
RiffMates/local_settings/import_redirect
RiffMates/local_settings/secrets/
```

The code in settings.py that does the importation work can be seen in the following listing.

Listing B.1   Code for dynamically importing local settings and secret modules

```
# RiffMates/RiffMates/settings.py
...
# ---- local settings import overrides

# detect if in dev server mode
import sys
DEV_SERVER = (len(sys.argv) > 1 and \
    sys.argv[1] == 'runserver')
```
Detect if you're running the development server.

```
redirect = (BASE_DIR /
    'RiffMates/local_settings/import_redirect')
```
The file containing the name of other files to import

```
with open(redirect, 'r') as f:
    import_file = f.read().strip()
```
Read import_redirect, and get the name of the other imports.

```
action = 'from RiffMates.local_settings.%s import *' \
    % import_file
```
Build the Python code that imports all values from the requested local settings file.

Execute the import command.

```
exec(action)
if DEV_SERVER:
    print('Importing settings: s' % import_file)

action = ('from RiffMates.local_settings.secrets.'
    '%s import *' % import_file)
exec(action)
if DEV_SERVER:
    print('Importing secrets: %s' % import_file)
```

If this is the development server, print some info about the import.

Repeat the process but for the corresponding secrets file.

Another alternative combines elements of these two options. The third-party library django-environ reads from a .env file in you project directory and populates the variables within, allowing you to access them. You can also use an environment variable to specify a different name for .env, meaning an operating system environment variable can cause .dev_env to be loaded in one place and .prod_env in another.

B.4.2 *Configuring email*

In chapter 6, you were introduced to the idea of an email backend. Django comes with several ways of "sending" email, including outputting what would normally be sent to the development server's console. If your Django project uses email, you're going to want to connect to an actual email server.

Email can be a little tricky. Email gets sent using the *Simple Mail Transfer Protocol* (SMTP). For small volumes, your hosting provider may include an SMTP server. Staying out of your user's spam folder can be a challenge, and properly configuring a server so that it isn't suspected of spewing junk mail is important.

For larger volumes of email, you want a service provider. Companies such as Mailgun, SendGrid, and Mailchimp allow you to send mail through their systems and work with the common email clients, such as Gmail and Outlook, to help ensure you stay out of the spam folder.

Whichever service provider you choose, you need to change the configuration in settings.py to point at their system. A sample configuration is as follows:

```
# RiffMates/RiffMates/settings.py
...
EMAIL_BACKEND = \
    'django.core.mail.backends.smtp.EmailBackend'
EMAIL_USE_TLS = True
EMAIL_HOST = 'smtp.example.com'
EMAIL_PORT = 587
EMAIL_HOST_USER = 'username'
EMAIL_HOST_PASSWORD = 'password'
```

Email backend for connecting to an SMTP server

Use an encrypted connection.

Host of the SMTP service

Network port of the SMTP service

Username and password of your account on the SMTP server

Of course, storing a password in clear text or in a file in your code repository is not a recommended practice. The EMAIL_HOST_PASSWORD value should be set using an environment variable or imported from a separate file, as discussed in the previous section.

B.4.3   Logging

Whether you realize it or not, you've been using Django's logging functionality all along. The development server console messages indicating a view was visited are from the logging system. Django's logging is built on top of Python's logging, which is extremely configurable (read: a bit complicated to get going).

Python breaks the logging system down into four parts:

- Loggers
- Filters
- Handlers
- Formatters

The logger is what you interact with to log a message. The logger object has a variety of methods that correspond to the log level of the message you are logging. The log levels are

- DEBUG
- INFO
- WARNING
- ERROR
- CRITICAL

The logging filter is responsible for determining which messages get recorded in the logs. The simplest filters are based on the log level. If your filter is set to ERROR, only messages marked as ERROR or CRITICAL get recorded. You likely want different filters in different environments. In development, you want everything, which you can get by setting the log level to DEBUG. In production, that's a bit too noisy, and you may set it higher. The WARNING level is pretty typical on a production server. If a problem occurs in production, you might temporarily change the log level to capture information and help you debug the issue.

The logging handler determines where a message gets logged. The two most common destinations are the console and a file. A logging formatter specifies the format of the message when it is logged. In addition to the message getting logged, you can also add information, such as the date and time, the called function, the process and thread IDs, the source code line, and the current phase of the moon. (That last one is a joke, but there are over 20 log attributes you can choose from: https://docs.python .org/3/library/logging.html#logrecord-attributes). You specify the format using a `%s` style string that names the attributes. For example, `"%(message)s"` is the format for logging only the message.

Django's own code uses different logging objects for different kinds of messages. The `django.request` logger logs the messages you've seen when using the development server. The `django.db.backends` logger is for database interactions. This classification allows you to determine which messages make it into your logs. It is also hierarchical; configuring for the `django` logger gets both the `.request` and `.db` `.backends` content, along with everything else.

Setup for logging is done in settings.py using a configuration dictionary. At a minimum, you want a handler and a logger. Most often, you'll set up a handler for the console, a separate handler for writing to a file, and a couple of formatters. This allows you to log to different places in different hosting environments. The following listing contains a logging configuration that has both a console and file-based handler and a formatter for each, and it sends all messages in the system to both handlers.

Listing B.2   Logging configuration for both the console and a file

```
LOGGING = {
    'version': 1,
    'disable_existing_loggers': False,
    'formatters': {
        'console': {
            'format': '%(levelname)-8s %(message)s'
        },
        'file': {
            'format': \
            '%(asctime)s %(levelname)-8s %(message)s'
        }
    },
    'handlers': {
        'console': {
            'class': 'logging.StreamHandler',
            'formatter': 'console'
        },
        'file': {
            'level': 'DEBUG',
            'class': 'logging.FileHandler',
            'formatter': 'file',
            'filename': '/tmp/debug.log'
        }
    },
    'loggers': {
        '': {
            'level': 'DEBUG',
            'handlers': ['console', 'file']
        }
    }
}
```

Specifies the version of the log configuration format should always be 1

Configuration section for log formatters

A formatter named console that outputs the log level and the message

A formatter named file that outputs the current date and time, log level, and message

Configuration section for handlers

Defines a handler named console that outputs to a stream (which, by default, goes to standard-out)

The name of the formatter to use with this handler (the handler and associated formatter are usually named the same thing, but this isn't required)

Defines a handler named file that outputs to a file

Name of the formatter to use with this handler

Extra configuration used by this handler specifying the full pathname of the logging file

The empty string specifies to record messages from all loggers. This includes your own loggers as well as all those used by Django.

A log level of DEBUG catches all messages.

This logger uses both the console and file handlers. All messages will be sent to both the console and the log file.

The configuration in listing B.2 is a nice example, but it is probably not the best choice for your production system. In production, you don't want to log to console, and in development, you typically only log to console. This configuration is also trapping all log levels, which is likely a little verbose for a production setup.

The logging classes specified in the handler configurations point to objects in the Python standard library. I recommend using `logging.RotatingFileHandler` instead of `logging.FileHandler`, as it is smart enough to change to a new file when your current log gets too big. To use the rotating handler, you must specify an additional argument of `maxBytes` that specifies the file's size limit.

There are plenty of sources to dig into for more information on logging:

- *Django's logging documentation*—https://docs.djangoproject.com/en/dev/topics/logging/
- *Python's logging documentation*—https://docs.python.org/3/library/logging.html
- *Python's logging cookbook*—https://docs.python.org/3/howto/logging-cookbook.html

If all that isn't enough, there are also centralized log-management services. These providers are API based, and you send your log messages to their systems. They typically include log-analysis tools and allow you to have all of your servers log to the same place, giving you an overview of your entire deployment. Two popular log management services are Datadog and Sematext, and the cloud providers have centralized logging within their offerings as well.

B.4.4   Custom 404 and 500 pages

The Django development server provides a lot of handy information when something goes wrong. The `404` page displays which URLs were attempted, and the `500` page shows a complete stack trace. Neither of these are things you want your users to see. With `DEBUG=False`, this information isn't shown, but the default pages won't look like your site. This is simple to remedy. Create files named *404.html* and *500.html* inside your templates folder, and Django will automatically use them to display the corresponding errors. These files are Django templates, so you can extend your base template and have the errors look like your project's other pages.

If this isn't sufficient for your error-handling needs, Django allows you to override the views called when errors have been triggered. You can replace them with your own views and perform whatever actions you want. For details on how to write custom error views, see https://docs.djangoproject.com/en/dev/topics/http/views/#customizing-error-views.

B.5   Static file management

In chapter 7, you learned how to use static files, such as CSS and JavaScript, within your Django project. The two key configuration values in settings.py for static files are the following:

```
# RiffMates/RiffMates/settings.py
...
STATIC_URL = '/static/'            ◁──┘ The base URL for
STATICFILES_DIRS = (                     serving static files
    BASE_DIR / 'static',          ◁──┐ The location where static files
)                                       are found in the project
```

In production, you want the web server to be responsible for hosting static files; it is just far more efficient. The settings in the example are the same, but you also need to configure your web server. Inside the web server, you map URLs to directories, so /static/ maps to where your static files are located.

Web server permissions are typically associated with the directory of the files being served. You don't want your Django code served by the web server, only the static files. For this reason (and another I'll get to in a second), it is best practice to copy the static files somewhere outside the project directory for serving by the web server.

Django provides a management command for copying the static files to their production location. This command is `collectstatic`. As part of your deployment process, you run this command, and then Django copies all the static files to the production location. You inform Django of the destination location by setting `STATIC_ROOT`, as in the following example:

```
# RiffMates/RiffMates/settings.py
...
STATIC_ROOT = OUTSIDE_DIR / 'static'
```

In chapter 7, you learned how I typically have a directory named *outside* at the same level as the project directory. I put user-uploaded files in this directory, and in the example configuration, I've done the same with the production static files.

How static files get managed is determined by a pluggable component. Web servers—and web browsers, for that matter—like to cache things. If you update your site's logo, just because you replaced it on the web server doesn't mean it will get served or the browser will even ask for it; it may use a cached copy. Enter `ManifestStatic-FilesStorage`. The class name may be a mouthful, but what it does is automatically rename your static files to include their MD5 hash. An MD5 hash is a short string that represents the content of a file: changing the file changes the hashed string. By appending the hash to the filename, any change to the file changes the filename, meaning it won't be cached. As you're using the `{% static %}` tag to serve your static files, Django takes care of name translation in the URL for you.

Django allows for the customization of other kinds of storage handlers as well, and when configuring to use the MD5 static handler, you have to be careful not to overwrite the other settings. To use the MD5 static handler, include all the following in settings.py:

```
# RiffMates/RiffMates/settings.py
...
STORAGES = {
  "default": {
      "BACKEND": "django.core.files.storage.FileSystemStorage",
  },
  "staticfiles": {
    "BACKEND": \
        "django.contrib.staticfiles.storage.ManifestStaticFilesStorage",
  },
}
```

> **Prior to Django 4.2**
>
> The STORAGES configuration value was introduced in Django 4.2. Prior to that, a different configuration value was necessary:
>
> ```
> # RiffMates/RiffMates/settings.py
> ...
> STATICFILES_STORAGE = \
>     'django.contrib.staticfiles.storage.ManifestStaticFilesStorage'
> ```
>
> This setting has been deprecated and will be removed in a future version of Django.

Using copies of static files in production means extra steps are required, and it complicates simple deployments, but it allows you to do fantastic things at scale. For example, you could have your static files served from an Amazon S3 bucket or a *content delivery network* (CDN). Both of these require custom handlers, and there are third-party packages that integrate the handling. For a bit more information and some pointers to other libraries, see https://docs.djangoproject.com/en/dev/howto/static-files/deployment/#staticfiles-from-cdn.

B.6   *Other databases*

Throughout the examples in this book, you've been using SQLite as your database, but Django supports four other databases out of the box:

- PostgreSQL
- MariaDB
- MySQL
- Oracle

There are also a number of third-party packages available that plug more database engines into your Django project. The ORM provides a common abstraction across all these databases, but it is just an abstraction. When you write code in a Model, Django is mapping your Python into SQL equivalents.

Different databases may handle the same SQL statement differently. For example, SQLite implements both the CharField and TextField as a text blob with no size limit, so it ignores the max_length attribute of the CharField. The Model still validates the length, but in a complicated set-up where multiple programs are sharing the database, you could end up with a CharField containing more characters than max_length value.

SQLite is the default database, with db.sqlite3 being the default database file. You've seen this file in your project, and if you were brave, you may have even deleted it. The configuration that determines this filename is in settings.py. The DATABASES configuration item specifies which database engine to use and what parameters that engine expects. The default Django puts in your settings.py when your project gets created looks like this:

```
# RiffMates/RiffMates/settings.py
...
DATABASES = {
    'default': {
        'ENGINE': 'django.db.backends.sqlite3',
        'NAME': BASE_DIR / 'db.sqlite3',
    }
}
```

Django is capable of interacting with multiple databases at one time. Doing so is outside the scope of this book, but this is why there is a nested dictionary inside the DATABASES configuration. You can end up with more than just default configured.

To use a different database, you change the ENGINE subproperty to point at a different backend. The other key–value pairs in the configuration are database specific. SQLite, being a file-based database, has a simple configuration: just the filename. The other databases interact over the network. To configure for a PostgeSQL database, you provide an OPTIONS dictionary instead of the NAME argument. The contents of that dictionary specify a service configuration file and a password storage file. The service configuration file contains network information, a username, and the database name to connect with. The password storage file contains your connection password. More details on interacting with specific databases can be found in the Django documentation: https://docs.djangoproject.com/en/dev/ref/databases/.

B.7   Caching

For a small project with a few users, your web server will likely be snappy enough that you'll get sufficient performance for your page. As you scale, you may need to introduce caching. A *cache* records the previous output of a computation and serves the recording up instead of rerunning the computation.

In Django's case, the computation is the view. With caching turned on, the first time a user hits a view, the result gets stored in the cache. Subsequent visits to the same view get served out of the cache instead, reducing the amount of code that needs to be run.

Django can use three different types of caches, based on

- Servers
- Databases
- Files

A cache server is a dedicated piece of software that provides caching functionality. Two popular choices are Memcached and Redis. Your hosting provider may offer these as add-on packages or cloud-based instances.

You can also have Django use your database to cache content. To do this, you need to create an extra table in your database to store the content; this can be accomplished using the createcachetable management command.

Alternatively, you can use files to store the cached contents. In this case, you point Django at a directory to use for the cache files. This directory should not be inside your project.

In all three cases, you set the `CACHES` value in your settings.py file to turn on caching, indicate your style of caching backend, and provide any additional parameters your backend requires. The following example is for a Memcached server running on port `11211` on the same machine as the Django instance:

```
# RiffMates/RiffMates/settings.py
...
CACHES = {
    "default": {
        "BACKEND": "django.core.cache.backends.memcached.PyMemcacheCache",
        "LOCATION": "127.0.0.1:11211",
    }
}
```

For more details on caching in Django, including the specific settings you need for different backends, see https://docs.djangoproject.com/en/dev/topics/cache/.

B.8   Putting it all together

If you think you're ready to go, look at the Django documentation's "Deployment Checklist": https://docs.djangoproject.com/en/dev/howto/deployment/checklist/.

If you are set up, and your infrastructure is all in place, there are a series of actions necessary for each deployment:

- Update your project code on the server.
- Install any third-party packages that were newly added to your project.
- Optionally, upgrade third-party packages.
- Copy static files to the production location.
- Sync the project's ORM with the production database.

B.8.1   Builds and releases

In the case of a PaaS, much of this is taken care of for you. For a VPS, you may want to write a script or two, ensuring a consistent process with each release. Some PaaS providers split the deployment process into two steps: *build* and *release*. When using containers, the build process is what builds the container object, while the release process pushes it into the infrastructure. Even if you're not using containers, thinking of deployment as a two-phase process can be beneficial.

If updating your code or any associated third-party libraries fails, you don't want to run the database migration command. Grouping the code updates, package updates, and static file management into a build script, while putting the migration call in a release script, means you won't be triggering changes in the database unless everything else went smoothly.

How you update the server's copy of your project code depends on your infrastructure. For simple systems, having a clone of your Git repo on the server means you simply do `git pull` on the branch used for production (typically `main` or `master`). For a PaaS like Heroku, this is done for you automatically. For more complex systems, with multiple servers being load balanced, you need to look into configuration management tools, such as Chef and Puppet. This doesn't become important until you're scaling, though, and scaling means your server is popular, which is a nice problem to have.

Packages in Python are not a solved problem. There are a variety of tool kits out there that do this and help deal with dependency management. As your project changes over time, you need to ensure your production environment continues to meet the dependency requirements of your project. Failure to do so might cause bugs in production. In some cases, it could cause the project to crash, resulting in a `500` error. Tools like Pipenv, Poetry, and Hatch help manage package dependencies, and each has its own strengths and weaknesses.

B.8.2   *Monitoring*

Even when everything goes well and your code gets happily deployed, there is a chance of a failure some time in the future. Servers run out of disk space, shared VPS environments have their CPU monopolized by bad neighbors, and cosmic particles rain through the ether and blow up processors and disk drives. That last one doesn't happen very frequently, but it has been known to happen.

Once your server is running, you want to make sure it stays running. Or, at least, you want to be notified if it stops running. Monitoring is the process of keeping an eye on your running systems. A simple version of this might be a shell script that uses `curl` once a minute to hit your web server, and if it gets no response, it kills and restarts your process.

Web services like Uptime and Pingdom monitor your pages and notify you when a page becomes unreachable. Most monitoring sites even hit your project from a variety of places on the planet and log information about the response time. If you end up with a lot of users in a foreign country, you might consider deploying a local server for them to reduce their response time. These kinds of tools only provide an outside view, a binary Service Is Up or Service Is Down perspective, but they tend to be inexpensive. Your hosting provider may offer more detailed services that are integrated with notification tools.

PagerDuty, Dynatrace, and other services allow you to add calls to their API within your code. This is somewhat like logging but with a view to monitoring your system. Alarms can be set up for different events as well as when events, like a server heartbeat, are not received in a timely fashion.

appendix C
Django template tag
and filter reference

This appendix is a reference guide for the built-in tags and filters available in the Django template language. For a full reference, see the online documentation: https://docs.djangoproject.com/en/dev/ref/templates/builtins/.

C.1   Tags

Table C.1   Built-in Django template tags

Tag	Description

`{% autoescape off %}`
`    {{ venue_listing }}`
`{% endautoescape %}`
	By default, Django escapes characters in variables that are reserved for HTML. The `{% autoescape %}` tag allows you to control this behavior by turning it on or off for a block. In this example, if `{{ venue_listing }}` contained HTML tags, they could be rendered without being escaped inside `{% autoescape off %}`.
	`{% autoescape %}` expects an argument of either on or off.

`{% block footer %}`
`    {{ block.super }}`
`{% endblock %}`
	Declare a block to be used in inheritance. Templates that extend other templates can override the contents by declaring a `{% block %}` with the same name—footer, in this example. Within a block, a special variable `{{ block.super }}` is available that contains the content of parent block.

`{% comment "Optional note" %}`
`    This content is not rendered`
`{% endcomment %}`
	The contents of a `{% comment %}` block are not included in the rendered content. This tag takes an optional argument that can be used as an additional note, which can be handy if you're commenting out a chunk of code and want to remind yourself why you did so. Comment blocks cannot be nested.
	The template language also supports the `{#` and `#}` pair as comment characters.

Table C.1 Built-in Django template tags

Tag	Description
`{% csrf_token %}`	This tag is part of Django's cross-site request forgery (CSRF) protection and should be included in any forms.
`{% cycle "red" "blue" %}`	Each time this tag is called, it produces its next listed argument. When the list is exhausted, it resumes from the start. It is typically used inside a `{% for %}` tag, changing its value on each iteration. One common use is creating a zebra-stripe effect by changing the style of an `<li>` element or the class of a `<tr>`.
`{% debug %}`	This outputs a large amount of debug information, including text component parts of the page, user information, and every loaded module. It only works if you have `DEBUG=True` in settings.py.
`{% extends "base.html" %}`	Part of the template inheritance mechanism, `{% extends %}` is used at the top of a file to indicate a template is a child of the named template, `"base.html"` in the example. Any `{% block %}` tags in this instance will override `{% block %}` tags of the same name in the parent.

`{% filter force_escape|lower %}`
   `This content will have the named`
  `filters applied before rendering`
`{% endfilter %}`
	This allows the use of one or more filters on the body of the tag. Filters to be applied are named as arguments; multiple filters can be applied through the use of the pipe (`|`).

`{% firstof is_leapyear is_winter is_week` `day "default" %}`	This outputs the value of the first value in its list that is not false-y, where *not false-y* means *it exists, is not empty, is not* `False`, *and is greater than zero if numeric*. A final string value can be provided to force a default result (all nonempty strings are `True`).

`{% for person in people %}`
   `{{ person.name }}`
`{% empty %}`
   `<i> No people </i>`
`{% endfor %}`
	This is the template equivalent of a Python `for` statement, and it loops over an iterable (`people`) and places the current instance in a value (`person`). The optional `{% empty %}` clause is run if the iterable is empty.

`{{ forloop.counter }}`
`{{ forloop.counter0 }}`
`{{ forloop.revcounter }}`
`{{ forloop.revcounter0 }}`
`{{ forloop.first }}`
`{{ forloop.last }}`
`{{ forloop.parentloop }}`
	These values are defined within the context of a `{% for %}` block, giving information on the current state of the loop. They correspond to the current count (1-based), current count (0-based), number of iterations from the end (1-based), number of iterations from the end (0-based), `True` if the first iteration, `True` if the last iteration, and the context value of a parent loop in the case of nested `{% for %}` tags. For a nested `{% for %}` tag, `{{ forloop.parentloop.counter }}` contains the counter of the parent loop.

Table C.1 **Built-in Django template tags** *(continued)*

Tag	Description

`{% if count > 50 %}`
    `It is big`
`{% elif count > 20 %}`
    `It is medium`
`{% else %}`
    `It is small`
`{% endif %}`
	This is the template equivalent of a Python `if` statement. The Boolean condition supports `and`, `or`, `not`, `==`, `!=`, `<`, `?`, `>`, `>=`, `in`, `not in`, `is`, and `is not` operators. Values in the condition support the use of filters through the pipe (`|`) operator and can be grouped with parentheses.

`{% ifchanged minute %}`
    `More than a minute went by`
`{% else %}`
    `Less than a minute went by`
`{% endifchanged %}`
	This checks whether a value has changed since the last time the same tag was executed. It is used within a `{% for %}` tag to determine if a value is different on a subsequent iteration. The `{% else %}` tag is optional.

`{% include "subtemplate.html" %}`
or
`{% include "subtemplate.html" with`
  `name="Connor" %}`
	This loads and renders a subtemplate. Using `with` sets values within the subtemplate's context.

`{% load taglibrary %}`	This loads a custom tag/filter library for use. It is equivalent to a Python `import` statement.
`{% lorem 10 w %}`	This outputs placeholder text, using the traditional "lorem ipsum" text. Arguments are optional, specifying the amount of content, the type of content (`w` for words, `p` for HTML paragraphs, and `b` for plain-text paragraph blocks), and the word `random` to generate random text instead of lorem ipsum.
`{% now "Y/m/d" %}`	This outputs the current date, using the specified format. This example outputs the date in ISO 8601 format, such as `"1999/12/25"`. Date string specifiers can be found here: https://docs.djangoproject.com/en/dev/ref/templates/builtins/#std-templatefilter-date
`{% regroup value by key as result %}`	This takes a list of dictionaries (`value`) and creates a new list, where items with the same key are grouped together. For example, if `value` contained a list of dictionaries with city information, where each city had a key named `country`, regrouping on `country` creates a new list, containing a nested list for each unique country found.
`{% resetcycle %}`	This resets a previous cycle tag so that it begins at the start of its argument list again. It is typically used in nested `{% for %}` tags, so the inner `{% for %}` starts at the beginning of a cycle rather than the state from the previous iteration.

`{% spaceless %}`
  `<p>`
    `<b>This is some content</b>`
  `</p>`
`{% endspaceless %}`
	This removes whitespace (including newlines) *between* HTML tags. Note that it does not remove spaces *within* HTML tags. The example renders as `<p><b>This is some content</b></p>`.

Table C.1   Built-in Django template tags *(continued)*

Tag	Description
`{% templatetag value %}`	This outputs one of the special characters normally reserved for the template tag language. It accepts an argument naming the special character, which is either openblock (`{%`), closeblock (`%}`), openvariable (`{{`), closevariable (`}}`), openbrace (`{`), closebrace (`}`), opencomment (`{#`), or closecomment (`#}`).
`{% url 'name' arg1 arg2 %}`	This looks up the named URL and returns an absolute path reference. Arguments after the name are optional and are passed to the URL look-up for URLs containing values.

`{% verbatim %}`
    `{% if count > 50 %}`
`{% endverbatim %}`
	The contents of a `{% verbatim %}` tag are rendered as is. This is typically used to include JavaScript templating syntax that uses similar characters as Django's template language. An optional name can be provided in both the open and close tag, allowing you to nest `{% verbatim %}` tags using pairs of names.

`{% widthratio value max max_width %}`
or
`{% widthratio value max max_width as my_ration %}`
	This calculates a value for a width based on the ratio of `value` to `max`. For example, if `value` is 50, `max` is 100, and `max_value` is 60, the result would be 30 (50 ÷ 100 * 60). Also accepts an "as" argument to put the result into a variable instead.

`{% with name="Mike" %}` `{% endwith %}`	This defines a context variable for use within the block.

C.1.1   Loadable tags

Django's built-in tags are available without using a `{% load %}` tag. Django also ships with other tags that are inside modules that need to be loaded to be used.

Table C.2   Loadable Django tags

Tag	Module	Description
`{% static "images/photo.jpg" %}`	static	This returns a link to the named static file.
`{% get_static_prefix %}`	static	This returns the relative path portion of a static URL.
`{% get_media_prefix %}`	static	This returns the relative path portion of a media URL.

`{% translate "Text for translation" %}`
or
`{% translate "Text for translation" as my_translation %}`
	i18n	This returns the translated text equivalent looked up within the translation files. It supports both string constants and named variables as well as an `as` clause to have the result put into a variable instead of being rendered.

Table C.2 Loadable Django tags *(continued)*

Tag	Module	Description

`{% blocktranslate %}`
    `A translated string with a {{ value }}.`
`{% endblocktranslate %}`
	i18n	This returns the translated text equivalent looked up within the translation files. It supports bound variables for look-up within the translation system.

`{% get_available_languages %}`	i18n	This returns a list of available languages from the translation system. The list contains tuples pairing the language code with the name of the language.
`{% get_current_language %}`	i18n	This returns the current language as a language code based on the user's preferred value.
`{% get_current_language_bidi %}`	i18n	This returns the current language's rendering direction—`True` for right-to-left languages.
`{% get_language_info for "en-ca" as lang %}`	i18n	This puts language information for the named code (`"en-ca"`) in the value (`lang`). Language information is an object with attributes for the language code (`lang.code`), language name (`lang.name_local`), language name in English (`lang.name`), language bi-direction (`lang.bidi`), and name in the active language (`lang.name_translated`).
`{% get_language_info_list for` `available_langs as langs %}`	i18n	This creates a list (`langs`) of language info data structures for each language code in the `available_langs` iterable.

`{% localize on %}`
    `{{ value }}`
`{% endlocalize %}`
	l10n	This activates (`on`) or deactivates (`off`) localization within the block contents.

`{% localtime on %}`
    `{{ value }}`
`{% endlocaltime %}`
	tz	This activates (`on`) or deactivates (`off`) conversion of aware datetime objects contained within the block to the current time zone.

`{% timezone "America/Toronto" %}`
    `{{ value }}`
`{% endlocaltime %}`
	tz	This converts any datetime objects contained within the block to the named time zone.

`{% get_current_timezone as my_zone %}`	tz	This puts the name of the current time zone in the named argument (`my_zone`).

C.2   Filters

Table C.3   Built-in Django template filters

Filter	Description
`{{ value|add:"2" }}`	This adds the argument (2) to the contents being filtered. It supports variables as an argument. If both the filtered value and the argument are lists, the lists will be concatenated (their values aren't added).
`{{ value|addslashes }}`	This adds backslashes before quote characters in a string. It is used to write content that is escaped, so the user can copy it to the clipboard.
`{{ value|capfirst }}`	This capitalizes the first character.
`{{ value|center:"15" }}`	This adds whitespace to center the contents for the given width. Note: this is only visible in HTML inside certain tags, as HTML normally ignores whitespace.
`{{ value|cut:" " }}`	This removes characters in the argument from the value. The example removes all spaces in the value.
`{{ value|date:"Y/m/d" }}`	This formats the value as a date using the given date specifier string. Specifiers can be found in the docs: https://docs .djangoproject.com/en/dev/ref/templates/builtins/#date.
`{{ value|default:"nothing" }}`	If `value` evaluates to `False`, it renders the contents of the filter's arguments instead.
`{{ value|default_if_none:"nothing" }}`	If `value` is `None`, it renders the contents of the filter's arguments instead.
`{{ value|dictsort:"name" }}`	This sorts a list of dictionaries, using the argument's key. In the example, a list of dictionaries in `value` would be sorted by the `"name"` key.
`{{ value|dictsortreversed:"name" }}`	This sorts a list of dictionaries in reverse order, using the argument's key.
`{{ value|divisbleby:"3" }}`	This returns `True` if `value` is divisible by the argument.
`{{ value|escape }}`	This performs HTML character escaping on `value`. If escaping has already been done on `value` it does not double-escape.
`{{ value|escapejs }}`	This performs JavaScript character escaping on `value`. It does not make the content safe for use as HTML.
`{{ value|filesizeformat }}`	This renders numbers using file size suffixes. For example, `123456789` is rendered as `117.7 MB`.
`{{ value|first }}`	This renders the first item in a list.

Table C.3 Built-in Django template filters *(continued)*

Filter	Description
`{{ value|floatformat }}` or `{{ value|floatformat:3 }}` or `{{ value|floatformat:"-3" }}` or `{{ value|floatformat:"3g" }}` or `{{ value|floatformat:"3u" }}`	This formats float values. With no argument, it displays a single decimal place. Integer arguments specify the number of decimal places. String arguments are converted to integers. Negative arguments specify the number of decimal places but show an integer if the number is precise (e.g., `7.1` becomes `7.100`, while `7.0` becomes `7`). A `g` suffix adds a thousandths separator. A `u` suffix turns localization off.
`{{ value|force_escape }}`	This performs HTML escaping on `value`, even if it has already been escaped.
`{{ value|get_digit:"2" }}`	This returns the nth digit of an integer from the right.
`{{ value|iriencode }}`	This converts an Internationalized Resource Identifier (IRI) to a string that can be included in a URL.
`{{ value|join:"," }}`	This returns a string composed of all the elements in a list, putting the argument between each item. It is equivalent to Python's `str.join()`.
`{{ value|json_script:"my-id" }}`	This converts a Python object to JSON wrapped in a `<script>` tag. The tag will have an `id` attribute corresponding to the argument.
`{{ value|last }}`	This returns the last item in a list.
`{{ value|length }}`	This returns the length of a string or list.
`{{ value|linebreaks }}`	This converts plain text into a paragraph, wrapping the content with `<p>` and `</p>` tags. A single newline within the content is converted to a ` `, while double newlines are converted into a second set of paragraph tags.
`{{ value|linebreaksbr }}`	This replaces newlines in a string with HTML ` ` tags.
`{{ value|linenumbers }}`	This prefixes each line in `value` with a line number.
`{{ value|ljust:"15" }}`	This adds whitespace to left justify the contents for the given width. Note: this is only visible in HTML inside certain tags, as HTML normally ignores whitespace.
`{{ value|lower }}`	This converts all characters to lowercase.
`{{ value|make_list }}`	This converts `value` into a list. For strings, the characters become items in the list; for integers, the digits become their character equivalents in the list.
`{{ value|phone2numeric }}`	This converts a phone number containing letters to its numeric equivalent. It does not validate the format of the phone number.

Table C.3   Built-in Django template filters *(continued)*

Filter	Description

`{{ value|pluraize }}`
or
`{{ value|pluraize:"es" }}`
	This returns s if value is 2 or greater. Given an argument, it returns the argument instead of s. The second example returns "es" if value is greater than 1.

`{{ value|pprint }}`	This is a wrapper around Python's pprint.pprint() function, which is useful when debugging.
`{{ value|random }}`	This returns a random item from a list.
`{{ value|rjust:"15" }}`	This adds whitespace to right justify the contents for the given width. Note: this is only visible in HTML inside certain tags, as HTML normally ignores whitespace.
`{{ value|safe }}`	This marks a string as not requiring HTML escaping. It has no effect if auto-escaping is turned off.
`{{ value|safeseq }}`	This applies the | safe filter to each item in a list.
`{{ value|slice:":2" }}`	This performs Python list slicing.
`{{ value|slugify }}`	This converts value into a newspaper slug. It removes any character that isn't an alphanumeric, underscore, or hyphen; converts it to lowercase; and removes any leading or trailing whitespace.
`{{ value|stringformat:"E" }}`	This performs printf-style string formatting on value. Note the argument does not use the percent symbol. For example, the argument "03d" is the equivalent of the format string %03d.
`{{ value|striptags }}`	This attempts to strip XML or HTML tags from a string. Note that there are tricky things users can do to get around this; do not assume the result of this filter can be marked as safe. If you absolutely must allow user input HTML, use a third-party HTML sanitizer library.
`{{ value|time:"H:i" }}`	This converts a time object to a string, using the argument as a string formatter. See the |date filter.
`{{ value|timesince:comparison }}`	This returns the amount of time that has expired between value and comparison, in human-readable format (5 days, 3 hours).
`{{ value|timeuntil:comparison }}`	This returns the amount of time remaining between value and comparison, in human-readable format.
`{{ value|title }}`	This converts a string to title case.
`{{ value|truncatechars:7 }}`	This truncates a string to the given number of characters. Truncated strings end with an ellipsis (…).
`{{ value|truncatechars_html:7 }}`	This is an HTML-aware version of |truncatechars.
`{{ value|truncatewords:7 }}`	This is like |truncatechars but counts the number of words instead of the number of characters.
`{{ value|truncatewords_html:7 }}`	This is an HTML-aware version of |truncatewords.

Table C.3   Built-in Django template filters *(continued)*

Filter	Description
`{{ value|unordered_list }}`	This converts a list into a series of `<li>` tags. It supports nested lists with inner lists converted into a sub `<ul>` collection. Note that the outermost output does not have `<ul>` tags wrapped around it.
`{{ value|upper }}`	This converts a string into all uppercase.
`{{ value|urlencode }}`	URL encodes a string.
`{{ value|urlize }}`	This converts text containing a URL into its clickable HTML equivalent. URLs are detected based on prefixes of *www.*, *http://*, or *https://*. Additionally, domain-only links are detected if they end in a recognized top-level domain (*.com*, *.edu*, *.gov*, *.int*, *.mil*, *.net*, or *.org*). Note that `value` may contain content besides the URL, such as a full sentence. For example `'Visit manning.com today'` is converted to `'Visit <a href="manning.com">manning.com</a> today'`.
`{{ value|urlizetrunc:"15" }}`	This is like `|urlize` but truncates the display portion of the URL if it exceeds the length given in the argument.
`{{ value|wordcount }}`	This returns the number of words in `value`.
`{{ value|wordwrap:"20" }}`	This adds newlines into a string to wrap at the given width.

`{{ value|yesno }}`
or
`{{ value|yesno:"yeah,nope" }}`
or
`{{ value|yesno:"yeah,nope,maybe" }}`
	This returns `yes` or `no` for `True` or `False`. An optional argument provides comma-separated alternate values for `yes` and `no`. A third value can be included in the argument to check `value` against `None`.

C.2.1   Loadable filters

Djangos has built-in filters that are available without using a `{% load %}` tag. Django also ships with other filters inside modules that need to be loaded to be used.

Table C.4   Loadable Django filters

Filter	Module	Description
`{{ value|apnumber }}`	humanize	This returns a number using Associated Press style, where numbers less than 10 are spelled out, while numbers greater or equal to 10 are presented as integers.
`{{ value|intcomma }}`	humanize	This converts an int or float to a string with thousands-based comma separators.
`{{ value|intword }}`	humanize	This converts large values to their written equivalent. For example, `1200000` becomes `1.2 million`.

Table C.4 Loadable Django filters

Filter	Module	Description
`{{ value|naturalday }}`	humanize	This converts a date into `today`, `yesterday`, or `tomorrow` if applicable; otherwise, it returns the date, using the same format as the `{% date %}` tag.
`{{ value|naturaltime }}`	humanize	This converts a datetime object into a natural string. Possible results include `now`, `29 seconds ago`, and `1 week, 2 days from now`. It uses the `|timesince` format if no conversion is possible.
`{{ value|ordinal }}`	humanize	This converts an integer into its ordinal text equivalent. For example, 1 becomes `1st`, 2 becomes `2nd`, and so on.
`{{ LANGUAGE_CODE|language_name }}`	i18n	This returns the name of the language for the filtered language code—for example, `German`.
`{{ LANGUAGE_CODE|language_name_local }}`	i18n	This returns the name of the language in its own language for the filtered language code—for example, `Deutsch`.
`{{ LANGUAGE_CODE|language_bidi }}`	i18n	This returns `True` for right-to-left languages and `False` otherwise.
`{{ LANGUAGE_CODE|language_name_translated }}`	i18n	The name of this language is displayed in the currently active language.
`{{ value|localize }}`	l10n	Forces localization on a single value.
`{{ value|unlocalize }}`	l10n	This disables localization on a single value.
`{{ value|localtime }}`	tz	This forces conversion of `value` into the local timezone.
`{{ value|timezone:"America/Toronto" }}`	tz	This forces conversion of `value` into the named timezone.
`{{ value|utc }}`	tz	This forces conversion of `value` into UTC.

appendix D
Django ORM field reference

This appendix is a reference guide for Django's built-in Database ORM fields. For a full reference, see the online documentation: https://docs.djangoproject.com/en/dev/ref/models/fields/.

D.1 Field options

Table D.1 contains the constructor arguments that can be used in all ORM field types.

Table D.1 Arguments common to all fields

Argument	Description
`null`	When `True`, empty values are stored in the database as NULL.
`blank`	When `True`, the value is allowed to be blank. Note: this is different from `null`, which is related to database storage. This field is used during field validation—for example, in the Django Admin.
`choices=[("en", "English"), ("fr", "French")]`	If present, this argument restricts the values allowed. The restriction is applied during the Model's validation step. The argument takes a sequence of `tuples`, with the first item in each tuple being what is stored in the database (`"en"` or `"fr"`) and the second item in each tuple being the value displayed to the user (`"English"` or `"French"`) in forms, including the Django Admin.
`db_column`	This is used to force the name of the database column; when it is not given, Django bases the column name on the field's name.

Table D.1   Arguments common to all fields

Argument	Description
db_comment	This sets the column comment, if supported by the database.
db_index	When True, this creates a database index for this column. To index across multiple columns, use the Meta.indexes property instead.
db_tablespace	The name of the database tablespace to be used if this field is indexed.
default	This is a default value for this field if no value is provided at construction. This can also be a callable—if so, it is called for each construction of a new object.
editable	When False, this field is not displayed in forms or the Django Admin and is ignored during Model validation. It defaults to True.
error_messages	If provided, this overrides the field's default error messages. It takes a dictionary with a message per key. Error message keys are null, blank, invalid, invalid_choice, unique, and unique_for_date. Other keys may be available for specific Model fields.
help_text	This provides extra help text to be displayed in forms for this field.
primary_key	When True, this marks the field as the primary key in the model. By default, the primary key is the ID field automatically added by Django.
unique	When True, each instance in the table must be unique from all others. Unique fields are automatically indexed.
unique_for_date	This takes the name of another field in the model of type DateField or DateTimeField and ensures the value in this field is unique for that date. For example, the value of a title field must be unique for a corresponding publication date.
unique_for_month	This is similar to unique_for_date but only restricts the month portion of the corresponeing date field.
unique_for_year	This is similar to unique_for_date but only restricts the year portion of the corresponeing date field.
verbose_name	This provides a human-readable name for the field. If not given, Django generates a value based on the field's name.
validators	This provides a list of validators to run for this field. For a full list of Django validators, see https://docs.djangoproject.com/en/dev/ref/validators/.

D.2 Field types

Table D.2 contains the fields that ship with the Django ORM. All fields support common field arguments described in D.1. Field-specific arguments are highlighted in the field's description in the table.

Some fields, like EmailField and URLField, automatically use a field validator. For a complete list of validators, see https://docs.djangoproject.com/en/dev/ref/validators/.

Table D.2   ORM field types

Field	Description
AutoField(**options)	An IntegerField that automaticaly increments. This is not typically used explicitly, as Django includes an ID field using this option automatically.
BigAutoField(**options)	This is a 64-bit version of AutoField; newer versions of Django use this as the ID field by default.
BinaryField(max_length=None, **options)	This stores raw binary data. An optional max_length argument specifies storage size in the database.
CharField(max_length=None, **options)	A string field, the max_length option maps to the VARCHAR column size in some databases and may be required. It uses a TextInput widget in forms by default (rendered as <input>).
DateField(auto_now=False, auth_now_add=False, **options)	This stores a Python datetime.date instance. If auto_now is True, the field is set to the current date each time a Model is saved. If auto_now_add is True, the field is set to the date the Model is created.
DateTimeField(auto_now=False, auth_now_add=False, **options)	This is similar to DateField, but it stores a Python datetime.datetime object.
DecimalField(max_digits=None, decimal_places=None, **options)	This stores a fixed precision decimal number represented by a Python Decimal object. Both max_digits and decimal_places are required arguments, with the first representing the number of digits in the number (including the decimal points) and the second representing the number of decimal digits.
DurationField(**options)	This stores a Python timedelta object to capture periods of time.
EmailField(max_length=254, **options)	This is a CharField instance that validates the contents against an EmailValidator.

Table D.2   ORM field types

Field	Description
`FileField(upload_to="", storage=None, max_lenth=100, **options)`	This stores the path to a file that was uploaded. The `upload_to` argument indicates the directory for uploading. The `storage` argument indicates the object that handles file storage; if `None`, the default Django storage mechanism is used. Full details on storage objects are available in the documentation: https://docs.djangoproject.com/en/dev/topics/files/#storage-objects. The `max_length` argument restricts the length of the filename. Instances of this field have attributes that contain more information about the file: `.name` is the file name, `.path` is the file path, `.size` is the file size, and `.url` is the URL used to access the file. Field instances also support several methods—`.open()`, `.close()`, `.save()`, and `.delete()`— which correspond to the equivalent file operations.
`FilePathField(path="", match=None, recursive=False, allow_files=True, allow_folders= False, max_lenth=100, **options)`	This is a `CharField`, whose choices are restricted to the names of files at a given path. The `path` argument is required and points to the directory used to inspect for allowable values. All other arguments are optional. The `match` argument can contain a regular expression to restricts the names of the paths. Set `recursive` to `True` to include subdirectories. Values for `allow_files` and `allow_folders` incidate whether file and directory paths are included as possible values.
`FloatField(**options)`	Stores a floating point number.
`GenericIPAddressField(protocol= "both", unpack_ipv4=False, **options)`	Stores an IPv4 or IPv6 IP address as a string. The `protocol` argument can be one of `both`, `IPv4`, or `IPv6`. Setting `protocol` to `IPv4` or `IPv6` restrict the field to that kind of address. When `protocol` is `both` and `unpack_ipv4` is `True`, packed IP4 addresses are unpacked when accessed (e.g., `::ffff:192.0.2.1` becomes `192.0.2.1`).
`ImageField(upload_to=None, height_field =None, width_field=None max_length=100, **options)`	An instance of a `FileField` that validates the uploaded file is an image. It requires the Pillow library to be installed. The `height_field` and `width_field` arguments optionally name other fields in the table that get automatically updated with the image's height and width values.

Table D.2   ORM field types

Field	Description
`IntegerField(**options)`	This stores an integer in the range of −2,147,483,648 to 2,147,483,647.
`JSONField(encoder=None, decoder=None, **options)`	This stores JSON-encoded data while allowing access to the field as if it were its Python equivalent. This field may not be supported by all databases or may require a plugin for the database. The `encoder` and `decoder` arguments can be used to specify a custom encoder or decored class, according to the `json` module in the standard library.
`PositiveBigIntegerField(**options)`	This stores an integer in the range of 0 to 9,223,372,036,854,775,807.
`PositiveIntegerField(**options)`	This stores an integer in the range of 0 to 2,147,483,647.
`PositiveSmallIntegerField(**options)`	This stores an integer in the range of 0 to 32,767.
`SlugField(max_length=50, allow_unicode=False, **options)`	A slug is a short label used in newspaper articles and is often used as part of a URL. The `allow_unicode` option indicates Unicode values can be accepted— the default `False` restricts slugs to ASCII.
`SmallAutoField(**options)`	This is an `AutoField` restricted to values between 1 and 32,767.
`SmallIntegerField(**options)`	This stores an integer in the range of -32,768 to 32,767.
`TextField(**options)`	This is a large text storage field. The underlying column type may or may not be different from a `CharField`, depending on the database. It uses a `Textarea` widget in forms by default (rendered as `<textarea>`).
`TimeField(auto_now=Flase, auto_now_add=False, **options)`	This is similar to `DateField` but stores a Python `datetime.time` instance.
`URLField(max_length=200, **options)`	This `CharField` validates its contents using a `URLValidator`.
`UUIDField(**options)`	This stores universally unique identifiers from Python's `UUID` class.

D.3   Relationship field types

This section contains the fields that specify inter-Model relationships. All fields support the common arguments described in table D.1. Field-specific arguments are highlighted in the description that follows.

D.3.1 *ForeignKey*

```
class ForeignKey(to, on_delete, limit_choices_to=None, related_name=None,
    related_query_name=None, to_field=None, db_constraint=True, **options)
```

This specifies a many-to-one relationship, pointing to the Model associated with this object. The to and on_delete arguments are required, with to specifying the Model of the related object. The on_delete argument specifies the behavior when the corresponding Model is deleted. The choices are CASCADE, which deletes the associated object; PROTECT, which prevents the deletion of the associated object; RESTRICT, which allows the deletion if there is another ForeignKey field on the same object that is also being deleted through a CASCADE; SET_NULL, which sets the value to NULL; SET_DEFAULT, which sets the field to its default; SET(value), which sets the value to that given; and DO_NOTHING, which takes no action, possibly causing a database integrity error.

The limit_choices_to argument allows you to restrict the choices for this field during validation. It takes a dictionary, specifying field names and values for the corresponding Model. For example, {"is_staff":True} restricts the relationship to objects that have an is_staff field set to True. This argument can also be a callable that returns a dictionary.

The related_name argument specifies the name to be used as the backward relationship between the foreign object and this one. This allows you to override the default name—for example, song_set on an Album Model pointing to a Song Model. It can be set to + to stop a related name from being generated. Similarly, the related_query_name argument specifies the name of the attribute for the forward relationship.

The to_field argument indicates which field on the related object contains the value to store, indicating the relationship. It defaults to the ID field of the object. If given, the field must point to a primary key.

The db_constraint argument controls whether a constraint is created in the database for the inter-table relationship. It defaults to True and may need to be turned off for tables with legacy data not generated by Django or for database sharding.

D.3.2 *ManyToManyField*

```
class ManyToManyField(to, realted_name=None, related_query_name=None,
    limit_choices_to=None, symetrical=None, through=None,
    through_fields=None, db_constraint=True, db_table=None, **options)
```

This represents a many-to-many relationship between objects. It creates an extra table that maps the keys between related objects. The to argument is required, and it points to the related Model.

The related_name, related_query_name, limit_choices_to, and db-constraint arguments are all the same as ForeignKey.

When using a ManyToManyField to define a relationship between a Model and itself, the symmetrical argument indicates whether both the forward and backward relationship is put in the database. Setting it to False indicates a one-way relationship;

relating `Model` instance A to `Model` instance B would not add another row for relating B back to A.

The table used to store a many-to-many relationship is automatically generated by Django. You can stop this and specify a different `Model` object to customize the relationship, using the `through` argument. This is normally done to add extra fields associated with the relationship. When doing so, the `through_fields` argument specifies names of the fields that form the relationship. This is only necessary if there are multiple `ForeignKey` fields pointing to the same `Model`, making the relationship ambiguous.

D.3.3 *OneToOneField*

```
class OneToOneField(to, on_delete, parent_link=False, **options)
```

This is similar to a `ForeignKey`, but it enforces a unique relationship constraint. A related `Model` can only be connected to a single instance of the owning object. The `to` and `on_delete` arguments are the same as `ForeignKey`.

The `parent_link` argument can only be used if the `Model` inherits from another concrete model. In this case, if `parent_link` is `True`, the field relates the parent class rather than the otherwise automatically created field. For more information on model inheritence, see https://docs.djangoproject.com/en/dev/topics/db/models/#model-inheritance.

index

D